Confucian Perfectionism

THE PRINCETON-CHINA SERIES
Daniel A. Bell, *Series Editor*

The Princeton-China Series aims to publish the works of contemporary Chinese scholars in the humanities, social sciences, and related fields. The goal is to bring the work of these important thinkers to a wider audience, foster an understanding of China on its own terms, and create new opportunities for cultural cross-pollination.

Ancient Chinese Thought, Modern Chinese Power, by Yan Xuetong, translated by Edmund Ryden
A Confucian Constitutional Order: How China's Ancient Past Can Shape Its Political Future, by Jiang Qing, edited by Daniel A. Bell and Ruiping Fan, translated by Edmund Ryden

Confucian Perfectionism

A Political Philosophy for Modern Times

Joseph Chan

PRINCETON UNIVERSITY PRESS
Princeton and Oxford

Library of Congress Cataloging-in-Publication Data

Chan, Joseph Cho Wai, 1960–
  Confucian perfectionism : a political philosophy for modern times / Joseph Chan.
    pages cm. — (Princeton-China series)
  Summary: "Since the very beginning, Confucianism has been troubled by a serious gap between its political ideals and the reality of societal circumstances. Contemporary Confucians must develop a viable method of governance that can retain the spirit of the Confucian ideal while tackling problems arising from nonideal modern situations. The best way to meet this challenge, Joseph Chan argues, is to adopt liberal democratic institutions that are shaped by the Confucian conception of the good rather than the liberal conception of the right.Confucian Perfectionism examines and reconstructs both Confucian political thought and liberal democratic institutions, blending them to form a new Confucian political philosophy. Chan decouples liberal democratic institutions from their popular liberal philosophical foundations in fundamental moral rights, such as popular sovereignty, political equality, and individual sovereignty. Instead, he grounds them on Confucian principles and redefines their roles and functions, thus mixing Confucianism with liberal democratic institutions in a way that strengthens both. Then he explores the implications of this new yet traditional political philosophy for fundamental issues in modern politics, including authority, democracy, human rights, civil liberties, and social justice. Confucian Perfectionism critically reconfigures the Confucian political philosophy of the classical period for the contemporary era"— Provided by publisher.
  Includes bibliographical references and index.
  ISBN 978-0-691-15861-7 (hardback)
  1. Political science—China—Philosophy.   2. Confucianism—Philosophy.   3. Philosophy, Chinese.
  I. Title.
  JA84.C6C468 2013
  320.01—dc23

                              2013022474

British Library Cataloging-in-Publication Data is available

This book has been composed in Minion Pro

Printed on acid-free paper. ∞

Printed in the United States of America

10 9 8 7 6 5 4 3 2 1

For Sharifa

CONTENTS

FOREWORD BY SERIES EDITOR

The first two books in the Princeton-China series—by Yan Xuetong and Jiang Qing—were written by influential Chinese intellectuals in mainland China. Yan and Jiang use values and concepts in ancient Chinese political thought to draw implications for social and political reform in China today. Yan's book is meant to provide standards for evaluating China's foreign policy, and Jiang's is meant to provide standards for evaluating domestic constitutional reform in China. Joseph Chan's book also draws on values and concepts in ancient Chinese political thought, but he integrates them with arguments and theories developed in the West. Chan has spent most of his life in the more liberal environment of Hong Kong, a hybrid society that has shaped his intellectual and normative orientations:

> The kind of society I grew up in provided me with the natural soil to adopt integration thinking. Hong Kong became a British colony after the First Opium War (1839–42). To many Hong Kong people, the colonial rule from 1842 to 1997 was both a curse and a blessing: curse because the local Chinese were unjustly discriminated against by the British; and blessing because the colony provided a relatively safe haven from the civil wars in China, and from the economic and political turmoil of the first three decades of communist rule since 1949. As the colony started to take off economically and politically in the 1970s, Hong Kong people began to experience the benefits of albeit limited civil liberties and participation, the rule of law, as well as the vitality and prosperity of market capitalism. At the same time, the local traditional, Confucian Chinese culture was largely left untouched by colonial noninterventionist policies—unlike in mainland China, where it was denounced by the entire society in government-led campaigns. Many Hong Kong people's experience of Chinese Confucian culture was positive, and that of British culture not negative, despite its domination through colonial rule. What they experienced was not so much a clash of cultures as their mutuality. Through persistence, creativity, and pragmatism, the men and women of Hong Kong—both Chinese and British—turned what would otherwise be dogmatic antagonism into productive integration. (Joseph Chan, "Notes on the Methods of Philosophical Reconstruction," 2012)

Chan was brought up in a Cantonese-speaking household. He did an undergraduate degree at the Chinese University of Hong Kong and won a scholarship to pursue graduate studies at the University of Oxford. At Oxford he sharpened his analytical skills and wrote a doctoral thesis on Aristotle's political philosophy. He returned to teach at the University of Hong Kong in 1990 and has been teaching there since then. Chan published several articles on Western political philosophy in leading journals, such as *Philosophy and Public Affairs* and *Ethics*, and also began to immerse himself in the Confucian tradition.

Hong Kong was the base for major Confucian philosophy in the twentieth century, and great thinkers such as Mou Zongsan wrote works that integrated modern Western and traditional Chinese traditions. Mou, however, was influenced primarily by continental European philosophy, and he was most concerned by metaphysical issues. His writing style was often difficult and dense, if not impenetrable. In contrast, Chan has been influenced by the Oxford analytical tradition, with its emphasis on clarity and rigor of argumentation, and his concerns are more directly political (another difference is that Mou wrote academic works in Chinese, while Chan can write in both Chinese and English). Rather than aiming to provide a brand new metaphysical theory that would underpin social and political thinking, Chan engages in what he calls "piecemeal" appropriation and reinterpretation of the Confucian tradition, with detailed argumentation for why and how parts of the Confucian tradition can enrich liberal democratic thinking (and vice versa). Chan's project may be less ambitious than Mou's, but it does not rest on any one foundation that can be chopped away to undermine the whole work.

This book draws on more than two decades of thinking about how Confucian political philosophy can be modernized and enrich liberal democratic theories and political practices. Chan aims to defend liberal democratic political institutions, but he asserts that traditional liberal arguments for those institutions need to be modified and enriched by integrating modernized Confucian values. In that sense, his theory is more universal compared to both theories that draw exclusively (or mainly) from Chinese political theory and theories that draw exclusively (or mainly) from theories developed in Western societies. The book thus poses a challenge not only to Western liberals who argue that their universal theories and values are applicable in China, but also to Western liberals who argue that their theories and values best fit Western societies. Just as Chinese should be open to the possibility that Western liberal ideas can improve political thinking and practice in China, so too Westerners should be open to the possibility that Confucian ideas can improve political thinking and practice in Western societies. Chan's book is thus an outstanding and original contribution that will challenge traditional ways of political theorizing in both China and the West.

Daniel A. Bell

PREFACE

This book is a critical reconstruction of certain Confucian political ideas of the classical period for modern times. It is an unusual project, so it is important to explain at the outset what it is and what it is not. The book is not an introduction to Confucian political thought; neither is it a work in the history of Chinese philosophy or intellectual history. I do not intend to provide detailed and systematic interpretations of Confucian political thought by closely analyzing the texts or examining the changing historical contexts in which these texts evolved. This project is normative political theory of a special kind—and its chief purpose is to explore the implications of a traditional political philosophy for a number of fundamental issues of modern politics, such as authority, democracy, human rights, civil liberties, and social justice. Understood as such, this project does not belong to any well-defined disciplinary inquiry: neither the history of philosophy nor contemporary political philosophy, it lies somewhere in between as an attempt to bridge the gap between these two fields. I shall call this project "philosophical reconstruction," a method of inquiry explained in appendix 1. The project may also be regarded as an exercise in comparative political theory, a newly developing area of inquiry that brings two or more traditions of political thought into contact and dialogue.

Ultimately the project seeks to ascertain whether Confucianism, after suitable reconstruction and revision, can re-present itself as a contemporary political philosophy for modern times. Modern China has been in search of a suitable political philosophy for more than a century. Several schools of thought have been given trials but without much success: Western liberalism has been unable to gain much ground, and Marxism, though its tenets were once enthusiastically adopted as the country's guiding principles, attracts little public attention today. Confucianism, however, is experiencing a steady revival in politics and society.[1] Today some scholars in China and other parts of the world are investigating Confucianism as an intellectual, ethical, and cultural resource for the development of a modern political philosophy.[2] But even those most sympathetic to Confucianism believe that it can regain its intellectual significance

---

1 See Daniel A. Bell, *China's New Confucianism: Politics and Everyday Life in a Changing Society* (Princeton: Princeton University Press, 2008).

2 For an account of the scene of contemporary Confucian political philosophy, see Stephen C.

in contemporary society only after systematic reconstruction and significant revision, including, some argue, suitable integration with other political philosophies such as liberalism or socialism.

This book aspires to contribute to the development of such a reconstructed Confucian political philosophy, although I am acutely aware of the difficulties in doing so. One challenge lies in the fact that China and the world have changed so much over the past century that traditional Confucianism no longer speaks effectively to the new social and political environment. Another is posed by the huge developments that Western political philosophy, especially its liberal and democratic variant, has undergone in terms of conceptual innovation and new theoretical arguments since the 1970s. The advanced development of Western political philosophy makes any attempt to reconstruct a viable contemporary Confucian political philosophy both difficult and rewarding because any such reconstruction would, at its best, draw on the rich resources available in contemporary Western political philosophy and at the same time critically respond to the arguments of that tradition. I have tried to meet this high standard but have no illusion about my limitations. Because this book is a philosophical reconstruction of a very old and complex traditional school of political thought, I do not have the space to fully develop the normative and conceptual arguments to the extent that would be normally expected of a contemporary work in political philosophy. I am satisfied if I have succeeded in developing an outline of a contemporary Confucian political philosophy that is philosophically distinctive, interesting, and plausible.

In the many years that I have worked on this project, friends and colleagues have often asked me about my reasons for undertaking it. Two questions in particular are regularly posed, and I will report them here, with my answers, in the hope that this will help the reader better understand the spirit behind the book.

The first question is: "If you believe that Confucian political ideas and values are philosophically attractive and promising, why not simply develop a contemporary political philosophy of your own, without referring to Confucian classics and using the language of Confucianism?" My short answer to this is that my interest in Confucianism is cultural as well as philosophical. Even if it were possible to develop the kind of political philosophy I find promising without drawing on Confucian ideas and terminologies, I would still be interested in constructing a contemporary political philosophy that is recognizably connected to the Confucian tradition. This interest reflects my cultural commitment as a Chinese scholar, and my desire to see this traditional school of thought—one that has influenced China and other societies for more than two thousand years—remain alive and vital, and develop and flourish into an at-

---

Angle, "Introduction: Contextualizing Progressive Confucianism," chap. 1 in *Contemporary Confucian Political Philosophy* (Cambridge: Polity, 2012).

tractive vision for modern life and society. Other things being equal, the continuation of a great tradition of thought and culture is a splendid thing.

The second question put to me is: "Do you regard yourself as a Confucian scholar?" My answer may be yes or no, depending on what is meant by the term "Confucian scholar" in today's context. If being a Confucian scholar today requires a person to be well versed in the long tradition of Confucian classics and thoroughly committed to traditional Confucian beliefs and values, then I am not a Confucian scholar—I do not possess a vast knowledge of the classics or accept without reservation all the fundamental tenets of Confucianism. I am, at most, a "Confucian-inspired scholar," one who finds many Confucian values inspiring and is interested in working out the implications of these values for modern politics. However, the term "Confucian scholar" could also be understood in a dynamic and engaging sense—namely, as someone who engages in the activity of *making sense* of Confucian thought, and develops, revises, and improves it as a tradition—in other words, someone who participates in the *making* of Confucian thought. I regard myself as a Confucian scholar in this sense, however inadequate I may be as a participant.

There is, however, another, deeper motivation behind this project. For a long time I have had a strong intellectual interest in the modern relevance of ancient thought, both Eastern and Western. For my D.Phil. degree I studied Aristotle's political theory and examined the modern relevance of its approach and basic tenets. My more recent study of Confucian political thought is a continuation of this broader research agenda. While the political theories proposed by Aristotle and other ancient Greek philosophers differ substantially from Confucian political thought in their substantive content, their structural features are strikingly similar. They are what I would call perfectionist theories of ethics, society, and politics. On ethics, these traditions of thought base ethical judgments about values, virtues, and norms—in short, conceptions of the good life—on their understanding of human nature or humanity (I call this ethical perfectionism). On society, these theories regard social groups and institutions as important sites where people develop the ethical capacities and skills necessary for the good life (social perfectionism). On politics, these theories hold the view that one of the major aims of the state is to help people pursue the good life by means of law, education, rituals, provision of resources, and coordination of social groups and their activities (political perfectionism).[3] I find this traditional perfectionist perspective on human life and society, in particular its emphasis on the connection between politics and the good life, insightful and profound. I do not mean, for any moment, to belittle the achievements of modernity. Liberal democratic institutions, for example, have provided hope and assurance for many people suffering from political oppression and exploitation.

---

3 As used in this book, the concept of political perfectionism does not imply making people perfect. It just says the state should help people live better lives.

The language and substance of perfectionism certainly need to adapt to some of the core values and institutions of modernity, but it would be a great loss to modern people and civilization if these perfectionist perspectives on ethics and politics disappeared from our intellectual horizon.

In this project I revive and reconstruct for modernity one such traditional perfectionist philosophy.[4] In the eighteenth century many progressive European intellectuals regarded Confucianism as the best philosophy of ethics and governance in the world. Less than two centuries later many progressive Chinese intellectuals judged it to be one of the worst philosophies. As the contents of Confucianism have undergone no fundamental changes, these diametrically opposed evaluations can only be explained by the changes of circumstance within which Confucianism was situated, namely, the drastic transformation of values and politics in the Western world and China in the nineteenth and twentieth centuries. If Confucianism is compared with other premodern philosophies of ethics and governance, it ranks as one of the best philosophies known to humankind. When compared with modern liberal democratic traditions of thought, however, it is judged by many modern thinkers to be outdated and wrongheaded. Nevertheless, it has been said that modernity is like an adolescent struggling for liberation from the bondage of tradition. When the young man matures, he learns to appreciate the wisdom of tradition. With this in mind, if we try to predict the dominant philosophical perspective half a century from now, we may find that rather than having replaced the traditional language of virtue, responsibility, and benevolent care, the modern language of freedom, rights, and democracy will have been enriched by it, and that modern values and ancient wisdom will have blended to form a more mature mode of human thinking and living. It is this hope that underlies this project of the critical reconstruction of Confucian political philosophy.

In writing this book, I have benefited tremendously from the help and advice of many colleagues, students, and friends. I owe a huge debt to the two readers for Princeton University Press, who provided searching criticisms and detailed comments. One reader remains anonymous, but the other is Jane Mansbridge, whose scrupulous reading of the manuscript and extremely useful suggestions have led me to make a few important changes in the presentation of the argument of the book. I am also very grateful to Rob Tempio, editor at the Press, and Daniel A. Bell, editor of the series in which this book is appearing, for their stewardship of this book. Stephen Angle, Sor-hoon Tan, and Ci Jiwei generously read the entire manuscript and offered many useful comments and corrections. For discussions and comments on individual chapters that helped

---

4 In other words, if we conceive of modernity as having multiple forms, then this project aims to explore a form of modernity that retains considerable continuity with traditional values. For discussions on multiple modernities, see Dominic Sachsenmaier and Jens Riedel with Shmuel N. Eisenstadt, eds., *Reflections on Multiple Modernities: European, Chinese and Other Interpretations* (Leiden: Brill, 2002).

make this a better book, I thank Daniel A. Bell, Chan Keung Lap, Chan Sin Yee, Peter Chau, Chen Lai, Yvonne Chiu, Ian Holliday, Leigh Jenco, Li Qiang, Hui-chieh Loy, Randy Peerenboom, Kwong-loi Shun, Chin-liew Ten, and David B. Wong. I ask forgiveness of anyone else whose name I have unintentionally omitted. Thanks also to Vikki Weston for excellent copyediting and Man-ying Ho, Larry Lai, and Sophia Chan for helping with the manuscript. I owe special thanks to two gifted students and friends at the University of Hong Kong, Elton Chan and Lorraine Lui. Elton has given me enormous help in research assistance and offered insightful feedback and suggestions over the years, and Lorraine did a superb job in helping produce the manuscript and assisted me in numerous ways during the final stage of writing.

Equally important is the support I have received of other kinds. I could not have finished this book without unloading my administrative responsibilities as head of department on Danny Wai-fung Lam for a semester. I have also relied on the support of staff, especially Sharon To, in the University of Hong Kong's Department of Politics and Public Administration. My work on this manuscript was generously supported by a grant from the Research Grants Council of the Hong Kong Special Administrative Region, China. For several decades I have been very fortunate to have a number of teachers and friends whose encouragement and support have been invaluable. My teachers Kuan Hsin Chi, Shih Yuan-Kang, and Andrew Wong Wang Fat (Chinese University of Hong Kong), John Charvet and Frederick Rosen (LSE), and Jonathan Barnes and David Miller (Oxford University) set me on the path of political philosophy and helped me appreciate its joy, importance, and rigor. The unfailing encouragement of Chan Kin Man, Wong Tak Sang, Wu Sin Kwan, and Kam Lap Kwan and the companionship and constant advice of Elaine Chan have meant much to me. Finally, I am deeply grateful to my mother for her continuing love. My greatest debt of all is to Sharifa. Her joyful presence, good humor, and steadfast support and care lifted me through the highs and lows of writing this book.

I am grateful to several publishers for permission to incorporate previously published material, which has been revised in light of the framework developed in the introduction and integrated into the overall line of argument:

Chapter 5 draws on my essays "A Confucian Perspective on Human Rights for Contemporary China," in *The East Asian Challenge for Human Rights*, edited by Joanne R. Bauer and Daniel A. Bell (Cambridge: Cambridge University Press, 1999), 212–37; and "Confucianism and Human Rights," in *Religion and Human Rights: An Introduction*, edited by John Witte, Jr., and M. Christian Green (New York: Oxford University Press, 2012), 87–102.

Chapter 6 draws on my essay "Moral Autonomy, Civil Liberties, and Confucianism," *Philosophy East and West* 52, no. 3 (July 2002): 281–310.

Chapter 7 draws on my essay "Is There a Confucian Perspective on Social Justice?" in *Western Political Thought in Dialogue with Asia*, edited by Takashi Shogimen and Cary J. Nederman (Lanham, MD: Lexington Books, 2008), 261–77.

Chapter 8 draws on my essay "Giving Priority to the Worst Off: A Confucian Perspective on Social Welfare," in *Confucianism for the Modern World*, edited by Daniel A. Bell and Hahm Chaibong (Cambridge: Cambridge University Press, 2003), 236–53.

Interplay between the Political Ideal and Reality

The Task

This book examines Confucian political thought from a perspective that explores the intricate interplay between political ideal and reality. This perspective is not unique to the study of Confucianism but common to much of the political theorizing carried out under the name of "political philosophy." Political philosophy has a dual character: viewed as a philosophical field of study, it searches for an ideal social and political order that expresses the best aspects of humanity and our most deeply held values;[1] viewed as a political field of study, it aims to illuminate our understanding of the real world and give principled guidance as to how we should act here and now. Any form of political theorizing that lacks an ideal is like a ship embarking on a voyage without destination, and political theorizing that is insensitive to the constraints of reality is like a ship on rough seas without competent navigation.

A political philosophy of comprehensive scope takes seriously this dual character, despite the almost irreconcilable demands of ideal and reality, and the fact that adapting an ideal vision to reality also necessitates lowering the sights and revising the content. To address both demands, a political philosophy needs to develop two tracks of theorizing—one track that explains or justifies an ideal conception of social and political order, bracketing off practical questions about feasibility and compliance, and another that develops a nonideal conception that addresses these practical questions. The challenge of such two-track theorizing is twofold: to demonstrate the attractiveness of the ideal even though it is unlikely to work in the real world, and to show that a feasible nonideal conception of order still tallies with the ideal conception, in the sense that people who live under the nonideal order are nonetheless aware of the ideal and regard it as an aspiration.

---

1 Admittedly this is a controversial statement. Political realists deny that it is the business of political theorizing to search for an ideal political order or ideal political morality. For a recent account of realism in political theory, see William A. Galston, "Realism in Political Theory," *European Journal of Political Theory* 9, no. 4 (2010): 385–411. For a defense of the function of ideals, see Nicholas Rescher, *Ethical Idealism: An Inquiry into the Nature and Function of Ideals* (Berkeley: University of California Press, 1992), esp. chap. 6; and Adam Swift, "The Value of Philosophy in Nonideal Circumstances," *Social Theory and Practice* 34, no. 3 (2008): 363–87.

Since its inception, Confucianism has always faced this challenge. Historically the strength of Confucianism lies in the long-lasting appeal of its ideal conception of ethical, social, and political order.[2] I shall describe this ideal conception in detail later; for the purpose of illustrating the challenge, let me first give a loose description. It consists of some ideal ends and ideal means, although the two are tightly linked, as we shall see. The ideal ends include the flourishing of human virtues, of social relationships based on mutual trust and care, and of public-spiritedness in society, all of which form part of a grand ideal of social harmony. The ideal means to attain those ends include: governance by people who are virtuous and competent; moral edification by example and persuasion; rites as a method of socialization and governance; and benevolent rule to ensure material sufficiency for all people. A few words are needed to explain the notion of rites, as it plays an important role in the Confucian conception of society. The Chinese word for rites is *li*, a rich and elastic concept frequently used in Confucian texts. In its most basic meaning, *li* refers to rites or rituals (these two terms are used interchangeably in this book) that guide behavior in religious ceremony, the court, family, and many other social relationships and contexts. However, Confucian masters believe that rites are not just a form of social etiquette but also perform important social functions—they help moral cultivation by regulating unhealthy desires and refining feelings and attitudes (*li jiao*, ritual education); they express the basic principles of human relationships and roles (*li yi*, ritual principles) and help regulate society according to these principles (*li zhi*, ritual system); these functions in turn help achieve a harmonious, ethical society, which is the goal of Confucian governance (*li zhi*, ritual rule) that cannot be achieved by the use of penal law.[3]

---

2 No doubt the dominance of the Confucian ideal in traditional China owes much to the fact that many rulers and political elites used it to justify their power to rule, although in reality they often adopted the strategies of an opposing thought—Legalism—to cope with problems in the real world. Despite this, the Confucian conception of social order captured many Chinese people's moral imagination and evoked their support for governance for more than two thousand years.

3 For historical and philosophical accounts of Confucian conceptions of li and its ethical, social, and political functions, see Michael Nylan, "The Three *Rites* Canons," chap. 4 in *The Five "Confucian" Classics* (New Haven: Yale University Press, 2001), esp. 188–201; Stephen C. Angle, "Neither Ethics nor Law: Ritual Propriety as Confucian Civility," chap. 6 in *Contemporary Confucian Political Philosophy*; Ruiping Fan, "Rites as the Foundations of Human Civilization: Rethinking the Role of the Confucian *Li*," chap. 11 in *Reconstructionist Confucianism: Rethinking Morality after the West*, (Dordrecht: Springer, 2010); Sor-hoon Tan, "The *Dao* of Politics: *Li* (Rituals/Rites) and Laws as Pragmatic Tools of Government," *Philosophy East and West* 61, no. 3 (2011): 468–91; and Anthony Kwok-wing Yeung 楊國榮, "Shi fei qu zhi: ren li gong cheng de jia zhi guan" 是非曲直: 仁禮共成的價值觀 [Right and Wrong, Straight and Crooked: Co-Realization of *Ren* and *Li* and Its Value System], chap. 7 in *Xian mei yu he le—Dui sheng ming yi yi de ni liu tan suo* 顯魅與和樂—對生命意義的逆流探索 [Revealing the Sacred Dimension of Life and Enjoying Harmony: A Search for the Meaning of Life] (Hong Kong: Joint Publishing HK, 2010). For a comparative account of rituals and reverence in Chinese and Western traditions of thought, see Paul Woodruff, *Reverence: Renewing a Forgotten Virtue* (New York: Oxford University Press, 2001).

Today this ideal conception is subject to severe criticisms: some people argue that it fails to include important values such as individual rights and personal autonomy; many more regard the ends as utopian, the means as impractical, and the overall ideal—the fusion of the ethical and the political—as irrelevant to the real world at best or oppressive at worst. In reality, they argue, people are selfish, those in power are often corrupt or incompetent, and human behavior cannot be restrained by rites alone. The solution these critics offer is a fundamental separation of the ethical and the political, a replacement of the old ideal with liberal democracy as both a normative ideal and a set of feasible institutions.

Although the liberal democratic solution is relatively new in the history of Chinese political thought, the problem of how to address the ideal and the actual is not. As early as the third century BCE, the Legalists bitterly attacked Confucianism. Han Feizi (ca. 280–233 BCE), for example, argues that "people are submissive to power and few of them can be influenced by the doctrines of righteousness [*yi*]" because "few people value humanity [*ren*] and it is difficult to practice righteousness." He ridicules Confucius (551–479 BCE) as someone who "cultivated his own character and elucidated his doctrines and traveled extensively within the Four Seas" and yet attracted only seventy people as his devoted pupils, while Duke Ai of Lu, whose moral character was obviously inferior to Confucius's, was easily able to subdue people with his power as sovereign of the state—even Confucius had to subordinate himself to Duke Ai.[4] Similarly, in the famous Han dynasty (206 BCE–220 CE) *Salt and Iron Debate* (*Yan tie lun*) in 81 BCE, government officials harshly criticized Confucian scholars for stubbornly holding on to ancient teachings that were perceived to be inadequate for the real business of the time.[5]

All these criticisms, both ancient and modern, point toward a similar proposal, namely, to abandon the high-sounding Confucian ideal and replace it with goals that are workable and effective in the nonideal world. Ironically, the Confucian masters were themselves keenly aware of the fact that their ideal—the Way of politics and humanity—was unlikely to be realized in their times. In *The Doctrine of the Mean (Zhong yong)*, Confucius is reported to have said that the Way (*Dao*) was not pursued.[6] In *The Analects*, his student Zilu comments that "as for putting the Way into practice, the gentleman knows all along that it is hopeless" (18.7).[7] Indeed Confucius is known to be the person "who keeps working toward a goal the realization of which he knows to be hopeless" (14.38).

---

4   "Wu du" 五蠹 (Five Vermin), in *The Han Feizi* 韓非子. Cited in "Legalism," chap. 12 in Wing-tsit Chan, comp. and trans., *A Source Book in Chinese Philosophy* (Princeton: Princeton University Press, 1969), 258.

5   Chap. 10, "Cifu" 刺復.

6   *The Doctrine of the Mean* 中庸 [Zhong yong], chaps. 4–5.

7   From D. C. Lau, trans., *Confucius: The Analects*, rev. bilingual ed. (Hong Kong: Chinese University Press, 1992), bk. 18, sec. 7 (hereafter 18.7). Unless otherwise stated, all translations of *The Analects* 論語 are adapted from Lau's. The system of notation of *The Analects* also follows Lau's.

The masters know why their ideal is hopeless—its realization requires that sages or gentlemen be in power, but these people are rare in the real world. Confucius says he has "no hopes of meeting a sage" or "a good man" (7.26). Mencius (fourth century BCE) says a Sage King appears only once every five hundred years (*Mencius* 2B.13),[8] and Xunzi (third century BCE) laments that "the rulers of men have never awakened to [the Way] in the last thousand years" (*Xunzi* 11.7d).[9]

Why, then, did the Confucian masters continue to hold fast to their ideal even though they were deeply pessimistic about its chance of success? What use is the ideal if it can never come into existence? Should the ethical norms of the ideal be followed even in unfavorable conditions, or should a different set of norms guide people's behavior? And how should the latter set of norms relate to those in the ideal conception? I shall show that these questions were as pertinent to the early masters as they are to anyone interested in the relevance of Confucianism in today's world, and that therefore, in this regard, there is continuity between traditional and contemporary Confucian political philosophy. To begin with, I will present a historical analysis of how early Confucians answered these questions. However, the main interest of this book is contemporary—namely, to construct a two-track approach to contemporary Confucianism and investigate whether a proper interplay between the Confucian ideal and the reality of modernity can be maintained. I will pursue this task by placing the interplay between the ideal and reality in the context of three sets of issues—political authority and democracy, human rights and civil liberties, and social justice and welfare.

This task does not involve developing any *ideal theory*, which, as John Rawls defines it, "assumes strict compliance and works out the principles that characterize a well-ordered society under favorable circumstances."[10] The task of an ideal theory, for Rawls, is to choose and justify principles of justice that define a perfectly just society, and to determine their lexical ordering if they conflict,

---

8   From D. C. Lau, trans., *Mencius,* rev. bilingual ed. (Hong Kong: Chinese University Press, 2003), bk. 2B, sec. 13 (hereafter 2B.13). Unless otherwise stated, all translations of *Mencius* 孟子 are adapted from Lau's. The system of notation of *Mencius* also follows Lau's.

9   From John Knoblock, *Xunzi: A Translation and Study of the Complete Works,* 3 vols. (Stanford: Stanford University Press, 1988–94), bk. 11, sec. 7d (hereafter 11.7d). Unless otherwise stated, all translations of *Xunzi* 荀子are adapted from Knoblock's. The system of notation of *Xunzi* also follows Knoblock's.

10   John Rawls, *A Theory of Justice* (Cambridge: Harvard University Press, 1971), 245. Rawls discusses the distinction and roles of ideal and nonideal theory on 8–9, 245–47, 351–52. For an account of Rawls's distinction of ideal and nonideal theories of justice, see A. John Simmons, "Ideal and Nonideal Theory," *Philosophy and Public Affairs* 38, no. 1 (2010): 5–36. In recent years there has been an interesting debate on the proper roles of ideal theory and nonideal theory in political philosophy. See, for example, Zofia Stemplowska, "What's Ideal about Ideal Theory?" *Social Theory and Practice* 34, no. 3 (2008): 319–40, and Ingrid Robeyns, "Ideal Theory in Theory and Practice," *Social Theory and Practice* 34, no. 3 (2008): 341–62. I see no necessity to enter this debate in this book.

assuming that these principles "will be strictly complied with and followed by everyone."[11] In my view, the classical Confucian ideal, being a loose and abstract conception of society, does not admit the same kind of theorizing of principles as Rawls does for his ideal theory of justice. My interest is not to work out the details of the Confucian ideal, but to take it as a "regulative ideal" and develop a Confucian nonideal political theory that retains the spirit of that ideal. Here I use "regulative ideal" in the Kantian sense, namely that it sets the standard for judging existing practices and serves as an aspiration for our endeavors, even when the standard or aspiration is *not achievable in its full sense*.[12] Kant speaks of the sage of the Stoics as an ideal that provides us "no other standard for our actions than the conduct of this divine human being, with which we can compare ourselves, judging ourselves and thereby improving ourselves, even though we can never reach the standard."[13] In the words of a contemporary commentator, a regulative ideal "is not so much a condition to be achieved . . . but rather a personal or institutional value to be always taken seriously in any practical deliberations."[14] My task, then, is to consider whether it is possible to connect practices in nonideal circumstances to the Confucian regulative ideal.

Two Ideals: The Grand Union and the Small Tranquility

In the early stages of its development, Confucian thought has already propounded different levels of ideal in response to the challenges of reality. For example, *The Book of Rites* (*Liji*) talks about two levels of ideal, and the *Gongyang Commentary of The Annals of Spring and Autumn* (*Gongyang zhuan*) talks about three. The best place to examine these ideals is the "Li yun" chapter in *The Book of Rites*. The chapter reports a dialogue between Confucius and his student Ziyou, in which Confucius first gives a description of the Golden Age—the Grand Union (*da tong*), an ideal society said to have existed in the

11 *A Theory of Justice*, 351.

12 I thank Jane Mansbridge for pointing me to this Kantian concept of a "regulative ideal." For a definition and references to Kant and the contemporary literature on this notion, see Jane Mansbridge et al., "The Place of Self-interest and the Role of Power in Deliberative Democracy," *Journal of Political Philosophy* 18, no. 1 (2010): 65. Mansbridge et al. define "a 'regulative' ideal, unachievable in its full state, as an ideal to which, all else equal, a practice should be judged as approaching more or less closely."

13 Immanuel Kant, *Critique of Pure Reason*, trans. and ed. Paul Guyer and Allen Wood (Cambridge: Cambridge University Press, 1998), 552, A569/B597.

14 Simmons, "Ideal and Nonideal Theory," 27. Here Simmons describes one possible function of ideals, which he draws from Joel Feinberg, who "argued that many apparent claims of right (or justice) are in fact only applications of 'right names' to what are better understood as '*ideal directives*, addressed to those in appropriate positions to do their best for a particular kind of human value . . . ' As such, the ideal at issue (in this version of 'ideal theory') has a more aspirational status, functioning in certain ways like a Kantian 'regulative ideal.'"

distant past—and then describes a "lesser" ideal, the Small Tranquility (*xiao kang*) in the more recent past. The Confucian authenticity of this famous chapter has been disputed in the history of Chinese thought, for it contains ideas from not only Confucianism but also the Daoist yin-yang school that only became popular in the late Warring States (Zhanguo) period (475–221 BCE). However, the general consensus today is that, whether or not the dialogue ever took place, the paragraphs describing the Grand Union and Small Tranquility are basically no different from the early Confucian masters' understanding of ideal politics and society, and so it would not be wrong to regard the ideal of the Grand Union and Small Tranquility as part of Confucian thought.[15] The description of the ideal of the Grand Union is worth quoting in full:

> Zhongni [Confucius] was once present as one of the guests at the *Ji* Sacrifice; when it was over, he went out and paced back and forth on the terrace over the Gate of Proclamations, looking sad and sighing. What made him sigh was the state of Lu. Yan Yan was by his side and asked him, "Master, why are you sighing?" Confucius replied, "I have never seen the practice of the Grand Dao and the eminent men of the Three Dynasties, but I aspire to follow them. When the Grand Dao was pursued, a public and common spirit ruled all under the sky [*tian xia wei gong*]; they chose men of talent, virtue, and ability for public service; they valued mutual trust and cultivated harmony. They did not treat only their own parents as parents, nor treat only their own sons as sons. Provision was secured for the aged till their death, employment for the able-bodied, and the means of growing up for the young. People showed kindness and compassion to widows, orphans, childless men, and those who were disabled by disease, so that they were all sufficiently provided for. Men had work and women had homes. Possessions were not wastefully discarded, nor were they greedily hoarded. People enjoyed laboring for others. In this way selfish schemings were discouraged and did not arise. Robbers, thieves, and rebellious traitors were unknown, and doors remained open and unlocked. Such was the Grand Union."[16]

15 For commentators who hold this view, see Kung-chuan Hsiao 蕭公權 [Xiao Gongquan], *Zhongguo zheng zhi si xiang shi* 中國政治思想史 [The History of Chinese Political Thought] (Taipei: Chinese Culture University, 1980), 68–69; Kuang Yaming 匡亞明, *Kongzi ping zhuan* 孔子評傳 [A Critical Biography of Confucius] (Nanjing: Nanjing University Press, 1990), 245–47; Wang E 王鍔, *Liji cheng shu kao* 《禮記》成書考 [An Investigation on the Creation of *The Book of Rites*] (Beijing: Zhonghua, 2007), 239–46.

16 Author's translation after consulting translations by James Legge, as well as Ch'u Chai and Winberg Chai—see James Legge, *The Li Kî*, part 3–4 of *The Texts of Confucianism*, vols. 3–4 of *The Sacred Books of China*, vols. 27–28 of *The Sacred Books of the East*, ed. Max Müller (Oxford: Clarendon Press, 1885), available at http://oll.libertyfund.org/index.php?option=com_staticxt&static file=show.php%3Ftitle=2014&Itemid=27; and Ch'u Chai and Winberg Chai, eds. and trans., *The Sacred Books of Confucius and Other Confucian Classics* (New Hyde Park, N.Y.: University Books, 1965). Unless otherwise stated, all translations of *The Book of Rites* 禮記 [*Liji*] are adapted from Legge's.

A brief comparison shows the distinctiveness of the Confucian ideal described above. For example, Marx's ideal society postulates a high degree of technological advancement and material abundance that makes possible the free development of individuality. Plato's ideal postulates a philosopher-king who knows the truth and puts it into practice by building a just and efficient society based on a strict division of labor. The Confucian ideal, in contrast, is not based on superior technology, abundant material resources, or expert knowledge but postulates an ethic of public-spiritedness and mutual care that reigns throughout society: people conduct affairs in sincerity and faithfulness with the aim of cultivating harmony; the virtuous and competent are chosen to work for the common good; people look after not only their family members but also others outside their family; different needs are satisfied at different stages of life; the least advantaged receive care and support from society; adults labor for others as well as for themselves; goods are not kept merely for personal use; and wastage is frowned upon. In an ideal society there is no mention of the existence of laws or rites, and, even if they exist, they need not be enforced. In short, the Confucian ideal society is primarily ethical in nature. It does not assume the best possible conditions of human life and circumstances, nor does it assume favorable natural conditions or human control of nature. The ideal consists of nothing but a thriving ethical spirit and a set of flourishing social and political relationships that spring from this spirit.

The ideal of the Grand Union echoes many of the thoughts of the early Confucian masters, and for this reason it can be properly regarded as a Confucian ideal. Putting the virtuous and competent in office is an important principle of governance repeatedly mentioned in *Mencius* and *Xunzi*.[17] Similarly, trustworthiness[18] and harmony[19] are common themes in *The Analects*, *Mencius*, and *Xunzi*. The idea of mutual care is also shared. Confucius says he longs to "bring peace to the old, to have trust in my friends, and to cherish the young" (*Analects* 5.26). In Xunzi's ideal society, "the young grow to maturity, and the old are cared for" (*Xunzi* 10.6). And in a similar manner to the "Li yun" chapter, Mencius says, "Treat the aged of your own family in a manner befitting their venerable age and extend this treatment to the aged of other families; treat your own young in a manner befitting their tender age and extend this to the young of other families" (*Mencius* 1A.7). Lastly, both Mencius and Xunzi share the Grand Union ideal that the least advantaged people—those who have few to turn to for help—should be taken care of by society (*Mencius* 1B.5; *Xunzi* 9.1, 9.4)

In the next chapter I will discuss in greater detail the features of the perfect ideal, especially those related to politics, but first let us consider a lesser ideal, the Small Tranquility, and see how the two are related.

17   See, for example, *Mencius* 2A.5; *Xunzi* 9.15.
18   See, for example, *Analects* 17.6; *Mencius* 1A.5; *Xunzi* 11.6.
19   See, for example, *Analects* 1.12; *Mencius* 2A.1; *Xunzi* 4.12.

Now that the Grand Dao has fallen into disuse and obscurity, hereditary families rule over the whole land. People love only their own parents as parents, and cherish only their own sons as sons. Goods and labor serve self-interests. Noblemen believe in their right to hereditary power. They build city walls, trenches and moats for security. Rules of propriety and righteousness are used to enforce the relationship between ruler and minister; to ensure affection between father and son, harmony between brothers, and concord between husband and wife; to establish institutions and measurements; to organize farms and hamlets; to honor the brave and the wise; and to bring merit to oneself. Selfish schemes and enterprises multiply, and armed conflicts arise. And so it was that Emperor Yu, King Tang, King Wen, King Wu, King Cheng, and the Duke of Zhou obtained their distinction. *Each of these six great men attended to the rules of propriety to manifest their righteousness and demonstrate their good faith. They defined what constituted excess, exemplified benevolence, and promoted the courtesy of concession, thus promoting good behavior by example. Rulers who did not act accordingly were driven out and condemned. Such was the Small Tranquility.* ("Li yun," *Book of Rites*, italics added)[20]

During times of the Small Tranquility, the spirit of impartiality and mutual care weakened. People were more concerned about the well-being of their own family members than the well-being of others. Political authority was passed on according to the principle of inheritance rather than the principle of abdication to the most virtuous and competent. As the desire to advance one's own interests came to the forefront, tactical behavior and armed conflicts began to occur. In response to these nonideal conditions, people built walls and ditches to protect themselves and established rules of propriety to guide behavior and regulate basic human relationships.

Interestingly, the author of the "Li yun" chapter does not portray the Small Tranquility as a fallen state completely at odds with the past. One very important feature of the Small Tranquility is that its rules of propriety perform *a dual function*—they not only discourage and curb improper behavior but also express and promote the ethical values that characterize the Grand Union, such as "harmony," "concord," "good faith," "benevolence," "righteousness," and "the courtesy of concession." In this sense, the lesser ideal of tranquility still keeps alive the ethical spirit of the Grand Union. The major Qing dynasty (1644–1911) commentator of *The Book of Rites*, Sun Xidan, insightfully observes that there are important connections between the two ideals. In the Small Tranquility, he argues, although the establishment of institutions and distribution of farmland primarily serve people's self-interests, it can enhance people's strength and productivity to such an extent that it benefits and supports everyone; the

---

20   Author's translation after consulting translations by Legge as well as Chai and Chai.

practice of benevolence and concession is conducive to the spirit of mutual trust and harmony in the Grand Union; and even though authority and power are hereditary, rulers act according to the rules of propriety and those who do not are driven out, so that the resulting situation retains the Grand Union's spirit of choosing men of talent and virtue for public service.[21]

The discussion above aims not to show that the Small Tranquility as described did actually exist in Chinese history, but that the author of the "Li yun" chapter is of the opinion that rites can be used to tackle problems arising from nonideal situations in a way that is compatible with the spirit of the Confucian ideal. A fundamental aim of Confucius's teaching in *The Analects* is also to help people see the deeper ethical values of rites—values such as harmony, benevolence, righteousness, and deference—which are very close to the spirit of the Grand Union.

> Of the things brought about by the rites, harmony is the most valuable. (1.12)
> What can a man who is not benevolent do with the rites? What can a man who is not benevolent do with music? (3.3)
> The gentleman has righteousness [yi] as his basic stuff and by observing the rites puts it into practice, by being modest gives it expression, and by being trustworthy in word [*xin*] brings it to completion. Such is a gentleman indeed. (15.18)
> For a man who is unable to govern a state by observing the rites and showing deference [*li rang*], what good can the rites be to him? (4.13)

We have seen two ideals, namely, the Grand Union as the perfect ideal and the Small Tranquility as the lesser ideal developed in response to unfavorable conditions. But how can we best describe the relation between these two ideals? The Small Tranquility is not a *transitional* stage toward the Grand Union, which Confucius regards as a bygone. The Small Tranquility might be described as *the second best* and the Grand Union as *the first best*, but even that is not entirely correct. Conceptually, the "second best" does not necessarily aim at the "first best" or retain any important connection with it. (I may choose an orange if an apple is not available, but nothing of the order of my selection suggests that the two have anything important in common, except that they are both fruits.) The Small Tranquility, however, does aim to keep alive the ethical spirit of the Grand Union. In tackling problems arising from unfavorable conditions, the lesser ideal adopts new measures and norms that still retain the ethical spirit of the perfect ideal as its ultimate aspiration. Thus, the best description of the relation between the Small Tranquility and the Grand Union is this: the Small Tranquility takes the Grand Union as its *regulative ideal* and partially achieves it.

---

21   Sun Xidan 孫希旦, *Liji ji jie* 禮記集解 [Collected Commentaries on *The Book of Rites*] (Beijing: Zhonghua, 1989), 584.

The Impasse

The "Li yun" chapter claims that the lesser ideal of the Small Tranquility was a reality in the Three Dynasties of Xia (ca. 2000–ca. 1600 BCE), Shang (ca. 1600–ca. 1100 BCE), and Western Zhou (ca. 1100–771 BCE). At the time of Confucius, however, things were much worse. The Zhou dynasty and its political setup had disintegrated, and its rituals had failed to control the behavior of both the people and the powerful feudal lords, many of whom had become corrupt and undisciplined. Even the notion of the Small Tranquility was an ideal far removed from reality. Confucius concludes that his mission to convince rulers of the necessity to implement the imperfect ideal has failed. And Mencius and Xunzi also remain pessimistic.

If this is the case, why were the early masters so reluctant to abandon their ideal? The ancient texts provide a few reasons that are also worth considering from a contemporary point of view. First, for the early masters, the fact that the rulers were not persuaded by the ideal does not imply that there are inherent problems with the ideal or that it should be dropped. Nor does it necessarily imply that the ideal is difficult to carry out. According to Mencius, the ideal is problematic only in that it fails to attract adherence from the political elite. When King Xuan of the state of Qi asks Mencius whether someone like Xuan himself can practice the Way of a true king and bring peace and protection to the people, Mencius replies that since the king cannot bear to see an ox trembling on the way to a religious sacrifice, his benevolence can also be extended to care for the people. Although Xuan still doubts that he can be a true king and practice the Way, Mencius's response has much implication for our discussion about ideal and reality: "That the people have not been tended is because you fail to practice kindness. Hence your failure to become a true king is due to a refusal to act, not to an inability to act" (*Mencius* 1A.7). When King Xuan then asks, "What is the difference in form between the refusal to act and the inability to act?" Mencius says,

> If you say to someone, "I am unable to do it," when the task is one of striding over the North Sea with Mount Tai under your arm, then this is a genuine case of inability to act. But if you say, "I am unable to do it," when it is one of breaking a twig for an elder, then this is a case of refusal to act, not of inability. Hence your failure to become a true king is not the same in kind as "striding over the North Sea with Mount Tai under your arm," but the same as "breaking a twig for an elder." (1A.7)

Mencius here distinguishes between what is physically impossible and what is physically easy to do. If someone fails to do what is physically easy, it is only because he or she refuses to do so. Mencius is of the opinion that the blueprint for his ideal—the Way of a true king—is not difficult to implement, and that what a ruler ought to do to protect and care for his people is to distribute sufficient land to each household so that they can maintain a decent standard of living; educate them about the five basic social relationships; consult their opinions in important matters; impose light taxes; prevent market monopoly; ensure the sustainability of common-pool resources; and share his joy with them. He maintains that as these policies had been successfully implemented by the early Sage Kings, there can be no question regarding their feasibility. If King Xuan failed to bring peace to the people, it would not be because the ideal and its policies were impossibly difficult for any ruler to carry out, but because Xuan himself was unwilling to do so. In other words, there is no reason to discard an ideal or relax what is demanded of rulers simply because some may refuse to act as good rulers. Although ways may need to be found to deal with weak, immoral, or selfish rulers, the solution should not be to abandon altogether the ideal standards of rulers.

Effective governance based on benevolence is only one aspect of the Confucian ideal. Another is the moral development of the common people, namely, that they should be encouraged to act virtuously in the spirit of harmony, righteousness, benevolence, and deference. However, the Confucian masters are not optimistic about the ability of the people to attain a high degree of moral understanding and development. For example, Confucius says, "Supreme indeed is the Mean as a moral virtue. It has long been rare among the common people" (*Analects* 6.29). And Mencius thinks that "the multitude can be said never to understand what they practice, to notice what they repeatedly do, or to be aware of the path they follow all their lives" (*Mencius* 7A.5). He also says that ordinary people "make the effort only when there is a [Sage King like] King Wen", while "outstanding men make the effort even without a King Wen" (7A.10). Xunzi is even more pessimistic. For him the common people are weak in their moral strength and unlovely in their feelings (*Xunzi* 23.6A).

Despite their pessimism, the masters attribute the inability of ordinary people to achieve advanced moral development to a lack of willpower and commitment, rather than to any inherent impossibility of the ideal of moral development. According to Mencius, everyone—common people and rulers alike—has the potential to become someone like Emperor Yao or Shun if they are willing to make the necessary effort: "The trouble with a man is surely not his lack of sufficient strength, but his refusal to make the effort"; "The Way of Yao and Shun is simply to be a good son and a good younger brother"; "The Way is like a wide road. It is not at all difficult to find. The trouble with people is simply that they do not look for it" (*Mencius* 6B.2). Xunzi also holds the view that it is possible for everyone to become a gentleman, but that not everyone is willing to do so. A sage can reach a high state of moral development through accumulated effort; common people, however, are "unwilling to do so" and "cannot be induced to do so" (*Xunzi* 23.5b).

Although we may agree with Mencius and Xunzi that it is empirically possible for everyone to become a Yao or Shun, it is certainly not as easy as "breaking a twig for an elder." The Way of Yao and Shun requires an utmost degree of filial piety and selfless devotion to the well-being of others—one's willpower has to be exceptionally strong and one's effort exceptionally strenuous. However, the fact that a moral ideal is demanding should not mean that we abandon it as an ideal. There are two reasons for this. First, Confucian thinkers never advocate the use of drastic measures to enforce people to be good, recognizing that such strategies are not only unworkable but also counterproductive. Second, it is unclear whether the masters ever expected ordinary people to reach the level of Sage Kings, and in any case, the political vision of a true king does not require common people to attain this level. So, unlike the Way of the true king, the high moral ideal for ordinary people remains, on the whole, an aspiration rather than an enforceable blueprint.

Even if the Confucian ideal is not impossible to attain or unreasonably harsh, it nevertheless remains "hopeless" in the sense that it has only a slight chance of ever being realized. If this is the case, would it be more logical to abandon two-track theorizing and adopt a single vision that is normatively attractive and has a good chance of success? The masters' answer seems to be no. To abandon the ideal—the greater one or the lesser one—is to abandon the Way of humanity. For the masters, people's ability to understand and practice benevolence, righteousness, and rituals marks the difference between humans and animals, and it is such ability that gives human beings worth (*Mencius* 4B.19, *Xunzi* 9.16a). To abandon an ideal that aspires to develop human potential is equivalent to abandoning humanity. Even if the Way of humanity is beyond the full reach of many people because of their weak willpower, it should not be compromised. In a conversation with Gongsun Chou, Mencius clarifies this point as follows:

> Gongsun Chou says, "The Way is indeed lofty and beautiful, but to attempt it is like trying to climb up to Heaven which seems beyond one's reach. Why not substitute for it something which men have some hopes of attaining so as to encourage them constantly to make the effort?"
>
> "A great craftsman," says Mencius, "does not put aside the plumb-line for the benefit of the clumsy carpenter. Yi did not compromise on his standards of drawing the bow for the sake of the clumsy archer. A gentleman is full of eagerness when he has drawn his bow, but before he lets fly the arrow, he stands in the middle of the path, and those who are able to do so follow him." (*Mencius* 7A.41)

According to Mencius, the standards of an art should not be lowered for the sake of clumsy learners. Similarly, the standards of the Way should not be lowered for the sake of the common people. Mencius emphasizes that the standards of benevolence and righteousness are not impossible to attain, but that people fail to live up to the standards in their full sense because they are weak-willed. As contemporary theorist David Estlund has said, "People could be good, they just aren't."[22] Similarly, the masters believe that if the ideal fails to be

---

22   David Estlund, *Democratic Authority: A Philosophical Framework* (Princeton: Princeton University Press, 2008), 264.

realized, it is due to the limitations of the people rather than problems with the ideal itself.

As we have seen, the lesser Confucian ideal of the Small Tranquility, though adapted to deal with nonideal conditions, still retains the Grand Union as its aspiration. However, if the nonideal conditions worsen so that even the lesser ideal becomes unachievable, what remains for Confucians to hold on to? Although there are aspirational reasons for maintaining the ideals, Confucians nonetheless need to find more feasible solutions to problems in reality. The question, then, becomes whether there is an alternative that retains benevolence and righteousness as an aspiration and yet effectively tackles problems in the nonideal world. The alternative advocated by the Legalists—namely, a complete reliance on rewards and, more especially, punishments administered through the instrument of law to shape people's behavior and strengthen the state—is categorically rejected by later Confucians. They argue that such a strategy would not only fail to ensure peace and stability but make people become "shameless" and hence move them farther away from moral development. As Confucius says, "Guide them by edicts, keep them in line with punishments, and the common people will stay out of trouble but will have no sense of shame. Guide them by virtue, keep them in line with the rites, and they will, besides having a sense of shame, reform themselves" (*Analects* 2.3). It is not difficult to understand this view. Moral character or virtue has to come from within, as it were. To be a virtuous agent, the agent must act with the right motivation and for the right reasons. People whose acts are motivated by the desire to conform to social pressure, to win praise, or to avoid punishment lack proper moral motivation and do not act virtuously. Confucians call these people "small men" or "village worthy" (*Analects* 17.12–13). In a similar vein, Mencius says that in order to be true kings, state rulers should be motivated by benevolence and righteousness rather than their own profit (*Mencius* 6B.4).

It should be noted that Confucius's position does not imply that he would never agree to the use of force or punishment. As will be discussed below, it is clear that Confucian masters treat punishment and litigation as a last resort, something to fall back on only when rituals, education, or mediation fail to regulate people's behavior. The primary aim for Confucians is always moral cultivation. Although different masters characterize the interplay between ideal means (such as education and rituals) and nonideal means (such as punishment, litigation, and military defense) in slightly different ways, they all affirm the primacy of the ideal means.[23] So the difference between Legalism and Confucianism is not that one allows the use of punishment as a means of social

---

23 Confucius says, "In hearing litigation, I am no different from any other man. But if you insist on a difference, it is, perhaps, that I try to get the parties not to resort to litigation in the first place" (*Analects* 12.13). Mencius says, "Good government does not win the people as does good education. He who practices good government is feared by the people; he who gives the people good education is loved by them" (*Mencius* 7A.14). Xunzi says, "If one only reproves and does not instruct, then punishments will be numerous but evil will still not be overcome. If one instructs but does not reprove, then dissolute people will not be chastened" (*Xunzi* 10.10).

control and the other does not. It is rather that Legalism adopts a single vision in which punishment plays the chief role, while Confucianism adopts a two-track vision in which punishment is always secondary to moral cultivation by means of rites and education.

Confucians thus face a difficult situation. On the one hand, they cannot agree with the Legalist strategy because it abandons the aim and means of moral cultivation. On the other, they acknowledge that their preferred means—the rites, the Kingly Way of governance, and virtues—have failed to control the behavior of the rulers and the common people. They are unable to envision a viable alternative that can simultaneously retain the spirit of the ideal and deal with the problems arising from nonideal situations, and they insist that the ideal can be realized without much difficulty if enough good people are in office—despite there being no way of ensuring that the good people will be put in power or that there are any to begin with. At the end of the day, without an acceptable nonideal alternative to their ideal, Confucian masters can only resign themselves to fate, or Heaven's will, over the chance of success of their ideal. For this reason Confucius says, "It is Destiny if the Way prevails; it is equally Destiny if the Way falls into disuse" (*Analects* 14.36). Similarly Mencius says that the Way's success is a matter of Heaven's will: "Confucius went forward in accordance with the rites and withdrew in accordance with what was right, and in matters of success or failure said, 'There is the Decree'" (*Mencius* 5A.8). For the masters, if the Way is destined not to prevail, there is nothing that humans can do. Confucians cannot lower the standard of the Way to adapt to reality, for it represents the Truth or Humanity. If they cannot move the fallen world closer to the Way, the only choice is to withdraw from it or sacrifice their lives for it. "When the Way prevails in the empire, it goes where one's person goes; when the Way is eclipsed, one's person goes where the Way has gone. I have never heard of making the Way go where other people are going" (*Mencius* 7A.42).

Breaking the Impasse

This, then, is the predicament facing early Confucianism. And it may not be too far off the mark to say that this predicament has not changed much in the past two thousand years or so. Today any attempt to revitalize Confucianism in the context of modern society faces the same task as that faced by the early masters, that is, how to develop a nonideal approach to society and politics that keeps alive the ideal as an aspiration while effectively dealing with problems that arise in nonideal conditions. The early thinkers became mired in their lesser ideal of the Small Tranquility and found no other way out. Can we do better today? And how should we set about doing so? In what follows I shall outline three general considerations that may serve to guide this process of constructing a Confucian political philosophy for a modern society. The first has to do with the importance of correctly capturing the spirit of the Confucian ideal. The second concerns Confucian attitudes in tackling the problems of reality. The third is about the proper relation of ideal and nonideal concerns.

Let me begin with the first consideration, the importance of correctly capturing the spirit of the Confucian ideal. It is not easy to pin down the elements that constitute the Confucian ideal (if we intend to go beyond the Grand Union and Small Tranquility), for Confucianism is a complex tradition of thought that evolved in response to changing historical circumstances. In this long process it has developed many views that were pitched at different levels, ranging from the most down-to-earth guidelines or recommendations for tackling changing circumstances (for example, behavioral prescriptions of rituals and the making of context-specific choices) to the highest-level ideals (for example, the spirit of benevolence and public-spiritedness). Many of these views fall somewhere between these two extremes, such as certain views about political institutions and economic policies, and it is not always easy to tell whether such views belong to the level of ideal (that is, those whose spirit needs to be kept) or the level of nonideal (that is, those whose contents and challenges vary with changing circumstances). For example, in politics, while the principle of selecting the virtuous and competent to work for public interest seems to be a part of the Confucian ideal, it is unclear whether the Confucian idea of having one Sage King to exercise supreme authority is necessarily a part of this ideal or merely a product of adaptation to nonideal conditions. Similarly, it is unclear whether Confucian distributive and retributive justice is on a par with benevolence in the ideal scheme of things, or merely a remedial virtue of less value than benevolence. Because of the multilevel character of Confucian views, it is easy to make unfair assessments of Confucian thought. In later chapters I shall attempt to answer some of these questions.

Second, despite the fact that Confucians hold tightly to their ideal conception of society and politics, they are relatively flexible when dealing with problems in the nonideal world. They know that although it is one thing to aspire to an ideal, it is another to practice it without regard to actual circumstances. When dealing with unfavorable conditions, the three Confucian masters all counsel people on the importance of acting flexibly and timely, even to the extent as to act contrary to rites and principles in order to prevent harm. Confucius says that "the gentleman is steadfast in purpose but he is not inflexible" (*Analects* 15.37). He also praises Guan Zhong, who helped save innocent lives by assisting Duke Huan, who, to gain power, killed his own brother Prince Jiu, whom Guan Zhong served, and was thus able to forge deals among conflicting feudal lords and successfully avoid interstate wars and bloodshed. Confucius's disciples question the integrity of Guan Zhong for willingly serving someone who had killed his lord. But Confucius insists on recognizing him as a benevolent man because of his contribution to peace and stability, the larger goals that a gentleman should pursue (*Analects* 14.16–17). Mencius also writes much about the necessity of discretion when facing conflicting demands. In a situation where a rite of lesser importance (for example, that a man should not touch a woman) conflicts with a more important goal (for example, that of saving a life), Mencius says that the more important goal should be pursued even if a lesser rite is violated (*Mencius* 4A.17). More generally, in making a choice between competing demands, we should not look abstractly at the nature of those demands, but rather at the concrete circumstances in which they are pertinent. We should also consider their trade-offs in terms of quantity, weight, or seriousness in the particular circumstances (*Mencius* 6B.1). Similarly, in praising a great *ru* (Confucian gentleman), Xunzi says, "He handles dangerous situations, responding, changing, and adapting as is suitable; he modifies and adjusts at the proper time and initiates or desists with the proper season; through a thousand affairs and ten thousand changes, his Way is one" (*Xunzi* 8.9). In modern terms, we could say that the Confucian Way, functioning as a regulative ideal, signifies not so much a rigid hierarchy of values and principles that can be mechanistically applied as a clarity of purpose and a firm grasp of what is truly significant and important. The rest is contextual thinking and judgment.

The third general consideration to guide the process of working out a Confucian political philosophy for modern times has to do with the relation between ideal and nonideal concerns. We have seen that early Confucianism displays a good degree of realism and flexibility toward the nonideal world. However, this realism and flexibility are not unprincipled but appropriately linked to ideal aspirations. To illustrate how early Confucians deal with these dual demands of flexibility and ideal aspirations, I will give two examples, both related to the use of force in nonideal conditions. The first example is taken not directly from Confucian classics but from the traditional Chinese discourse on martial virtue (*wu de*), which was heavily influenced by Confucian thought. The very term of "martial virtue" suggests a striking reconciliation of idealist and realistic demands, an interplay of the ideal and nonideal. Martial arts and the use of force are supposed to be the very antithesis of the Confucian ideal of benevolence and harmony, yet they are necessary in the nonideal world and can, and should, be practiced with a view to the ideal. The idea of martial virtue is that martial arts must be guided by virtue, in the sense both that the person practicing martial arts must possess virtue in order to attain the highest level of the arts and gain due respect from others, and that the use of force is permitted only in achieving ethical ends, such as saving lives and maintaining peace and justice.[24] According to traditional Chinese views, the martial arts are not merely a set of practices involving certain skills or techniques, they are also practices involving virtue and an ethical purpose.

---

24 See Liu Shujun 劉樹軍, "Chuan tong wu de si xiang de ji ben nei rong" 傳統武德思想的基本內容 [The Basic Content of Traditional Wu De Thought], in *Chuan tong wu de ji qi jia zhi chong jian* 傳統武德及其價值重建 [The Reconstruction of Traditional Wu De and Its Values] (Changsha: Central South University Press, 2007), 87–96. I thank Jeffrey Martin for mentioning wu de when I explained to him the theme of this chapter.

My second example is criminal punishment.[25] In Confucian vocabulary, there is a range of words to describe different types of social means to guide behavior. As *The Book of Rites* says, rituals (li) should cultivate moral character and manifest morality; music (*yue*) should achieve harmony among people; government directives and decrees (*zheng*) should coordinate collective action; and penal law and punishment (*xing*) should guard against people's tendency to do evil ("Yue ji," *Book of Rites*). The preferred means of achieving the Confucian ideal of society are rituals and music, as it is only through these that people can acquire genuine moral attitudes and character. But punishment becomes necessary when these means fail to prevent wrongdoing. What, then, should be the proper interplay between the ideal and the nonideal means? As Confucius says, "When rites and music do not flourish, punishments will not be exactly right; when punishments are not exactly right, the common people will not know where to put hand and foot" (*Analects* 13.3). Traditional commentaries on the meaning of "punishments will not be exactly right" suggest two readings that are not mutually inconsistent but rather complementary. The first reading maintains that without the flourishing of rites and music, no proper standard of right and wrong conduct will be readily available to determine the right level of sentencing and punishment. The second reading says that without effective rites and music, rulers will tend to overly rely on severe punishments to prevent wrongdoing or maintain social stability. So the use of punishment must be guided by the rites and applied only when the preferred means of rites, music, and education have been tried.

The Argument of This Book

From its inception to modern times, Confucianism has always faced the problem of the serious gap between its social and political ideal and reality. This book argues that the problem is not the regulative ideal itself, but how to develop a viable method of governance that retains the spirit of the Confucian ideal and at the same time effectively addresses the problems of nonideal contemporary situations. Without a doubt, modern society and its institutions present new opportunities and challenges for dealing with the nonideal world. Liberal democratic institutions, human rights apparatus and civil liberties, and measures to promote social justice are new means of coping with social problems both old and new. When considering these methods of tackling social problems, we should exercise the same flexibility and adaptability as early Confucian masters counsel. I shall argue that Confucians should embrace modern

25   A third example may be the use of force in military action. For an instructive analysis of early Confucian views on just war from the perspective of ideal vs. nonideal, see Daniel A. Bell, "Just War and Confucianism: Implications for the Contemporary World," in *Confucian Political Ethics*, ed. Daniel A. Bell (Princeton: Princeton University Press, 2008), 226–56.

institutions and measures if they are effective and tie them to the Confucian ideal in the same way early masters deal with the use of force in the above examples. It may be argued that many modern institutions and measures, having often originated in the West, necessarily carry normative and philosophical ideas and values that run counter to the Confucian ideal. However, such an argument makes controversial interpretations of both Western practices and the nature of Confucianism. I shall critically examine such interpretations and show how modern institutions and measures can promote a number of Confucian goals and how such institutions can be modified to keep alive the spirit of the Confucian ideal.

The main strategy that I shall use to tie modern institutions with the Confucian ideal is to develop what I call a Confucian *perfectionist* approach to politics. Political perfectionism is the philosophical view that the social and political order—including political rights and duties—are to be judged by their contribution to the human good life.[26] Confucian perfectionism, then, assesses social and political institutions with reference to the Confucian conception of the good. The best way for Confucians today to meet the challenge, I argue, is to adopt some liberal democratic institutions but justify them with the Confucian perfectionist approach, that is, to ground and shape these institutions in terms of the Confucian conception of the good rather than the liberal conception of the right. This approach decouples liberal democratic institutions from those popular liberal philosophical packages that base liberal democratic institutions on fundamental moral rights or principles, such as popular sovereignty, political equality, human rights, and individual sovereignty.

I will adopt this approach to examine issues of political authority and democracy, human rights and civil liberties, and social justice and welfare. In doing so, I aim to reconstruct both Confucianism and liberal democratic institutions, blending them to form an outline of a new Confucian political philosophy, which I call *Confucian political perfectionism*. This philosophy incorporates a number of basic institutions of liberal democracy, grounds them on Confucian perfectionism, and redefines their roles and functions. It mixes Confucian values with liberal democratic institutions in a way that hopefully strengthens both.

This book is divided into two parts. The first part discusses issues of political authority and institutions. The second examines issues to do with relations between the state and the people—human rights, civil liberties, social justice, and social welfare. The scope and method of the book are discussed in appendix 1.

In chapter 1 I examine early Confucian views on the nature, purposes, and justifications of authority. I first reject an interpretation of Confucianism that treats authority as an ownership right to be possessed by the monarch or the people. (Appendix 2 evaluates this interpretation in detail.) I then develop a

---

26 For an account of political perfectionism, see Joseph Chan, "Legitimacy, Unanimity, and Perfectionism," *Philosophy and Public Affairs* 29, no. 1 (2000): 5–42.

Confucian perfectionist perspective that takes the well-being of the people and their willing acceptance of political rule as fundamental to the legitimacy of political authority. According to this perspective, political authority exists *for* the people and is partly justified by its ability to protect and promote the people's well-being. But the authoritative relationship between the governed and those who govern is also constituted by mutual commitment on both sides— those who govern are committed to serve the people, and the governed willingly and gladly accept and support the governance. The Confucian perfectionist perspective therefore makes two connections between authority and the good life. First, authority instrumentally serves the well-being of the people. Second, the constitutive mutual commitment of the governing and governed is an ethically valuable and satisfying relationship that contributes to the good life. This perfectionist perspective differs importantly from Lockean liberalism—authority is not derived from the consent of people who possess political rights that are naturally given or morally basic but is part and parcel of a good political relationship that contributes to the good life of the people.

Chapter 2 explores a paradox—although early Confucianism endorses the idea that authority exists to serve the people and that authority cannot be based on the arbitrary will of the one who holds the authority, it implicitly or explicitly embraces the notion that authority must be monist and supreme and not be subject to any higher legal constraints. In other words, early Confucianism would not accept the modern ideas of limited government and the separation of powers. The chapter reconstructs certain early Confucian arguments for authority and the importance of a monist and supreme conception of authority. I propose that these arguments cannot reject limited government and the separation of power, and that the notion of monist and supreme authority must be given up if Confucian political thought is to have any potential today. Instead of hoping for the appearance of a godlike figure to assume a position of utmost prestige and power, we should lower our sights and adopt a political system that brings together people with flawed but above-average levels of virtue and intelligence in positions of power, allowing them to cooperate, check among themselves, and also be checked by the people.

While chapters 1 and 2 are studies of Confucian conceptions of authority on the ideal level, chapters 3 and 4 deal with problems of authority on the nonideal level. Chapter 3 puts forward the argument that although the Confucian ideal of the authoritative ruler-ruled relationship, one marked by mutual commitment and trust, is an insightful and attractive ideal that would appear to be relevant even in contemporary democratic societies, in reality not all officials are trustworthy and genuinely care for the people. Here the challenge of how to properly handle the interplay between the ideal and reality arises—on the one hand, we must find a social device that helps prevent officials from abusing power and removes bad officials from office; on the other hand, such a device must be able to express the Confucian ideal relationship and hopefully also promote it. The solution, I argue, lies in the nature of institutions, which are devices that at once perform socially useful tasks to tackle real-life problems *and* uphold standards of normative appropriateness that express ideal aspirations. I argue that one kind of political institution, namely, democratic elections, can perform this dual function. Drawing on the work of contemporary political scientists, I argue that democratic elections can perform both as a device to select virtuous and competent politicians for the common good (the selection function) and as a mechanism to reward and sanction them (the sanction function). While the sanction function of elections addresses nonideal problems, the selection function expresses the spirit of the Confucian ideal of political relationship.

Chapter 4 examines more comprehensively the relationship between Confucian political perfectionism and democracy. I argue that the two are complementary and can strengthen each other. On the one hand, democracy instrumentally promotes Confucian political ends such as the improvement of people's well-being and directly expresses the Confucian ideal political relationship—in this sense democracy can be instrumentally and expressively justified in Confucian terms. On the other hand, the Confucian perfectionist approach to ethics and politics provides a robust ethical foundation for a well-functioning democracy. In ideal situations, democratic elections will be conducted in a civil and respectful manner consistent with the spirit of the selection model. In real, nonideal situations, however, democratic elections may breed and reinforce hostile antagonism, and the democratic political process may become a trading of narrow interests at the expense of the common good. Although Western theorists have long pointed out the importance of civic virtues or civility as an essential condition for democracy, contemporary theorists have tended to adopt a liberal, knowledge-based approach to civic education, the effectiveness of which is questionable. I argue that Confucian moral education, which is humanity-based rather than citizen-based, provides a stronger incentive for citizens to cultivate civility than liberal civic education, as well as a more comprehensive foundation of virtues. Lastly, I argue that Confucian political perfectionism can also offer some reflection on how to select virtuous and competent people to serve in politics. I suggest, by way of example, a second chamber of legislature whose members would be selected by colleagues. If suitably formed, this chamber would not only be a governing institution in its own right but also play an important part in the moral education of the society at large.

The second part of the book reconstructs and develops a Confucian perfectionist perspective on the issues of human rights, civil liberties, social justice, and social welfare. In chapter 5 I adopt a two-track approach to human rights. I argue that the idea of human rights is compatible with the Confucian understanding of ethics and society, but that in the ideal society people will be guided by precepts of benevolence and virtues rather than by considerations of human rights. Thus human rights do not play an important practical role in ideal society, for the same reason that rites are not important in the Grand Union. In nonideal situations, where virtuous relationships break down and mediation fails to reconcile conflicts, human rights can become a powerful fallback apparatus for the vulnerable to protect their legitimate interests against exploitation and harm by powerful actors, especially the state. The importance of human rights thus lies in its instrumental function. But unlike liberalism, Confucian ethics would not take human rights as constitutive of human worth or dignity. Furthermore, just as early Confucianism states that the use of penal law must be governed by considerations of virtue and ethical propriety, the practice of human rights must not eclipse the moral vocabularies of the common good, virtues, and duties. To avoid the rise of "rights talk" and a rights-centered culture, I argue that Confucian perfectionism should keep the list of human rights short and restrict it to civil and political rights—not because social and economic rights are less important but because civil and political rights are more suitable for legal implementation and because they redress a strong tendency within traditional Confucianism to place too much power in the hands of political leaders.

Chapter 6 develops a new Confucian perfectionist approach to individual autonomy and civil liberties. Confucianism has often been criticized for failing to recognize individual autonomy. I argue, however, that Confucian ethics does promote individual moral autonomy, in the sense that the moral agent must voluntarily accept the demands of morality and reflectively engage in the moral life. To a considerable extent, this notion supports toleration and freedom, since a highly restrictive or oppressive moral environment is harmful to the development of a genuine moral life. However, traditional Confucian moral autonomy is compatible with only a narrow range of life choices. To cope with the demands of a fast-changing, pluralistic society, Confucian ethics should incorporate a moderate notion of personal autonomy in the wider sense that people should have the freedom to form life goals and chart a personal path of life. This should not be a moral right or, in liberal terms, an individual sovereignty, but a valuable aspect of the good life. A Confucian perfectionist ethics that incorporates this notion is receptive of the pluralism of values and ways of life in modern society. A Confucian perfectionist political theory sees civil liberties as instrumentally useful for the promotion of the good and expressive of the ideal of personal autonomy and attempts to balance the two when they conflict. This perfectionist perspective, however, rejects the strong liberal view that gives sovereign protection to the individual insofar as his or her personal life is concerned.

Chapters 7 and 8 develop a Confucian perfectionist perspective on justice and welfare. In chapter 7 I argue that the principles of resource distribution in *Mencius* can be conceived as principles of justice, which I call principles of sufficiency. The aim of social justice, according to this perfectionist view, is to enable every member of a community to live a good life. What is morally significant is whether each person has sufficient resources to lead a good life, not whether each has the same amount. The Confucian conception of the good life sets a rough standard for sufficiency—namely, the amount a person generally needs to live a decent material life and feel materially secure enough to pursue the higher, ethical life. On the matter of distribution of resources, Confucian justice is not of an egalitarian but a *sufficientarian* view, to use the jargon of contemporary political philosophy. Justice as sufficiency for all, however, is only part of the larger Confucian conception of the social ideal. In chapter 8 I argue that Mencius envisages a multilevel social system of provision in which the family, the village or commune, as well as the government all have specific roles to play—social justice is the foundation of this social system; the family and commune (or social relationships and networks) provide familial care and mutual aid; and when they are not sufficient, the government steps in to provide direct welfare assistance. This Confucian social ideal integrates justice and care, recognizing both individual merit and personal responsibility.

The conclusion summarizes the arguments of the book and integrates them into the political philosophy described in previous chapters, namely, Confucian political perfectionism. It explains how perfectionism runs through the reconstruction of this philosophy. Taken as a whole, Confucian political perfectionism makes a radical departure from European and American liberal democratic theory, although it makes use of certain liberal democratic institutions to cope with nonideal problems. It differs most noticeably from a rights-based approach to politics. In the rights-based approach, democracy is understood as an embodiment of the idea that the people are sovereign—it not only *means* rule by the people but is also *justified* by that idea. In Confucian political perfectionism, the concept of democracy still means rule by the people, but it is not justified by the idea that people are sovereign. Rather, it is justified by its service to the people and by a perfectionist view of a political relationship of mutual commitment and trust between the people and those they have elected to govern. According to Confucian perfectionism, morality based on integrity and virtue is essential to the health of democratic politics and has important implications for the duties of both citizens and representatives. In the rights-based approach, human rights and civil liberties are both similarly justified by the fundamental idea that people have sovereign rights over their bodies and actions. In Confucian political perfectionism, however, human rights and civil liberties are important insofar as they protect or promote fundamental individual interests, in particular the interest in leading an ethical life and a non-Confucian ideal of moderate personal autonomy. Rights and liberties must be exercised with a balanced consideration of these two interests. Lastly, in the rights-based approach, social justice is premised either on the self-ownership right (as in libertarianism) or on the right to equal respect and concern (as in egalitarianism). In Confucian political perfectionism, however, social justice is justified by its contribution to the good life—it provides resources sufficient for all people to live an ethical life, while allowing economic inequality to arise from merit and contribution.

The conclusion also discusses appropriate ways of promoting Confucianism in the context of a modern pluralistic society. I argue that in public political discourse, one should not present Confucianism as a comprehensive and packaged doctrine and ask people to accept policy proposals as implications of that package. Promoting Confucianism in this way undermines the ability of a liberal democratic society to function well and is not in accord with the spirit of Confucian civility. Rather, the Confucian perfectionism in political philosophy and politics that I develop takes the form of moderate perfectionism. In political philosophy, Confucian perfectionism develops its arguments and institutional proposals through a bottom-up process of examining the specific Confucian values and principles relevant to each political issue under discussion, rather than a top-down application of a comprehensive doctrine to the issue. In politics and public policy making, Confucian perfectionism asks citizens and officials to appeal to individual and specific values and principles in Confucian thought and justify them in terms that do not require prior acceptance of Confucianism. It fashions not a winner-take-all politics but a piecemeal politics in which both the gains of winners and losses of losers are limited and their positions can reverse in different policy domains.

The philosophy and politics of Confucian political perfectionism that this book espouses, I hope, are a viable approach for dealing with the quandary of Confucian political thought, a desirable way to refashion both Confucian values and liberal democratic institutions in modern society, and an attractive philosophical alternative to liberal democratic theory.

PART I

Political Authority and Institution

CHAPTER 1

What Is Political Authority?

In this and the following chapters, I shall attempt to develop a Confucian conception of political authority by answering a number of questions, namely: What is political authority? What are its purposes? How can it be justified? Do people who are ruled play any role in the justification? What scope of authority should a state or government have? What institutional structure of authority should a state adopt? Viewed together, the answers to these questions will form the backbone of a theory of political authority. Although the texts of early Confucian thinkers do not outline anything close to a systematic theory of political authority, they share similar core ideas and views that can be reconstructed and developed into a more or less coherent perspective. My aim is to expound this perspective and assess its philosophical plausibility.

This chapter deals with the first four questions of authority—its nature, its purposes, its justifications, and the role of the people in these justifications. It develops a perfectionist perspective that takes the well-being of the people and their willing acceptance of political rule as fundamental to the legitimacy of political authority. In the first section I start with the Western Zhou dynasty conception of Heaven's Mandate (*tianming*), which says that the right to rule is based on Heaven's Mandate.[1] I reject two interpretations that treat the right bestowed by Heaven as a *dominium* or ownership right. The second section argues that for early Confucians, political authority exists for the benefit of the governed and is justified by its ability to protect and promote the people's well-being. I call this view of authority the service conception and explain its main features and implications. The third section argues that according to the service conception, political rights are justified instrumentally by the contribution they make to the betterment of people's lives, and thus no persons, be they rulers or

---

1   One might wonder why I do not start with an analysis of absolute monarchy, which early Confucian thinkers either embraced or did not reject. The reason is that I believe the normative basis of authority, which is captured by the idea of Heaven's Mandate, is a more fundamental notion than types of authority (in terms of its form and scope). But I do discuss in details two most important dimensions of absolute monarchy—its monist and supreme power and its hereditary principle—in chapter 2 and appendix 2, respectively. For an analysis of early Confucian political thought that does take monarchy as one of its central focuses, see Yuri Pines, "The Ruler," pt. 1 in *Envisioning Eternal Empire: Chinese Political Thought of the Warring States Era* (Honolulu: University of Hawaii Press, 2009).

the people, have any natural political right to rule. I defend this view of political rights and point out problems with the opposing idea of popular sovereignty. The fourth section argues that early Confucianism also contains a noninstrumental justification of authority, in the sense that an authoritative political relation is constituted in part by the people's willing acceptance of and compliance with the political rule. The final section integrates the instrumental and constitutive aspects of political authority by developing a perfectionist approach and laying out the approach's key features. This approach, as we shall see in chapters 3 and 4, plays a critical role in my strategy to relate the Confucian ideal to democratic political institutions.

The Dominium Conception

Political authority is taken here in a normative sense, namely, as a legitimate right to rule at the highest level within a jurisdiction. What is the source of political authority for early Confucians? The best starting point is the idea of tianming, arguably the single most important political idea of the Western Zhou period and one that shaped the subsequent political thinking of the entire traditional Chinese political thought.[2] The term *tianming* expresses the notion that the right to rule is based on Heaven's Mandate. In *The Book of History* (*Shang shu*), the Duke of Zhou frequently invokes this idea to justify his country's revolt against the Shang regime. This shows that the people in Zhou already knew the distinction between sheer might and legitimate authority to rule. Might was thought to be necessary for authority, but it was Heaven's Mandate that ultimately conferred legitimacy on rulership.

However, what does political authority or the right to rule amount to? What rights and duties are associated with political authority in this theory of Heaven's Mandate? There seems to be textual support for two interpretations of tianming—the ownership interpretation and the democratic rights interpretation—and scholars have argued for both interpretations. The first interpretation says that Heaven bestows on the chosen ruler an ownership right to the people and land over which the ruler rules. The second interpretation holds an opposite view, namely, that Heaven bestows a fundamental moral right to rule to the people themselves, with the right to own the territory in which they live. These two incompatible interpretations, however, share the same *conception* of political authority (or sovereignty) as an entitlement of dominium or ownership. They differ only in the identity of the dominus or owner—that is, whether those entitled to political authority are the rulers or the people. On this dominium

---

2   See Herrlee Glessner Creel, *The Western Chou Empire*, vol. 1 of *The Origins of Statecraft in China* (Chicago: University of Chicago Press, 1970), 93. Mencius makes heavy use of this concept in his discussion of political authority.

conception, political authority is something that can be owned and passed on, and it contains entitlements to resources within the jurisdiction of the dominus. Since an examination of these two interpretations requires detailed textual analyses that might detract from the thrust of the overall argument in this chapter, I shall only state the main conclusions of this examination here and leave the exegetical arguments to appendix 2. I argue there that early Confucianism does not endorse the dominium conception of political authority, whether the dominium is vested in a person or a people. Political authority, or the right to rule, according to the Confucian view, does not contain any ownership claim over the people, land, or authority itself. It is not a dominium but an *imperium*—that is, the legitimate right to govern within a jurisdiction. When a ruler is said to have received Heaven's Mandate, it is this right to rule that he has received. This right is no more than the power to make and implement laws and policies within a certain territorial jurisdiction and is *conditional* on the ability of the ruler to protect and promote the people's well-being. Political authority exists for this purpose, and its justification depends on its ability to serve this purpose well. In appendix 2 I also argue that early Confucian texts, especially *Mencius*, do not take the people as the natural dominus—the people do not possess any natural fundamental right to rule. The democratic idea of popular sovereignty cannot be found in the texts. While the conclusions of my analysis in appendix 2 are primarily about what Confucianism is not, they also point toward a highly interesting, albeit rudimentary, alternative conception of political authority. The rest of this chapter is devoted to a further analysis and development of this conception.

The Service Conception

The Zhou dynasty concept of Heaven's Mandate says that Heaven gave the right to rule to the Zhou dynasty in order that the people could receive proper protection under its authority. And it is the protection of the people that is also the key condition for Zhou being able to keep the mandate.[3] A similar idea can be found in a passage of a lost chapter of *The Book of History*, which is quoted in *Mencius*: "*The Book of History* says, 'Heaven populated the earth below, made the people a lord, and made him their teacher, that he might assist Heaven in loving them'" (1B.3). Zhou's idea that the purpose of tianming is to protect the people has been further developed in later periods, for example, in this well-known passage by Mencius which states that the people are more important than the ruler: "The people are of supreme importance; the altars to the gods of earth and grain come next; last comes the ruler" (*Mencius* 7B.14), and in Xun-

---

3   The other condition is for the ruler to be virtuous and practice virtuous rule—both related to the task of protecting the people.

zi's often cited idea that "Heaven did not create the people for the sake of the lord; Heaven established the lord for the sake of the people." Xunzi writes,

> Heaven did not create the people for the sake of the lord; Heaven established the lord for the sake of the people. Hence, in antiquity land was not granted in fiefs of ranked sizes just to give honored position to the feudal lords and for no other purpose. Offices and ranks were not arranged in hierarchical order and provided with suitable titles and emoluments just to give honored status to the grand officers and for no other purpose. (*Xunzi* 27.68)

If we combine the ideas of these two thinkers, we have the following view of political authority: the people have independent worth (Mencius), and the authority of the ruler and all other officials is an instrument to serve them (Xunzi). Borrowing a term from the contemporary British legal and political philosopher Joseph Raz, I shall call this combined idea the "service conception" of political authority. The service conception states that the point of setting up political authority, and more generally a regime, is to serve the ruled, who have worth in themselves.[4] Political offices of all levels—along with the associated power, status, and emoluments—are created to benefit the ruled rather than the officeholders themselves.

The Confucian service conception of authority has several important implications that are worth exploring here. First, there are two hierarchies in the ruler-ruled relationship as understood by this conception. One is the hierarchy of power—the ruler rules while the ruled respects and obeys. However, there is also a more fundamental hierarchy of value or worth. The service conception states that the people—the ruled—have worth independent of the ruler-ruled relationship, whereas the ruler's worth is only derivative. Of course, we need to distinguish between the ruler as an office and the ruler as a person holding the office. The service conception states that the office's value is entirely instrumental to, or derived from, the worth of the people, and the features of the office—the power, respect, and emolument that come with it—are justified ultimately with reference to its instrumental function. But the service conception does not deny that the person holding that office has independent worth, who may indeed have great worth if he possesses superior abilities and virtues to effectively

---

4 "The service conception of the function of authorities [is] the view that their role and primary normal function is to serve the governed." Joseph Raz, *The Morality of Freedom* (Oxford: Clarendon Press, 1986), 56. It should be noted that the exact meaning and implication of the service conception and justification of authority developed by Raz is different from what I am expounding here, which is based on ideas already present in Confucian texts. It should also be noted that the idea of "serving" the people, when applied to the Confucian tradition, should not be taken to mean serving the preexisting desires of the people, whatever these desires may be. As noted below, the good life of people, according to Confucian thought, consists of not only material well-being (the desire for which is perfectly reasonable) but also moral cultivation and virtuous social relationships. Serving the people includes creating an environment conducive to these ethical pursuits as well.

discharge his office. It also does not deny that the ruler (rather than the office) should develop a noninstrumental, ethical relationship with the ruled—a point I shall develop later in this chapter.

Second, the service conception is clearly in opposition to the ownership interpretation of tianming, namely, that tianming grants the ruler an ownership right to the land and people. The service conception not only rejects this but also affirms the instrumentality of political authority, namely, that political authority serves the interests of the people (in today's terms, the public interest or common good) rather than the private interests of the ruler. A similar notion that appears in *Shuo yuan* states that Heaven establishes rulership for the sake of the people and not for the sake of the position itself; if the ruler governs for his private interests (*si yu*) and not for the interests of others, he has failed to act according to Heaven's decree and has forgotten what it truly means to be a ruler.[5]

Third, according to the service conception, the raison d'être of political authority—to serve the people—is also the very basis for Heaven's Mandate and hence the ruler's legitimacy. The following passage from *Chun qiu fan lu* expounds Xunzi's idea and explicitly links the ruler's service to the people to the basis of Heaven's Mandate: "If a person's virtue is sufficient to ensure peace and contentment for the people, Heaven will give its mandate to him to govern, but if the vice of a serving ruler is sufficient to seriously harm the people, Heaven will take away the mandate from him."[6] This apparently religious justification of legitimacy has a thoroughly worldly character—what ultimately matters is the well-being of the people and whether they are well served by the ruler. It is important to note that although this justification of authority is instrumental and consequentialist, it is not the maximizing form of consequentialism. The passage does not imply that if a serving ruler is less than perfect in terms of virtue and competence, we must keep searching for a better one. It implies that the criterion for legitimacy is one of sufficiency—a ruler should possess *sufficient* virtues and abilities (which should be reflected by a good track record)— and that any vices demonstrated by a ruler must be serious enough to significantly harm the people's interests in order for him to be removed.[7] This makes good political sense as continuity and stability are fundamentally important in politics and constant changes of leadership only cause confusion and undermine effective governance. This point also has important bearing upon the

5   Bk. 1, "Jun dao" 君道.

6   Chap. 25, "Yao Shun bu shan yi, Tang Wu bu zhuan sha" 堯舜不擅移、湯武不專殺. My own translation.

7   In the most extreme case, Heaven waited five years for the corrupt ruler Jie to correct his behavior before finally removing him from office—see "Duo fang" 多方 (Numerous Regions), *The Book of History*. The somewhat slow response could be explained by two factors: (1) that it takes time for the performance and level of corruption of a ruler to become evident and to deteriorate to the extent that it is no longer tenable; and (2) that it takes time to find and establish an effective alternative power to replace the corrupt ruler.

evaluation of regime types, especially the principle of monarchical heredity, as I discuss in appendix 2.

A Non-Rights-Based Justification

According to the service conception I have developed thus far, political authority exists to serve the ruled, and the political rights attached to this authority are justified instrumentally by the contribution they make to the betterment of people's lives. These political rights are not fundamental moral rights that belong to individuals but are more on a par with the rights of officials such as the police, who have rights because their proper exercise of them can protect and promote the well-being of the people. Theoretically one could extend this view to a general view about all political rights, a view that is not articulated in Confucianism but which can be regarded as a natural extension of, or at least fully compatible with, its core political ideas. The general view is that the distribution of political rights or powers, and the institutional form that these rights or powers take, should be evaluated by the service conception. A person possessing political rights or a share in an institution of political authority must have this possession justified by reference to the good of the people. In this sense there is no natural right to political power as such. There is no natural ruler whose right requires no justification with regard to the interests or needs of other people.

But this idea applies even to the governed insofar as they also possess certain political rights. When the ruled take turns to rule (as in classical Athens), or when citizens cast votes to elect their leaders (as in a democracy), they are sharing in and exercising political power and are therefore actively engaging in the act of ruling. However small the portion of power an individual citizen possesses, the aggregate effects of their individual powers can be tremendous. Collectively, citizens assert a great deal of influence on the choice of rulers, the making of laws and policies, and hence the livelihood of the people. There is a great deal of truth in what the American judge Louis Brandeis said: in a democracy, the most important office is the office of citizen.[8] Because citizenship is a form of political office, it too needs to be justified according to the service conception. It is necessary to ask whether such an institutional arrangement serves the well-being of the people. There is no natural citizenship just as there is no natural rulership.[9] It is important to note that this view is not a rejection of

8 Cited in Barack Obama, *The Audacity of Hope: Thoughts on Reclaiming the American Dream* (New York: Three Rivers Press, 2006), 135.

9 This is an uncommon view in contemporary Western political theory. Many scholars believe that citizens have a basic moral right to vote (as a human right) or that they possess popular sovereignty, as a kind of basic natural or moral right. Richard Arneson is one of the small minority of theorists who rejects the majority view and gives a clear statement of a purely instrumental view of political rights. See his "The Supposed Right to a Democratic Say," chap. 11 in *Contemporary*

democracy as a set of political institutions but a rejection of a certain way of justifying democracy, one that appeals to a fundamental moral right of political participation or sovereign rule of the people. Rejecting such a rights-based justification of democracy is entirely compatible with justifying democracy instrumentally as a means of achieving certain goods, such as the protection and promotion of the people's well-being. Whether Confucianism would find any instrumental justification of democracy compelling will be discussed in chapters 3 and 4.

The service conception affirms the primacy of the people, not in terms of their political rights, but in terms of their worth. Political rights, whether those of the rulers or those of the ruled, are justified by the fact that they promote the well-being of the people. One may question whether this service conception is defective as a normative vision precisely because it does not recognize the political rights of citizens as being fundamental natural or moral rights (which are often expressed in terms of the notion of popular sovereignty, i.e., that the people collectively are the ultimate source of political authority and laws). As I argue in appendix 2, Confucianism does not recognize this notion of popular sovereignty. So the question we need to ask is this: From a normative perspective, should Confucianism endorse and incorporate a notion of popular sovereignty even if traditionally it does not have one? If people today no longer think that ultimate authority or sovereignty belongs to the ruler, should it therefore belong to the people instead? One could go further and argue that the Confucian service conception of political authority can be best explained by the more fundamental notion of popular sovereignty. The conception holds that political authority exists to serve the people and is justified according to the extent that it does so. An intuitive rationale for this conception is precisely that because political authority ultimately belongs to the people, they can legitimately expect authority to be held and exercised in such a way as to bring them benefit, in the same way a piece of property is used to benefit its owner.

Whereas the service conception of authority requires that authority be grounded in the service of the people, popular sovereignty goes beyond that and asserts that the *will* of the people as a *juridical* notion is the final basis for political authority, just as the will of a property owner ultimately determines how a piece of property is to be disposed of or used. But the will of a people is a difficult concept to define. Both "the people" and "the will of the people" have no straightforward empirical references. "The people" have to be defined, often artificially and arbitrarily, by those in power. Constitutionalists have argued that it is the constitution that defines the people, not the other way round. Once a constitution is laid down, the people can only legitimately change it according

---

Debates in Political Philosophy, ed. Thomas Christiano and John Christman (Oxford: Wiley-Blackwell, 2009). Jean Hampton also denies Locke's view that "political authority resides naturally in the individual, such that she can confer it (as a loan) on the ruler." See her *Political Philosophy* (Boulder: Westview Press, 1997), 76.

to the stringent rules and procedures set by the constitution itself. Nationalists have argued that it is the nation that defines the people. However, the nation is an even more "imagined community" and contested notion than "the people," and hence liable to manipulation and abuse.

Similarly, although often invoked, the will, or the voice, of the people cannot be precisely defined. Although referendums can be used to give direct voice to the people, their responses in such situations consist merely of a "yes" or "no" to preselected questions written and placed before them by political elites.[10] The malleable nature of the notion of "the will of the people" thus reveals its weakness rather than its strength. In history it has been used to justify guardianship and one-party rule—considering themselves unable to practice self-rule, the people choose to delegate their authority to an agent who governs them on their behalf. Popular sovereignty can thus be made compatible with an authoritarian regime as long as it can be deemed to have the "consent" of the governed.[11]

A more serious problem of popular sovereignty is that the will of the people, however this may be constructed, is supposed to be the source of all laws and powers within a jurisdiction. If absolute monarchy is rejected on the grounds that the exercise of political authority—the enactment of laws and the determination of justice—should not be based on the will of a single person, is it then acceptable to base the exercise of political authority on the will of many people? What guarantees that the will of the people would be any less arbitrary or mistaken than the will of a monarch? In fact, even when absolute monarchy was practiced in Europe in the sixteenth and seventeenth centuries, the monarch was never thought to be above all laws but was bound by the divine and natural law that served as a critical standard by which to judge the laws he made. If a complete secularization of human affairs implies a rejection of the validity of any laws that are not "man-made," popular sovereignty in a secularized form would imply sovereignty in its most absolute form, in that the will of the people becomes the single source of all official powers and laws in the human realm. As Hannah Arendt writes, "absolute power becomes despotic once it has lost its connection with a higher power than itself"; and "in the realm of human affairs sovereignty and tyranny are the same."[12]

It may be argued that "tyranny" is a misleading term to use in this context because when the people as a whole rule over themselves and give themselves laws to follow, they are, at worst, "tyrannizing" only themselves. But self-tyranny, the argument continues, is not tyranny. Even when the people's will is arbitrary and their laws poorly made, there are no people other than themselves

10   Robert Jackson, *Sovereignty: The Evolution of an Idea* (Cambridge: Polity, 2007), 81.

11   For historical examples of such use of popular sovereignty, see Quentin Skinner, "The Rediscovery of Republican Values," chap. 2 in *Renaissance Virtues*, vol. 2 of *Visions of Politics* (Cambridge: Cambridge University Press, 2002).

12   Hannah Arendt, *On Revolution* (London: Penguin, 2006), 153, 144.

who suffer—a form of collective self-harm rather than despotism. Further-more, if sovereignty is understood as a dominium, the people as the dominus have the right to use their property (jurisdictional powers and territory) as they please—including to dispose of it in a wasteful way, to use it in a way harmful to themselves, to destroy it, or to give it to others. What they do may be folly or hurtful to themselves; nevertheless they have a right to do so. A dominium implies a right to do wrong to themselves.

However, the view that the people are a single body or entity, and that the people's rule is self-rule, is deeply misleading. The people are always a plural-ity—they speak in different voices, and they seldom act in unison. If the will of the people is the source of authority and law, we need to ask: Of the many voices, which one has the ultimate say? Whose voice should dominate? Could the will of those people that ultimately forms the basis of the law be considered arbitrary or unreasonable? Can it be justified to those who are unsuccessful in determining the law? These are broad questions about the legitimacy of major-ity rule and the status and rights of the minority in a system of politics governed by the principle of people's rule. The debates on constitutionalism, individual liberties, the minority's right to protection and secession, and so forth center on how best to protect the minority in the face of the power of the majority, which, if not restrained, can be as despotic as that of an absolute monarch. A limited government, whether a limited monarchy or a constitutional democracy, is bet-ter than an unlimited one, whether the unlimited government is rule by one or by many. What matters more than the will of men and women is government by a law that is right and just, which is why, from early modern Western politi-cal thought until today, thinkers have tried hard to reconcile the will of the people with ideas that appear to be objectively right: the General Will (Rous-seau), the common good (Founders of the U.S. Constitution), or the reasonable-(Rawls). In this tradition, when the will of the people is disconnected from a notion of rightness, it is doubtful whether it can be regarded as a true source of legitimate authority and law. The recognition that the people's power needs to be restrained, and that their will has to be reasonable, shows that popular sov-ereignty should not be understood as a dominium or the people as a dominus. I therefore believe that it is right for Confucianism to reject the dominium con-ception of political authority, whether it resides in the Sage King, the monarch, or the people. And insofar as popular sovereignty is understood in light of the dominium conception, it should be rejected.

The Role of the People

The Confucian service conception justifies authority not by popular sover-eignty or other notions of people's natural political rights, but by its ability to effectively serve the well-being of the people. However, we also need to look at whether early Confucian thinkers view the promotion of people's well-being as a necessary condition for legitimizing authority or a sufficient one. If it is a *sufficient* condition, it may be argued that the service conception is too permissive and instrumental to define the relationship between the ruler and the ruled: too permissive, in that it justifies the imposition of authority on the people against their will as long as such an imposition effectively promotes their well-being; and too instrumental, in that it portrays the ruler-ruled relationship as having no intrinsically valuable features that can play some role in justifying authority. So, according to early Confucianism, do the people play any role in making a putative authority an authoritative one? If their role is not one of *authorization* (which presupposes prior political rights), what is it?

The answer to this question, I believe, lies in the fact that Confucians are not interested in authority merely as an institution justified externally by certain objective reasons such as the promotion of people's well-being. Authority is also a kind of *relationship* or *bond* between the ruler and the ruled (or in contemporary terms, between those who govern and the governed). What makes the relationship truly authoritative is not just the ruler's ability to protect and promote the people's well-being, but the willing acceptance of his rule by the people. That is to say, authority is not merely externally justified but is internally constituted by mutual commitment on both sides—the ruler's commitment to care for the people and, most important, the people's willing acceptance.[13]

As authority is constituted by the attitudes and commitments of both the ruler and the ruled, early Confucian thinkers can be interpreted as regarding authority as a precarious and fragile relationship that can be harmed or undermined by any one side of the relationship withdrawing the attitudes that constitute authoritativeness. The Duke of Zhou understood this point painfully well, as he struggled hard to legitimize and secure the newly established regime of Zhou after its successful revolt against Shang (or Yin). In *The Book of History*, the Duke reiterated his concern that even though Zhou had been given Heaven's Mandate to rule the people of Yin, the mandate could easily be lost if the new regime failed to win the people's hearts. The Duke said to the young prince of Zhou, "O prince, have I not spoken in accordance with reason in these many declarations? I am only influenced by anxiety about (the appointment of) Heaven, and about the people."[14] In an early chapter of *The Book of History* it is stated, "The people are the root of a country; when the root is firm, the country

13   As in reality it is hard to obtain unanimous submission from the people, authority and legitimacy must be viewed in terms of the degree of acceptance. See the discussion at the end of this chapter.

14   "Jun Shi" 君奭 (Prince Shi) chapter; brackets in the original. Translation adapted from James Legge, *The Shû King, The Religious Portions of the Shih King, The Hsiâo King*, part 1 of *The Texts of Confucianism*, vol. 1 of *The Sacred Books of China*, vol. 3 of *The Sacred Books of the East*, ed. Max Müller (Oxford: Clarendon Press, 1879), available at http://oll.libertyfund.org/index.php?option=com_staticxt&staticfile=show.php%3Ftitle=2162&Itemid=27. All translations of *The Book of History* 尚書 [*Shang shu*] are adapted from Legge's.

is tranquil. . . . In [his] dealing with the millions of the people, [the ruler] should feel as anxious as if [he] were driving six horses with rotten reins. The ruler of men—how should he be but [take his governing duties] most reverently?"[15]

This analogy vividly illustrates the precarious nature of authority. The people are like horses under no secure command—they can easily topple the driver (the ruler) if the two parties do not work in harmony. A ruler who cannot command willing submission from the people is but a powerless individual on thin ice. It is interesting to note that the Song dynasty (960–1279 CE) thinker and politician Su Dongpo makes the same point when he quotes this analogy to counsel Emperor Shenzhong:

> It is said in *The Book of History*, "In ruling over the people, I feel as if I were holding six horses with worn-out reins." *This means that no one in the nation is in a more precarious position than the emperor [ren zhu] himself.* When the emperor and the people come together, they are ruler and subjects; when they detest each other, they become foes. But the line of division, determining whether the people go with the ruler or against him, is extremely tenuous. *He who is able to command the support of the millions becomes a king, while he who alienates their support becomes a solitary private individual [du fu]. The basis of the ruler's [authority] [ren zhu] lies, therefore, entirely in the support of the people in their hearts. . . . And when an emperor loses the support of the people, it spells his ruin.* This is an inexorable law from whose consequences no ruler can hope to escape.[16]

The passages above from *The Book of History* and Su Dongpo both indicate that the authority of the ruler and his regime is based on the compliance of the people. However, it is not based on the people in the *juridical* sense of authorization by the people, as suggested by the notion of people's sovereignty. It is also not understood in the *empirical* sense of what political scientists today call "political support." People can give political support for reasons that do not constitute an authoritative relationship between the ruler and the ruled, such as self-interest or habitual compliance. In my opinion, authority is based on the people in the *ethical* sense that authority ultimately resides in the "hearts of the people"—true authority can only be accepted, recognized, and willingly complied with by the people. Confucians recognize that the willing acceptance of the people cannot be obtained through might or institutional office alone. To be truly authoritative, an officeholder must win the hearts of the people.

The early Confucian masters use words such as *min fu*, *min yue*, and *min gui* to describe the notion of people's willing and glad acceptance of political rule.

---

15 "Wu zi zhi ge" 五子之歌 (Songs of the Five Sons) chapter.

16 Su Dongpo 蘇東坡, "Memorial to His Majesty Emperor Shengtsung" 上神宗皇帝萬言書, in *Lin Yutang Chinese-English Bilingual Edition: Selected Poems and Prose of Su Tungpo*, trans. Lin Yutang (Taipei: Cheng Chung Book, 2008), 33–35. Italics added. The original translation of *ren zhu* 人主 is the ruler's power, which is better translated as rulership or the authority of the ruler.

Let us consider a list of passages taken from *The Analects* and *Mencius* in which these words appear.

The Analects

The Governor of She asked about government. The Master said, "Ensure that those who are near are *pleased* [*yue*] and those who are far away are attracted." (13.16, italics added)

If a man is tolerant, he will win the multitude. If he is trustworthy in word, the common people will entrust him with responsibility.... If he is impartial, the common people will be *pleased* [yue]. (20.1, italics added)

When distant subjects are *unsubmissive* [*bu fu*] one cultivates one's moral quality in order to attract them, and once they have come one makes them content. (16.1, italics added)

Raise up the true and place them over the crooked, and *the allegiance of the people* [min fu] will be yours; raise up the crooked and place them over the true, and the people will not be yours. (2.19, italics added)[17]

Restore the states that have been destroyed, revive interrupted dynastic lines, reinstate political exiles, and you will *win the hearts of the people* [*min gui xin*] all over the world. (20.1, italics added)[18]

Two points are noteworthy in the above passages. First, for Confucius, the ideal ruler-ruled relationship or true authority is based on the voluntary and glad acceptance of the people. Second, the ruler should actively behave and do things that can win the people's hearts. More specifically, he should be trustworthy, impartial, and fair in dealing with the people in order to keep those who are close content and to attract others to come under his rule.[19] The same points appear in *Mencius*.

Mencius

One who uses force while borrowing from benevolence will become leader of the feudal lords [*ba*], but to do so he must first be the ruler of a state of considerable size. One who puts benevolence into effect through the transforming influence of virtue [*de*] will become a true king [*wang*], and his success will not depend on the size of his state. Tang began with only seventy *li* square, and King Wen with a hundred. When people submit to force they

---

17 Translation taken from Roger T. Ames and Henry Rosemont, Jr., *The Analects of Confucius: A Philosophical Translation* (New York: Ballantine, 1998).

18 Translation taken from Simon Leys, trans., *The Analects of Confucius* (New York: Norton, 1997).

19 For an interesting analysis of the notions of authority and obedience in *The Analects*, see Sor-hoon Tan, "Authoritative Master Kong (Confucius) in an Authoritarian Age," *Dao* 9, no. 2 (2010): 137–49.

do so not willingly but because they are not strong enough to resist. When people submit to the transforming influence of virtue they do so sincerely, with admiration in their hearts [*xin yue cheng fu*]. An example of this is the submission of the seventy disciples to Confucius. (2A.3, italics added)

In this passage, Mencius mentions two methods of obtaining compliance from the people: the first, the use of force disguised by the language of benevolence, relies on a certain type of action; the second, practicing benevolence "through the transforming influence of virtue," relies on a certain type of attitude. As he explains, however, compliance brought about by the first method lasts only as long as the force is applied since the people have not submitted willingly. To achieve lasting and stable compliance, the one in power must have a virtuous attitude and sincerely practice the policies of benevolent rule. In other words, for the people to willingly and gladly accept his rule, the ruler must genuinely care for the people and not act out of a desire to gain power. The expression used in this passage to imply willing and glad submission is *xin yue cheng fu*, which literally means "the heart is pleased and submission is sincere" and echoes Confucius's remarks about glad and willing submission.

The need for rulers to "win the hearts of the people" by cultivating and displaying virtues is also emphasized by Xunzi (*Xunzi* 6.10). He makes a similar distinction between *ba* and *wang* as Mencius, saying that hegemons use tactics, deception, and "the appearance of humaneness [ren]" as a means of triumph only. They do not "develop what is highest and most noble," nor are they "able to win over the hearts and minds of men." True kings, however, being the worthiest and strongest of men, "are able to help the unworthy" and "to be magnanimous toward the weak" (7.1).

To sum up, Mencius's use of the phrase *xin yue cheng fu* nicely captures the spirit of the early Confucian masters' conception of authority as a relationship. On the one hand, authority is hierarchical. On the other, it is not top-down or one-sided, but mutual—political authority has to be earned, and submission must be sincere and willing. When the ruler is trustworthy and caring, the ruled will gladly support and work for the ruler. This relationship may have desirable political consequences; as Mencius says, "Practice benevolent government and the people will be sure to love their superiors and die for them" (*Mencius* 1B.12; see also 1B.13). But more important, Confucian masters view this relationship as ethically valuable and satisfying in itself.

Toward a Perfectionist Perspective

In the second section of this chapter, I said that political authority must be justified by its contribution to the well-being of the people. This seems to be an instrumental justification, in the sense that political authority and its associated political rights and powers are treated as a means to an independent end, namely, the well-being of the people. In justifying political authority, priority is given to the instrumental effects of the institutional arrangement of powers and offices. In the previous section we saw that the justification of authority also lies in the ethical attitudes and commitments of rulers and the ruled. Ultimately authority lies in the people's willing and glad submission to the ruler. No ruler enjoys full and legitimate authority—or is truly authoritative—unless the ruled willingly and gladly accept his rule. And no ruler can win the hearts of the people and obtain their acceptance if he is not trustworthy, virtuous, and genuinely solicitous of their well-being. Thus there are two ways of justifying authority—the first is with reference to the instrumental effects of authority on the well-being of the people, and the second with reference to people's willing and glad submission, which in turn is engendered by the virtue and commitment of the ruler. If the first justification focuses on the instrumental effects of authority as institutional offices and powers, the second focuses on the attitudes and commitments of the ethically valuable authoritative relationship between the ruler and the ruled.

There need not be any paradox or contradiction in claiming that instrumental effects and constitutive attitudes and commitments are both essential to authority. In fact, these two aspects of authority are often inextricably bound. Offices, powers, and rules—on which authority is based—are not self-effectuating or unconditionally authoritative in themselves. They can be disputed, challenged, and changed in the political process. The very ability of the rulers to serve the ruled depends to a large extent on the personal qualities of those who exercise authority and the attitudes of those who receive commands. Zhou's political figures were painfully aware that even when entrusted with Heaven's Mandate and empowered by military strength, their rule was never secure unless they could win the hearts of the people over whom they ruled. A ruler cannot effectively exercise power to promote the welfare of the ruled for long if the latter do not support his rule.

Confucians understand very well that *agency* matters a great deal in political rule, in the sense that the personal qualities of officials can greatly undermine or enhance their ability to command the acceptance and support of the people.[20] A personal quality essential to authority is trustworthiness. Confucians think that ultimately the effectiveness of political power rests on the level of trust the people have in their ruler. A government must have the people's cooperation and compliance in order to accomplish its tasks. While pure coercion may bring about short-term compliance, only trust can ensure stable cooperation. Confucius says, "Without the trust [xin] of the people, no government can

---

20 Contemporary British political theorist Mark Philp makes this point well: "Authority is central to political rule, and central to its development of a broader legitimacy and stability, but it is also intricately linked to political agency. While it regulates that agency, it is also in turn shaped and structured by it. Indeed, at times, it may be wholly a creation of such agency." See his *Political Conduct* (Cambridge: Harvard University Press, 2007), 59.

stand" (*Analects* 12.7).[21] Confucius's point is not that the people should always trust their governments, but that those in power must earn the people's trust by being trustworthy. As he says, "good faith [xin] inspires the trust of the people" (20.1).[22] In *The Analects*, Zixia, student of Confucius, also says, "Only after he has gained the trust [xin] of the common people does the gentleman work them hard, for otherwise they would feel themselves ill-used" (19.10). Xunzi writes, "One whose governmental ordinances and edicts are trustworthy [xin] will be strong; one whose ordinances and edicts are not trustworthy will be weak" (*Xunzi* 15.1c).

The instrumental and constitutive elements of authority are therefore mutually reinforcing. A ruler must demonstrate a good track record in serving the public in order to command the recognition and support of the people, but to claim full and legitimate authority he must display virtue and skill and win the people's willing support in order to strengthen the ability to serve. In building and exercising authority, the ruler's ability to serve is intertwined with the people's willing acceptance of his rule.

In the process of establishing authority, Confucian thought defines no one clear point at which authority becomes legitimate—rather, the conception of legitimate authority should be viewed as a continuum. At one end is a person with no right to rule, for example, someone like Confucius who lacks the necessary political power and resources to be recognized even as a de facto authority, or a ruler who has ruled ruthlessly and selfishly and thus lost all right to authority. Confucian masters call the latter person a "solitary man" (*yi fu*,[23] *du fu*[24]), such as Zhou of Shang. At the other end of the continuum is a person with the requisite effective power to promote the good of the people and the virtue to attract their voluntary submission. Confucian masters call such a person a "true king" (wang). Most early Confucian masters make little mention of the situations that may exist between these two extremes. Xunzi, however, uses the term "hegemon" (*ba*) to describe someone who does not possess the qualities of a true king but is nevertheless acceptable as a ruler—someone who, though lacking the virtue to win the hearts of the people, is trustworthy and fair and can thus maintain effective rule (*Xunzi* 11.1c). The emphasis of most Confucian thinkers, however, is on the ideal end of the continuum: the ideal political relationship that is marked by mutual commitment and in which true authority reigns.[25]

---

21 Simon Leys's translation.
22 Simon Leys's translation.
23 *Mencius* 1B.8.
24 *Xunzi* 15.1d.
25 For reason of space I cannot discuss another possible dimension of legitimacy in the early Confucian conceptions of authority—institutional rules of recognition. Justin Tiwald interestingly argues that Mencius is of the view that "we need widely recognized and relatively clear conventions that determine who the political authorities are." See his "A Right of Rebellion in the *Mengzi*?" *Dao* 7, no. 3 (2008): 275. Elsewhere I have used an institutional conception of authority to explain how

I shall briefly highlight a few distinctive features of this Confucian perspective on authority by contrasting it with one Western conception. As I have just said, the Confucian perspective focuses on the ideal relational approach to authority in which trust and voluntary submission play an important part in constituting authority. Within Western traditions of political thought, Locke comes closest to this perspective in stressing trust and voluntary submission in politics. He draws a close connection between the people's consent, willing submission, and trust and the legitimacy of political authority. However, there are fundamental differences between the two perspectives. Locke's perspective is one of political voluntarism, which can be defined as "the view that political relationships among persons are morally legitimate only when they are the product of voluntary, willing, morally significant acts by all parties."[26] This perspective is built on a theory of moral rights, which holds that people are born with full-blown claim-rights in the state of nature and that political authority can be legitimated only by the consent and trust of these right-holders. As Locke writes, "Men being . . . by nature, all free, equal and independent, no one can be put out of this estate, and subjected to the political power of another, without his own consent"; "No government can have a right to obedience from a people who have not freely consented to it."[27] As I argued earlier, Confucian thought does not assume the existence of natural or moral political rights, neither for rulers nor for the people. Although Mencius does talk about the approval of the people, as I argue in appendix 2, he does not treat this as a rights-based idea.

The difference between the Confucian perspective and that of Locke can be clearly seen in the respective definitions of the notion of trust. Locke uses "trust" as a quasi-legal concept to describe the relations between government and the people. He calls the power of government "fiduciary," which suggests a trustee-and-beneficiary relationship. The people, who possess rights prior to the set up of government, choose to entrust some of their rights to the government in order to receive its protection. To quote Locke,

> The legislative being only a fiduciary power to act for certain ends, there remains still *in the people a supreme power to remove or alter the legislative*, when they find the *legislative* act contrary to the trust reposed in them. For all *power given with trust* for the attaining an *end*, being limited by that end, whenever that *end* is manifestly neglected, or opposed, the *trust* must necessarily be *forfeited*, and the power devolve into the hands of those that gave it,

a perfectionist state could have legitimate authority. See Joseph Chan, "Political Authority and Perfectionism: A Response to Quong," *Philosophy and Public Issues* 2, no. 1 (2012): 31–41.

26   A. John Simmons, *On the Edge of Anarchy: Locke, Consent, and the Limits of Society* (Princeton: Princeton University Press, 1993), 36.

27   John Locke, "Second Treatise of Government," in *Two Treatises of Government*, ed. Peter Laslett, 3rd ed. (Cambridge: Cambridge University Press, 1988), secs. 95, 192.

who may place it anew where they shall think best for their safety and security. (Emphasis in original)[28]

In the same vein, the people place in the executive a "fiduciary trust" for the safety of the people.[29]

According to the Confucian conception of political relationship, however, "trust" refers to the confidence and faith people have in their rulers, and trustworthiness is a virtue by which rulers gain the trust of the people. While Locke's notion of trust is juridical, the Confucian notion is ethical, and defined without reference to any prior notion of rights.[30] I am not suggesting here that the Confucian perspective would necessarily reject the language of rights in politics, or that it gives no objective reasons to require rulers to behave in a certain way (Heaven's Mandate and the importance of the people's well-being are such reasons, as seen earlier in this chapter); the point is rather that the Confucian ideal conception of political relationship moves beyond the outer sphere of objective reasons and rights and enters the inner sphere of the minds and dispositions of rulers and the ruled. From the Confucian point of view, an ideal political relationship should be ethically attractive and intrinsically satisfying. Only when both parties in the relationship are intrinsically motivated to do what they are supposed to do would this be the case. That is to say, the trustworthiness of rulers and their commitment to the people's well-being, as well as the submission of the people, should come from their hearts.[31] This, I suggest, is the distinctive aspect of the Confucian ideal conception of political relationship.

If the conception of political authority put forward by Locke, and many other thinkers subscribing to the consent theory, is rights-based, the Confucian conception is what I would call "perfectionist." Generally speaking, a perfectionist view of authority ties its moral acceptability to the promotion or realiza-

---

28　Ibid., sec. 149.

29　Ibid., sec. 156.

30　Note that Locke's "fiduciary trust" differs from contemporary Confucian philosopher Tu Weiming's concept of "fiduciary community," which he uses to characterize Confucian ideal society. Locke's notion is juridical, while Tu's "fiduciary community" refers to an ethical society based on mutual trust and concern and shared values. It may be possible to view the ideal ruler-ruled relationship based on mutual trust and commitment described in this chapter as an aspect of Confucian fiduciary community. For the notion of "fiduciary community," see Tu Wei-ming, "The Fiduciary Community," chap. 3 in *Centrality and Commonality: An Essay on Confucian Religiousness*, SUNY Series in Chinese Philosophy and Culture (Albany: State University of New York Press, 1989), rev. ed. of *Centrality and Commonality: An Essay on Chung-yung*, vol. 3 of Monographs of the Society for Asian and Comparative Philosophy (Honolulu: University of Hawaii, 1976). For a critical examination of Tu's concept, see Zhaolu Lu, "Fiduciary Society and Confucian Theory of Xin—On Tu Wei-ming's Fiduciary Proposal," *Asian Philosophy* 11, no. 2 (2001): 85–101.

31　The best statement of this account of Confucian thought is Xu Fuguan's essay from 1951. See Xu Fuguan 徐復觀, "Ru jia zheng zhi si xiang de gou zao ji qi zhuan jin" 儒家政治思想的構造及其轉進 [The Structure and Transformation of Confucian Political Thought], in *Xue shu yu zheng zhi zhi jian* 學術與政治之間 [Between Academics and Politics], rev. ed. (Taipei: Taiwan Student Book, 1985), 47–60.

tion of the human good or what contemporary theorists call "the good life." While there is no term in the classical texts that is equivalent to the notion of the good life, it would not be too far off the mark to say that early Confucians subscribe to a broad conception that takes material well-being, moral self-cultivation, and virtuous social relationships as constituents of "the good life" for a normal human being, with the ideal of sagehood as the highest good.[32] In the case of the Confucian perspective we are constructing here, there are two important ties between authority and the good life. First, authority instrumentally promotes the good life by making possible a social environment that helps people pursue material well-being and a virtuous life, a point that I shall develop in the next chapter. Second, the authoritative relationship itself contributes to the ethical life, for its constitutive mutual commitment of care and support makes the relationship ethically valuable and satisfying. So, while willing submission or consent according to Locke is a rights-transferring act, according to Confucian thought it is an indication of an ethically valuable and satisfying political relationship. According to the perfectionist view, political rights and duties are not the most fundamental categories in political morality. It is the good life—and the virtue and ethical relationships that constitute it—that is the foundation.[33]

It may be argued that the Confucian perfectionist perspective seems a high-minded approach to authority. While it gives priority of place to the ruler's virtue and the people's willing submission, many existing regimes and rulers would simply fall short of this high standard. But the Confucian perspective

32   Here I am concerned about the broad outline of the Confucian conception of the good life, leaving internal differences between thinkers aside. I discuss the views of Confucius and Mencius on material goods in people's lives in chapter 7. For an account of various Confucian conceptions of moral self-cultivation, see Philip J. Ivanhoe, *Confucian Moral Cultivation*, 2nd ed. (Indianapolis: Hackett, 2000). For an account of Confucian conceptions of sagehood, see Stephen C. Angle, *Sagehood: The Contemporary Significance of Neo-Confucian Philosophy* (New York: Oxford University Press, 2009). The notion of the highest good (*zhi shan*) can be found in *The Great Learning*.

33   It may be argued that the concept of paternalism, or more accurately a parent-children familial model, is a better way to characterize the Confucian conception of authority and its foundation. Elsewhere I have argued that the familial model is misleading in several important ways— see Joseph Chan, "Exploring the Nonfamilial in Confucian Political Philosophy," in *The Politics of Affective Relations: East Asia and Beyond*, ed. Hahm Chaihark and Daniel A. Bell (Lanham, MD: Lexington, 2004), 64–65. I also think that "perfectionism" is superior to "paternalism" as a characterization of Confucian politics, although both terms express a concern to promote people's well-being or good life. In contemporary political and legal philosophy, "paternalism" is commonly associated with the use of coercion by the state to promote the good of its citizens. Perfectionism in politics, however, does not necessarily carry this feature, and in fact many contemporary political perfectionists do not favor coercion as a means to promote the good life. It is also the case that Confucianism does not favor the use of force in promoting its conception of the good. In addition, the mutual commitment and ethical relationships of the ruler and the ruled, which are an important feature of the Confucian conception of authority, can be subsumed under "perfectionism" but not "paternalism." I define a noncoercive version of state perfectionism in "Legitimacy, Unanimity, and Perfectionism," 14–15.

that I have reconstructed here does not take the mutual commitment standard as a *threshold* for legitimacy. It does not say that any ruler who falls short of this threshold is necessarily an illegitimate authority. As noted above, legitimate authority is a continuum that admits of degrees, because the realization of aspects such as the well-being of the people, the virtue of a ruler, and mutual ethical relationships are a matter of degree. Only in relatively extreme cases can we be certain that particular rulers clearly do or do not possess authority. This apparent vagueness does not seem to be a concern for Confucian masters. Unlike many Western legal and political theorists, they do not seek to prove the existence or otherwise of the right to rule or the obligation to obey. Their high standard represents not so much a legalistic interest in clear answers as a keen awareness of the imperfection of reality and a reminder for existing rulers to take seriously the business of governing and the fragility of their authority.

The practical interest of the Confucian perfectionist approach explains why Confucian thinkers devote enormous intellectual energy to examining the dispositions and virtues that rulers should possess and the policies they should adopt in pursuing kingly (authoritative) rule. Apart from trustworthiness, the virtues these thinkers frequently mention are benevolence (ren) and righteousness (yi), but there are also other important virtues such as tolerance (*kuan*), impartiality (*gong*), and reverence (*gong*) (see *Analects* 20.1, 20.2; *Xunzi* 14.5). They also propose a long list of methods and policies[34] that are often termed "benevolent rule" (*ren zheng*) and "rite-based governance" (li zhi). Their ideas and discussions on these topics are generally regarded as the most insightful aspects of Confucian political thought. Politicians who desire to govern well and win the approval of the people would benefit much from following the advice of Confucian masters. Having said that, it must be noted that the masters provide little information on nonideal situations—namely, what politics and the structures of authority should be like if politicians are neither virtuous nor truly solicitous of the people. This issue will be examined in chapters 2, 3, and 4.

---

34 See, for example, *Mencius* 1A.7, 2A.5.

CHAPTER 2

Monism or Limited Government?

The previous chapter discussed the nature and justificatory basis of political authority in early Confucianism. The conclusion was that political authority is not a dominium, a form of property to be owned by the ruler or the people, but an imperium, a legitimate right to govern within a jurisdiction. This right to rule is grounded on its service to the good life of the people and on the people's willing acceptance of being ruled. In this chapter I discuss how early Confucian thought deals with two further issues related to political authority: the scope of authority of a ruler (or state), and the required institutional structures of authority. Specifically, I examine whether the early Confucian conception of authority is compatible with the idea of limited government and, as a way of achieving it, the idea of the separation of powers.

In chapter 1 I argued that legitimate authority cannot be based on the arbitrary will of the one who holds the position of authority.[1] Authority exists for the service of the people and therefore has to be exercised in a way that is consistent with that purpose. In an ideal scenario, the ruler is virtuous and competent, and authority is exercised for the right purposes and in the right way. In nonideal situations, however, the ruler may not be virtuous or competent, and authority may be misused or exercised arbitrarily. To prevent this from happening, authority should be limited or restrained in ways that protect the people. For this reason, any view that rejects the dominium conception of authority would also tend to defend a limited government of some kind in nonideal situations, whatever form the government takes (e.g., monarchy or democracy). If early Confucianism rejects the dominium conception of authority and justifies authority in terms of its service to the people, would it not also endorse the idea of limited political authority or limited government?

In its modern sense, limited political authority refers to a kind of authority or government that is effectively restrained by law, in the sense that the source, scope, and exercise of authority are defined and regulated by law. If we bear this in mind when considering the relationship between limited political authority and Confucianism, we come to see a disturbing paradox. On the one hand, Confucianism strongly embraces a set of ideas that imply that it should

---

1   The dominium conception, *ex hypothesi*, would not condemn any arbitrary use of property by its owner (as long as the use does not violate the property rights of others).

be able to endorse limited government. This set of ideas includes the service conception of authority and the rejection of the dominium conception, as we have examined. It also includes the notion that government should be bound by some form of higher principles, which we shall discuss shortly. On the other hand, however, Confucianism not only stops short of endorsing limited government, it actively opposes it by embracing the notion that political authority, even if not a form of property, should be monistic and supreme, and not subject to any higher legal constraints. To dissolve this paradox it is not enough to maintain that constitutionalism, a European concept and experience that emerged first in early modern Europe, was not available to traditional China. Indeed, one might even ask why the Chinese had not developed constitutionalism themselves prior to the modern revolution of 1911. We need to consider the main obstacles within Confucianism that prevent it from accepting limited government.

In the first section I look more closely at both sides of the paradox before searching for an explanation. The second section begins with the question of why political authority is needed and reconstructs certain early Confucian texts, especially *Xunzi*, to provide an answer. Two arguments in support of the need for political authority are considered—rulers are needed to provide administrative coordination of collective action, and sage-rulers are needed to set up principles of morality, interpret them in changing circumstances, and make contextual decisions. I argue that these arguments do not justify placing authority over the law, and hence they cannot reject the idea of limited government. The third section considers two Confucian arguments for a monist and supreme conception of authority—the argument that ultimate authority must reside in one person as divided authority leads to chaos, and that oneness (or unity) in Dao requires oneness in political authority. I argue that these arguments fail to reject the principle of separation of powers, which is an important corollary of the principle of limited government. The final section concludes that in the real, nonideal world we should not search for a godlike person and place him or her in a position of utmost prestige and power but adopt a system of governance that involves mutual cooperation and checks among people who are virtuous and intelligent.

The Paradox

Confucianism endorses the idea that government or authority should submit to ethical limits. In other words, Confucianism places authority under the constraints of particular independent, substantive principles of rightness. This has two implications: first, what the person in authority says or does is not beyond reproach; second, a ruler who seriously violates these principles of rightness loses his legitimacy to govern. We have already seen this idea at work in the Zhou rulers' attempt to use the notion of Heaven's Mandate to justify both their revolt against Shang and their claim to authority. In fact, the Heavenly Mandate is a two-edged sword—it both legitimizes and constrains political authority. After Zhou, this notion eventually became less bound to the elusive will of Heaven and more in keeping with higher principles within human grasp. Thinkers after the Duke of Zhou called these principles Dao and used them to assess the state of politics in their times.

According to early Confucian tradition, which includes the Five Classics as we know today,[2] *Dao*[3] is an umbrella term that describes some fundamental facts and principles (or norms)[4] about the cosmos and the human world—cosmic ordering patterns (*tian dao*) concerning the roles of Heaven, Earth and humans, and the five basic social relationships (*ren dao*). Two passages from *Xunzi* and *The Book of Rites* illustrate this:

> The relationships between lord and minister, father and son, older and younger brothers, husband and wife, begin as they end and end as they begin, share with Heaven and Earth the same organizing principle, and endure in the same form through all eternity. (*Xunzi* 9.15)

> (In the distinctions of the mourning) for the kindred who are the nearest, the honored ones to whom honor is paid, the elders who are venerated for their age, and as the different tributes to males and females; there are seen the greatest manifestations of the course which is right for men. (*Book of Rites*)[5]

Dao also describes the right norms and conduct in politics, which are sometimes called the "Kingly Way" (*wang dao*). Briefly stated, there are two types of

---

2 For a brief reference to the Five Classics, see appendix 1.

3 The concept of Dao in Chinese philosophy is multifaceted and complex. For a description of its meanings and usages in Chinese philosophy, see Zhang Dainian 張岱年, *Key Concepts in Chinese Philosophy*, trans. and ed. Edmund Ryden (New Haven: Yale University Press; Beijing: Foreign Languages Press, 2002), 11–26; originally published in Chinese as *Zhongguo gu dian zhe xue gai nian fan chou yao lun* 中國古典哲學概念範疇要論 [A Handbook of Categories and Concepts in Classical Chinese Philosophy] (Beijing: Academy of Social Sciences, 1989). For a comprehensive account of the various dimensions of Dao in Confucianism, see Xinzhong Yao 姚新中, "The Way of Confucianism," chap. 3 in *An Introduction to Confucianism* (Cambridge: Cambridge University Press, 2000).

4 Scholars who subscribe to a virtue-ethics reading of Confucianism might prefer "norms" to "principles" in describing the underlying things that guide human action. Whether there are moral "principles" in Confucian ethics is a complex issue that cannot be discussed here. A. S. Cua has argued that the notions of virtue and objective principles are complementary in Confucian ethics. See his "The Status of Principles in Confucian Ethics," *Journal of Chinese Philosophy* 16, no. 3–4 (1989): 273–96. A different view, one that sees Confucian ethics as offering guidelines for conduct rather than principles, is expressed in Roger T. Ames, "On the Source of 'Principles' and 'Virtues': Value as Growth in Relations," chap. 1 of pt. 4 in *Confucian Role Ethics: A Vocabulary* (Hong Kong: Chinese University Press, 2011).

5 "Sang fu xiao ji" 喪服小記 (Record of Smaller Matters in the Dress of Mourning) chapter; brackets in the original.

political norms connected to Dao, namely, li and ren.[6] *Li* is a rich and elastic term. It may refer to unchanging fundamental principles underlying the five human relationships (in politics, the ruler-minister-ruled relationship) and its constitutive virtues; it may also refer to everyday rituals (etiquette, codes of conduct, manners), which may evolve with time and changing circumstances. As Xunzi puts it, Dao "is just ritual and moral principles, polite refusals and deference to others, and loyalty and trustworthiness" (*Xunzi* 16.4). *Ren* is another rich and elastic term. One common usage refers to one's affective feelings (such as love and care) toward others. When applied to politics, it refers to a set of social and economic policies that aims at protecting and promoting the people's material and social well-being. Mencius calls governance that is based on such policies "benevolent rule" or the "Kingly Way." These two terms refer to the same set of policies, suggesting a close relation between Dao (in politics) and ren.

Early Confucians appealed to Dao as a critical standard to evaluate politics and guide political conduct.[7] When Dao prevails in the world under Heaven (*tian xia you dao*), or in a state (*bang you dao*), the world or state is good. When Dao does not prevail (*wu dao*), Confucius says gentlemen should hide away and refrain from serving in government;[8] Xunzi says a person should "follow the dictates of the Way rather than those of one's lord" (*Xunzi* 29.2); and Mencius says ministers should remonstrate with their lord, and if repeated remonstrations fall on deaf ears, ministers of the royal blood should depose him (*Mencius* 5B.9). In the extreme case where Dao is completely lost in a state, the ruler would lose his legitimacy (or mandate) (4A.9)[9] and could be forcibly overthrown (1B.8, 5A.6).[10]

For Confucians, then, Dao refers to the higher principles that morally bind political authority and guide government action. These general principles are not abstract ones whose moral force depends on people's intuitive recognition but are principles embodied in concrete models, norms, rules, and rituals developed by Sage Kings in the past. More specifically, Dao refers to the Golden Age model of governance (*xian wang zhi fa*) that began to evolve during the

---

6   This is not the place to offer a detailed analysis of these two central concepts in Confucianism. My purpose here is only to introduce them in order to illustrate the content and function of the Way in politics. There is a rich contemporary literature on ren and li and their relations with each other. For an introductory account of the concepts in early Confucian texts and the contemporary literature on them, see Karyn L. Lai, "Confucius and the Confucian Concepts *Ren* and *Li*," chap. 2 in *An Introduction to Chinese Philosophy* (Cambridge: Cambridge University Press, 2008). An influential philosophical account of the relations between the two concepts is Kwong-loi Shun, "*Jen* and *Li* in the *Analects*," *Philosophy East and West* 43, no. 3 (1993): 457–79.

7   Confucian Dao could be compared to the idea of the natural law in Western political thought, in that both refer to unchanging, objective principles that prescribe human conduct.

8   See *Analects* 8.13.

9   Compare also "Yin zhu jie" 殷祝解, *The Lost Book of Zhou* 逸周書 [*Yi Zhou shu*].

10   For an illuminating discussion of the complexity beneath 1B.8, and in particular whether Mencius thinks that the people have the right to revolt, see Tiwald, "A Right of Rebellion," 274–79.

times of Yao and Shun and continued to the Three Dynasties, of which Zhou represented the highest development.[11] Dao as embodied in this tradition and model of governance is described in detail in the ancient classics,[12] some of which acquired the status of State Classics in the Han dynasty. Emperors and officials alike were expected to study and follow the teachings in these Confucian canons. Thus we could describe Dao as representing not just a form of abstract natural law that is apart from and superior to actual politics and positive laws but also a set of everyday constitutional conventions (*li fa*) that rulers and officials were expected to honor.[13] In different periods of Chinese history, Dao as li fa was constantly appealed to in debates and discussions that took place in the imperial courtrooms. Some officials were even given the role of censor to remonstrate emperors who violated li. In certain periods of Chinese history, however short, the will of the emperor could not be turned into legislation or policy without the official endorsement of the relevant administrative ministries.

Having looked briefly at the nature and role of Dao in politics, we are now able to understand one side of the paradox, namely, why Confucianism should be inclined to endorse the idea of limited government. According to the reconstructions I have presented in this and the previous chapter, here are three main views in Confucianism that, if pulled together, would constitute a strong case for limited government (or constitutional government). These three views are:

1. Authority as imperium: Political authority is a legitimate right to rule (imperium) rather than an ownership right possessed by the ruler or people (dominium).
2. Service conception of authority: Political authority is justified by its service to the well-being of the people.
3. Dao-based perfectionist politics: Dao is a set of objective principles and rituals regarding the well-being (or the good life) of the people that is used to guide and assess politics.

These three views are congenial with each other; the second can be understood as a development of the first, and the third a development of the second. The Service Conception of Authority develops the conception of Authority as Imperium in that it states the condition for justifying authority as a legitimate

11 See *Mencius* 4A.1; "Ritual principles, moral duty, laws, and standards are all products of the sage" (*Xunzi* 23.2a).

12 "The sage is the pitch pipe of the Way. The Way of the world has its pitch pipe in the sage. The Way of the Hundred Kings is at one with the sage. Hence, the Way expressed in *The Book of Poetry, The Book of History, The Book of Rites*, and *The Classic of Music* returns to this oneness" (*Xunzi* 8.14).

13 Of course, as we shall see later, Confucians such as Xunzi also think that these laws and conventions are often subject to particularistic judgments as necessitated by changing circumstances.

right to rule; Dao-Based Perfectionist Politics develops the Service Conception of Authority by providing principles that define the good life of the people (ren dao) and tradition-based rituals and policies to promote it. By providing a particular objective conception of the good life, Dao is a position in ethical perfectionism, which, minimally defined, is the view that conceptions and judgments about the good life are not subjective and that there are better or worse conceptions and judgments.[14] Furthermore, Dao-based politics is a brand of political perfectionism, which, according to the contemporary literature of political philosophy, means that under certain conditions it is appropriate and legitimate for the state to promote the good life.

Each of the three views above could support the idea of limited government. As the conception of Authority as Imperium denies that authority belongs to rulers as their property, it leaves space for constitutional restraints of government authority. The Service Conception of Authority welcomes limited government insofar as it is shown to be more effective than unlimited government in protecting and promoting people's good life. Dao-Based Perfectionist Politics shares the spirit of the idea of limited government, in that both believe in the existence of fundamental moral and political principles that (1) are not subject to the mere likes and dislikes of people and should not be changed by the politics of the day, and that (2) should be put into effect to enable government to pursue its proper tasks and prevent it from abusing its power.

Viewed together, these three views strongly imply that Confucianism should be accepting of limited government: if authority derives legitimacy from its contribution to the people and is placed under the constraints of higher principles, it seems natural to accept that the authority of a government should also be restrained and guided by law. However, Confucianism not only has not embarked on such a journey but has also been steadfast in advocating an opposite view of government in which authority at the top enjoys supreme, undivided, and absolute powers unrestrained by the law. Here we come to the other side of the paradox. In Chinese history, although Dao and li did at times function as constitutional conventions, they were precisely that—conventions backed by no higher institutional authority to effectively bind rulers who chose not to follow them. Nothing in the Confucian canons or actual politics of traditional China suggests that rulers lacked the authority to sack disobedient officials, put them to death, or disestablish and reorganize ministries to increase their own power. Although from a *bureaucratic* point of view a ruler might, at times, be subject to certain procedural constraints from below, and from a *normative* point of view be subject to the higher authority of Dao, he was not subject to a higher

14   For a useful discussion of the different definitions of ethical perfectionism, see Steven Wall, "Perfectionism in Moral and Political Philosophy," *Stanford Encyclopedia of Philosophy*, ed. Edward N. Zalta, winter 2012 ed., http://plato.stanford.edu/archives/win2012/entries/perfectionism-moral/.

authority or restrained by any *institutional* or *legal* means. Thus, in reality, more often than not it was power that restrained Dao, not the other way round.

Although a centralized imperial monarchy did not take root until the Qin dynasty (221–206 BCE), early Confucian texts already contain views that emphasize the supreme status of authority and its undivided power. How did Confucianism come to this view of authority?[15] What is it about Confucian notions of authority and politics that prevent it from embracing limited government despite its apparent leanings toward it? To answer these questions, we need to take a look at some fundamental issues, such as the need for establishing political authority, the sort of authority required, and the best person to discharge the functions of authority. In the next section I reconstruct the early Confucian texts from which I attempt to extract some answers, and in doing so I also critically evaluate those answers, with the aim of revising and further developing the Confucian views of authority.

Arguments for Political Authority

Since the Han dynasty, Confucianism has justified the need for political authority in the following way: the people (*min*), who are created by Heaven, are not able to govern by themselves and face a number of challenges if they live together without a ruler or government. This notion is linked to an idea that first emerged in *The Book of History* and was later endorsed by Mencius, Xunzi, and other Confucians, namely, that Heaven created the people and put rulers in place to protect them and benefit them. *Mencius* reports a well-known passage in a lost chapter in *The Book of History*,[16] which states that Heaven created the people on earth and provided them with a lord and teacher so that he might assist Heaven in protecting and loving them (*Mencius* 1B.3).

The passage above, however, does not explain why Heaven needed to establish a lord for its people. This gap is filled by one Tang dynasty (618–907 CE) commentary on *The Book of History* that says that because "the multitude are not able to govern by themselves," Heaven established a lord to govern and teach them.[17] This explanation echoes a similar view expressed in two historical texts from the Han dynasty:

---

15   Yuri Pines's *Envisioning Eternal Empire* claims that "the notion of the ruler's exclusiveness as the final decision-maker reflects a very broad consensus among the thinkers of the Warring States." See his chap. 2, "Ways of Monarchism," 52. Pines and I have come independently to asking this question of why early Chinese thinkers had embraced a conception of supreme and undivided authority even though they realized that actual rulers were not all that great. Pines's answers is that the thinkers saw "the omnipotent sovereign, despite its evident shortcomings, as the least possible evil," 53. The alternative, they thought, was disintegration of the state and wars, as borne by historical experience. Sor-hoon Tan also suggested this explanation to me in a personal communication.

16   "Tai shi" 泰誓 (Great Oath) chapter.

17   My own translation. Kong Yingda 孔穎達, *Shang shu zheng yi* 尚書正義, bk. 11.

I heard that the people created by Heaven were unable to govern themselves; so Heaven established kingship to rule and manage them. The power to dominate all land within the Four Seas is not for the benefit of the emperor; establishing feudal states is not for the benefit of the feudal lords; these things exist for the benefit of the people. (*Book of Han*)[18]

As I have heard, the people created by Heaven cannot govern themselves, so Heaven established for them the ruler, so as to take up the duty of shepherding them. (*Book of the Later Han*)[19]

According to these two passages, rulership, or political authority, is necessary because people cannot govern themselves. Heaven therefore established lordship to govern them (*zhi*), teach them (*jiao*), and shepherd them (*mu*).[20] Yet we still need to know why people are thought to be unable to govern themselves, and whether this explanation can justify empowering rulers with the supreme authority that Confucian thinkers believe they should have. *The Analects* and *Mencius*, however, do not provide much help in answering these questions, as they simply take for granted the existence of political authority and only discuss how rulers should rule. *Xunzi*, however, offers an illuminating account of the human condition from which we can begin to reconstruct answers to the above questions. An analysis of his account also offers a good way to present and integrate similar ideas from other texts.

According to Xunzi, human beings have comparably little physical strength when compared to other animals. "In physical power [humans] are not as good as an ox, in swiftness they do not equal the horse" (*Xunzi* 9.16a). Nevertheless, they survive and flourish in face of the challenges posed by the natural world. It might be argued that it is human intelligence that enables them to devise tools and utilities to cope with the challenges—for example, making weapons to hunt animals, traps to catch them, and fences to keep and breed them. However, intelligence is not the only reason why humans are able to survive and flourish; for if they act individually and do not collaborate, their individual intelligence does not yield significant results. For Xunzi, the key of the explanation lies in the fact that "humans alone can organize themselves into communities [*qun*] and animals cannot." The word *qun* means something like "to organize oneself into a community or society"[21] and in the present context refers to a special kind of organization or collaboration that involves a distinction of roles and

18   My own translation. "Gu Yong Du Ye zhuan" 谷永杜鄴傳 (Biographies of Guyong and Duye) chapter.

19   My own translation. "Xiaohuan di ji" 孝桓帝紀 (Annals of Emperor Xiaohuan) chapter.

20   The notion of "shepherd" (*mu*) can be found in "Xianggong shi si nian" 襄公十四年 (The Fourteenth Year of Duke Xiang), *Chun qiu zuo zhuan* 春秋左傳.

21   I adopted this translation from the suggestion of the anonymous referee. Note that John Knoblock translates *qun* as "to assemble" or "to form societies," and Burton Watson translates it as "to organize himself in society" in his *Basic Writings of Hsün Tzu* (New York: Columbia University Press: 1963), sec. 9, 45 (hereafter *Hsün Tzu* sec. 9, 45).

division of labor (*fen*) or, in short, a human society. Only by acting collaboratively can humans gather superior strength to "put animals to their use" and "overcome all objects" (*Xunzi* 9.16a).

Xunzi further says that humans have the propensity to compete as well as to cooperate, and that if the former propensity is stronger than the latter, strife results and disorder ensues. The key to successful collaboration is that people are willing to accept their roles and divisions and accordingly constrain their desires. Xunzi argues that this is possible only if social distinctions and hierarchy are arranged and regulated by yi (there is no perfect translation of this term; the closest in this context would be "duty," or "moral duty," or simply "morality"). "How can social divisions be translated into behavior? I say it is because of yi. Thus, if yi is used to divide society into classes, concord will result" (9.16a).[22] In another passage, Xunzi makes a similar point, stating that the ancient kings regulated people's desires and social distinctions by principles of rituals and morality (li yi) so as to cause people "to perform the duties of their station in life and each to receive his due. . . . This indeed is the Way to make the whole populace live together in harmony and unity" (4.12).

Administrative and Coordinative Functions

Let us now consider the role of rulers in Xunzi's theory of society.[23] Rulers are those who are able to organize people into a society and assign them proper roles and stations, and under whose leadership the world is properly ordered to benefit the "myriad things" on earth. The following two passages give a clear view of rulership as the ability to organize people into a society:

> What is a lord? I say that he is one who can [organize people into a society]. Wherein lies his ability to organize? I say that it lies in expertise in providing a living for the people and in caring for them, expertise in arranging and ordering men, expertise in providing clear principles for the orderly disposition of the people, and expertise in constraining faults and in refining the people. (*Xunzi* 12.6)

22   In this passage Xunzi also makes the point that unlike animals, human beings can organize themselves into a society because they have yi while animals do not. It is not clear whether by "have yi" Xunzi means an *innate* sense of duty or moral capacity, in which case this might well contradict his general view that human nature is "evil" or bad, or an *acquired* sense or moral capacity, in which case Xunzi would have to explain why human beings whose nature is evil can possibly acquire a sense of duty or morality. This difficult interpretive and philosophical issue has generated a rich contemporary literature—see the many stimulating articles collected in T. C. Kline III and Philip J. Ivanhoe, eds., *Virtue, Nature, and Moral Agency in the Xunzi* (Indianapolis: Hackett, 2000), but it has no direct bearing on what I argue here. I thank the anonymous referee for raising this issue.

23   For a general account of Xunzi's conceptions of society and state, see Henry Rosemont, Jr., "State and Society in the *Xunzi*: A Philosophical Commentary," chap.1 in Kline and Ivanhoe, *Virtue, Nature, and Moral Agency.*

A lord is one who is accomplished at causing men to form societies. If the way of a society is properly structured, then each of the myriad things acquires its appropriate place, the Six Domestic Animals can properly increase, and every living thing will have its allotted fate. Thus, just as the Six Domestic Animals will multiply and increase if they are nurtured and bred according to the seasons, and just as plants and trees will flourish if they are cut and planted with the seasons, so too, if the acts and orders of government are according to the seasons, the Hundred Clans will be united and the worthy and good will offer their allegiance. (9.16a)

The essence of rulership, then, lies in the ruler's ability to organize people in society, or to make possible a society based on the distinction of roles and division of labor. But Xunzi goes beyond this abstract view of authority to lay out in detail the various functions and roles that a ruler and his government must perform in building up a society. Some of these functions are similar to those of governments in modern societies, such as security and defense, public works, management of common-pool resources (e.g., forestry and fishery), and production and trade (e.g., agriculture and crafts) (*Xunzi* 9.17). It is not difficult to see the connection between these functions and the idea of authority as the ability to coordinate. An agency empowered by authority and financed by taxation is necessary for collective works like security, defense, and public works, which cannot be achieved by individual action. Management of common-pool resources such as forestry and fishery is another area in which authority as a regulative agency is needed. Xunzi is keenly aware of the problem of the so-called tragedy of the commons, that is, in some situations where individual action is left uncoordinated, short-term individual rationality may lead to long-term collective irrationality. To overcome such problems, an authority is needed that can constrain individual action and ensure that everyone benefits in the long run. For this reason, in elaborating the regulations of a Sage King (*sheng wang zhi zhi*), Xunzi explains the need for the regulation of forestry and fishery in some detail:

If it is the season when the grasses and trees are in the splendor of their flowering and sprouting new leaves, axes and halberds are not permitted in the mountain forest so as not to end their lives prematurely or to interrupt their maturation. If it is the season when the giant sea turtles, water lizards, fish, freshwater turtles, loach, and eels are depositing their eggs, nets and poisons are not permitted in the marshes so as not to prematurely end their lives or interrupt their maturation. (9.16b)

We have seen that for Confucians, rulership is needed because people cannot govern themselves. The passage above supplies a partial answer as to why Xunzi thinks people are unable to govern themselves—not because of foolishness or incompetence but because, with regard to the administrative functions of government, there are limits to the strength, resources, and rationality of the people when they act individually. In this instance, the main responsibilities of political authority are coordination, regulation, and provision of services, and officials in roles of authority primarily require managerial leadership and skills. The necessity of these administrative functions and skills alone does not justify exalting political authority to the high levels proposed by Xunzi.

Transformative Political Leadership

Xunzi also provides other reasons for the necessity of political authority. For him, the norms of morality are fundamental to society, and he defines these norms as rituals (li) or duty (yi) according to the distinction of roles and division of labor. However, Xunzi does not believe that society is what Hayek has called a "spontaneous order," in the sense that its rituals, norms, and social orders emerge spontaneously, but that society and its rituals have to be created and applied. Only people with great virtue and high moral powers—gentlemen (*jun zi*) or sages (*sheng ren*) according to Xunzi—are up to this important task:

> Heaven and Earth are the beginning of life. Ritual and moral principles are the beginning of order. The gentleman is the beginning of ritual and moral principles. Acting with them, actualizing them, accumulating them over and over again, and loving them more than all else is the beginning of the gentleman. Thus, Heaven and Earth give birth to the gentleman, and the gentleman provides the organizing principle for Heaven and Earth. The gentleman is the triadic partner of Heaven and Earth, the summation of the myriad of things, and the father and mother of the people. (*Xunzi* 9.15)

> Ritual principles, moral duty, laws, and standards are all products of the sage. (23.2a)

Mencius shares a similar view about the important role of the sages, even though he does not agree with Xunzi that they are the sole instigators of moral norms and rituals. Mencius holds that morality and ritual have their seeds in human nature; nevertheless, like Xunzi, he believes that the ancient sages' thinking and deeds represent the culmination of humanity and human relationships. In fact, the three major Confucian thinkers—Confucius, Mencius, and Xunzi—all regard Yao and Shun as model sages and model rulers, who laid down a perfect set of principles and a perfect model of rituals and governance:

> The compasses and the carpenter's square are the culmination of squares and circles; the sage is the culmination of humanity. If one wishes to be a ruler, one must fulfill the duties proper to a ruler; if one wishes to be a subject, one must fulfill the duties proper to a subject. In both cases all one has to do is to model oneself on Yao and Shun. (*Mencius* 4A.2)

The ritual and moral principles created and perfected by the gentleman or sage are those that prescribe the roles and functions of the lord, minister, father, son, older brother, younger brother, farmer, knight, artisan, and merchant (*Xunzi* 9.15). Xunzi and other Confucian thinkers consider these roles and relationships the backbone of a society. By creating or perfecting the principles that govern these roles and relationships, the gentleman transforms the human condition from a primitive state, the state of nature so to speak, into a civilized society. It is here that the importance of political authority reaches its highest level—the kind of leadership shown by early sage-rulers like Yao and Shun (and those in the Three Dynasties) is not managerial but *transformative*. For this reason, Xunzi thinks that the Son of Heaven (*tian zi*), a person who possesses such transformative powers and complete virtue and perspicacious wisdom (*Xunzi* 18.5a), is worthy of the most prestigious and unrivaled position of governing the world. He is "without peer" (24.1), and "his position of power and authority is the most honorable in the empire, having no match whatever" (18.5a).

Now we may ask what this reconstruction of the rationale of political authority thus far can tell us about the question of limited government. Would the conception of transformative political leadership reject the idea of limited government? I think it would not; rather, it would support it. The reason is that since the principles of morality and models of governance have already been laid, they could well be crystallized or codified into a set of higher laws that define and regulate basic social and political institutions. If these principles and models have proved to be basically correct and good, why should they not be used to establish a constitution that binds the hands of future rulers? We might also argue that in conceiving the supreme status and power of the ruler or Son of Heaven, Xunzi may have confused the early stage of civilization, when Sage Kings enacted principles and established basic institutions, with later developments where such transformative leadership and unrivaled authority may no longer be necessary. As Xunzi believes that the Sage Kings established a basic framework for a civilized society that would be valid for many generations, it would follow that future Sons of Heaven would not be required to possess the same transformative power and exalted authority in order to rule effectively, as they could learn from and follow the framework that has been put in place. Why should rulers be given more prestige and authority than they need? Why should we not bind their hands with the principles and models of the Sage Kings?

Judgment More Important than Model

Xunzi does have an answer to these questions, which is in line with the position of many other thinkers in the Confucian tradition, and which could be taken as a possible reason for rejecting the idea of limited government. The answer is the view that leadership has a comparative advantage over the laws and methods of governance that Sage Kings have established over time. The gist of this view is that the "model" of governance (*fa*) established by Sage Kings, however perfect it may be, cannot itself apply and create order in society. "There are men who can bring order about, but there is no model that will produce order" (*Xunzi* 12.1). The model, being only "the first manifestation of order," cannot be applied uniformly and without careful knowledge of its working sequence as adjustments must always be made in response to changing circumstances. Only a gentleman cum ruler who has a deep understanding of the moral principles underlining the model knows best how to put it to use.

> The model cannot be established alone, nor can its categories for analogical extension apply themselves in particular instances. . . . The model is the first manifestation of order; the gentleman is the wellspring of the model. Accordingly, if there is a gentleman, however incomplete the model may be, it is sufficient to be employed everywhere. So too if there is no gentleman, then however complete the model may be, the loss of the proper application of the proper sequence of "first and last" and the impossibility of appropriate response to evolving affairs is sufficient to cause anarchy. One who, not understanding the moral principles underlying the laws, attempts to rectify the norms contained therein, however broad his view, is bound to produce anarchy in what he superintends. (12.1)

In another passage, Xunzi makes a similar point that it is the gentleman rather than a good model that is the guarantee for order and stability, saying that "although there have been cases in which a good legal model nonetheless produced disorder," he has never heard of a case "where there was a gentleman in charge of the government and chaos ensued." "Order is born of the gentleman; chaos is produced by the small man" (9.2).[24]

Although Xunzi's argument has a point, it does not justify the view that the ruler should not be bound by higher law.[25] The point is that moral and political judgment is essential in politics. Moral principles and rituals, laws and policies, are only general rules; they require interpretation, adaptation, revision, or extension in the face of changing circumstances, which in turn require judgment. On some occasions certain principles may come into conflict, and judgment will be needed to tackle this conflict. Principles and rules can guide us only up to a point, and beyond this we must rely on judgment. For this reason the ability to make sound judgment is essential to leadership. This ability does not come naturally—judgment has to be nurtured and guided by experience, learning, and virtue. Thus we need people of moral and intellectual caliber to assume political leadership.[26] Nevertheless, the need for judgment and leadership does

---

24 See also 19.2d.

25 I do not mean to suggest that Xunzi thinks rulers can rule arbitrarily. Xunzi certainly advocates fairness and impartiality (which often consist of correctly following rules) and opposes arbitrary rule. But he never conceives the use of a constitutional law to constrain a ruler at the very top level.

26 For a more general discussion of Confucian conceptions of leadership, see Joseph Chan

not conflict with the idea of binding government with law. A distinction can perhaps be made between basic law that defines political institutions and basic principles of morality and society, and more concrete policies and practices. Policies and practices may need to be adapted as circumstances change, but basic law and principles, being the basis of social and political organization, are more stable and generally require less skilled judgment in application.

Perhaps Xunzi would still maintain that (1) if we have a gentleman in power, we do not need power-restraining constitutional law, and (2) if the one in power is not a gentleman, then even a perfect constitutional law would be of no benefit. However, the second point is flawed. A ruler may lack the qualities of a gentleman in two ways: first, if he lacks the ability to make sound judgments, and second, if he lacks virtue or moral correctness. As I have argued above, the application or enforcement of constitutional law does not require difficult judgments, at least for clear constitutional cases, so even a ruler whose powers of judgment are less than ideal would have no problem enforcing or following constitutional law. If a ruler lacks virtue or moral correctness, an effective system of constitutional law is needed precisely in order to restrain him from abusing his power. Thus, even if we accept point 1, point 2 is mistaken, and hence the argument is unsound.

To conclude the discussion thus far, I have argued that Xunzi overestimated the perennial need for transformative leadership and its importance over the law. Although the role of good leadership is important in politics, good leadership would not be hindered by good constitutional law, while bad leadership requires it. Mencius perhaps comes closer to recognizing the correct balance of leadership and law, despite the fact that what he envisions is not power restraining constitutional law: "Goodness alone is not sufficient for government; the law unaided cannot make itself effective" (*Mencius* 4A.1).

Arguments for Monist Authority

The Problem of Divided Authority

Even if Confucians reject Xunzi's idea of the supremacy of authority, they may still not accept limited government, as the concept carries implications that may not be acceptable to them. It is important to note that the modern interpretation of limited government presupposes the existence of a working constitution and an independent judicial branch that interprets the constitution and has the power of judicial review. If government is to be effectively restrained by law, this restraint must be exercised by another power that has the authority to do so. In this sense limited government is often associated with the idea of the

---

and Elton Chan, "Confucianism and Political Leadership," in *The Oxford Handbook of Political Leadership,* ed. Paul 't Hart and R.A.W. Rhodes (Oxford: Oxford University Press, forthcoming).

separation of powers. Of course, conceptually, separation of powers means not just an independent judicial branch restraining the hands of government but also a split between executive and legislative authorities, whose institutional authority is derived from different sources, and whose powers partially overlap to create checks and balances. In practice, however, the system of separation of powers can be viewed as another way of limiting or restraining political authority. Limited government uses constitutional law to restrain authority, and separation of powers uses a system of checks and balances between different branches of government. Constitutionalism comprises both these elements.[27]

However, the adoption of a political system based on the idea of the separation of powers and checks and balances would be unacceptable to Xunzi and most other Confucian thinkers, who subscribe to a monistic view of authority. For them, ultimate political authority must reside in one person as divided authority leads to instability or chaos. Xunzi states this point clearly:

> The lord is the most exalted in the state. The father is the most exalted in the family. Where only one is exalted, there is order; where two are exalted, there is anarchy. From antiquity to the present day there has never been a case of two being exalted, contending for authority, and being able to endure for long. (*Xunzi* 14.7)

In another passage Xunzi says that when instruction comes from one authority it is a source of strength, but when it comes from two authorities it is a source of weakness (15.1c). Confucius is recorded to have stated a similar view:

> There are not two suns in the Heavens, nor two kings in a territory, nor two masters in a family, nor two superiors of equal honor; and the people are shown how the distinction between ruler and subject should be maintained. (*Book of Rites*)[28]

Mencius also approvingly quoted the same passage from Confucius: "According to Confucius, 'There cannot be two kings for the people just as there cannot be two suns in the Heavens'" (*Mencius* 5A.4). When asked about how to stabilize the world (i.e., the empire), Mencius makes the same point: that it can be

---

27 In a monarchical political system, we also need to ask who, if not the monarch, should have the power to amend the constitution and who to interpret it. For the power of amendment, we could imagine a constitution that gives power to the monarch to amend the constitution according to some stringent procedures and constraints as laid down in the constitution. This is actually the idea of constitutional government, which says that, legally speaking, final authority, including the power to amend the constitution itself, rests with the constitution rather than with any individual person, the monarch or the *demos*. Even in a full constitutional democracy, the people and the democratically elected legislature have no arbitrary power to change the constitution. The same can be said of a constitutional monarchy. As for the power of interpretation, the constitution can set up an independent court system, appointed by the monarch, that has the power to interpret the constitution and declare any law or government act unconstitutional.

28 "Fang ji" 坊記 (Record of the Dykes) chapter.

done only on the basis of "one," that is, one sovereign who can unify all people (1A.6).

There is something in the monistic view of authority that is true but trivial—it is not workable to have two equally supreme authorities governing the same set of issues within a jurisdiction without any specification as to how to resolve conflicting decisions. In this sense it is true that "there cannot be two kings for the people." But it does not follow that there cannot exist within a jurisdiction two or more equally supreme authorities commanding different sets of issues. The modern system of the separation of powers and checks and balances, championed by Montesquieu and the authors of the *Federalist Papers*, is precisely one in which the legislative, executive, and judicial powers fall into the hands of different people who enjoy no supreme authority over one another. Of course, the idea of the separation of powers does not imply that the three authorities act like monarchs within their own jurisdictions. Rather they operate in an elaborate framework in which each authority partially overlaps another and detailed rules exist to determine who has a final say over which matters. The reason for the overlapping among the three powers is that this is necessary to ensure mutual checks and balances. As James Madison explains, the separation of powers allows one authority or branch of government to have partial agency in, or control over, the act of the others.[29] What the separation of powers does mean is that the hands that hold the whole power of one branch cannot hold the whole power of another branch.

Although the system of separation of powers and checks and balances may not appear to have the same efficiency as a system of absolute authority, it can be stable and robust if the notion of rule of law is generally accepted in a society. In fact, one may argue that any system of absolute authority can also be unstable because an incompetent or corrupt ruler whose power is unconstrained could bring a great deal of harm to the people, who might rise in resistance or revolt. This is why Madison says, "The accumulation of all powers, legislative, executive, and judiciary, in the same hands, whether of one, a few, or many, and whether hereditary, self-appointed, or elective, may justly be pronounced the very definition of tyranny."[30] The system of separation of powers has proved to be an effective mechanism to prevent monopolization and abuse of power by one person or part of government.

Oneness in Dao

The Confucian monistic view of authority, then, rests on the somewhat shaky claim that a divided sovereign authority inevitably leads to instability or chaos. Absolute authority can also be a major source of such problems (*Xunzi* 9.2).

---

29   Frederick Quinn, ed., *The Federalist Papers Reader and Historical Documents of Our American Heritage* (Santa Ana, CA: Seven Locks, 1997), no. 47, 114.
30   Ibid., 113.

And Confucius is of the view that even one wrong saying of an absolute ruler unopposed by others can ruin his state (*Analects* 13.15). But there seems to be a deeper reason for Confucians to uphold the monistic view of authority, and one that is not consequentialist but metaphysical. Commentators have suggested that the monistic view of authority is part and parcel of Confucian metaphysics, according to which "one" is the fundamental ontological category of the universe.[31] "One" suggests unity and coherence. Things in the world that are apparently diverse are ultimately derived from, or based on, one single ontological source, the Heavenly Dao (tian dao). And since Dao is one, supreme political authority must also be one. Perhaps this is what Confucius means when he says "there are not two suns in the Heavens, nor two kings in a territory." The relationship between the Heavenly and worldly principle of monism is elaborated in detail in *The Annals of Lü Buwei* (*Lüshi chun qiu*) and *Chun qiu fan lu*.[32]

Nevertheless, it is unclear why oneness in Dao should require oneness in political authority, when Confucians themselves acknowledge that it is rare to find an ideal person who fully embodies Dao and has the ability to put it into practice. Xunzi also recognizes that it is very difficult for anyone to fully grasp the Way precisely because of its comprehensiveness. According to him, when people think they have grasped the Way, they may just have focused on one aspect of it and lost sight of other important aspects.

> The myriad things constitute one aspect of the Way, and a single thing constitutes one aspect of the myriad things. The stupid who act on the basis of one aspect of one thing, considering that therein they know the Way, are ignorant. Shen Dao had insight into "holding back," but none into "leading the way." Laozi had insight into "bending down," but none into "straightening up." Mozi had insight into "uniformity," but none into "individuation." (*Xunzi* 17.12)

Xunzi often criticizes previous great thinkers (including Laozi, Mencius, and Mozi) as having only partial insight into Dao. But this criticism can also be leveled against Xunzi himself: if even gifted thinkers inevitably suffer from partial understanding, how can any person other than a true sage claim to be the sole representative of the Way and thus deserve supreme and absolute authority to rule? Since comprehensive understanding of the Way is unlikely to be available to any but the most exceptional ruler, there is no reason that political authority should reside in one person. Thus, even if the Way is one, it does not follow that political authority should be one. Instead, we should try to devise a political rule that recognizes the limits of people's virtue and understanding

31   Zhang Fentian 張分田, *Min ben si xiang yu Zhongguo gu dai tong zhi si xiang* 民本思想與中國古代統治思想 [People-Based Thought and Ancient Chinese Thought on Governance], vol. 2 (Tianjin: Nankai University Press, 2009), 413–18.

32   See "Tian dao wu er" 天道無二, chap. 51 in *Chun qiu fan lu*.

and yet strives to utilize them in the governance of the Way.[33] This system should have a plurality of power centers, with offices taken up by those people who have the appropriate virtue and abilities.

Mutual Cooperation and Checks

To conclude the discussion on the Confucian monistic view of authority, there are two distinct reasons that we need a number of virtuous people sharing in governance, rather than one. First, as it is extremely rare to find a virtuous person possessing a full understanding of the Way, we need a political system that allows virtuous individuals to complement each other and collaborate to achieve a balanced view of the Way and put it into practice. Second, Confucians have long understood that virtue is in fact a form of power—a virtuous leader can persuade, inspire, and transform others. If, as I have argued above, Confucians can agree that any one form of power should be limited and checked by another form of power, then they should also agree with Montesquieu and Arendt that "even virtue stands in need of limitation,"[34] for it is also a form of power. Montesquieu says that to prevent abuse of power, "it is necessary from the very nature of things that power should be a check to power."[35] If virtue is a form of power, then virtue should also be a check to virtue. John Adams generalizes Montesquieu's point into a famous saying about balance of power: "Power must be opposed to power, force to force, strength to strength, interest to interest, as well as reason to reason, eloquence to eloquence, and passion to passion."[36] To this list we should add "virtue to virtue."

The zealous search for a godlike ruler is thus flawed in a number of ways. First, it is a search for someone who, at least since the Three Dynasties, has not been found to exist, a point that most Confucian thinkers including Xunzi have admitted. More serious, there are a number of dangers inherent in setting up a political office with the potential for such unrivaled authority and prestige when no individual exists who can live up to the demands or responsibility of such an office. No depth of insight is required to see that if a "small man" occupies a great office of unconstrained power, disastrous results will follow. The

---

33   Stephen C. Angle similarly argues that what is distinctive about Confucianism is its "simultaneous commitments to perfection and fallibility," and therefore that "none of us, including our leaders, can be relied upon to see all relevant sides of a given situation." Politics should therefore allow "multiple perspectives" and "institutions of protected political participation." See his *Sagehood*, 212.

34   Arendt, *On Revolution*, 143.

35   Montesquieu: "Constant experience shows us that every man invested with power is apt to abuse it, and to carry his authority as far as it will go. Is it not strange, though true, to say that *virtue itself has need of limits*? To prevent this abuse, it is necessary from the very nature of things that power should be a check to power." Italics added. From Baron de Montesquieu, *The Spirit of the Laws* (New York: Hafner, 1949), bk. 11, chap. 4, 150.

36   Cited in Arendt, *On Revolution*, 143.

emphasis on the search for a godlike political figure has meant that Confucian thinkers have lost sight of the real challenge in governance, namely, how to effectively groom and select people who, though they may never achieve the mystical level of a Sage King, may yet possess appropriate moral and intellectual capabilities to assume leadership. The real emphasis should be on bringing people with flawed but above-average levels of virtue together in positions of power, so that the weaknesses of one can be compensated by the strengths of another, and the strengths of all can be reinforced. Xunzi's notion of allowing only one person to occupy a single position of utmost prestige and power is not a solution that is feasible in the real nonideal world. A system of governance that involves mutual cooperation and checks among people who have more virtue and intelligence than the rest is more desirable than an absolute monarchy. This issue will be pursued in the following two chapters.

CHAPTER 3

The Role of Institution

In the previous two chapters I have rejected the dominion interpretation of the Confucian conception of authority and criticized the Confucian emphasis on a monist and supreme authority. I have reconstructed and further developed a conception that justifies authority by its service to the people and the people's willing acceptance. This conception expresses an ideal political relationship between the ruler and the ruled—the ruler is committed to governing the people in a trustworthy and caring manner, and the ruled, in return, express their willing endorsement and support of the ruler. This ideal relationship is marked by mutual commitment and trust.

Early Confucian thought, however, also expresses an acute awareness of the fact that authority in the real world is fragile. Rulers are not often virtuous and trustworthy, authority can be resisted, and political relationship broken. Early Confucian masters, however, do not discuss at great length how politics and authority should be structured in situations where rulers are not good enough; nor do they give much guidance on how good people could be selected into political offices. Their main preoccupation is to urge existing rulers to improve their virtues and methods of governing. According to the masters, if rulers are not convinced or motivated to improve themselves—if the Way does not prevail—there is little we can do except withdraw from the political world or sacrifice our lives for it. At the end of the day, Confucian masters can only resign themselves to fate, or Heaven's will, regarding the chance of success of their ideal. This is a highly unsatisfactory situation. Confucian political thought cannot get out of this predicament unless it develops a perspective on social and political order that effectively deals with the problems of reality while maintaining its ideal political relationship as a regulative ideal. This chapter and the next will do just that. In developing this perspective, we need to borrow from modern political experience and political science.

In the first section I argue that institutions seem particularly suited to mediate between real-world tasks and ideal aspirations, for they at once perform socially useful tasks that tackle real-life problems and uphold standards of normative appropriateness that express ideal aspirations. In the second and third sections I argue that democratic elections, understood in an appropriate way, are an institution that performs the dual function. However, the purpose of democratic elections can be understood in at least two ways: as a device to select virtuous and competent politicians for the common good (the selection model), or as a mechanism to reward and sanction politicians in general (the sanctions model)—a distinction drawn by contemporary political scientist Jane Mansbridge and others; or as both. While the sanction function of elections can compel elected officials to work for the public interest, I argue that it is the selection function that echoes the spirit of the Confucian ideal of political relationship. Whenever circumstances permit, democratic elections should be expressed and practiced more as a device of selection and less as a mechanism of sanction. In the fourth section I look further into certain issues about the selection model.

The Dual Function of Institutions

Despite its attractiveness, the Confucian conception of political relationship is a lofty ideal that is often at odds with reality. In the real world not every political leader is trustworthy, public-spirited, or genuinely mindful of the well-being of the people. Furthermore, it is hard to bring about—or engineer—these desirable attitudes and dispositions through deliberate social design. Early Confucians were keenly aware that benevolence and ethical behavior cannot be brought about by punishment or reward. Contemporary social and political theorist Claus Offe echoes this view by saying that cognitive and normative dispositions "are either present or absent in a given social context, but cannot easily be brought into being through strategic action. If knowledge is perceived to be lacking, we start doing research. But what do we do when trust, benevolence, or dispositions toward cooperation are perceived to be lacking?"[1] He argues that these normative dispositions cannot be strategically produced by any of the three major media of coordination that reproduce the social order of modern society, namely, the money-driven economic market, the democratically legitimated use of coercion, and the knowledge-based networks of professional organizations. In fact, trust and other such dispositions are the very cultural and moral resources that enable the existence of such forms of coordination.

So what can we do to promote trust, benevolence, and other normative dispositions? Early Confucians would say that we can promote them through the use of rites. As I argued in the introduction, rites can help provide the link between ideal and nonideal aspirations. On the one hand, they help control behavior by providing concrete guidelines (which are in turn backed up with mild forms of social sanction such as verbal commendation or condemnation); on the other hand, they shape the internal dispositions or intrinsic motivations of people by habituating them within a particular world of meanings and values. When rites are clear and effective, there are not only shared meanings among the populace but also shared norms for action, as well as shared expectations of

---

1   Claus Offe, "How Can We Trust Our Fellow Citizens?" in *Democracy and Trust,* ed. Mark E. Warren (Cambridge: Cambridge University Press, 1999), 43.

motives and responses that help reduce distrust to a minimum. But Confucians know that these strategies are unlikely to work when leaders themselves lack virtue, when trust is generally lacking in society, or when the world of shared meanings and values has disintegrated. In any of these conditions, it is extremely difficult to create or re-create rites that carry legitimacy and command respect. For example, to set up a government bureau to promote rites in a modern society that is devoid of the shared meanings and norms of rites would likely cause suspicion and cynicism. It is as hard to socially engineer rites as it is to engineer desirable attitudes and dispositions. If this is the case, is there any alternative in modern society that can supplement the role of rites, and connect ideal and nonideal aspirations?

The answer, I believe, is institution, insofar as an institution is understood to be a device that performs a socially useful task (or tasks) in a normatively appropriate way, rather than a mechanism that controls behavior.[2] Understood as such, the goal of an institution is "getting things done" and doing things "the right way."[3] And to achieve this, an institution must be informed by some "logic of consequentiality" and "logic of appropriateness."[4] An institution's powers and responsibilities, rules and regulations, and incentive and sanction mechanisms must be informed by the logic of consequentiality, in the sense that they are designed to bring about certain desired consequences related to the institution's task. But these things must also be informed by the logic of appropriateness, in that they have to express certain values and norms that are thought to be bound up with the institution's task. To illustrate: The university as an institution has the task to pursue and disseminate knowledge. To this end the university must set up governance structures and human resources and incentive systems. But it must also adhere to the values and norms internal to the practice of knowledge discovery, such as truthfulness, creativity, accuracy, and free inquiry. An institution therefore has two sides—the business side and the normative side, both of which are subsumed under the institution's task.

The view of institution I am developing here is slightly different from Alasdair MacIntyre's. What he calls a "practice" is similar to what I call the "normative side of an institution." According to MacIntyre, a practice "involves standards of excellence and obedience to rules as well as the achievement of goods

---

2 The account of institution offered below is influenced by the work of Claus Offe, in particular his "Institutional Design," in *Encyclopedia of Democratic Thought*, ed. Paul Barry Clarke and Joe Foweraker (London: Routledge, 2001), 363–69; "Designing Institutions in East European Transitions," in *The Theory of Institutional Design*, ed. Robert E. Goodin (Cambridge: Cambridge University Press, 1996), 199–226; and "Trust Our Fellow Citizens"; as well as Alasdair MacIntyre's "The Nature of the Virtues," chap. 14 in *After Virtue: A Study in Moral Theory* (London: Duckworth, 1981).

3 Offe, "East European Transitions," 201.

4 The phrases are from James G. March and Johan P. Olsen, *Rediscovering Institutions: The Organizational Basis of Politics* (New York: Free Press, 1989), 23–24; also cited in Offe, "East European Transitions," 201. My usage of these two phrases is not entirely the same as that of March and Olsen, who followed Alasdair MacIntyre.

[internal to the practices]."[5] He also clearly separates practices from institutions. We can illustrate his distinction again by the example of the university. The pursuit of knowledge is a practice, while the university is an institution. The practice of knowledge is constituted by certain standards of excellence (such as truthfulness, originality, and accuracy) and by rules that participants are expected to follow (such as citation and acknowledgment rules and rules of reasoning and proof). If participants in the practice act in accordance with these standards and rules, they will achieve certain goods that are internal to the practice, such as insight, creativity, and intellectual satisfaction. The university as an institution, according to MacIntyre, is simply a device to support the practice of knowledge and is characteristically and necessarily concerned with external goods, which he defines as money and other material goods, and power and status. Macintyre further says practices need institutions to be sustainable, and yet they may not be able to resist the corrupting power of institutions. He writes:

> For no practices can survive for any length of time unsustained by institutions. Indeed so intimate is the relationship of practices to institutions—and consequently of the goods external to the goods internal to the practices in question—that institutions and practices characteristically form a single causal order in which the ideals and the creativity of the practice are always vulnerable to the acquisitiveness of the institution, in which the cooperative care for common goods of the practice is always vulnerable to the competitiveness of the institution.[6]

MacIntyre helps us see the socially useful task of an institution as a practice having its own standard of excellence, norms, and internal goods, and that an institution may promote or corrupt the practice in question. But he draws too sharp a distinction between practices and institutions. For him, the relationship between the two is causal—institutions offer external goods, such as money and power, to support the internal goods of practices, and the former may also come to corrupt the latter. In my view, the relationship between institutions and practices is more than causal. Institutions—at least the good ones—not only provide resources and administrative support for a practice but also embody or reflect the internal values and excellences of that practice.[7] For example, the rules governing teaching and learning at a university must reflect the norm of free inquiry as an internal norm of the practice of knowledge inquiry; the ten-

---

5 MacIntyre, *After Virtue*, 177.

6 Ibid., 181.

7 As the anonymous referee points out, institutions, once up and running, may tend to take on a life of their own that undermines the internal values and excellences of the practices within them. I agree, which is why I hold that MacIntyre's warning about the negative effects of institutions on practices is important and valid. Nevertheless, MacIntyre also thinks that the long-term survival of practices cannot do without the support of institutions. So the choice is not whether to have institutions, but how to preserve their healthy functioning. I discuss ways of doing this with regard to democratic elections in the next chapter.

ure and promotion rules must uphold the values of truthfulness, accuracy, and originality. Similarly, the health-care rules and regulations of a hospital should embody the ideal relationship between health-care professionals and patients as envisaged by the practice of medicine.[8] So a practice is not only made possible by an institution but also finds its partial embodiment in it.[9] A bad institution is one that either fails to embody or actively corrupts the internal norms and values of a practice.

In the introduction I introduced the two-track approach to reconstructing Confucianism. Part of the aim, and challenge, of this approach is precisely to develop a perspective that simultaneously keeps alive the Confucian ideal as an aspiration and effectively deals with problems that arise in nonideal conditions. When Confucian rites do not flourish in modern society, what else do we have to promote the Confucian ideal? I suggest that the best alternative is the institution as understood in the above way. Since an institution bases its legitimacy on its ability to perform a socially useful task—or practice in MacIntyre's sense—in the right way, it must actively embrace and manifest the internal norms and values of that task (or practice). A successful institution will therefore have socializing effects on the participants within it (and even on third parties outside the institution, such as the general public). The participants will be exposed to, and habituated into, norms and regulations that endow them "with a sense of meaning and appropriateness, as well as an awareness of what is expected of them and what is likely to happen to them."[10] For this reason social scientists claim that institutions, like rituals, can shape people's behavior and normative orientations. In performing socially useful tasks, institutions blend together social values and ethical aspirations on the ideal level and practical concerns on the nonideal level. Institutions are neither wholly rites nor wholly sanction mechanisms, but a mixture of both. Unlike sanctions, institutions express values and embody norms; unlike rites and norms, they are constituted by rules and regulations and supported by compliance mechanisms.

Democratic Elections as an Institution

We may now return to the question of how to realize the Confucian ideal conception of political relationship in a modern society. The Confucian conception

---

8   Of course, insofar as there are different conceptions of the practice of medicine, there are also different rules governing the relationship between health-care professionals and patients.

9   Michael J. Sandel has also made a similar point in his discussion of the relation between political ideas and institutions: "Political institutions are not simply instruments that implement ideals independently conceived; they are themselves embodiments of ideas." In *Democracy's Discontent: America in Search of a Public Philosophy* (Cambridge: Harvard University Press, 1996), ix.

10   Offe, "Institutional Design," 363. In "Trust Our Fellow Citizen," 71, he writes, "The formative function of an institution is performed if people living in or under these institutions are both cognitively familiarized and effectively impregnated with the normative ideas embodied in the institution."

of political relationship can be regarded as a practice defined with reference to certain standards of excellence (such as the trustworthiness of politicians and policies that care for the well-being of the people) and certain internal goods (such as sincere and mutual commitment, sharing of fate, and harmony). For a practice to succeed, participants must be intrinsically motivated—they must sincerely submit to the standards of excellence and find those internal goods desirable for their own sake. And for an institution to succeed, its rules and regulations must be able to simultaneously tackle nonideal conditions, such as power use and abuse, and at the same time embody and manifest the aspirations of the ideal practice. What kinds of political institutions could do this today? In searching for institutions, we are naturally limited by our experience and horizon. Prudence counsels us to be cautious and piecemeal in proposing new institutions, for we have little knowledge of their effect. Also, it is difficult for new institutions to gain legitimacy and public support, unless they are developed within a legitimate institutional setting and adapted from successful precedents elsewhere, in which case they are not completely new.[11] So my strategy is to first consider existing institutions, and to discuss proposals of new institutions in the next chapter.

The most obvious existing institution to consider is electoral democracy. Given certain appropriate conditions, democracy is known to be more effective than other kinds of political systems in compelling political leaders to work for the interest of the electorate, removing leaders who are judged to be incompetent, and curbing power abuse. That is to say, democracy is rather good at addressing real-life problems. But can democratic elections also embody or manifest the ideal political relationship envisaged in early Confucianism? Although many people today believe democracy is the only legitimate form of government, many also experience a big gap between the ideal and the actual institution and feel alienated from the politicians and processes. There is strong evidence of mounting public dissatisfaction with representative democracies in many countries. A team of political scientists, led by Susan Pharr and Robert Putnam, have found that citizens' trust of politicians in twelve out of thirteen "Trilateral countries" (i.e., Japan, Europe, and North America) declined from 1974 to 1996, with a growing number of citizens being of the opinion that their politicians were interested in votes rather than the well-being of the people, and that elected representatives lost touch with those they had been elected to represent.[12] The public's attachment to particular political parties similarly seems to have declined in many of these countries, signaling "a growing disenchantment with partisan politics in general."[13] Even formal political institutions, such as parliaments and the executive branches of the government, have experienced

---

11 See Offe, "Institutional Design."

12 Susan J. Pharr and Robert D. Putnam, eds., *Disaffected Democracies: What's Troubling the Trilateral Countries?* (Princeton: Princeton University Press, 2000), 13–16.

13 Ibid., 18.

a dramatic drop in citizens' confidence. In the United States, for example, "in the mid-1960s a large proportion of Americans expressed a great deal of confidence in the Supreme Court, the executive branch, and Congress, but that confidence dropped dramatically by the early 1970s, and slid even further for the executive and Congress over the following two decades. Significantly, it is the Supreme Court, the least partisan and political institution, that has best retained the public's confidence."[14] In short, "most citizens in the Trilateral world have become more distrustful of politicians, more skeptical about political parties, and significantly less confident in their parliament and other political institutions."[15]

It may not be too far off the mark to speculate about what citizens expect of their political leaders by looking at the mirror image of politicians as perceived by citizens. When citizens complain that politicians care more about votes than about the voters' well-being, they are in effect saying that they expect politicians to care for their needs and well-being. When citizens complain that their elected representatives lose touch with them, it is because they expect them to be in touch. Politicians today are expected to share their citizens' joy in national celebrations and their sorrow in disasters, and they are heavily criticized if they fail to do so. Similarly, when citizens lack confidence in partisan politicians and institutions, they expect their leaders and institutions to be working for the common good and not for personal or party political gains. In these aspects at least, the public's yearning for good leadership and better political relationships in modern democracies is strikingly similar to the early Confucian conception of political relationship, in that it calls for trustworthiness, care for the well-being of the people, and a strong sense of sharing and mutuality. What the Confucian conception of political relationship portrays is not a parochial, old-fashioned understanding of politics but an insightful and attractive ideal that still has resonance in contemporary democratic societies.[16]

Before discussing how democratic institutions can embody and manifest the Confucian conception of political relationship, we need to take note of an important feature of institutions, namely, that their rules and regulations—along with the expressive values and symbolic meanings of these rules—are man-made. As such they are dependent on human construction and interpretation, and any one set of rules and regulations may allow for different interpretations. An institution has socializing effects only if its participants more or less share the same interpretation of its values and meanings.[17] Now, the purpose or function of democratic institutions is subject to different understandings, not all of

---

14 Ibid., 19.

15 Ibid., 21.

16 This is not to say that there are no problems with the Confucian conception, some of which I explored in the previous chapter.

17 There are at least two ways to facilitate a shared interpretation. The first is to rely on leaders defining and communicating one salient interpretation and setting a personal example to others; the second is to choose auxiliary rules and regulations to reinforce one interpretation over others.

which are consistent with the Confucian conception of ideal political relationship. Let us take elections as an example. One popular academic view of the function of elections is that they are a device to hold political leaders accountable by providing rewards (powers and privileges) and sanctions (removal from office). Behind this so-called sanctions model of elections is the notion that politicians are opportunistic agents motivated solely by self-interest. Periodic elections and other accountability mechanisms are therefore necessary to monitor elected officials and induce them to do what the voters want. The classic and most extreme statement on this sanctions model is Hume's maxim:

> In contriving any system of government, and fixing the several checks and controls of the constitution, every man ought to be supposed a *knave*, and to have no other end, in all his actions, than private interest. By this interest we must govern him, and, by means of it, make him, notwithstanding his insatiable avarice and ambition, cooperate to public good.[18]

Many contemporary public choice theorists basically follow Hume's maxim in understanding the working of constitutional democracy.[19] The sanctions model of democracy, and politics in general, is thus based on distrust and control. Government is regarded as a necessary evil, and politicians are regarded as knaves. Although authority is necessary for promoting the public good, subjection to authority is both dangerous and unpleasant. Authority therefore has to be subject to stringent democratic accountability devices. It is obvious that if distrust-and-control is the key point of democracy, then it goes deeply against the Confucian ideal conception of political relationship, which takes trustworthiness, sincerity, and mutual commitment of rulers and the ruled as an aspiration. For this reason, democratic institutions, as understood by the sanctions model, cannot perform the role of integrating Confucian ideal and nonideal concerns, even if these institutions are effective in tackling real-life problems.

A political constitution designed on the basis of the sanctions model not only fails to express the ideal political relationship; it also has highly undesirable consequences. In the real world, not all politicians or people who seek to enter professional politics are motivated purely by private interests. Many people may have both public- and private-interest motivations. As Bruno S. Frey has argued, to imply that all politicians are pure egoists is to crowd out the civic

---

18 David Hume, "Of the Independency of Parliament," essay 6 in pt. 1 of *Essays: Moral, Political and Literary*, ed. Eugene F. Miller, rev. ed. (Indianapolis: Liberty Fund, 1987), available at http://files.libertyfund.org/files/704/0059_Bk.pdf. This quotation might give an oversimplistic account of the views of Hume, who might not exclude a principle of promoting virtue in constitutional design. For this interesting point, see Baogang He, "Knavery and Virtue in Humean Institutional Design," *Journal of Value Inquiry* 37, no. 4 (2003): 543–53. I thank Baogang He and Stephen Angle for drawing my attention to this article.

19 A notable example is Geoffrey Brennan and James Buchanan, "Predictive Power and the Choice among Regimes," *Economic Journal* 93, no. 369 (March 1983): 89–105.

virtue of good politicians.[20] Pronouncements of good intentions and displays of good behavior would be looked at with suspicion or mockery by those who subscribe to the sanctions model, and good politicians would be made to follow rules and norms that assume they are knaves. Furthermore, democratic institutions modeled on the knavery principle would likely attract more people with low civic virtue to enter politics than altruistic people because they would find it less demeaning to operate in such a setting. As Adrian Vermeule puts it, "designing institutions for knaves creates a system in which knaves operate comfortably, while knights decline to take public office."[21] The result would be a vicious circle in which bad politicians would dominate the political scene because of the self-fulfilling effects of the system, and the public would be forced to invest more resources and create more rules to monitor them.

The Grand Union Ideal and the Selection Model

Is it possible to understand the point of democratic elections in a different way? I believe Confucianism can provide an alternative understanding, one that is drawn from the Grand Union ideal discussed in the introduction to this book. In *The Book of Rites*, the "Li yun" chapter describes the Way of politics as follows: "When the Grand Dao was pursued, a public and common spirit ruled all under the sky; they chose men of talent, virtue, and ability for public service; they valued mutual trust and cultivated harmony." The ideal described here is very similar to the Confucian ideal political relationship as summarized in the introduction of this chapter. The Grand Union ideal suggests a principle: to select the virtuous and competent to assume leadership, so that they can work for the public interest and cultivate trust and harmony with the people. *The Book of History* tells us what the process of selection looked like in the mythical Golden Age. In describing how Shun was chosen to succeed the throne of Yao, it says that Yao first asked his ministers to see who among them could succeed him. The ministers replied that they were not virtuous enough for the job and recommended Shun, a man who was from a lower level of society but known to be of good character. Yao accepted the recommendation and tested Shun by assigning him some major governing responsibilities and observing his conduct and ability. After three years of observation, Yao and many other people were satisfied with Shun's performance and Yao abdicated his position to Shun.[22]

20   Bruno S. Frey, "A Constitution for Knaves Crowds Out Civic Virtues," *Economic Journal* 107, no. 443 (July 1997): 1043–53.

21   Adrian Vermeule, "Hume's Second-Best Constitutionalism," *University of Chicago Law Review* 70, no. 1 (2003): 425. See also Jane Mansbridge, "A 'Selection Model' of Political Representation," *Journal of Political Philosophy* 17, no. 4 (2009): 379; and Frey, "A Constitution for Knaves," 1049.

22   "Yao dian" 堯典 (Canon of Yao) chapter.

I want to suggest that the meaning or point of elections can be understood in the light of the Grand Union ideal. That is to say, elections should not primarily be about monitoring or control, nor should they be seen as an accountability device to induce self-interested politicians to work for voters; they should rather be seen as a method for selecting people who have integrity, ability, and commitment to public service and who will cultivate trust and harmony with the people. As suggested by contemporary historian Yu Ying-shih, some Confucian scholars in the late nineteenth and early twentieth centuries viewed Western democracies in exactly this way. One example is Wang Tao (1828–1897), the Chinese assistant to James Legge (1815–1897, the first English translator of the Confucian classics), who gave the following characterization of the English government and people after a two-year trip to Great Britain and Europe in the late 1860s:

> The real strength of England, however, lies in the fact that there is a sympathetic understanding between the governing and the governed, a close relationship between the ruler and the people. . . . My observation is that the daily domestic political life of England actually embodies the traditional ideals of our ancient Golden Age. In official appointments the method of recommendation and election is practiced, but the candidates must be well known, of good character and achievements before they can be promoted to a position over the people. . . . And moreover the principle of majority rule is adhered to in order to show impartiality. . . . The English people are likewise public-spirited and law-abiding: the laws and regulations are hung up high (for everyone to see), and no one dares violate them.[23]

To Wang, the English elections were conducted in a spirit strikingly similar to the Confucian principle of selection and spirit of impartiality, so much so that he thought that the political life of England actually embodied the traditional ideals of the ancient Golden Age (the Grand Union) in China. My point here is not that Wang gave an accurate picture of English political life, but that some Confucians viewed Western democracy in a way consistent with the Confucian ideal. Yu provides further examples of Confucian scholars in the modern period who give high praise of Western democracies.[24]

The American Founding Fathers also took the point of democracy to be, in part, about the selection of the virtuous and competent. In the *Federalist Papers* no. 57, written in 1788, James Madison wrote:

> The aim of every political constitution is, or ought to be, first to obtain for rulers men who possess most wisdom to discern, and most virtue to pursue,

---

23   Ssu-yü Teng and John K. Fairbank, *China's Response to the West: A Documentary Survey, 1839–1923* (Cambridge: Harvard University Press, 1954), 140, cited in Yu Ying-shih, "The Idea of Democracy and the Twilight of the Elite Culture in Modern China," in *Justice and Democracy: Cross-cultural Perspectives*, ed. Ron Bontekoe and Marietta Stepaniants (Honolulu: University of Hawaii Press, 1997), 201.

24   Yu, "The Idea of Democracy"

the common good of the society; and in the next place, to take the most effectual precautions for keeping them virtuous whilst they continue to hold their public trust. The elective mode of obtaining rulers is the characteristic policy of republican government.[25]

Some political scientists and economists today call the Madisonian understanding of democratic elections and representation the "selection model," in contrast to the "sanctions model" championed by public choice theorists. The selection model has largely been rejected or ignored in much of the public choice literature in the past few decades.[26] But there is now a burgeoning literature that argues for the selection model as both normatively more attractive and empirically more valid than the sanctions model.[27]

According to James Fearon, the central idea of the selection model is that elections can be viewed "as a means of selecting the type of leader who will act competently and faithfully in the public interest, independently of reelection incentives."[28] There are three necessary conditions for this model to work:[29] First, that among the candidates there are people who belong to this good type of leader; second, that the candidates' policy direction or conception of the public interest more or less aligns with that of the voters (if they have any); third, that electoral mechanisms and processes can be designed to facilitate voters' selection of good leaders. As these conditions do not seem to be impossibly difficult to obtain, the selection model is not an unrealistic ideal. Moreover, advocates of this model, such as Jane Mansbridge, admit that both selection and sanctions may be present in reality—politicians may have both "the desire to make good public policy and the desire to be reelected," [30] and voters may want to select good leaders as well as to monitor them after selection. But Mansbridge argues that selection should work at the front end of the electoral system and sanctions should work at the edges of the system, so that the focal meaning of the electoral system remains one of selecting and trusting good

---

25   James Madison, "The Alleged Tendency of the New Plan to Elevate the Few at the Expense of the Many Considered in Connection with Representation," no. 57 in Alexander Hamilton, James Madison, and John Jay, *The Federalist Papers*, ed. Clinton Rossiter, with introduction and notes by Charles R. Kesler (New York: Signet Classic, 2003), 348.

26   See, for example, James Buchanan's view: "To improve politics, it is necessary to improve or reform rules, the framework within which the game of politics is played. There is no suggestion that improvement lies in the selection of morally superior agents who will use their powers in some public interest." Cited in Timothy Besley, "Political Selection," *Journal of Economic Perspectives* 19, no. 3 (2005): 44.

27   The most recent and comprehensive survey of this literature is Mansbridge, "A 'Selection Model.'"

28   James D. Fearon, "Electoral Accountability and the Control of Politicians: Selecting Good Types versus Sanctioning Poor Performance," chap. 2 in *Democracy, Accountability, and Representation*, ed. Adam Przeworski, Susan C. Stokes, and Bernard Manin (Cambridge: Cambridge University Press, 1999), 60.

29   Compare ibid., 59; Mansbridge, "A 'Selection Model,'" 377–84; and Besley, "Political Selection."

30   Mansbridge, "A 'Selection Model,'" 370.

politicians. "Monitoring need not be systematic and on-going . . . it is more efficient for individual citizens and interest groups to send in alarms when they come across wrongdoing ('fire alarm' oversight) rather than engage in continual monitoring ('police patrol' oversight)."[31]

The selection model, then, seems attractive in two ways. First, it breaks the vicious circle of "distrust, control, and more distrust" of politicians. Although no system or rule can control politicians completely, especially when they are self-interested agents, the selection model encourages people of integrity and public-interest motivation to enter politics, and the presence of such people fosters a culture of civic virtue and helps to monitor the behavior of those politicians who may act as knaves.[32] Second, as Mansbridge argues, in the selection model the electoral system can "normatively reinforce a commitment to the public good and a warranted relationship of trust and goodwill between representative and constituent."[33] She writes:

> Beyond efficiency, constituents can take some satisfaction from the quality of their relationship with an intrinsically motivated representative. A selection model privileges commitment to the common interest over the more self-interested motive of desiring reelection. . . . Without knowing each other personally, both partners in the relationship can wish the other well.[34]

It is striking that Mansbridge's description of the quality of the constituent-representative relationship in the selection model sounds so similar to the early Confucian ideal conception of ruler-ruled relationship outlined in the beginning of this chapter and in chapter 1. Both conceptions give pride of place to trust, goodwill, and mutual commitment to the common good. The selection model seems to offer an understanding of democratic institutions that have a chance to work in nonideal conditions and yet tallies with some ideal concerns of the early Confucian conception of politics.

Disagreement and Aristocracy

It may be argued that by contrasting sanction and selection models we have missed a third way of understanding democratic elections. In society, conflicting conceptions of public interest, justice, or virtue always exist, and there often seems no way to reach unanimity on these issues. Democratic elections, according to this third way of understanding, can provide a free process for public opinion formation and articulation and a fair procedure to address and resolve

---

31 Ibid., 385. In developing this point, Mansbridge cites Mathew D. McCubbins and Thomas Schwartz, "Congressional Oversight Overlooked: Police Patrols versus Fire Alarms," *American Journal of Political Science* 28, no. 1 (1984): 165–79.

32 See Frey, "A Constitution for Knaves," 1049.

33 Mansbridge, "A 'Selection Model,'" 371.

34 Ibid., 393.

disagreement. The rationale of democratic elections is not so much to select and empower those who are intrinsically motivated to pursue public interest, but to decide which conceptions of public interest should prevail in policy making.[35] This third view of democratic elections is certainly plausible, and I see no reason to reject it. But I do not see any irresolvable contradiction between this and the selection model, the main reason being that even if the rationale of democratic elections is to resolve conflicting conceptions of public interest, voters may still want to elect those who are intrinsically motivated, rather than induced or sanctioned, to pursue conceptions of public interest that are shared between the constituents and their representatives. In other words, it is perfectly consistent for voters both to elect publicly motivated and trustworthy candidates and to advance their conceptions of public interest through electoral competition.

In addition, if we shift from the voter's point of view to a societal perspective, then it seems that the selection of publicly motivated people to serve in the government is an important, independent social goal. Conceptions of public interest are often vague and need to be translated into policy proposals. Even enacted policies have to be regularly tested, reexamined, and revised according to changing circumstances. In real politics there is a great deal of room, and need, for political judgment. We should not, therefore, design a democratic political system that attracts politicians who mainly respond to sanction and control and but binds their hands by stringent accountability and transparency measures, as implied by the sanctions model. Rather, we should design a political system that attracts publicly motivated and trustworthy politicians and allows them space to make highly context-dependent judgments and policies and defend them in public forums.[36] So the selection of publicly motivated people to serve in the government is an important independent goal of democratic elections, even if we also accept the procedural-deliberative function as another goal of democracy. Advocates of the procedural-deliberative view of democracy should find more affinity with the selection model than with the sanctions model, as the selection model (as a normative model) encourages voters and candidates to seriously deliberate public interest—in much the same way as the procedural-deliberative view.

As we have seen, there are a number of different ways in which the rationale behind the institution of democratic elections can be interpreted, one of which is the selection model. However, the selection model itself can also be interpreted in several different ways. Mansbridge, for example, in her examination of the selection model, distinguishes two ways of viewing elected representatives. The first way she calls "Burkean." This assumes that the represen-

---

35 I thank Chin-liew Ten for suggesting this important alternative.

36 As Mansbridge writes, "We should favor not extreme *transparency in process* (for example, making all committee meetings public), but instead *transparency in rationale*—in procedures, information, reasons, and the facts on which the reasons are based." From "A 'Selection Model,'" 386 (italics and brackets in the original).

tative not only is intrinsically motivated to serve the public but also is someone who "has more wisdom, intelligence, or prudence than the voter." "For Burke and many others at this time, including many framers of the U.S. constitution," Mansbridge writes, "electoral representation implied what Bernard Manin calls 'the principle of distinction'—that representatives 'should rank higher than their constituents in wealth, talent, and virtue.' . . . Hanna Pitkin considered this conception of representation 'elitist' and anchored it in a theory of 'natural aristocracy.'"[37]

According to Mansbridge, the selection model does not necessarily carry any connotations of aristocracy on the part of the representative or incompetence on the part of the voters. The model assumes only that the representative is intrinsically motivated to seek the good of the whole society and is prepared to rely on his or her own judgment (because he or she is less responsive to sanctions). This assumption does not imply any notion of superiority of the representative vis-à-vis the voters. Mansbridge further argues that in Western societies, the old aristocratic view of representation has to some degree given way to a new and relatively egalitarian view. This version of the selection model eschews hierarchy and embraces the view that representatives should be more "like" their constituents and "possess their sentiments and feelings."[38] In her understanding, many representatives today "see themselves as 'like' their constituents, in demographic characteristics, political attitudes, or both."[39] Similarly, "Today when voters say they want to select a 'good man' or 'good woman' as a representative, they often seem to want someone like them, but with the interest, competence, and honesty to be a legislator."[40]

We need to ask whether the Confucian view is closer to the old or new understanding of the selection model. On the surface, the spirit of the Confucian view seems to be more in line with the old understanding, as Confucianism also talks about hierarchy and distinction. But it is important to note that Confucianism talks about difference in terms of virtue, wisdom, and understanding of the world, not in terms of social status or economic means. Moreover, Confucianism sees no differences in the moral character aspect of its ideal—it does not say that in the most ideal situation people should have different moral or intellectual abilities. On the contrary, the Confucian masters Mencius and Xunzi believe that every person has the potential to become morally good, even to become a sage. Ideally everybody can and should fulfill this potential. In reality, however, the moral and intellectual development of each are affected differently by both external factors, such as cultural environment, and internal factors, such as willpower and determination. Confucianism neither condemns nor praises these differences but accepts them as a fact of life and turns them to

---

37 Jane Mansbridge, "Clarifying the Concept of Representation," *American Political Science Review* 105, no. 3 (August 2011): 623.

38 "A 'Selection Model,'" 387.

39 "Concept of Representation," 623.

40 "A 'Selection Model,'" 387.

good use in politics and education. Confucians want those with the responsibility of governing to have the virtue and competence necessary for that task, and to set themselves as good examples for others.[41] To borrow from contemporary political economists Geoffrey Brennan and Alan Hamlin, who are not Confucians, "we could select, if not the ablest and the most conscientious and public-spirited, at least those who are more able and more conscientious and more public-spirited than average."[42]

I do not think that this Confucian view is incompatible with Mansbridge's favored understanding of the selection model. To quote her again, "Today when voters say they want to select a 'good man' or 'good woman' as a representative, they often seem to want someone like them, but with the interest, competence, and honesty to be a legislator."[43] A Confucian view of selection can accept this statement, if likeness or resemblance between representatives and constituents lies merely in demographic background or political opinion (for example, conceptions of public interest), but cannot accept the statement if likeness refers to ability, public-spiritedness or integrity. Clearly Confucians would not accept that a representative should be selected because he or she possesses a level of ability and public-spiritedness similar to that of the average constituent, whatever that may be. But this cannot be what Mansbridge has in mind either. In fact, Mansbridge adds an important clause in the statement about likeness— "with the interest, competence, and honesty to be a legislator." Without this condition the choice of representatives based on likeness does not qualify as a selection model. Confucians would agree with Mansbridge that we need the people in office to have sufficient public virtue and ability for their official tasks. If average voters do not possess public virtue and ability, then Confucians and Mansbridge should also agree that it is not morally problematic but desirable or even morally obligatory[44] for voters to choose people who have higher public virtue and ability than the average voter. It is not elitist to hold this view. To think otherwise would be a perverse kind of egalitarianism.

Conclusion

To briefly conclude, I have argued in this chapter that the reconstructed Confucian conception of authoritative ruler-ruled relationship is an insightful and attractive ideal. It is marked by mutual commitment—rulers genuinely care for the people and promote their well-being, and impress the people with their

---

41 I thank Elton Chan for instructive discussion of this point.

42 Geoffrey Brennan and Alan Hamlin, *Democratic Devices and Desires* (Cambridge: Cambridge University Press, 2000), 170.

43 "A 'Selection Model,'" 387.

44 For an interesting argument for this position that voters have a moral duty to vote for the common good, see Jason Brennan, *The Ethics of Voting* (Princeton: Princeton University Press, 2011).

trustworthiness and integrity. The people are subsequently moved to accept the rulers and support them. I have argued that this ideal relationship seems to have its resonance even in contemporary democratic societies. In reality, however, not all officials can live up to this ideal, and their authority can be constantly undermined by their own vice or folly. The challenge for Confucians is twofold. On the one hand, a social device must be found that helps prevent officials from abusing power and removes bad officials from office. On the other hand, such a device must be able to express the Confucian ideal relationship and hopefully also to promote it. The key to solving this issue lies in the nature of institutions, which are devices that perform socially useful tasks in a normatively appropriate way. I have argued that institutions seem particularly suited to mediate between real-world tasks and ideal aspirations.

To this end I have examined one particular kind of democratic institution, namely, elections. Because institutions are man-made and the purpose and values they represent can be subject to different interpretations, it is important to understand the rationale of democratic elections in a way that tallies with the Confucian conception of political relationship. Drawing on the work of contemporary political scientists and political economists, I have argued that we should favor the selection model of elections over the sanctions model. As an empirical theory, the selection model emphasizes the fact that the voters' key motive in an election is to seek publicly motivated politicians whom they trust to take office. As a normative theory, the selection model advocates that the rules and processes of electoral systems should encourage the appearance of this type of politicians in the political realm. It not only presents an empirically viable interpretation of the election of representatives and a desirable way of interpreting the rationale of elections, it strongly echoes the spirit of the Confucian ideal political relationship.

This chapter has not touched on other issues that may complicate the relationship between Confucianism and democracy. Even if Confucianism has affinity with the selection model of democratic elections, in imperfect reality democratic elections may lead to a lot of consequences that go against the spirit of the Confucian ideal. Whether Confucianism would accept the whole package of Western democratic institutions is a complex open question, and one that I shall explore in the next chapter.

CHAPTER 4

Mixing Confucianism and Democracy

This chapter takes another look at the relationship between the Confucian political ideal and democracy. In chapter 3 I focused on one aspect of this relationship—the way in which democratic elections can be understood as an institution that addresses real-world problems and yet tallies with the spirit of the Confucian conception of the ideal political relationship. Building on the conclusions of the previous chapters, I shall examine the complex relationship between Confucian political ideas and democracy in more detail, to see if there are affinities and tensions between the two in both ideal and nonideal contexts.

The overall argument of this chapter is that democracy and Confucian perfectionism help strengthen each other. In the first section I define democracy as a political system in which citizens have the right to take part in competitive elections to decide their government. I also explain why this definition is appropriate for the tasks of this chapter. In the second section I argue that democracy can be expressively and instrumentally linked to Confucian political ideas. In ideal situations democratic elections express the Confucian ideal political relationship. In nonideal situations, where not all officials are upright and virtuous, democratic elections help protect people's interests, thereby instrumentally promoting the Confucian service conception of authority, but without breaking the expressive relationship with the Confucian ideal. In the remaining sections I argue that Confucian perfectionist ethics can also work to the benefit of democracy. A well-functioning democracy needs its citizens to be virtuous and civil—without these ethical qualities, democracy can degenerate into dysfunctional partisanship and competition. Confucianism may offer help to democracy, first by providing moral teachings on virtues and civility to help develop a virtuous citizenry, and second by offering reflections on the search for virtue and talent in politics.

Defining Democracy

The core questions guiding my examination are these: Under what conditions, and to what extent, is democracy compatible with Confucianism? And can Confucianism contribute to the criticism or development of democracy? Before tackling these questions, it is important to explain how the term "democracy" will be used in this chapter. Several conceptual points need to be clarified. First, the issue of constitutional design has been the central focus in the debate on the compatibility of democracy and Confucianism since the late nineteenth century. This chapter therefore defines democracy as a political system rather than a set of values, a way of life, or a set of social and economic conditions. The key issues that first motivated this debate were related to the direction of political reform in modern China: What kind of constitutional structure is appropriate for China? Who should rule? Should citizens have the right to political participation? As these issues of political reform are still very much alive in China today, any discussion about the relationship between Confucianism and democracy that does not address these issues would be inappropriate for this reason.

Second, I make a distinction between the *constituents* of democracy and the *conditions* that make it work satisfactorily. In defining democracy as a political system, I leave out certain social, economic, moral, and cultural conditions that make the system work. In doing so, I am not suggesting that these conditions are not important in terms of the robustness and effectiveness of democracy. Indeed, the contemporary literature on political science agrees that certain conditions are essential to the consolidation and functioning of democracy (such as a culture of tolerance, civility and civic duties, readiness to compromise, a vibrant civil society, a participatory culture, public reason and deliberation, a developed state bureaucracy, a politically neutral army, the absence of deep social cleavages, an independent media, and a strong middle class[1]), and that democracy as a political system would be inappropriate for any society that lacks most or all of these conditions. Later in this chapter I shall discuss the importance of virtue and civic education in democracy. But these conditions, however important, are merely conditions of a democracy as a political system, not its defining constituents. Even if a political society possesses all these democracy-enabling conditions, it is not yet a democracy if its political system does not permit its citizens to have the right to take part in competitive elections to decide their government. A participatory society and a consultative government together do not make a democracy. This point is important for the purposes of this chapter, for according to some interpretations, Confucianism does endorse consultation, tolerance, civility, or even a participatory community. However, these interpretations, even if true, still do not prove that Confucianism can accept democracy as a political system.

Third, in defining democracy as a political system, I make a further distinction between democracy and liberal democracy. Some scholars have adopted what I shall call a *liberal view of democracy* in their discussion of the compatibility of Confucianism and democracy.[2] For them, democracy contains not only

---

1   See Larry Diamond, *Developing Democracy: Toward Consolidation* (Baltimore: Johns Hopkins University Press, 1999).

2   See, for example, Chenyang Li 李晨陽, "Confucian Value and Democratic Value," *Journal of Value Inquiry* 31, no. 2 (1997): 183–93. However, Li has adopted a narrower definition that does not

particular decision-making procedures and a particular distribution of political power, but also a set of laws and public policies that promote *liberal values* such as individual rights and freedoms, individualism, and personal autonomy. According to this view, "democracy" is equivalent to "liberal democracy." But this may not be the most desirable way to tackle the issue of compatibility. Using this inclusive definition, we could easily conclude that Confucianism is incompatible with democracy simply on the grounds that Confucianism does not endorse liberal values. Put in another way, for Confucianism to accept democracy, we would need to show that Confucianism would accept not only a certain set of political institutions but also a core set of liberal values. It may be the case, however, that Confucianism is compatible with just one set of principles, for example, that Confucianism endorses a form of democracy that does not embrace liberal values.

In the history of Western political thought, the concepts of democracy and liberalism track two different sets of concerns and issues. "Democracy" as a concept deals with the source and distribution of political power, whereas "liberalism" is primarily concerned with the scope and limits of political power (and hence the scope and limits of individual freedom). To adopt a liberal view of democracy (as liberal democracy) would turn our attention away from the question of power distribution—the focus of this and earlier chapters—to the question of human rights and civil liberties, issues that have independent importance and can be conceptually separated from the issue of democracy. The relationship between Confucianism and liberal freedoms is a different issue and will be tackled in part 2 of this book.

I do not mean to suggest that democracy is not conceptually linked to certain types of individual freedoms and rights. Indeed it is. But this fact is best comprehended not as an accidental marriage between the two sets of ideas but as the consequence of viewing democracy as a certain type of decision-making power and procedure. Following David Beetham, I shall define democracy as "a mode of decision making about collectively binding rules and policies over which the people exercise control."[3] Indeed, one of the most commonplace definitions of democracy—namely, democracy as *rule by the people*—is defined procedurally. The notion of *rule* is understood as the activity of making authoritative decisions (for example, laws and public policies), and the phrase

---

include liberal values in his recent article "Min zhu de xing shi he ru jia de nei rong—zai lun ru jia yu min zhu de guan xi" 民主的形式和儒家的內容—再論儒家和民主的關係 [Democracy as Form and Confucianism as Content—Revisiting the Relationship between Confucianism and Democracy], *Ru xue: xue shu, xin yang he xiu yang* 儒學: 學術、信仰和修養 [Confucianism: Scholarship, Faith, and Self-Cultivation], ed. Liu Xiaogan 劉笑敢, vol. 10 of *Zhongguo zhe xue yu wen hua* 中國哲學與文化 [Journal of Chinese Philosophy and Culture] (Shanghai: Ligang chu ban she 漓江出版社, 2012), 131–46.

3 David Beetham, "Liberal Democracy and the Limits of Democratization," in *Prospects for Democracy: North, South, East, West*, ed. David Held (Stanford: Stanford University Press, 1993), 55.

rule by the people should therefore be understood to mean the idea that the people as a whole are entitled to make authoritative decisions.[4]

As a procedural concept, democracy is concerned with the ways in which collective decisions should be arrived at, not with what constitutes the proper content of those decisions, except insofar as they relate to the procedure itself. As Brian Barry explains, "democracy" contains no constraints on the content of the decisions produced, such as respect for human rights, protection of individual liberty, rule of law, concern for the general welfare, or economic equality—*except those required by democracy itself as a procedure*.[5] Thus the idea of a democratic procedure *conceptually* presupposes that participants in the procedure have certain rights or liberties that are *constitutive* of the very procedure itself. The right to take part in a collective decision-making process presupposes the right to form, express, and aggregate political preferences, which in turn presupposes the civil right to free expression, communication, and association. But other individual rights or liberties cherished by liberals, such as freedom of choice with regard to marriage, occupation, and travel, are *not* conceptually presupposed or necessitated by the idea of a democratic procedure. A democratic procedure can still exist even if the participants collectively decide that they have no right of choice in these arenas. Confucianism may still embrace democracy even if it does not embrace full-fledged liberal values.

My fourth and final conceptual point is that I follow the literature of political science in further distinguishing between direct and indirect democracy. Direct democracy is a political system in which laws and major policies are made directly by every citizen by means of referendums. In indirect democracy, however, citizens themselves do not make laws and policies but elect legislators and executives to do so. The political system of indirect democracy is representative democracy based on universal franchise and free and fair competitive elections. In discussing the relationship between Confucianism and democracy, I shall focus on indirect democracy, which is the system commonly adopted in democratic countries today, as direct democracy is often thought to be feasible or desirable only in small-sized communities.

Expressive and Instrumental Relationships

There are two ways of looking at the relationship between Confucianism and democracy and hence two ways of justifying democracy within Confucian po-

4 People's rights to make public decisions can be expressed directly, through full democratic procedures where everyone participates, such as referendums, or indirectly, through representative democratic procedures. Representative democracy requires certain basic institutions, such as free, fair, competitive elections and universal suffrage, and some basic rights, such as freedom of association and expression.

5 Brian Barry, *Democracy, Power and Justice: Essays in Political Theory* (Oxford: Clarendon Press, 1989), 25.

litical thought. The first is to examine whether democracy as a political system expresses some normative ideal or value that Confucianism endorses. If it does, democracy can have a positive expressive relationship with Confucianism. The second is to examine whether democracy can bring about certain effects that are desirable in the view of Confucian thought. If it can, democracy can have a positive instrumental relationship with Confucianism. I shall discuss the expressive relationship first.

Democracy is often regarded as an institution expressing certain moral values or principles such as popular sovereignty or political equality. In previous chapters I have argued that Confucianism does not accept popular sovereignty or political equality as a fundamental moral principle. To briefly recap, Confucianism, at least the version that I have reconstructed, holds that political authority—whether it is in the hands of a few or in the hands of many—must be justified by its service to the well-being of the people. Having the right to vote within a democracy means having a share in authority, which needs to be justified in that way. According to the Confucian view, there is no natural or fundamental moral right to power. Political authority is first and foremost a responsibility toward others rather than a right for oneself.

No doubt democracy as a political system gives power to the people and distributes votes equally. But such a system need not be justified by, or be seen to express, popular sovereignty or political equality as a moral principle or ideal. As I argued in chapter 3, the meaning of institutions is a matter of human interpretation. I suggest that the institution of democracy can be disconnected from such moral principles. This does not imply that what is left for Confucianism and democracy can only be an instrumental relationship. Democracy can be understood in a way that expresses another political ideal that Confucianism endorses.[6] Recall that the Confucian ideal political relationship is marked by mutual commitment and trust—the rulers are committed to governing the people in a trustworthy and caring manner, and the ruled, in return, express their willing endorsement and support of their rulers. Democracy can also be understood as a political system that precisely expresses such an ideal political relationship. The point of democratic elections is to select those who are public-spirited and trustworthy and to make explicit the public's endorsement and support of those who are elected. The inauguration ceremony of a democratically elected state president, for example, often serves as a high point of this relationship—the people gather to celebrate and witness the swearing-in of a president whom they have elected and support, and the president pledges to "devote" himself or herself "to the service and well-being of the people"[7] and

---

6 This is a self-criticism of my earlier article "Democracy and Meritocracy: Toward a Confucian Perspective," which overemphasizes the instrumentality of democracy and ignores the possibility that democracy can express the Confucian political ideal. In *Journal of Chinese Philosophy* 34, no. 2 (2007): 179–93.

7 Taken from the oath of office of the president of India. See Constitution of India, art. 60

swears that he or she "will in no way betray the people's trust."[8] Elections are both a means of selecting good rulers and a way of expressing the mutual commitment of the ruler and the people. While democracy is not the only kind of political system that can express this Confucian conception of ideal political relationship, it provides the most direct and explicit form of institutional expression.

This ideal picture of democracy, however, is possible only if there are virtuous people who are willing to run for office, and if the voters not only are virtuous enough to want to put those people in office but also have enough knowledge of the candidates to select those who are most suitable. As James Madison says, to realize the republican principle, "the people will have virtue and intelligence to select men of virtue and wisdom. . . . If there be sufficient virtue and intelligence in the community, it will be exercised in the selection of these men. So that we do not depend on their virtue, or put confidence in our rulers, but in the people who are to choose them."[9] In fact, the Grand Union ideal, which informs my reconstruction of a Confucian way of looking at elections in the previous chapter, calls for similar conditions: "Men [all people] did not treat only their own parents as parents, nor treat only their own sons as sons." In this ideal community, people are filled with concern for the public and common good and for this reason choose men of virtue and ability for public service.

In nonideal situations, however, not every politician or voter possesses the virtue and ability necessary for achieving an ideal political relationship. Some may have few virtues, and many may have mixed motives based on public and self-interest. Nevertheless, I believe that democracy is valid for Confucianism even in these situations for reasons that are both expressive and instrumental. Elections can still be effective in situations where politicians and officials have mixed motives, as they not only act as an expression of an official's commitment to public service but also compel officials to work for the people if they wish to be reelected. Virtuous officials need no such compulsion, but those who have weak public-interest motives do. Moreover, if leaders prove to be obviously irresponsible or incompetent, the people can protect their basic interests by voting them out of office in the subsequent election. The sanction function of elections makes them compatible with Confucianism in that Confucians believe that leaders should work for the welfare of the people, and that they should lose their legitimate right to authority and be removed if they fail at this task. A political system that gives people the right to vote has the powerful function of protecting their legitimate interests against encroachment from bad rulers.

"Oath or Affirmation by the President," http://lawmin.nic.in/olwing/coi/coi-English/coi-index English.htm.

8   Taken from the oath of office of the president of Taiwan. See "Swearing-in Ceremony," Office of the President of the Republic of China (Taiwan): Inaugural Ceremony of the Thirteenth-Term (May 2012), http://www.president.gov.tw/Portals/0/president520/English/oath.html.

9   James Madison, "Virginia Ratifying Convention," vol. 1, chap. 13, document 36 of *The Founders' Constitution*, ed. Philip B. Kurland and Ralph Lerner (Chicago: University of Chicago Press, 2000), http://press-pubs.uchicago.edu/founders/documents/v1ch13s36.html/.

Confucians should therefore find the sanction function of elections useful for achieving some political goals in nonideal situations, even if elections are less ideal as a way of motivating leaders to do good for the people. As I illustrated in the introduction to this book, although there are aspirational reasons for maintaining the Confucian political ideal, Confucians are aware of the need to find a feasible mechanism to address problems in the nonideal world. The question is whether there is an alternative that tackles those problems and yet retains the Confucian ideal as an aspiration. Democratic elections seem to be the one institution that does precisely that, as they perform both selection and sanction functions.[10] In short, Confucianism and democracy can be expressively and instrumentally linked.

The Problems of Democracy in Nonideal Situations

This is not to say that there is no tension between democracy as a political system and Confucianism. In nonideal situations, although democratic elections provide incentives and sanctions for elected officials to work for the betterment of people's lives, they can also be fraught with a number of problems. At the risk of oversimplification and generalization, let me give a brief sketch of some of these problems.

In ideal situations, elections can be conducted in a civil and respectful manner consistent with the spirit of selecting virtuous and competent people to power—candidates respect each other and present themselves well to the public, and voters give their support to those candidates they think will work best for the common good rather than just for their own self- or group interests. However, as elections are a form of competition that necessarily produces winners and losers, nonideal situations, such as those in which politicians have mixed motives, may induce highly antagonistic rivalry among candidates. Opponents may engage in negative campaigning strategies to discredit each other and offer policy promises that are detrimental to the long-term good of society merely to win short-term electoral support. Elections are also conducive to the development of political parties as politicians with similar political orientations naturally band together to increase their political influence, compete for office, and form governments. As John Burnheim notes, "the worth of electoral democracy is closely bound up with the processes of party politics."[11] However, many people today are increasingly skeptical about whether the development of political parties actually fosters, attracts, and facilitates the selection of the

---

10 In reality the relative importance of the two functions depends on the distribution of motivations among political leaders. If there are a good proportion of public-spirited people among candidates and officials, the ideal political relationship expressed through the selection model of elections might take a more prominent place in the public culture of society than the realistic concerns expressed through the sanction function, and vice versa.

11 John Burnheim, *Is Democracy Possible? The Alternative to Electoral Politics* (Berkeley: University of California Press, 1985), 96.

best people to serve in politics. They argue that those who rise high in party organizations may not be the most capable, upright, and fair minded, or those most genuinely interested in working for the common good, but those who have learned to play the power games in party politics. Burnheim describes the problem in this way:

> It is, I think, fairly obvious that many of those who are elected to high office in most democratic countries are undistinguished in most relevant respects. The reason many abler and better people give for not going into politics is that they are not well equipped to deal with the continual jockeying for influence and position in party life, the toadying to those already in positions of power, the necessity of discrediting others rather than cooperating with them, the subordination of issues to tactics and so on.[12]

The fact that electoral campaigns require extremely high levels of financing and are increasingly influenced by corporations also contributes to the popular belief that parties serve only the interests of the powerful.

In addition, although democracy is generally effective in exposing corruption and administrative blunders, it is not always the best method of promoting quality deliberations and the politics of common good. As Amy Gutmann and Dennis Thompson noted, "In the practice of our democratic politics, communicating by sound bite, competing by character assassination, and resolving political conflicts through self-seeking bargaining too often substitute for deliberation on the merits of controversial issues."[13] Party politicians are often seen as opportunists who exploit or exaggerate their opponents' weaknesses for partisan gains, sometimes going to such extremes as to risk the good of the country for the good of their party. Commenting on the extremely partisan ways in which American politicians in Washington, DC, handled the nation's debt problems in August 2011, the public affairs commentator Fareed Zakaria writes,

> Americans have demonstrated to themselves, the world and global markets that their political system is broken and that they are incapable of conceiving and implementing sensible public policy. What they have instead is the prospect of more late-night cliffhangers, extreme tactics, budget guillotines, filibusters and presidential vetoes. It makes for good TV news specials, but it is a sorry picture of how the world's leading country governs itself.[14]

The performance of the voters and citizenry in established democracies can also often leave much to be desired, and many citizens are apathetic and have lost interest in voting. If they do vote, many are ill informed and some vote ir-

---

12 Ibid., 101.

13 Amy Gutmann and Dennis Thompson, *Democracy and Disagreement* (Cambridge: Harvard University Press, 1996), 12.

14 Fareed Zakaria, "The Debt Deal's Failure," *Time Magazine*, August 15, 2011, 22.

responsibly pursuing narrow self-interests at the expense of the common good.[15] Many democratic theorists have argued that these problems could be cured by more citizen participation and that people would become better citizens through active participation. However, active participation does not necessarily produce deliberative attitudes and abilities, and often it results in the opposite—with people's political views becoming hardened and more polarized, and proponents of opposing views becoming less respectful of each other. Drawing on Diana Mutz's empirical research results, Jason Brennan says that

> deliberation and participation do not come together. Deliberative citizens do not participate much, and participatory citizens do not deliberate much. The people who are most active in politics tend to be (in my words, not Mutz's) cartoon ideologues. . . . They seek out and interact only with others with whom they already agree. . . . The empirical evidence suggests that the people most willing to bear the personal costs (in terms of time and effort) of participation are those with the most extreme views. Extremists are interested in politics and tend to be the most dissatisfied with the status quo, and thus tend to be the most highly participatory citizens.[16]

Active participation may then in fact lead to more dispute and greater conflict, not less. Ronald Dworkin also expresses his frustration about the poor quality of debate and deliberation in American politics:

> American politics are in an appalling state. We disagree, fiercely, about almost everything. We disagree about terror and security, social justice, religion in politics, who is fit to be a judge, and what democracy is. These are not civil disagreements: each side has no respect for the other. We are no longer partners in self-government; our politics are rather a form of war.[17]

We can understand why Louis Brandeis says that the most important office in a democracy is the office of citizen,[18] for the quality of democratic governance ultimately depends on the virtue and intelligence of the people. When political leaders are not good, citizens can sanction them through elections and other constitutional devices. But if the citizens themselves are not good, elections do not change this. In an extreme scenario, where voters are highly partisan, shortsighted, ill informed, and susceptible to bribery (as in vote buying), elections are not only ineffective in curbing such behavior but may in fact feed it into the political process, resulting in policies that abuse minority interests,

---

15 See Bryan Caplan, *The Myth of the Rational Voter: Why Democracies Choose Bad Policies* (Princeton: Princeton University Press, 2007); and Brennan, "How Well Do Voters Behave?" chap. 7 in *Ethics of Voting*.

16 Brennan, *Ethics of Voting*, 176, citing Diana C. Mutz, *Hearing the Other Side: Deliberative versus Participatory Democracy* (New York: Cambridge University Press, 2006).

17 Ronald Dworkin, *Is Democracy Possible Here? Principles for a New Political Debate* (Princeton: Princeton University Press, 2006), 1.

18 Cited in Obama, *Audacity of Hope*, 135.

reinforce corruption, escalate social conflicts, or seriously undermine long-term economic or environmental sustainability. Quoting Madison again, democracy works only if the people "have virtue and intelligence to select men of virtue and wisdom. Is there no virtue among us? If there be not, we are in a wretched situation. No theoretical checks—no form of government can render us secure. To suppose that any form of government will secure liberty or happiness without any virtue in the people, is a chimerical idea."[19]

Combining Democracy and Confucian Values

Confucians would be very concerned about the negative picture of political leaders and citizens as described by Zakaria and Dworkin, for it goes deeply against the Confucian values of common good, sincerity, trust, and harmony, especially as described in the Grand Union ideal: "When the Grand Dao was pursued, a public and common spirit ruled all under the sky [*tian xia wei gong*]; they chose men of talent, virtue, and ability for public service; they valued mutual trust and cultivated harmony." Confucians would also find it deeply troubling if, in nonideal situations, democracy bred and reinforced hostile antagonism, and if the democratic political process became a trading of narrow interests at the expense of the common good.

Nevertheless, in my opinion democracy should not be rejected, for although it may not be a perfect form of government, it is also not the worst. Unless citizens are very corrupt, irresponsible, and uncivil, democracy is still "a guarantee against bloody revolution and effective in preventing the government from systematically ignoring the interests or flouting the wishes of the governed. It avoids the worst abuses and makes the government responsive to large shifts of public opinion."[20] What needs to be done, I think, is for democracy to be supplemented with a strong ethical foundation and alternative institutions, and Confucian resources can be drawn upon to supply these. In the rest of this chapter I shall explore these two areas, starting with the ethical foundation, as this is the most important according to Confucian thought.

Western theorists have long pointed out the importance of civic virtues or civility as an essential condition for democracy, which otherwise can be a highly adversarial political process. People need civility to prevent contestation from turning into deeply divisive antagonism. Civility is important for people who are not intimately related but need to interact with one another, be they acquaintances, colleagues, or strangers encountered in meetings, discussion forums, the market place, or streets. Civility is especially important when people find themselves in disagreement. Some people say civility is a virtue that dis-

---

19 Madison, "Virginia Ratifying Convention."
20 John R. Lucas, *Democracy and Participation* (Harmondsworth, UK: Penguin, 1976), 200.

poses people "to be polite, respectful, tolerant, and decent to one another."[21] Others say it is "behavior in public which demonstrates respect for others and which entails curtailing one's own immediate self-interest when appropriate."[22] Still others say it is a civic orientation "that does not duck conflict entirely, but that simultaneously embraces the importance of maintaining harmonious social relationships."[23] Whatever the exact definition, can Confucian ethics offer anything close to civility? Many people think that Confucian ethics is a form of familial and clan ethics for close-knit relationships, one that gives no guidelines on how to treat acquaintances or strangers. Because of this deficiency, it is sometimes said that the Chinese lack public virtues and that they treat strangers and unknown foreigners "coldly" and "rudely."[24]

This seems a misunderstanding of Confucian ethics. If one looks at the Confucian conception of the ideal moral person as articulated in *The Analects*, namely the jun zi, commonly translated as the "gentleman,"[25] one will find that the gentleman is not only a person with filial piety but also one who possesses a variety of virtues and character traits that enable him to deal appropriately with nonintimates in many different social circumstances. I shall mention some of these virtues and character traits that are particularly relevant to our concern about civility in the context of disagreement and difference. Let me start with this well-known passage in *The Analects*:

1. The Master said, "The gentleman seeks harmony not sameness, the petty person seeks sameness not harmony." (13.23)[26]

The precise meaning of this passage is somewhat vague and open to interpretation. One common interpretation says that, on the one hand, the gentleman will not seek sameness or conformity without principle; on the other hand, although being a principled person, the gentleman is not imposing or competitive but maintains harmony with others. By contrast, the petty person seeks conformity without principle in order to pursue personal gains or increase per-

---

21   Nina Eliasoph, "Civil Society and Civility," chap. 18 in *The Oxford Handbook of Civil Society, ed. Michael Edwards* (New York: Oxford University Press, 2011), 220.

22   Nicole Billante and Peter Saunders, "Six Questions about Civility," Occasional Paper 82 (July 2002), Centre for Independent Studies, 3.

23   Mutz, *Hearing the Other Side*, 75.

24   Lucian Pye 白魯恂, "Ru xue yu min zhu" 儒學與民主 [Confucianism and Democracy], trans. Chen Yinchi 陳引馳, chap. 3 in *Ru jia yu zi you zhu yi* 儒家與自由主義 [Confucianism and Liberalism], ed. Harvard-Yenching Institute and SDX Joint Publishing, SDX & Harvard-Yenching Academic Series (Beijing: SDX Joint Publishing, 2001), 176.

25   Ames and Rosemont translate *jun zi* as "the exemplary person" in their translation of *The Analects*.

26   Translation adapted from Ames and Rosemont, *Analects of Confucius*. Another useful translation is that of Chichung Huang: "The gentleman is harmonious but not conformable; the small man is conformable but not harmonious." See his *The Analects of Confucius* (New York: Oxford University Press, 1997).

sonal influence by banding together with those who share similar interests. The petty person does not care for genuine harmony and associates with others purely on the basis of sameness of interests.

There are actually two qualities involved in the above description of the gentleman, both of which are relevant to civility. First, unlike the petty person, the gentleman does not form cliques to pursue narrow group interests. Implicit in this attitude is a concern and respect for righteousness, which, in the context of public duties, we might today call the common good. This quality of nonpartisanship is echoed in two other passages often mentioned in historical interpretations of the passage.

> 2. The Master said, "The gentleman associating openly with others is not partisan; the petty person being partisan does not associate openly with others." (2.14)[27]
>
> 3. The Master said, "The gentleman is self-esteeming but not contentious, gregarious but not factious." (15.22)[28]

The three passages above indeed describe a quality very close to civility or civic-mindedness. People with civility do not push their own self-interests at the expense of the interests of others. Civic-minded people have the common good at heart. This quality is very important to democracy—without it democratic politics is a mere power game.

There is a second quality in the description of the gentleman above. Being a principled person concerned for the common good, the gentleman is not contentious or competitive but seeks harmony with others. Harmony, however, is not based on sameness or conformity but recognizes differences and even disagreements. But how does the gentleman remain true to his principles and maintain a harmonious relationship with others in a context marked by differences or disagreements? Passage 1 does not give an answer, but another passage suggests a clue:

> 4. The Master said, "Gentlemen are not competitive, except where they have to be in the archery ceremony. Greeting [*zuo yi*, bowing with hands folded in front of the chest] and making way for each other [*rang*], the archers ascend the hall, and returning they drink a salute. Even in competition, they are gentlemanly." (3.7)[29]

For Confucius, competition can be gentlemanly if it is embedded with rituals that express a spirit of respect and civility. Greeting an opponent before a competition and drinking together afterward are precisely the type of rituals that keep contending parties within a civil relationship. The Chinese word *rang*,

27 Translation adapted from that of Ames and Rosemont. Compare Huang's translation: "The gentleman is all-embracing and not partial; the small man is partial and not all-embracing."

28 Huang's translation. Compare Ames and Rosemont's: "Exemplary persons are self-possessed but not contentious; they gather together with others, but do not form cliques."

29 Translation adapted from that of Ames and Rosemont and Huang.

however, can mean something more than respectful and civil behavior. It can mean more substantive disposition and action like yielding, conceding, compromising, and deferring for the sake of maintain a good relationship with others or for the greater good of all. Of course, in sporting competitions, rang in the sense of yielding is not expected of contending parties. But in social relations and public affairs, rang is important. Consider this passage:

5. The Master said, "If rulers are able to effect order in the state through the combination of observing ritual propriety [li] and deferring to others [rang], what more is needed? But if they are unable to accomplish this, what have they to do with observing ritual propriety?" (4.13)[30]

According to this passage, ritual propriety must be accompanied by a real readiness to defer and yield to others, without which it is hard to effect order in the state. If rang is absent in society, if people do not yield or compromise, they will band together to press for their own demands to be heard above those of others, different sides will harden their positions, and conflicts will escalate. In the end people will resort to power to resolve conflicts—through voting or extralegal means of influence. The losing side will feel crushed and look for opportunities to fight back. Confucius fears that a state that descends to this level is simply ungovernable.

There are many occasions where yielding is appropriate—yielding to the common good, yielding to the weak and underprivileged, and yielding to the old, for example.[31] But there is one form of yielding that is particularly relevant in politics—yielding to people with virtue and ability. As the Confucian classics state:

6. Select the virtuous and give [power] to the able [xuan xian yu neng]. ("Li yun," Book of Rites)
7. Recommend the virtuous and yield to the able [tui xian rang neng]. (Book of History)[32]

Confucians strongly believe that positions of authority should be taken by the virtuous and able. In the context of democratic elections, for example, a gentleman should yield and not compete with another whom he thinks is more virtuous and able than he is himself.[33] This kind of yielding can perhaps be subsumed under the idea of yielding to the common good, because letting the more virtuous and able rule can better promote the common good.

---

30   Translation from Ames and Rosemont.

31   Cf. Stephen C. Angle's discussion of deference in his *Contemporary Confucian Political Philosophy*, 127–32.

32   My own translation. "Zhou guan" 周官 (Officers of Zhou) chapter.

33   This is exactly what Tang Junyi 唐君毅 [Tang Chun-i] said about democratic election in his "Min zhu li xiang zhi shi jian yu ke guan jia zhi yi shi" 民主理想之實踐與客觀價值意識, chap. 20 in *Zhong hua ren wen yu dang jin shi jie* 中華人文與當今世界 (Taipei: Dongfang ren wen xue hui 東方人文學會, 1975).

But when a person thinks that he is better able to promote the common good, or is more benevolent, than others, or when his judgment on the common good differs from that of others, he should not easily yield. As *The Analects* states,

> 8. The Master said, "Standing up for humanity [ren], do not yield the precedence even to your teacher." (15.36)[34]

Applying these points to politics in general and elections in particular, we have these precepts:

1. Priority of the common good: The gentleman should put the common good before his own personal interests. He can work with others to promote the common good, but not form cliques to pursue narrow group interests. (passages 1–3)
2. Yielding: In running for office, the gentleman should yield to those whom he thinks can better serve the common good. (passages 6–7) More generally, people should practice yielding and deference whenever appropriate. (passage 5)
3. Duty to promote the common good: In running for office or taking part in general political action, the gentleman should not yield if he thinks he is more able than others to promote the common good, or if he disagrees with others in his judgment about the common good. (passage 8)
4. Respect and civility: In competition or contention in elections or debates, the gentleman should act in accordance with rituals of respect and deference so as to maintain a civil and harmonious relationship with others. (passages 4–5)

These precepts may sound idealistic to today's reader. In my opinion, however, the extent to which these precepts are thought to be idealistic is inversely proportional to the health of a society. In a healthy society these precepts are perceived as everyday norms that people willingly follow. The health of democratic institutions and governance depends on people's willing observance of these precepts, not the other way round. After all, as Madison says, if there is no virtue among us, we are in a "wretched situation"—no form of government, not even democracy, can render us secure.[35]

Moral or Civic Education?

My analysis seems to have come full circle. In the early chapters I began by depicting the Confucian ideal conception of political authority and the ruler-ruled relationship. As this ideal situation is difficult to obtain, realistic and feasible alternatives are needed that can at once address real-life problems and

34   Translation adapted from Huang.
35   Madison, "Virginia Ratifying Convention."

express ideal aspirations. I have suggested democracy, as a system of political institutions, as one such alternative. However, institutions such as elections, representation, rule of law, and separation of powers are no guarantee for good governance as they also depend on the kind of ethical resources that, in bad times, can appear to be as idealistic and demanding as any other social and political ideal. Thus I began with one idealistic aspiration and seem to have ended with another.

Nevertheless, unless we wish to claim that a purely institution-based solution that simultaneously addresses the Confucian ideal and reality is possible, or that the success of democracy does not depend on ethical and cultural conditions, the circular route we have traveled thus far conforms fully to the fundamental insight in Confucian social and political philosophy: that in the ultimate analysis it is people, not institutions, that count—namely, it is people's virtues and character traits and the cultural environment in which these things are nourished that are essential to good social and political order. Institutions are necessary, and, as I argued in the previous chapter, they can shape people's value orientation and guide their behavior. But in order to work, institutions need to be embedded in an ethical and cultural habitat. This is why discussions on virtue, moral education, and rituals occupy a prominent place in Confucian thought.

For Confucian masters, the teaching of precepts must be accompanied by the cultivation of character traits and the practice of rituals. This is a rather substantive kind of moral education that may be quite foreign to mainstream thinking in contemporary liberal democratic societies. For even though contemporary liberals are convinced of the necessity of education for democracy, they are generally skeptical of substantive programs of this nature, preferring to talk about *citizen* virtue rather than *human* virtue, about participation as a springboard for virtue, and about civic education rather than moral education. It is my opinion that this form of liberal strategy raises serious questions.

Traditional participatory democratic theorists believe that the foundations for citizenship and civic virtue education lie in civic associations, town hall meetings, and political campaigns. For them, participation in these arenas is an educational experience that enables participants to acquire a strong sense of citizenship along with an accompanying civic-mindedness and deliberative skills. In his influential book *Strong Democracy: Participatory Political for a New Age*, Benjamin Barber proposes a series of old and new participatory institutions as "a program of participation and civic renewal," ranging from "neighborhood assemblies" and "television town meetings" at the local level, to "universal citizen service" and "legislative initiative and referendum process" at the national level.[36] Yet, as Jane Mansbridge shows, participation can lead to serious conflicts if participants adopt an "adversarial" mindset that discourages rea-

---

36 Benjamin R. Barber, "The Real Present: Institutionalizing Strong Democracy in the Modern World," chap. 10 in *Strong Democracy: Participatory Politics for a New Age* (Berkeley: University of California Press, 1984).

soned discussion among people of good will.[37] Or as Diana Mutz argues, political talk among people of different views can lead to polarization of positions, animosity, and resentment if participants do not conduct the talk in the spirit of civility.[38] So participation does not necessarily breed virtues but rather presupposes them.

Even when liberals talk about the necessity of education, they generally prefer the term "civic education" to "moral education," wishing to steer clear of questions about personal morality and conceptions of the good person or the good life that might be regarded as controversial. Typically liberals hold a narrow view of civic education that focuses on the acquisition of knowledge of public affairs and critical-thinking abilities. For example, for Barber, civic education primarily means "equal access to civic information" and holding of local and national discussions;[39] for Dworkin, it means making "a Contemporary Politics course part of every high school curriculum" so as "to instill some sense of the complexity of [political controversies of the day], some understanding of positions different from those the students are likely to find at home or among friends, and some idea of what a conscientious and respectful argument over these issues might be like."[40] Clearly, cognitive training and knowledge acquisition are an important part of any kind of civic education, but they cannot constitute the whole of such an education. Civic education should also instill virtues such as respect, civility, and a commitment to the common good—these are ethical commitments and character traits that are not purely rational but are, more importantly, learned traits that need to be nourished and instilled.

When liberals talk about the importance of civic virtues, they tend to mean only, as Cass Sunstein puts it, that such virtues are "necessary for participation in public deliberation," and "instrumental to a well-functioning deliberative process."[41] Paul Weithman usefully calls this brand of republican thought "political republicanism," as it identifies certain civic virtues as instrumentally necessary for republican government. For the political republicans, civic virtues are

> the traits citizens need to talk with one another as equals in the public fora of a contemporary pluralistic society. These neorepublicans stress that citizens must be willing to participate in politics, that they must offer public-regarding justifications for the policies they favor, that they should attempt to understand points of view different from their own, and that they should be prepared to "reconsider [their] ends and commitments."[42]

37 Jane Mansbridge, *Beyond Adversary Democracy* (New York: Basic Books, 1980).

38 Mutz, *Hearing the Other Side.*

39 Barber, "The Real Present," 278–79, 285–86.

40 Dworkin, *Is Democracy Possible Here?* 148–49.

41 Cass R. Sunstein, "Beyond the Republican Revival," *Yale Law Journal* 97, no. 8 (1988): 1541, n. 8. Cited in Paul Weithman, "Political Republicanism and Perfectionist Republicanism," *Review of Politics* 66, no. 2 (2004): 294.

42 Weithman, "Political Republicanism," 294.

Weithman contrasts this political approach with what he calls "perfectionist republicanism," a traditional Western perspective that can be traced back as far as to Cicero. This perspective does not make a clear distinction between personal and civic virtues but regards them all as human virtues or "genuine human excellences." The most central feature of this perspective is the claim that "effective and lasting self-government requires citizens to develop and exercise traits of character which are genuine human excellences."[43]

Confucianism is not a republican thought system, but it is a system of perfectionist ethics akin to perfectionist republicanism in its insistence on the cultivation of human virtues. The Confucian precepts discussed above define the way in which people, as moral persons, should behave. According to the Confucian view, there are important virtues that the gentleman should cultivate and practice wherever he is. Consider the following passages:

9. When Fan Chi asked about humanity [ren], the Master said, "Conduct yourself with respect; perform your duties with reverence; treat others with wholehearted sincerity. Even if you should journey to the Yi and Di barbarians, you cannot abandon these." (*Analects* 13.19)[44]

10. When Zizhang asked Confucius about humanity [ren], Confucius said, "To be able to practice five things under Heaven constitutes humanity." When further questioned about what these five things were, he said, "Respectfulness, lenience, truthfulness, industry, and beneficence. Be respectful and you shall not be humiliated; be lenient and you shall win the multitude; be truthful and the people will trust you; be industrious and you shall score successes; be beneficent and you shall be fit to employ the people." (17.6)[45]

Confucius said the virtues of respectfulness, lenience, truthfulness, industry, and beneficence are what constitute ren—not ren as it is in imperfect reality, but as it can and should be in the ideal. These human virtues go hand in hand with the precepts above that aim to guide the actions of the gentleman in his interactions or work with others. Confucians today would join the perfectionist republicans in claiming that moral education is more effective than a political version of civic education in engendering the virtues necessary for a well-functioning democracy. There are several reasons for this claim.

First, these two conceptions of education provide different forms of motivation and convey different messages. According to the moral conception, one should cultivate these virtues in order to be a good *person*. According to the civic conception, one should cultivate them in order to be a good *citizen*. In other words, if someone fails to develop these virtues, the moral conception believes that he or she has failed to be a good person while the civic conception

43 Ibid., 293.
44 Translation (slightly modified) from Huang. The passage is numbered 17.5 in Huang.
45 Translation (slightly modified) from Huang.

believes that he or she has only failed to be a good citizen. For many people, the desire to be (or to appear to be) a good person is stronger than the desire to be a good citizen.[46] People who are not concerned with public affairs may not care to cultivate the virtues of a good citizen in their daily life and, finding themselves in situations where they have to vote or debate with others, may discover that they lack the necessary virtues to deal with the task they face. According to the Confucian conception of moral education, however, people should cultivate these virtues whether they choose to participate in public affairs or not. These virtues make people better persons and guide them in their interactions with family members, friends, colleagues, and fellow citizens.

Second, as human virtues are relevant in many different social contexts besides the public arena, people not only have numerous opportunities to learn and practice them but also are expected to learn and practice them. In fact, Confucius goes so far as to claim that ren and its virtues are so closely bound with personhood that one can, and should, practice ren in all situations.

11. The Master said, "If a gentleman abandons humanity [ren], how can he fulfill that name? A gentleman will not, for the space of a meal, depart from humanity. In haste and flurry, he always adheres to it; in fall and stumble, he always adheres to it." (*Analects* 4.5)[47]
12. The Master said, "Is humanity [ren] so remote? If I desire humanity, there comes humanity!" (7.30)[48]

Civic education has a higher chance of success if its norms and virtues owe their authority to humanity, which can and should be practiced everywhere.

Third, political republicans face "an assurance problem"[49] that perfectionists do not, as Weithman insightfully points out. Citizenship, like justice, is a conditional virtue or duty, in the sense that one is obliged to act in accordance with the requirements of citizenship only if one has some assurance that other citizens will do the same. If civic virtues are tied only to citizenship, citizens may not see a reason to behave civilly and respectfully to others, especially if assurance from others is not forthcoming. According to the perfectionist conception, however, people should not easily discard virtues or duties just because others are not virtuous—if they do so they would not only cease to be responsible citizens but become quite different persons. This point is important, for in electoral debates and public discussions people do not always behave with respect and civility and do not always put common interests before their own. A gentleman who chooses not to retaliate against uncivil behavior

---

46 In Weithman's words, "the identity of republican citizenship is *reflectively escapable*." "Political Republicanism," 306.

47 Translation from Huang.

48 Huang's translation. The passage is numbered 7.29 in Huang.

49 Weithman, "Political Republicanism," 308.

but remains steadfast in virtue can prevent an escalation of antagonism and a cycle of confrontation.

To conclude the above discussion, a humanity-based moral education seems more effective than a citizenship-based civic education in instilling the virtues that promote the health of democratic institutions and processes. Moral education is directed at people as persons and is thus more relevant to their personal lives; it gives stronger motivation to people to cultivate the virtues, and it reinforces assurance of compliance in society. I shall not discuss the methods of moral education in modern society, except to point out that, for Confucians, role modeling is the most powerful method of moral education. Moral education should thus begin in the family and be taught in the first instance by the parents. Children should also receive moral education in schools through stories and precepts, manners and rituals, and from the personal example of teachers themselves. As a theorist I shall defer to scholars in the field of moral education on matters of curriculum design and implementation.[50] What I shall briefly dwell on in the rest of this section is a residual but important normative issue about moral education.

Liberals prefer the narrow notion of civic education to the robust notion of moral education because they wish to avoid controversies about what makes people good and what makes their lives better. By contrast, the perfectionist view on moral education seems to presuppose what John Rawls has called the "comprehensive doctrines" of the good life, about which there is often deep disagreement among people in a pluralistic society. Liberals may therefore raise questions about the legitimacy of any government-enforced moral education based on a perfectionist conception of the good life. The legitimacy of perfectionism is an important question for our project, for the modern version of Confucian political philosophy that I am reconstructing in this book is a perfectionist theory, one that has implications not only for moral education but also for a number of other issues this book addresses, such as authority, democracy, human rights, civil liberties, and justice.[51] In the conclusion to this book I shall provide a detailed reply to the question of the legitimacy of perfectionist politics. Here I shall just briefly indicate the line of argument that I shall develop in the conclusion. I believe it is possible to appeal to judgments about the good life without basing them on any comprehensive doctrine. Elsewhere I

50 For the pros and cons of, and the methods of implementing, moral education, see Robert E. Carter, *Dimensions of Moral Education* (Toronto: University of Toronto Press, 1984); Eamonn Callan, *Creating Citizens: Political Education and Liberal Democracy* (Oxford: Clarendon Press, 1997); Tianlong Yu, *In the Name of Morality: Character Education and Political Control*, vol. 26 of *Adolescent Cultures, School, and Society* (New York: Peter Lang, 2004); Holly Shepard Salls, *Character Education: Transforming Values into Virtues* (Lanham, MD: University Press of America, 2006); Joseph L. DeVitis and Tianlong Yu, eds., *Character and Moral Education: A Reader* (New York: Peter Lang, 2011).

51 I have defended the legitimacy of political perfectionism in "Legitimacy, Unanimity, and Perfectionism."

have distinguished between comprehensive and moderate political perfectionism.[52] The former comprehensively ranks human goods, experiences, and ways of life; connects them to a tradition of thought; and proposes policies and laws on that comprehensive basis. Moderate perfectionism, however, appeals to individual judgments about human goods and experiences in a piecemeal way and whenever they are relevant to a policy issue under question; it does not attempt to pursue a comprehensive doctrine of the good life through political action. In other words, moderate perfectionism steers a middle path between comprehensive doctrines and what Rawls calls "public reason"—a kind of shared political value within the political culture of a liberal society. I believe that traditional perfectionist philosophies such as Confucianism have rich insights and ethical resources to offer modern societies, but they took the form of a comprehensive doctrine that causes problems of legitimacy and harmony for modern-day politics. The best way to make these insights and resources relevant to a modern pluralistic society is through moderate perfectionism. The moderate way of conducting moral education, for example, is to promote specific human virtues that constitute the good life, without basing them on a comprehensive doctrine. It is, I believe, possible to understand and appreciate the value of such Confucian virtues as respect, reverence, trustworthiness, sincerity, and beneficence without accepting the whole philosophy of Confucianism. I will argue further in favor of the legitimacy of moderate perfectionism in the conclusion.

A Nondemocratically Elected Second Chamber

I have argued that a well-functioning democracy requires the people's commitment to civility and the common good, and one way to foster these ethical commitments is by promoting human virtues through moral education. Confucianism has a long tradition of rich reflections on the virtues that we can draw on to develop a modern conception of moral education. *The Analects* itself is already a source of profound insight. In this final section I shall explore another way in which Confucian ethical and political ideas can supplement democratic politics. Remember that in the Confucian political ideal, the virtuous and competent are selected to serve the people. In an ideal situation, democratic elections can serve this function well as long as there are virtuous and competent people running for office and voters are competent enough (or have enough information) to identify and elect them. In a nonideal situation, however, not all candidates or voters possess virtues and competence. Furthermore, if the elected officials in a democratic regime lack virtues or competence, the public governance of that regime will be poor. How can the governance of democratic regimes be improved? In the previous section I suggested a bottom-up

52 Ibid., 10–20.

method of promoting a virtuous citizenry through moral education. Of course, we also need the kind of civic education proposed by Dworkin—one that aims to improve citizens' cognitive competence, including knowledge of public affairs and critical-thinking abilities, in such a way that citizens are able to appreciate the force of competing arguments and to differentiate good ones from bad. But democratic governance can also be improved in other ways, for example, by finding ways to increase the pool of virtuous and competent politicians among the elite and to utilize their talents to improve public governance. Few contemporary political scientists or democratic theorists have given much thought to this issue. Many are pessimistic about the ability of existing political institutions (including political parties) to foster and select high-caliber politicians, to the extent that they seem to have given up hope that these institutions can be refashioned or reformed. They turn, instead, to the people, whom they hope can rejuvenate themselves by participating in deliberative forums or social movements. The limitations of this strategy, especially if it is not accompanied by moral education, have been discussed above.

However, I see no reason not to emphasize the importance of the education and recruitment of political leaders. For Confucians, the quality of governance depends mainly on the quality of political leaders. If, in nonideal situations, democratic elections cannot furnish enough high-quality politicians, public interest compels us to find alternative means to supplement the electoral method of selecting legislators and officials. One possible institution is a nondemocratically selected second chamber (hereafter called "second chamber") in a bicameral legislature, a notion that has been proposed by scholars of different traditions of political thought. I shall offer a rough proposal of my own below. Before doing this, I will briefly explain the value of the second chamber. Assuming that the design and implementation of the second chamber are shown to be plausible and desirable, such a chamber has two kinds of value. The first one, naturally, is to contribute to governance through discussing and passing bills and government budget and spending, balancing the views of the democratically elected chamber (hereafter called "first chamber"), and monitoring the government. The second value is educational. If the second chamber is filled with politicians who are thought to be of high quality (i.e., virtuous and competent), they can serve as role models for other politicians and the entire citizenry, as the manner in which they debate on public affairs, the viewpoints they bring into public discussion, and the judgments and decisions they make can have an educational influence on other people. Confucian thinkers have long held the view that a key function of political leaders is to set themselves as moral examples for people to emulate so that they too can later become gentlemen who are fit for taking on the responsibilities of governance. In this light, the second chamber is not only a governing institution in its own right but also an important part of the moral education of society at large.

Needless to say, there are some issues concerning this kind of institution. The first issue is related to the legitimacy of the second chamber. The second relates to the existence of a reliable method of identifying and selecting the virtuous and competent. The third relates to the powers and responsibilities of the two chambers and the possible conflicts between them. A full defense of the second chamber must adequately address all these issues. However, owing to the limitations of space, I will just look briefly at each of these issues to show its initial plausibility and desirability. Let us begin with the issue of legitimacy. For democrats who believe in political equality or popular sovereignty as a moral principle, any proposal put forward for a nondemocratically formed political institution would be met with serious suspicion if not downright dismissal. Confucians, however, do not share these democratic moral principles, as I argued in chapter 1. They believe that if one accepts the service conception of authority (i.e., that authority has to be justified by its service to the people), then no individual has any fundamental moral right to have a share in political authority. Any institutional arrangement of political authority is to be assessed by its contribution to the well-being of the people. For this reason, the legitimacy of the second chamber has to be based on an assessment of how well it would work by itself and how well it would fit with other parts of the overall political system. Of course, from the Confucian perspective, we also need to look at the extent to which people would accept this kind of institution—not because people have prior political rights and their consent must be obtained, but because Confucians regard people's willing and glad acceptance of authority as an important part of the ideal political relationship. If the majority of people are strongly against the second chamber, the latter would carry little authority and not be able to effectively perform its given tasks.

People may still reject the second chamber if it is ill conceived or ill designed. One of the most commonplace criticisms of the concept of the second chamber is that there is no reliable way of identifying virtuous and competent rulers. This assertion may be supported by two reasons. The first is that there is no objective basis for differentiating people according to their virtue and competence. The second is that there is no reliable institutional mechanism to identify and select the virtuous and competent. The first reason, I believe, is too extreme to be tenable. The virtues and competence we expect of political leaders are neither mysterious nor highly contestable. We want leaders to be knowledgeable about their tasks, to have the ability to think and express clearly and understand complex arguments, and to possess such virtues as public-spiritedness, sense of responsibility, integrity, trustworthiness, civility, benevolence, and so forth. These virtues are human virtues that can be known and experienced in many social contexts. It is possible to judge whether people do or do not possess these abilities and character traits, and we make this sort of judgment about the people with whom we work or interact—our colleagues, fellow members of a committee or group, or friends. For example, we judge the virtues of our colleagues when we evaluate them for appointment of positions or tasks and we know that some people are better qualified than others. We are confident in our ability to judge because we know the people we are evaluating.

Through an extended period of interaction, we have observed how they think, decide, and execute their duties, and how they treat other people. If we do not possess this ability to evaluate people, then there is no objective basis to the selection of any leaders in any institutions, including political ones.

However, when we know only a little about the people we are evaluating, as in the case of external work applicants who are not personally known to a selection committee, we are less confident about passing this sort of evaluative judgment. Interviews and personal references may help, but only to a limited extent. This point actually illustrates that democratic elections, when they take place within a constituency of considerable size, are unreliable as a mechanism for selecting good leaders, as the electorate usually have little interaction with or personal knowledge of the candidates. Although voters can acquire some knowledge of candidates through town hall or televised debates or pamphlets of self-introduction, this method is far less reliable than the way in which we get to know the colleagues we interact with on a regular basis. Voters often cast their votes based on highly impressionistic observations of the candidates. And to some extent, smart candidates can fool voters by pretending to be virtuous and caring.

The second reason for rejecting the second chamber is that there is no reliable institutional mechanism to select good people, either because no mechanism can acquire or supply the amount of accurate information about candidates needed to assess them, or because, if such a mechanism did exist, it could be abused by interested parties. This reason cannot be assessed in the abstract without having some institutional mechanism as a focus. I shall therefore first discuss one influential proposal for the second chamber made by Daniel A. Bell before proceeding with my own. Bell has made a strong case for valuing and incorporating virtue and talent in political decision making in contemporary societies. "Political decision makers in contemporary societies," he writes, "should be intelligent, adaptable, long-term minded, and public-spirited—traits not all that different from the traditional virtues of Confucian exemplary persons."[53] He argues that "modern societies . . . face the challenge of combining dual commitments to democracy and decision making by talented and public-spirited elites. More specifically in the East Asian context, societies must try to reconcile rule by 'Confucian' exemplary persons with democratic values and practices."[54] Bell then proposes a selection mechanism—the use of competitive examinations to select people with virtue and talent to be members of the second chamber, which he calls "House of Virtue and Talent." The examinations, according to Bell, "should test for both memorization and independent thought." Essay questions should be tailored to test for "economic and political

53 Daniel A. Bell, "Taking Elitism Seriously: Democracy with Confucian Characteristics," chap. 6 in *Beyond Liberal Democracy: Political Thinking for an East Asian Context* (Princeton: Princeton University Press, 2006), 160.

54 Ibid., 162.

knowledge of the contemporary world," "knowledge of philosophy and literature that have inspired great leaders of the past," as well as "problem-solving
ability." There should also be "essay questions on ethics to help filter out political demagogues and brilliant but morally insensitive technocrats."[55] When applying his model to China, he suggests elsewhere that "the examinations would
test for the Confucian classics, basic economics, world history, and a foreign
language."[56]

There is considerable merit in Bell's proposal. Examinations do seem to be
an effective way of testing for knowledge relevant to public affairs and critical
thinking. They also filter out the effects of personal networks and political loyalty, which are an important concern in a context like China. More important,
as members of the House do not need to respond to immediate political pressure from the electorate, they are in a politically more secure position than
those in the first chamber to tackle long-term policy issues that require short-
term sacrifices on the part of the voters. They are also in a better position to care
for the interests of nonvoters, whether these are young people or foreign work-
ers. However, as Bell's critics have pointed out, the major weakness of examinations is that they cannot effectively test for virtues such as civility, public-
spiritedness, trustworthiness, and integrity, for the simple reason that ethical
knowledge is not equivalent to a well-developed disposition to act.[57] Bell is not
unaware of this problem, although he does not seem to think it is a very serious
one. As he puts it, "examinations won't test perfectly for these virtues." His defense of this model, despite this inadequacy, is that "deputies chosen by such
examinations are more likely to be virtuous than those chosen by democratic
elections"[58] and that "this procedure is more effective than other methods of
political selection currently on offer."[59] But it is very doubtful if examinations
are a more reliable test for virtue than are democratic elections. It seems that it
would be easier for intellectually bright candidates to fake virtue in anonymous
examinations by making what appear to be ethically correct judgments and
arguments than to fake it in public democratic elections by simulating virtuous
behavior.

Nevertheless, it is not easy to find alternative mechanisms that are more effective than examinations and democratic elections. Early Confucians were
well aware of the practical difficulties in assessing a person's virtue and competence. Confucius, for example, says that when assessing someone, we must

55   Ibid., 168.

56   Daniel A. Bell, "Toward Meritocratic Rule in China? A Response to Professors Dallmayr,
Li, and Tan," *Philosophy East and West* 59, no. 4 (2009): 558.

57   See Chenyang Li, "Where Does Confucian Virtuous Leadership Stand?" *Philosophy East
and West* 59, no. 4 (2009): 531–36; and Sor-hoon Tan, "Beyond Elitism: A Community Ideal for a
Modern East Asia," *Philosophy East and West* 59, no. 4 (2009): 537–53.

58   Bell, "Toward Meritocratic Rule," 558.

59   Bell, *Beyond Liberal Democracy*, 169.

carefully observe his actions and motives, consult others who know that person, and then make an independent judgment.[60]

> The Master said, "See what a man does; watch his motives; examine what he is at ease with. How, then, can he conceal himself? How, then can he conceal himself?" (*Analects* 2.10)[61]

> Zigong asked, "The people of the prefecture all love him—what do you think about such a man?" The Master said, "Not good enough." "The people of the prefecture all loathe him—what do you think about such a man?" The Master said, "Not good enough, either. It would be best if the prefecture's good people loved him and its evil people loathed him." (13.24)[62]

> The Master said, "If the multitude loathes him, it must be looked into; if the multitude loves him, it must be looked into." (15.28)[63]

In the Tang dynasty Lu Zhi (754–805 CE), a famous senior Confucian official whose political writings were held in high regard by later generations of Confucian thinkers, also wrestled with the difficult problem of identifying and selecting people of virtue and talent. In the following important passage, Lu examines various methods, including the kind of state examinations introduced in Tang, and finds them wanting in terms of reliability.

> The most urgent matter for bringing about the Way is to get the right people. Yet identifying the right people is so difficult a task that even the sages found it problematic. Listening carefully to someone's speech does not guarantee that he really possesses virtuous conduct; but judging a person only according to virtuous conduct may on the other hand lead to neglecting his talent. If examinations are used for selection, people will engage in crafty hypocrisy and as a result the righteous man of principle will seldom get promoted. If fine reputation is followed as the standard, the problem of popularity contest will only worsen, and the subtle-cautious talents will never rise to high positions.[64]

Lu says that examination results do not effectively distinguish between principled people and those who "engage in crafty hypocrisy." Meanwhile, speech,

---

60 Bell puts forward the assumption that learning in classics improves the virtue of the learner. I am prepared to accept this assumption in a purely educational context, but when learning of this kind is done for an extrinsic cause such as competing for positions or offices, I doubt if the assumption can stand.

61 Translation from Huang with slight modifications.

62 Huang's translation.

63 Huang's translation.

64 Lu Zhi 陸贄, "Qing xutaisheng zhang guan ju jian shu li zhuang" 請許台省長官舉薦屬吏狀 [A proposal to allow ministers to select their own staff], *Wikisource*, http://zh.wikisource.org/zh-hant/%E8%AB%8B%E8%A8%B1%E5%8F%B0%E7%9C%81%E9%95%B7%E5%AE%98%E8%88%89%E8%96%A6%E5%B1%AC%E5%90%8F%E7%8B%80.

action, or reputation *alone* does not provide sufficient evidence. Lu maintains, in the same spirit as Confucius, that the only way to fully grasp a person's character is to get to know him and observe him for an extended period of time and from all angles.

> Indeed, it is only when a person has befriended someone for a long time, knowing comprehensively his fundamental as well as superficial sides, having a good grasp of his sternest will and intention, seeing thoroughly his capacity for practical matters, that one can be certain that he really has kept the Way and preserved his talents for future use. And only under such condition will crafty pretenders find no room for their hypocrisy. This is why Master Confucius says, "See what a man does; watch his motives; examine what he is at ease with. How, then, can he conceal himself?" Adequate observation cannot be hastened within a day and a night.[65]

Having stated the principle one should follow in identifying the right people, Lu goes on to propose what he regards as a workable selection method, and one that was put into practice in early dynasties.

> This is why, in previous dynasties, "recommendation by prestigious local elderly and officials" was established as the method of selection and promotion. Adopting this method has many benefits: it verifies clearly the actual political/administrative performance of each official, extends the range of talent selection, encourages the cultivation of virtuous conduct and competence, and, lastly, puts the ambition that arises from pride to rest.[66]

Confucius's and Lu's basis for identifying virtue and talent is close acquaintance and careful observation. For Lu the people best skilled at this are prestigious elderly people and officials in local districts—people who have observed the fellow citizens in their districts and have the credentials and knowledge to select and recommend people to higher authorities. In my view Lu's suggested model can easily be transposed to contemporary situations. In the following paragraphs I shall propose a selection mechanism for the second chamber that I call "selection by colleagues" (with "colleagues" understood in the widest sense of the term). I shall then briefly describe the functions and terms of the chamber.

As constitutional design is a contextual matter that cannot be fruitfully discussed at a general level such as this, the proposal I am about to put forward serves merely as an invitation for further discussion. Any proposal, however attractive it may seem in the abstract, may prove unfeasible in a particular social context if it fails to win the favor of the people. A proposed new institution must also function as part of a coherent constitutional package, but any discus-

---

65   Ibid.

66   Ibid. I thank Elton Chan for drawing my attention to this article by Lu and for providing a translation of the quotations.

sion about the desirability and feasibility of such a package is bound to be highly controversial, for the package involves too many interrelated factors whose overall effects are extremely difficult to predict with certainty. For these reasons, then, any proposals for a new political institution, including mine below, must be considered with a healthy dose of skepticism. My aim is mainly to introduce a hypothetical example of a proposal based on the Confucian ideas of selection outlined above.

Rationale, Approach, and Selection Method

To ensure that any selection of the virtuous and competent is effective, the selection method must meet two requirements. First, there must be suitable people available for selection into the second chamber, and second, the selectors must be able to identify them and be willing to make a disinterested choice. To see the distinctiveness of a selection method based on the opinions of colleagues, let us contrast it with the examinations method. The examinations method is targeted at political beginners whose virtues and talents are relatively unknown to their peers. However, not only is this method unreliable, it unnecessarily excludes available information about the distribution of virtue and talent in a society.

The colleague-based selection approach, however, would be targeted not at people at the *ex-ante* of public service but at those near the *ex-post*. Similarly to J. S. Mill, in his proposal to reform the House of Lords to reflect the experience of the Roman Senate,[67] I think the best pool of virtue and talent comes from seasoned participants in public service—those who have had a long and rich experience of public service in the legislature, courts, civil service, government advisory bodies, statutory bodies, and diplomatic services. In terms of candidate qualifications, we might set different lengths of service and levels of seniority for different public service sectors. The general principle would be that senior public servants who meet the qualification requirements would have the opportunity to select each other to serve in the second chamber. The selectors, however, would not need to be confined to this group of people. Those who have worked with some of these senior public servants for an extended period of time in one capacity or another could also be included, for they would presumably possess a more reliable knowledge and assessment of those public servants than would other people in society. The selectors might include senior

---

67   John Stuart Mill, "Of a Second Chamber," chap. 13 in pt. 3, "Considerations on Representative Government," of *Utilitarianism, On Liberty, Considerations on Representative Government*, ed. H. B. Acton (London: Dent & Sons, 1972). For a brief proposal of a "third chamber" in addition to the bicameral Congress in the context of the United States, see also Daniel Bell (American sociologist 1919–2011), "The Old War: After Ideology, Corruption," *New Republic*, August 23 and 30, 1993, 20–21. Different proposals suggest different credentials to qualify as members of the second chamber. Mill includes not only senior or retired public service officials but also professors. Bell apparently confines membership to retirees of the first two chambers.

secretariat staff serving in any of the public institutions mentioned above or experienced political affairs journalists who interact with senior public servants on a regular basis. Direct employees of the public servants would be excluded as selectors, as selection of one's own boss would constitute a conflict of interest.

Any qualified senior public servants would be able to stand as candidates—and might volunteer themselves or be nominated by others. Once a list of candidates has been drawn up, eligible selectors from the three sources (senior public servants, senior secretariat staff, and experienced journalists) would be asked to evaluate the candidates' virtue (most notably in terms of public-spiritedness, sense of responsibility, fairness, integrity, and civility) and competence (in terms of the ability to understand complex arguments from diverse points of view, open-mindedness, knowledge of some fields of public service, etc.) by giving each candidate an overall mark for each of these two dimensions. Marks would then be aggregated, and those candidates whose overall marks are above a set threshold would be selected to serve in the second chamber.

Powers, Size, and Terms

Before we can decide on the powers of the second chamber vis-à-vis the democratically elected first chamber, we have to look at the role it would play in a democratic society. The second chamber could play a strong role (i.e., as a *guardian* of public interest with overriding powers over the democratically elected first chamber), an equal role (i.e., as a *partner* having the same powers as the first chamber), or a weak role (i.e., as an *adviser* and *role model* for society as a whole, having the power only to delay and return bills to the first chamber for another round of discussion). In my view the role it should play depends a great deal on the level of virtue and competence of the democratic citizenry.[68] The lower the level of virtue and competence the citizenry reaches, the stronger the role the second chamber should take. However, the second chamber should be able to exert healthy influence on society even if it plays only a weak role, for the most unique and valuable function it can serve is to act as a role model of public deliberation for politicians and citizens. The following hypothetical description of the size and terms of the second chamber is based on the weak role scenario.

The second chamber would have no fixed number of seats that should be filled. The number would depend entirely on the number of qualified senior public servants appointed by the colleague-based selection method. The im-

---

68 Another way to determine the relative power of the second chamber vis-à-vis the first would be to look at the nature of the work performed by each chamber. For example, the second chamber might have more power in policy areas such as environmental and population issues that affect future generations or other nonvoters. I thank Daniel A. Bell for this suggestion.

portance of the chamber would be measured by the quality of deliberation rather than the sheer number of voices or votes. Members would serve a maximum of two terms. To fulfill the advisory and role-modeling functions, deliberative meetings would be fully broadcast via free public television and radio channels. Members of the second chamber would exert their influence mainly through their justly obtained reputation and prestige as virtuous and competent citizens, through the force of their arguments, and through their power to criticize the government and the first chamber and to delay bills.

As second chamber members would be near the *ex-post* of their public service life, temptations of corruption or power abuse might be lessened. Their incentives would not come from a strong desire for more power or fame, for presumably they would have satisfied their taste for these things through long years of public service. Also, as the constitutional powers of the members of the second chamber would be limited (at least in the weak-role scenario), such positions would be less likely to attract ambitious politicians still hungry for power. Their main incentive to serve would, we hope, be a desire to utilize their virtue and competence to contribute to society in another capacity. Nevertheless, the standard corruption prevention measures that apply to the first chamber would also apply to the second chamber.

One commonplace criticism of the notion of a nondemocratically selected second chamber asserts that although people would like to select good leaders, they are often unable to agree on an evaluation of the virtue and competence of candidates. For this reason, the criticism continues, power should not be given to those people whose virtue or competence is disputed. Instead it may be argued that every citizen should be allowed to vote for the members of a legislature, as democratic voting is a fairer, and hence preferable, way of settling disagreements. In my opinion, however, the fact that there are disagreements on the quality of candidates does not mean that we should put aside our concern for making good selection judgments and simply adopt whatever content-independent voting principle seems fair to everyone involved. After all, if all we wanted was procedural fairness, we could simply settle disagreements by flipping a coin.[69] Flipping a coin may be an appropriate decision-making principle if we are not too concerned about the qualitative differences of the options to choose from. In situations where we are indeed concerned, such as selecting people to take up public offices, we do want our decision-making procedure to help us make better evaluations about the quality of the candidates. So whatever decision-making procedure is adopted, its legitimacy should be based in good part on the care and quality of the discussion about the candidates prior to the moment of decision making.

---

69 For a detailed argument against a pure procedural justification of democracy, see Estlund, "The Limits of Fair Procedure," chap. 4 in *Democratic Authority*.

Conclusion

In this chapter I have suggested ways of supplementing democracy by drawing on Confucian values and thought and have demonstrated that Confucianism and democracy can be linked expressively and instrumentally, in both directions. In an ideal situation democracy directly expresses the Confucian ideal political relationship and other political values; in nonideal situations democracy serves as a useful instrument to pursue Confucian goals without breaking the expressive relationship with the Confucian ideal. Nevertheless, a well-functioning democracy needs a virtuous citizenry to prevent it from degenerating into an antagonistic political competition based solely on narrow self-interests. In this regard, Confucian ethical insight and reflection can help make democracy ethically more attractive and practically more feasible. I have briefly sketched two ways in which Confucianism may offer help—through its moral teachings on virtues and its reflections on the search for virtue and talent. I have argued that Confucian humanity-based moral education seems more effective than liberal citizen- and knowledge-based civic education in instilling civic virtues. To further supplement electoral institutions, I have also provided Confucian reflections on how to select the virtuous and competent to serve in politics and suggested, by way of example, a second legislative chamber whose members are selected by colleagues.

PART II

Rights, Liberties, and Justice

CHAPTER 5

Human Rights as a Fallback Apparatus

Modern Challenges to Confucianism

One of the most complex issues involved in developing a contemporary Confucian ethical and political theory is the question of human rights and individual autonomy. Since the May Fourth Movement (1915–1926), Confucianism has been criticized for failing to recognize the dignity of the individual and the value of individual autonomy as understood in the Western liberal traditions of political thought. Some critics have even contended that Confucianism not only fails to recognize but actively suppresses individual autonomy. The most forceful critic in this regard was Chen Duxiu (1879–1942), who argued powerfully that Confucianism is inappropriate as a model for modern times because its ethics seriously undermines individual autonomy and self-respect. Similarly, contemporary critics claim that Confucianism is incompatible with human rights and civil liberties as it does not respect the autonomy of the individual.[1]

In this and the following chapter, I shall discuss how contemporary Confucian-inspired scholars should respond to the question of human rights and individual autonomy. As these concepts are primarily modern and Western, and there is little in traditional Confucianism that we can draw reference from, it is therefore necessary to tackle the relations between Confucian thought and these two concepts through elaboration and emendation. It is my hope that my interpretive analysis will capture the spirit of the tradition and that my emendation will strengthen the philosophical appeal of Confucianism to people in modern times.

The relationship between Confucianism and human rights is a complex one that raises a number of questions: Is Confucianism compatible with the notion of human rights? Is there a place for human rights in an ideal society as understood in Confucianism? Under what conditions would Confucianism accept human rights, if at all? Can Confucianism accept the specific human rights as

---

1 For powerful contemporary challenges along similar lines, see Randall P. Peerenboom, "Confucian Harmony and Freedom of Thought: The Right to Think versus Right Thinking," chap. 13 in *Confucianism and Human Rights*, ed. William Theodore de Bary and Tu Weiming (New York: Columbia University Press, 1998); and Ci Jiwei 慈繼偉, "*Cong zheng dang yu shan de qu fen kan quan li zai xian dai xi fang he ru jia si xiang zhong de cha yi*" 從正當與善的區分看權利在現代西方和儒家思想中的差異 [The Right, the Good, and the Place of Rights in Confucianism], in *Guo ji ru xue yan jiu* 國際儒學研究 [International Confucian Studies], vol. 6 (Beijing: China Social Sciences Press, 1999).

listed in the Universal Declaration of Human Rights? The answers to these questions vary according to each individual's understanding or evaluation of both Confucianism and human rights. For example, some scholars holding an incompatibilist position present Confucianism rather positively and human rights rather negatively, arguing that Confucianism as an ethics of benevolence and harmonious social relationships has no place for rights that are premised on individualism and self-assertiveness; whereas others holding the same incompatibilist position argue that Confucianism preaches an authoritarian form of morality and politics that should be rejected and replaced by a political philosophy of human rights and democracy. The compatibilists, however, argue that while Confucianism may accept the notion of human rights, it may not accept the full-blown conception of human rights as expounded by certain contemporary liberal philosophies of rights or as developed in contemporary international laws. In this chapter I shall develop and defend this moderate compatibilist position.

With regard to the question of compatibility, it is important to detach the idea of human rights from the doctrines or philosophies that have become associated with it in recent centuries. Although Western natural law theories and various liberal schools of thought have contributed much to the development of human rights, today the idea of human rights—minimally defined as rights that human beings have by virtue of their humanity—has gained currency in many different religions and cultures and is supported by people who subscribe to various philosophical and religious traditions of thought. As will be seen later, some of the attacks on human rights made by Confucian-inspired scholars might better be seen as attacks on the kind of rights talk commonly found within certain strands of liberalism. Of course, the extent to which human rights as developed in international laws today can be separated from Western liberalism may be an open question, but it is a mistake simply to assume or assert an equivalence of the two.

The overall argument of this chapter is that while the idea of human rights is compatible with Confucian ethics, the Confucian perfectionist approach understands the value and proper function of human rights in ways that are different from mainstream liberalism. In the next section I discuss and reject several arguments for the incompatibility view. In the third section I adopt a two-track approach to examine the value and function of human rights. In Confucian ideal society people are more or less virtuous and act in the spirit of benevolence; thus the notion of human rights has no practical importance, and human rights are not needed to express human worth. In nonideal situations, however, where people fail to act virtuously and social relationships break down, human rights are important instruments for protecting the legitimate interests of the people. In the fourth section I argue that Confucian perfectionism would resist the development of the type of rights talk that has the effect of impoverishing people's moral vocabularies and encouraging a culture of rights claims and litigation. There are two ways to resist the trend of rights talk—first, to encourage a perspective that sees both human rights and virtue as important and mutually dependent, and second, to discourage the development of a long list of rights. For several reasons I argue that Confucians should prefer to restrict rights to civil and political rights.

Refuting the Incompatibility View

One of the most common arguments in support of incompatibility holds that the idea of human rights carries certain presuppositions that are either philosophically problematic or fundamentally at odds with Confucianism. This view is well represented in the work of Confucian scholar Henry Rosemont, Jr., who points out that it is "a bedrock presupposition of [Western] moral, social, and political thinking that human beings have rights, solely by virtue of being human." According to him, every human being

> has a definite sex, a color, an age, an ethnic background, certain abilities; and we all live in a specific time and a specific place. From these facts some disturbing considerations follow. The first is that if rights are borne by human beings regardless of these differentiations, then those rights must obtain for human beings altogether independently of their culture. But then it becomes extremely difficult to imagine actual bearers of rights, because there are no culturally independent human beings.[2]

According to Rosemont, the concept of human rights presupposes *acultural* (or *asocial*) human beings, that is, human beings as existing in a cultural and social vacuum, a view not only antithetical to the Confucian conception of personhood but also philosophically untenable. Roger Ames also argues that Confucianism cannot accept human rights because they protect interests that are "independent of and prior to society."[3]

But such arguments give a mistaken representation of the nature of human rights. Rosemont is right in defining human rights as the rights people have solely by virtue of being human, irrespective of their sex, ethnicity, culture, and historical background. He is mistaken, however, in arguing that this definition of human rights implies that human beings can be thought of as having none of these attributes. This definition of human rights is not a *descriptive* claim about human nature but a *moral* view about the distribution of rights—one's sex, race, or culture is a morally irrelevant consideration insofar as one's entitlement to basic human rights is concerned. Neither are international charters of human rights guilty of the charge that human rights presuppose acultural or asocial

2   Henry Rosemont, Jr., "Why Take Rights Seriously? A Confucian Critique," chap. 10 in *Human Rights and the World's Religions*, ed. Leroy S. Rouner (Notre Dame: University of Notre Dame Press, 1988).

3   See Roger T. Ames, "Rites as Rights: The Confucian Alternative," in Rouner, *Human Rights and the World's Religions*, 205.

human beings. The International Covenant on Economic, Social and Cultural Rights protects people's interests in a meaningful social and cultural life. The freedoms of expression and of religion laid down in the International Covenant on Civil and Political Rights, which are taken by Rosemont and others as individualistic rights, are in my opinion designed to protect people's *social* interests: freedom of expression protects an individual's interest in communicating with others, especially in the public sphere; freedom of religion protects one's interest in joining religious associations. These rights are based on the fact that human beings are social and cultural animals. We must not confuse the basis of individual rights with the content of those rights. Although it is the *individual's* interest, not *society's* interest, that justifies a human right, the content of the individual's interest may be *social*.[4]

Rosemont goes on to argue that even if the concept of human rights does not presuppose acultural or asocial beings, it is

closely related to our view of human beings as freely choosing autonomous individuals, a view which is at least as old as Descartes and which is reaffirmed in the 1948 United Nations Declaration of Human Rights. But this concept is overwhelmingly drawn from the culture of the Western industrial democracies and is concerned to propose a particular moral and political perspective, an ideal, appropriate to that culture.[5]

In his view, other cultures or moral perspectives do not affirm this idea of a free, autonomous self. In early Confucianism, according to Rosemont, "There can be no *me* in isolation, to be considered abstractly: I am the totality of roles I live in relation to specific others. I do not *play* or *perform* these roles; I *am* these roles. When they have all been specified I have been defined uniquely, fully, and altogether, with no remainder with which to piece together a free, autonomous self."[6] In a similar vein, Ames argues that "There is much in the Confucian tradition that might be a resource for rethinking our notion of *autonomous individuality*, especially that aspect of the individual which, given its priority over society and environment, effectively renders context a means to individual ends."[7]

This argument is problematic in both its understanding of the Universal Declaration of Human Rights (UDHR) and the Confucian conception of personhood.[8] For example, the UDHR makes no direct mention of the concept of freely choosing autonomous individuals, and none of the major ideas in the

4 For more discussion on this point and the relationship between individual rights and common goods, see Joseph Chan, "Raz on Liberal Rights and Common Goods," *Oxford Journal of Legal Studies* 15, no. 1 (1995): 15–31.

5 Rosemont, "Why Take Rights Seriously?" 167-68.

6 Ibid., 177

7 Ames, "Rites as Rights," 212.

8 See "The Universal Declaration of Human Rights," United Nations, http://www.un.org/en/documents/udhr/.

document can be easily construed as promoting a liberal-individualistic ideal of autonomy. Neither is individual freedom defined as an absolute value or as license to do whatever one pleases. The first article in the UDHR stipulates that "All human beings are born free and equal in dignity and rights" but continues, "They are endowed with *reason* and *conscience* and should act towards one another in a spirit of *brotherhood*" (italics added). The last article also states that "everyone has duties to the community in which alone the free and full development of his personality is possible," and that the exercise of one's rights and freedoms must meet "the just requirements of morality, public order and the general welfare in a democratic society." In addition, the UDHR does not define the basis of civil rights other than associating it with "the dignity and worth of the human person." There is no autonomy-based justification of these rights. Moreover, in the West, freedom of expression is often justified on the grounds that it contributes to the pursuit of truth, arts, democracy, the monitoring of government, and so forth—grounds not directly related to personal autonomy as such. Similarly, the right not to be subjected to torture, arbitrary arrest, detention, or exile, the right to fair hearing, and the right to be presumed innocent until proven guilty are typically justified on the basis of our interests in a minimal notion of freedom, physical security, and fair treatment rather than any robust liberal idea of autonomy.

It is also problematic to describe the early Confucian conception of personhood as purely role-based. Rosemont says, "I am the totality of roles I live in relation to specific others. I do not *play* or *perform* these roles; I *am* these roles." If by this Rosemont means that Confucian individuals have no internal capacity to step back from social conventions to reflect on, affirm, or reject their social roles and associated norms, then this is an incorrect interpretation of Confucian thought. There is no shortage of discussion in the classical texts as to whether people should accept or continue to play their roles and how they should do so: whether a ruler should give up his throne, a gentleman join the government, a son/minister follow his father's/ruler's instruction, and so forth. All this presupposes that Confucian individuals have the capacity to reflect critically on their roles.[9]

To be sure, Confucianism does place significant ethical constraints on human actions, and many of these are based on social roles. But it would be a mistake to think that Confucianism sees all duties, or rights, as arising solely from social roles, as Rosemont's description of the Confucian conception of personhood seems to imply. Although Confucianism places great emphasis on particular social roles, it is not a purely role-based ethics. The Confucian ethics of benevolence is ultimately based on a common humanity rather than differ-

---

9 An instructive discussion of this point can be found in Kwong-loi Shun, "Conception of the Person in Early Confucian Thought," chap. 8 in *Confucian Ethics: A Comparative Study of Self, Autonomy, and Community*, ed. Kwong-loi Shun and David B. Wong (Cambridge: Cambridge University Press, 2004).

entiated social roles—it carries ethical implications beyond these roles. The Confucian view is that human persons are first and foremost moral agents capable of realizing ren, which means, among other things, a certain ability or disposition to care for and sympathize with others. Although the sites for the realization of ren are commonly found in personal relationships, such as those between father and son or husband and wife, there are *nonrelational* occasions where moral actions are also required by ren. That is to say, not all moral duties in Confucianism arise from social institutions or relationships.

Take for example Confucius's golden rule, "Do not impose on others what you yourself do not desire" (*Analects* 15.24)—a moral precept applicable to everyone irrespective of social role or status. Mencius also says, "A gentleman retains his heart by means of benevolence [ren] and the rites [li]. The benevolent man loves others, and the courteous man respects others" (*Mencius* 4B.28). In this passage the "others" are unspecified. This notion of loving all others can also be found in book 7 of *Mencius*, where Mencius says, "A benevolent man loves everyone, but he devotes himself to the close association with good and wise men" (7A.46). A more telling example of a non-role-based or nonrelational morality is Mencius's discussion of a child on the verge of falling into a well (2A.6). For Mencius, a man with ren would be moved by compassion to save the child, not because he is acquainted with the child's parents, nor because he wants to win the praise of his fellow villagers or friends, but simply because of his concern for the suffering of another human being. Mencius's point is that no man is devoid of ren in the sense of "sensitivity to the suffering of others." These "others" are not confined to those personally known but may also include all people within the Four Seas—namely, everywhere in the world.

Some might argue that the example of the child about to fall shows only that we are moved to save a child in danger only if we see the child, that is, that there is some kind of "interaction" or relationship between the child and the one who saves him or her. However, in my opinion this stretches the notion of relationship too far—a personal relationship does not begin instantaneously upon first eye contact. Moreover, even if the sight of a child in danger arouses feelings of benevolence or empathy and moves me to action, my compassion for complete strangers could be similarly triggered by the audiovisual images of their suffering I encounter in the media. Benevolence may also compel us to respond to this awareness. Although it is true that Confucian ethics favors a graded concern for others and emphasizes that we should care for our family and friends above strangers, Confucians also believe that benevolence is not confined to those personally known but can reach all people within the Four Seas. Later Confucians even talk about the benevolent heart being able to encompass nature and Heaven. Confucian ethical concern for human suffering is potentially unlimited in scope. Benevolence motivates and commands us to respond to our awareness that there are people in need, even if they are strangers and live far away from us.

Nothing I have said thus far shows that Confucianism recognizes that human individuals have rights irrespective of their roles. Rather, it shows that the argument for the charge that Confucianism is *unable to accommodate* universal human rights is unsound, for it is based on a *false* premise, namely, that Confucianism subscribes to a purely role-based view of morality.[10]

Contemporary Confucian scholar Kwong-loi Shun also disagrees with the purely role-based interpretation of Confucian ethics but seems hesitant to endorse the compatibility of human rights and Confucianism for a slightly different reason. He agrees that "Confucian thinkers regard human beings as autonomous in having the capacity to reflect on, assess and shape their lives without being determined by external influences." But "the exercise of this capacity," according to his interpretation of Confucian ethics, is "intimately linked to the social order" rather than to the fact that individuals have separate interests to protect or ends to pursue. In particular, he believes that the fact that any claim individuals can make on others in such an order is "based on an understanding of the social dimensions of human life rather than on a conception of human beings as individuals who need protection in the pursuit of their individual ends." Shun says that the basis for making a legitimate claim on others "is not a view of human beings as individuals whose interests require protection either because of competing interests among people or because their freedom to choose their own ends needs to be preserved."[11] In other words, if, according to Confucianism, people should not make claims on the basis of their individual interests or ends, then the fact that human rights do allow people to make claims on such a basis would not be welcome by Confucian ethics.

What should we make of this view? I believe it is fair to say that Confucianism does not give importance to the idea of individuals freely choosing their own ends, whatever these ends may be. The emphasis is on acting rightly rather than freely, and to act rightly is to act in accordance with one's best understanding of the requirements of Confucian morality. Nevertheless, Confucianism never denounces or belittles individual interests that are understood as the legitimate needs and desires of individuals as human beings (not just as parents, sons and daughters, or officials). One discourse in Confucianism that does denounce "interests" refers to the self-interests (often selfish interests) of rulers, not those of the people; rulers should care for the basic interests of their people above their own interests. As Xunzi says, lordship is established for the people, not for the ruler (*Xunzi* 27.68). For Confucianism, one of the most important functions of a ruler is to "benefit" (*li*) the people. As the classical texts clearly show, the ruler's task is to protect the interests of the people in terms of subsistence and pursuit of material goods, fair treatment in the allocation of rewards and punishments, and proper familial and social relationships. Shun claims

---

10   Roger Ames has further developed his view of Confucianism as a kind of "role ethics" in *Confucian Role Ethics: A Vocabulary* (Hong Kong: Chinese University Press, 2011), which I am not able to discuss here.

11   Shun, "Conception of the Person," 194–95.

that "the focus of Confucian thinkers when viewing the legitimate claims that an individual has on others is less on how the claims serve to protect that individual, but more on how they are part of a social setup that is to the communal good." This claim seems to be overstated, for he also notes, rightly in my view, that it is not true that Confucian thought "downplays individual interest and subordinates it to the public good"; rather, "there is no genuine conflict between individual interest and the public good."[12]

One reason for the absence of genuine conflict between individual interests and the public good is that the public or communal good is partially constituted by individual needs and entitlements. As I shall show in chapter 7, peace and harmony are based on the recognition of each individual's due, or the fair treatment of individuals. Mencius and Xunzi take the fair treatment of individuals as a moral imperative that trumps political goals such as the gaining of an empire. Mencius says that it is wrong to "kill one innocent man" or "take what one is not entitled to" in order to gain an empire, for doing so is contrary to righteousness (yi) and benevolence (ren) (*Mencius* 2A.2, 7A.33). Xunzi is of the same view, namely, that a gentleman (ru) "would not commit a single act contrary to the requirements of justice nor execute a single blameless man, even though he might thereby obtain the empire. Such a lord acts with justice [yi] and faithfulness [xin] toward the people" (*Xunzi* 8.2).

In light of this understanding, we may conclude not only that Confucian thought would not oppose the idea that basic individual interests constitute the common good, but that it would take these interests as the basis of a legitimate social and political order. Confucianism would not reject human rights on the grounds that they protect fundamental individual interests and would in fact support the civil rights laid out in the UDHR, such as the right not to be tortured or subjected to arbitrary arrest and the right to a fair hearing, precisely because they protect the fundamental individual interests of physical security and fairness. As the UDHR's notion of human rights does not presuppose the notion of freely choosing autonomous individuals without regard for community responsibilities or social relationships, and as Confucian ethics see no opposition between the individual good and the common good (i.e., social order and harmony can only be pursued by affirming and protecting people's interests in terms of security, material goods, social relationships and fair treatment), then it follows that, with regard to these issues at least, there is no incompatibility between Confucianism and the concept of human rights.

Human Rights in Ideal and Nonideal Situations

While there is no strict incompatibility between Confucianism and the idea of human rights, the tensions between the two lie in the more subtle issues of how Confucians understand the value and proper function of human rights, as well

12 Ibid., 195.

as which of the many rights laid out in international human rights treaties they accept as fundamental. There are two common approaches to understanding the value and function of fundamental human rights: one is an instrumental approach that takes human rights as an important device for protecting people's fundamental interests; the other does not deny the instrumental value of human rights but insists that they also have an important noninstrumental value, in the sense that they are necessary expressions of human dignity or worth. In this section I shall argue that Confucianism can accept the first approach but not the second.

Joel Feinberg has made an influential argument for the expressive value of human rights.[13] He asks us to imagine "Nowheresville," a world in which "the virtues of moral sensibility" and "the sense of duty" flourish, and which is filled with "as much benevolence, compassion, sympathy, and pity as it will conveniently hold without strain." What is lacking in this world is individual right— people have no right to make claims against each other. In Feinberg's view, having a right enables the right-holder to make certain claims against others, to make a complaint and demand for compensation if he or she is wronged, and so forth. In Nowheresville, however, if people are treated inappropriately, they can make no claims against others, which results in a lack of self-respect and human dignity—for having the capacity to assert rights claims is a necessary condition for self-respect and human dignity. Feinberg writes:

> Having rights enables us to "stand up like men," to look others in the eye, and to feel in some fundamental way the equal of anyone. To think of oneself as the holder of rights is not to be unduly but properly proud, to have that minimal self-respect that is necessary to be worthy of the love and esteem of others. Indeed, respect for persons (this is an intriguing idea) may simply be respect for their rights, so that there cannot be the one without the other; and what is called "human dignity" may simply be the recognizable capacity to assert claims. To respect a person then, or to think of him as possessed of human dignity, simply *is* to think of him as a potential maker of claims.[14]

Feinberg does not, however, give any argument for the claim that human dignity "may simply be the recognizable capacity to assert claims." In any case, Confucians would resist any view that links human dignity solely with rights and the capacity to make claims against others. The concept of human dignity is broad and vague and allows for various conceptions. If one minimally defines the concept as the inner moral worth of a human being that entitles him or her to a certain moral status and respect that no other living things or material objects possess,[15] then clearly different cultural or philosophical perspectives

---

13   Joel Feinberg, "The Nature and Value of Rights," *Journal of Value Inquiry* 4, no. 4 (1970): 243–60.

14   Ibid., 252.

15   See Rhoda E. Howard, "Dignity, Community, and Human Rights," chap. 4 in *Human Rights in Cross-Cultural Perspectives: A Quest for Consensus*, ed. Abdullahi Ahmed An-Na'im (Phil-

will have different views of the source of inner moral worth and hence different conceptions of human dignity. According to Mencius and Xunzi, the source of inner moral worth that makes human beings *gui* (translated as noble, honorable, or valuable) is the human capacity for benevolence and righteousness (*ren yi*). Mencius says, "Every man has in him that which is exalted [gui]," namely, his "benevolence and righteousness [ren yi]" even if "the fact simply never dawned on him" (*Mencius* 6A.17). For Xunzi, among all living things, only humans possess "a sense of duty [yi],"[16] and for this reason they are "the noblest [gui] beings in the world" (*Xunzi* 9.16a). This inner worth of human beings allows Mencius to say that in politics "people are of supreme importance" (*Mencius* 7B.14), and that innocent life should never be sacrificed merely to gain political power (2A.2). As we see, Confucians regard human beings as having an inner moral worth that gives them a special status, and they believe that the source of this worth lies in each person's potential capacity for benevolence and righteousness, rather than in the possession of rights.[17]

Even if human rights are not needed to express the dignity of an individual, it does not follow that human rights do not or should not exist. Nevertheless, human rights do not have any practical importance in an ideal Confucian society, and it seems inappropriate to invoke the notion of rights in such a context. In the ideal Confucian society, people are more or less virtuous and act in the spirit of benevolence—a graded notion of care or love for one's family and friends and for all strangers as brothers within the Four Seas. People in virtuous relationships should not need to think of themselves as individuals possessing rights that they can evoke to make claims against their partners; they should think of themselves as participating in a relationship of reciprocal commitment or mutual caring. To introduce considerations of rights is inappropriate in such relationships, as it might motivate us to see the interests of others as limitations on our own interests rather than as separate interests that we might wish to promote.[18]

For Confucians, human virtue and virtuous relationships are not dependent on rights. This point has important implications for certain strands of contem-

---

adelphia: University of Pennsylvania Press, 1992), 83; and Doron Shultziner, "Human Dignity: Functions and Meanings," chap. 7 in *Perspectives on Human Dignity: A Conversation*, ed. Jeff Malpas and Norelle Lickiss (Dordrecht: Springer, 2007), 81.

16   As I discussed in chapter 2, note 22, Xunzi's notion of a "sense of duty" might contradict his general view that human nature is bad or evil. One possible way to get around this apparent contradiction is that even though human beings have no innate sense of duty or morality, they can somehow acquire it through socialization and learning, although it is not clear how this can be possible. In any case, Xunzi might argue that the fact that human beings can acquire a sense of duty or morality is what separates them from animals and gives them an exalted status in the world.

17   For another critique of Feinberg's view from a Confucian perspective, see Craig K. Ihara, "Are Individual Rights Necessary? A Confucian Perspective," chap. 1 in Shun and Wong, *Confucian Ethics*.

18   Hugh LaFollette, *Personal Relationships: Love, Identity, and Morality* (Oxford: Blackwell, 1996), 146.

porary rights talk prevalent in some Western countries, where some liberals have adopted an inflated view of rights and argue that even the most valuable forms of mutual caring and love can flourish only in a relationship based on rights. Simon Caney, for example, argues that "benevolence as a virtue is more desirable if based on knowledge of one's rights and entitlements. It has a greater degree of intentionality."[19] John Tomasi gives the following example to support Caney's general point:

> Imagine a marriage relation in which one spouse is utterly deferential to the other. Consider a "deferential wife" whose most every act toward her husband would be perceived by others as being beyond her reasonable duty, as being—apparently, at least—supererogatory (we could as easily imagine a "husband"). However uncomfortable, she nonetheless always wears clothes she knows he prefers; however much they annoy her, she always invites guests he enjoys; however ill suited for her schedule, she always rises and retires when he does. . . . It seems clear that the deferential wife . . . does not act in a way properly called "virtuous" . . . She does not recognize that she is most often in a good position to act otherwise; she has forgotten—and likely would prefer not to be reminded—that she even has rights.[20]

One may agree with Tomasi that, in this example, the wife lacks self-respect or self-worth. The basis of self-respect, however, need not lie in the fact that she has rights, but in the belief that she is worthy of care and concern and that her well-being matters. Therefore she has a legitimate basis, namely, the ideal of mutual caring and love, to complain about her husband—the husband is not treating her with care and is not recognizing her needs and aspirations.[21] The wife need not think in terms of rights in order to assess the relationship. In fact, once she begins to think in these terms, she starts to distance herself from the persons on whom she may press her claims. What she ought to do, according to the Confucian view, is to remind her husband of the ideal of mutual love and caring.

For Confucians, therefore, rights do not play an important role in virtuous relationships, where the focus is on mutual caring and love. But what if the relationship turns sour? Do we need rights to repair it in this instance? Probably not, since it would still be best to repair the relationship by refreshing both

---

19 Simon Caney, "Sandel's Critique of the Primacy of Justice: A Liberal Rejoinder," *British Journal of Political Science* 21, no. 4 (1991): 517

20 John Tomasi, "Individual Rights and Community Virtues," *Ethics* 101, no. 3 (1991): 533. See also Joel Feinberg, *Harm to Self*, vol. 3 of *The Moral Limits of the Criminal Law* (New York: Oxford University Press, 1986), 238.

21 Some might say that the husband violates the norm of reciprocity, which is one form of fairness. But reciprocity, as I understand it, is a minimum notion embedded in many kinds of ethics. One can say that the ideal of mutual caring and love, and Confucius's notion of *shu*—not to impose on others what we ourselves do not desire, and establish and enlarge others insofar as one seeks to establish and enlarge oneself—embody some notion of reciprocity. In any case, reciprocity as a form of "fairness" is still very different from the notion of a right.

partners' commitment to the ideal of mutual caring, rather than by introducing or invoking rights.[22] However, if the relationship breaks down to a point of no return, rights may be relevant and useful in protecting the interests of both parties. Consider again the example of the breakdown of a marriage: if a husband's love for his wife has died and in many ways he has harmed her interests, it would be highly desirable and even necessary for the wife to have formal and legal rights (marriage rights as well as human rights) to fall back on in order to protect her interests.[23]

Thus in nonideal situations rights can play an important role even in familial relationships, and I think Confucianism would endorse rights in this sense. No ethics of benevolence and care would seek to diminish the needs of individuals. After all, when we care for a person, what are we supposed to care for if not that person's needs and interests? There is no reason why Confucianism would prohibit an assertion of rights that is necessary to protect important individual interests. And if familial relationships require rights as a fallback position, this should be reason enough to support the greater community with an apparatus of rights. In the workplace, market, government, court, and other less personal social spheres, people's motivations to act virtuously toward each other may not be as strong as within the context of the family. In nonideal situations rights are important instruments with which the vulnerable can protect themselves against exploitation and harm.

Early Confucian thinkers reacted in a similar way to problems of moral wrongdoing in nonideal situations. When things go wrong and people misbehave in a nonideal society, Confucians first appeal to each other's sense of benevolence and righteousness and reaffirm the norms and rituals that they are expected to follow, hoping that those who go astray will return to the path of benevolence and righteousness. If conflicts or inappropriate conduct persist, the parties involved are brought before those who enjoy an exalted status and command respect from all parties (typically village elders) for mediation, in the hope of reconciling conflict and restoring social harmony.[24] If mediation does not work, Confucians allow the issue to be litigated in court, although they prefer to avoid this where possible. Confucius says, "In hearing litigation, I am no different from any other man. But if you insist on a difference, it is, perhaps, that I try to get the parties not to resort to litigation in the first place" (*Analects* 12.13). But Confucius does not say that litigation should be avoided absolutely or at all costs. When people no longer act according to virtues or rituals—when

---

22   LaFollette, *Personal Relationships*, 146.

23   The notion of rights as a fallback apparatus is taken from Jeremy Waldron, "When Justice Replaces Affection: The Need for Rights," chap. 15 in *Liberal Rights: Collected Papers 1981–1991* (Cambridge: Cambridge University Press, 1993), 374.

24   For a detailed discussion of the Confucian practice of mediation in traditional and modern China, see Albert H. Y. Chen, "Mediation, Litigation, and Justice: Confucian Reflections in a Modern Liberal Society," chap. 11 in *Confucianism for the Modern World*, ed. Daniel A. Bell and Hahm Chaibong (Cambridge: Cambridge University Press, 2003).

they harm others, for example—there is a need to fall back on some institutional apparatus to protect the legitimate interests of those involved. More important, Confucius does not say that we should always yield to others at all times, particularly when we are unjustly harmed.[25] There is a passage that may correct this popular misunderstanding of Confucius: "Someone said, 'Repay an injury with a good turn. What do you think of this saying?' The Master said, 'What, then, do you repay a good turn with? Repay an injury with straightness, but repay a good turn with a good turn'" (*Analects* 14.34). When we are wronged, injured, or harmed by others, Confucius says that it would be appropriate to react by recourse to "straightness," which might be interpreted today as including such measures as seeking justice and compensation through litigation.

The Confucian preference for mediation, reconciliation, and compromise, therefore, does not imply that human beings do not have rights or that they should never use them to protect themselves when harmed. Nevertheless, the Confucian favoring of nonlegal methods of conflict resolution is worth mentioning in the contemporary discourse of human rights. As Randall Peerenboom writes,

> Although far from perfect, traditional methods [of conflict resolution] such as mediation offer many advantages. Both parties save face, fully participate in the proceeding, and shape the ultimate solution. The process, usually faster and cheaper than more formal methods, allows for a more particularized justice and for the restoration of social harmony, with both sides feeling they have received their due.[26]

In fact, the Confucian concern for nonlitigation can be understood as an objection not to human rights as such but to the abuse of rights. However, in order not to abuse rights, we need a theory of virtues to guide right-holders in the exercise of their rights. Confucianism, being a rich theory of virtues, therefore complements a theory of human rights in this regard.[27]

Confucians today, therefore, would approach the value and function of human rights in the same way that early Confucian thinkers approached litigation. Human rights are not necessary to the expression of human dignity, nor are they constitutive of virtues or virtuous relationships. In a nonideal situation, however, they can serve as an important fallback apparatus to protect one's

---

25   And so, on the level of states, defensive wars can be morally legitimate, according to Mencius. For a detailed account of Mencius's view, see Bell, *Beyond Liberal Democracy*, 23–51.

26   Randall P. Peerenboom, "What's Wrong with Chinese Rights? Toward a Theory of Rights with Chinese Characteristics," *Harvard Human Rights Journal* 6 (1993): 55.

27   For more discussion, see Michael J. Meyer, "When Not to Claim Your Rights: The Abuse and the Virtuous Use of Rights," *Journal of Political Philosophy* 5, no. 2 (1997): 149–62; Jeremy Waldron, ed., *Nonsense upon Stilts: Bentham, Burke and Marx on the Rights of Man* (London: Methuen, 1987); and Seung-hwan Lee, "Liberal Rights or/and Confucian Virtues?" *Philosophy East and West* 46, no. 3 (1996): 367–79.

basic interests and needs. In a modern society, human rights function both as a normative principle and a legal instrument, but what ultimately gives human rights their significance and impact is the latter. As a legal instrument, they protect powerless individuals from harm by governments, corporations or social groups. Human rights laws are no ordinary laws; they are higher laws that trump ordinary laws or policies made by governments. Human rights laws cannot be effective without the rule of law and an independent court system with powers of judicial review. But when human rights laws are not yet in place or effective, human rights serve as a powerful normative principle to critique the status quo and demand change, with the ultimate aim of turning human rights aspirations into effective positive laws.[28]

Rights Talk and the List of Rights

There is still one important issue to address before Confucians can fully accept human rights as a fallback apparatus. In the Confucian view, the need for claim-rights emerges only when virtues fail, rituals break down, and mediation becomes ineffective. But such rights, if frequently evoked, can create a snowball effect that causes further social strain and encourages divisive ways of thinking and adversarial tactics. The more readily people can access the rules and procedures of human rights, the more likely they are to use them in the first instance. In this scenario, rights would be brought from the background to the foreground, becoming the first resort rather than the last.[29]

Let us look carefully at this problem. The first point to note is that a culture of litigation and adversarial actions may develop even without the introduction of a human rights apparatus. When the level of general trust is low in a society and ordinary social norms and mechanisms are too weak to guide behavior, litigation might become the only effective way to protect one's interests in cases of conflict, whether or not human rights laws exist. To prevent a culture of litigation from developing, we should try to rebuild social capital, revitalize social norms and mechanisms, and above all make sure that the law is enforced in a fair and effective manner.

Second, whether the human rights apparatus will encourage rights talk and litigious behavior or not, and how likely this is, depends on a number of factors, namely, how human rights are perceived, how wide-ranging the scope of these rights is, and whether there are alternative mechanisms in place to resolve con-

---

28 Of course, the human rights legal apparatus goes much further than the traditional Chinese penal and administrative law system in the following structural aspects (not to mention the difference in content): the distinction between higher and ordinary laws, the concept of a limited government, judicial review, and perhaps a democratic political system. I argued in chapters 2–4 that Confucianism today should accept these institutions.

29 For this argument, see Justin Tiwald, "Confucianism and Human Rights," chap. 22 in *Handbook of Human Rights*, ed. Thomas Cushman (Abingdon, UK: Routledge, 2012).

flict or prevent abuse of power. A culture of rights talk and litigious behavior is more likely to develop in a society if human rights are given an exalted status and human rights protection covers a wide range of aspects of people's lives. In recent decades the number of international human rights treaties and laws has significantly increased, expanding from the "first generation" of civil and political rights, to social and economic rights, to minority and group rights, and environmental rights. New bodies and mechanisms have been created to monitor compliance and implementation. These developments have encouraged rights movements and rights talk in international and national contexts. Many philosophers have challenged the long list of human rights that has been enumerated, questioning the coherence of the so-called new generations of rights. What is worrying is that in public and academic discourse, rights talk seems to have eclipsed traditional moral vocabularies such as justice, the common good, virtue, and duties and rights have become the main moral currency to tackle social problems. James Griffin, for example, has argued that "the fairly recent appearance of group rights is part of a widespread modern movement to make the discourse of rights do most of the important work in ethics, which it neither was designed to do nor . . . should now be made to do."[30] Coupled with the exalted status of human rights, this rights talk trend could have the effect of impoverishing people's moral vocabularies and encouraging a culture of rights claims and litigation.

In my view, Confucianism should resist such a development. We have already examined the fact that Confucians see human rights as an instrumental fallback apparatus rather than an abstract ideal that expresses human dignity. To avoid the problems above, Confucians should emphasize the importance of educating people in the value of virtue—and right-holders should possess virtues to guide them in the exercise of their rights. I also believe that Confucians would prefer a short list of human rights consisting of (1) those rights whose violation (often by governments) poses serious setbacks to social order and individual interests, and (2) those rights that can most easily be implemented and protected by law. The first generation of rights—civil rights and political rights—appears to fit these two criteria more so than social, economic, or other types of rights. Confucians certainly do not belittle the social and economic interests of people. Although these interests may arguably be more basic than certain civil liberties such as freedom of speech and association, unlike civil rights, they are hard to protect through litigation and need to be secured through politics and policies.[31] What governments need to do is to make and enforce sound policies and institutions to promote economic growth and a fair distribution of resources. Appealing to the language of rights in these matters

---

30   James Griffin, *On Human Rights* (New York: Oxford University Press, 2008), 256.

31   I do not want to claim that there cannot be any economic and cultural rights that can be effectively implemented by law—this is a difficult empirical question and needs to be discussed case by case.

can risk turning a complicated balancing of competing values—such as social justice, basic needs, equal opportunity, efficiency, and general utility—into simplistic legalistic reasoning. More important, the introduction of civil and political rights can help prevent violations of social and economic rights, for the latter are often a result of government corruption, maladministration, and mismanagement of economic policies. Amartya Sen has famously argued that famines are almost always associated with authoritarian political rule and that democracy plays an important instrumental role in their prevention: "Famines are easy to prevent if there is a serious effort to do so, and a democratic government, facing elections and criticisms from opposition parties and independent newspapers, cannot help but make such an effort." He continues: "The positive role of political and civil rights applies to the prevention of economic and social disasters in general."[32]

The nature of traditional Confucianism also makes civil and political rights a priority. As I argued in chapter 2, a long-standing feature of traditional Confucian thought (and Chinese political tradition) was the ruler's unchecked supreme status and authority. Although in theory people enjoyed supreme importance, in reality they were not protected by legal institutions or empowered to protect themselves through political participation. The introduction of a human rights apparatus in the civil and political sphere would therefore help to redress the heavy imbalance of power between the ruling and the ruled. Relatively easy access to the legal apparatus to assert one's civil and political rights and legally challenge rights-violating laws and policies is actually something to be welcomed rather than deterred, for it provides powerless individuals with a powerful means to defend themselves.[33]

---

32 Amartya K. Sen, "Democracy as a Universal Value," *Journal of Democracy* 10, no. 3 (1999): 8. This point goes some way to resist a common argument made by some Asian governments in the so-called Asian Values debate, which holds that civil and political liberties need to be sacrificed in order to meet more basic material needs. For a detailed discussion of the trade-off argument and other points of contention in the debate, see Bell, "Human Rights and 'Values in Asia': Reflections on East-West Dialogues," chap. 3 in *Beyond Liberal Democracy*. Bell, however, points out that while "the general claim that civil and political rights must be sacrificed in the name of economic development may not stand up to social scientific scrutiny, East Asian governments also present narrower justifications for curbing *particular* rights in *particular* contexts for *particular* economic or political purposes. These actions are said to be taken as a short-term measure to secure a more important right or more of that same right in the long term." Ibid., 56–57.

33 It should be noted that there are two kinds of civil freedom: one kind concerns political matters such as political speech, public demonstration, and association, while the other has more to do with cultural and moral matters such as pornography, assisted suicide, and homosexuality. Elsewhere I have argued that Confucians would favor a more liberal approach to the first sort of freedom and a more conservative one to the second, which is another issue often discussed in the "Asian Values" debate. For a detailed discussion of the issue about human rights and cultural and ideological differences, see Joseph Chan, "Hong Kong, Singapore and 'Asian Values': An Alternative View," *Journal of Democracy* 8, no. 2 (1997): 35–48; Joseph Chan, "Thick and Thin Accounts of Human Rights: Lessons from the Asian Values Debate," chap. 3 in *Human Rights and Asian Values: Contesting National Identities and Cultural Representations in Asia*, ed. Michael Jacobsen and Ole

Rich cultural and ethical resources already exist within a Confucian society to deal with the sort of concerns raised by social and economic rights. As we shall see in chapters 7 and 8, a long-standing feature of Confucian thought is the emphasis on the government's responsibility to cater for people's material needs. A large part of the Confucian ideal of benevolent rule requires the setting up of social and economic policies to distribute land and economic opportunities for the ruled. Mencius's influential idea of a well-field system articulates what we may call today the sufficiency principle of social justice, which holds that the government has a responsibility to provide for each household a certain amount of land to own and plow so that members of that household can live a decent material life and have spare time to learn and practice virtues when dealing with family members and neighbors. It is interesting to note that Mencius, like Sen, attributes poverty and famines to political factors rather than natural ones. Mencius is keenly aware of the seriousness of poverty and inequality of wealth in his times. He refers to situations in which some people have food "so plentiful as to be thrown to dogs and pigs," while others "drop dead from starvation by the wayside" (*Mencius* 1A.3). He also says, "Nowadays, the means laid down for the people are sufficient neither for the care of parents nor for the support of wife and children. In good years life is always hard, while in bad years there is no way of escaping death" (1A.7). The cause of such situations, according to Mencius, lies with "despotic rulers and corrupt officials" (3A.3). He goes so far as to claim that if people die of starvation under a particular ruler, then that ruler has not only failed in his obligations as ruler but has also behaved no differently than if he had killed them (1A.3; see also 1A.4).

Conclusion

In this chapter I have argued that there is no incompatibility between Confucianism and the notion of human rights. In the Confucian ideal society there is no need for human rights, and they are not necessary for human dignity or constitutive of human virtues. In nonideal situations, where virtuous relationships break down and mediation fails to reconcile conflict, human rights can serve as a fallback apparatus for the protection of fundamental individual interests. But human rights should not be exalted to eclipse other moral vocabularies such as duty and virtue, or exercised without regard for the interests of other people. To avoid the rise of rights talk, Confucians prefer to restrict rights to civil and political rights—not because social and economic needs are less important but because civil and political interests are more easily protected by litigation. The promotion of economic rights, on the other hand, requires sound economic institutions and policies that cannot easily be ensured through the

---

Bruun, vol. 6 in Nordic Institute of Asian Studies: Democracy in Asia Series (Surrey: Curzon Press, 2000). In chapter 6 I discuss the basis and limits of liberties related to cultural and moral issues.

legal language of human rights. In addition, there are three reasons for giving civil and political rights priority over social and economic rights in a Confucian-inspired society. First, the adoption of civil and political rights redresses a strong tendency within Confucianism to overempower political leaders. Second, there are rich conceptual and ethical resources in a Confucian-inspired society to protect and promote people's material needs and social relationships (i.e., the concerns of social and economic rights). Third, similarly to contemporary thinkers, early Confucian thinkers such as Mencius recognized that the chief causes of severe poverty and famine are political corruption and despotism, which require sound political solutions. Today, political corruption and despotism are prevented by a robust set of civil and political rights and legal apparatus that protect not only people's physical security and freedom but also their fundamental material needs and interests.

CHAPTER 6

Individual Autonomy and Civil Liberties

Individual Autonomy: Moral and Personal

May Fourth intellectual Chen Duxiu argued that Confucian ethics is incompatible with modernity. Modern life, he said, is based on recognition of the individual, or the independence of individual personality and property. The spheres of modern society—the family, economy, and politics—are organized by the principle of respect for individual autonomy, whereas Confucianism preaches the opposite: the son is not independent of the father, the wife is submissive to the husband, and the people are subjects to the rulers.[1] But is it true that Confucianism does not recognize individual autonomy? Some contemporary Chinese scholars have argued that although Confucianism may not incorporate the liberal notion of individual autonomy, it nevertheless contains a concept of moral autonomy that can support civil liberties.[2] This argument is important. If sound, it can be useful in revising the dark and pessimistic picture of Confucianism painted by the May Fourth thinkers. In this chapter I seek to critically examine the Confucian conception of moral autonomy and explore its implications regarding civil liberties.

The concept of moral autonomy is, unfortunately, vague and ambiguous, and many of the arguments that make use of it do not help remove its vagueness or ambiguity. The question of whether Confucian ethics has a conception of moral autonomy often invites two replies. The first argues that as the term "moral autonomy" was coined and popularized by Kant, it should also be de-

---

1   See Chen Duxiu 陳獨秀, *De sai er xian sheng yu she hui zhu yi: Chen Duxiu wen xuan* 德賽二先生與社會主義：陳獨秀文選 [Mr. Democracy and Mr. Science and Socialism: Selected Writings of Chen Duxiu], ed. Wu Xiaoming 吳曉明 (Shanghai: Shanghai Yuandong 上海遠東, 1994), esp. "Dong xi min zu gen ben si xiang de cha yi" 東西民族根本思想的差異 [Fundamental Differences in Thinking between East and West], 25–29, and "Kongzi zhi dao yu xian dai sheng huo" 孔子之道與現代生活 [The Way of Confucius and Modern Life], 56–62. For an analysis of Chen Duxiu's view, see Lin Yü-sheng, *The Crisis of Chinese Consciousness: Radical Antitraditionalism in the May Fourth Era* (Madison: University of Wisconsin Press, 1979), esp. chap. 4.

2   This line of argument can be found in the works of Mou Zongsan 牟宗三 [Mou Tsung-san] and Tang Junyi 唐君毅 [Tang Chun-i]. See also Lin Yü-sheng, "The Evolution of the Pre-Confucian Meaning of *Jen* 仁 and the Confucian Concept of Moral Autonomy," *Monumenta Serica: Journal of Oriental Studies* 31 (1974–75): 172–204; and his "Reflections on the 'Creative Transformation of Chinese Tradition'" in *Chinese Thought in a Global Context: A Dialogue between Chinese and Western Philosophical Approaches*, ed. Karl-Heinz Pohl (Leiden: Brill, 1999), 73–114, which appeals to the Confucian concept of moral autonomy in arguing that Confucianism can accept human rights.

fined in his terms. Therefore, as Kant rejects anything other than one's practical reason as the source of morality, and as Confucian ethics views morality as grounded in human nature and Heaven, Confucianism cannot contain a concept of moral autonomy. The second reply argues the opposite extreme, namely, that as conceptions of moral autonomy range from the very minimal—for example, that moral autonomy requires only the agent's voluntary endorsement of morality—to the more demanding—that morality is a free creation of the individual's will—the spectrum is broad enough to encompass any Confucian conception of moral autonomy, however narrow.

Both replies are problematic in that they direct our attention away from substantive issues to terminological ones. A more fruitful strategy, I believe, is to ask whether the elements commonly found in conceptions of moral autonomy can also be found in Confucian ethics, without necessarily concluding that those elements present in Confucian ethics amount to a *genuine* conception of moral autonomy. To what extent can those elements found in Confucian ethics support civil liberties? This is a substantive question. Although for the sake of convenience I shall use the phrase "a Confucian conception of moral autonomy" rather than "the elements in Confucian ethics that are present in other common conceptions of moral autonomy," I do not intend to settle the terminological dispute. Rather, I shall discuss some aspects of moral autonomy that are commonly found in different conceptions and examine whether they are present in Confucian ethics.

Individuals are autonomous if they are in some sense master of their own lives. Individuals are *morally* autonomous if they are in some sense master of their *moral* lives. In the next section I suggest that for an individual to be master of his or her own moral life, the individual must be in control of one or more of the following elements:

- the voluntary endorsement of morality
- a reflective engagement in moral life
- the recognition of morality as self-legislation
- the recognition of morality as radical free expression of the individual's will

In the third section I try to show that the first two elements—voluntary endorsement and reflective engagement—are present in Confucian ethics, while the last two—self-legislation and radical free expression of the individual's will—are not only foreign to Confucian ethics but also incompatible with it. The first two elements together form what I shall call, for brevity's sake, the Confucian conception of moral autonomy. In the fourth section I argue that although this is a minimal conception, it does support civil liberties to a certain degree and to a certain point. Confucian moral autonomy does not support an oppressive moral community, but it also does not support a liberal-open society. In the fifth and sixth sections I argue that to supply a stronger case for civil liberties, we need to incorporate a modern conception of individual autonomy as personal autonomy. "Personal autonomy" has often been confused with "moral autonomy," but these two capture different concerns and carry different implications. It is the former notion that more strongly supports liberties. I argue that personal autonomy should be understood not as a right but as a value, and that the acceptance of this value would strengthen the contemporary appeal of Confucianism as an ethical and political theory. Such an inclusion need not imply the abandonment of Confucian ethics but can be seen as an internal revision in response to new social circumstances.

Before examining the various elements of moral autonomy, it should be noted that it is not my aim to offer a comprehensive examination of civil liberties and Confucianism but to look at this question from the angle of the Confucian conception of moral autonomy and determine the usefulness of this idea in justifying civil liberties. Certainly there are other elements or reasons in Confucian ethics that also have bearing on civil liberties, but I will refer only to those that have direct connection with the argument of moral autonomy, especially those that set limits to this argument. In addition, I do not intend to cover all the liberties mentioned in the standard national and international charters of human rights.[3] Rather, I will focus mainly on freedom of expression and, more generally, freedom of action and confine my examination to two areas: the extent to which these freedoms should be restricted by law for the sake of promoting morality or punishing immorality; and whether Confucian moral autonomy provides resources to support these freedoms.

Elements of Moral Autonomy

Voluntary Endorsement

The first element of autonomy, voluntary endorsement of morality, captures the most minimal meaning of the concept of moral autonomy but is not a sufficient account of the concept. This element is best understood in the negative sense: moral agents cannot lead a moral life if they are coerced into it. Such a life not only lacks autonomy but is not a moral life at all. Why is this so? The answer has to do with the nature of moral life. A life is not genuinely moral if agents do not endorse the moral life they lead or are not driven by morality. Those who comply with moral commands through fear of punishment are acting involuntarily: they are not motivated by morality and therefore do not lead a moral life. Similarly, those who comply solely for their own benefit do not lead a moral life. Leading a moral life means not only behaving appropriately outwardly but also acting with proper motivation and with a genuine appreciation of the intrinsic demands of morality. A moral life must stem from internal personal motivation, that is, the precondition of a moral life is the voluntary endorsement of

---

3 Civil and political liberties were discussed in the previous chapter.

morality. A morally autonomous life must include, among other things, the agent's voluntary endorsement of the demands of morality. Most ethical theories converge at this point.[4]

I do not mean to imply that morality becomes true or valid simply because of an individual's voluntary endorsement. To say this would be to see morality as self-legislation, a view that claims more than voluntary endorsement and will be analyzed shortly. Endorsement here is compatible with the realist metaethical view that a morality is true whether or not one endorses it. Endorsement is a precondition of moral life, not moral truths.

Reflective Engagement

Voluntary endorsement is not necessarily reflective or deliberative and can be compatible with unreflective habituation. According to some accounts, moral autonomy requires more than voluntary endorsement. To be morally autonomous, an individual must lead his or her moral life according to his or her own understanding of what morality requires. A moral understanding is an individual's own if it is developed through reflective engagement, which consists of personal reflection, deliberation, and judgment. A person who is brainwashed to believe in a certain morality or who unreflectively follows social conventions does not lead a morally autonomously life. Viewed in this way, an individual has moral autonomy only if his or her moral acts can ultimately be traced back to, and supported by, reflective engagement.

It is important to emphasize that, like voluntary endorsement, reflective engagement need not be the source of moral truths. Reflective engagement is fully compatible with a realist account of morality. Why, then, is reflective engagement important to a moral agent if the standard of morality can be independent of his or her own personal view? The answer is twofold: first, it is an individual's reflective engagement that makes his or her moral life, values, and acts genuinely his or her own, and that makes him or her morally autonomous; second, although it is true that an individual can lead a moral life without reflection, such an unreflective moral life would probably not be successful. Human morality, as we understand it, is a complex matter. There is always the possibility of error or failure—for example, individuals who do not fully understand morality, make inappropriate moral decisions, or fail to live up to the demands of morality.[5] Many ethical theories claim that a successful moral life requires intelligent ethical understanding and a virtuous disposition, both of which have to

---

4 A clear statement of this can be found in Aristotle, *Nicomachean Ethics*, 1110a–1111b.

5. This is especially true if morality is objective and hence admits of understanding that is true or false. But even if morality is not objectively valid and is, as a Humean would say, a projection of human feelings, there might still be room for rational reflection and hence a possibility of error. For example, Simon Blackburn claims that an individual's reflection on his or her feelings and desires, which is the basis of morality, can admit of rational scrutiny, and that it is therefore possible for an individual to make improper (i.e., irrational or subrational) moral judgments. See Simon Black-

be developed through learning, habituation, and reflection. Of course, the existence of a moral expert or sage who can advise us in our behavior would ease the need for reflection—but moral sages are rarely present, and their teachings rarely cover all possible moral situations. In addition, if the teachings of a moral sage are not transparently clear and have no clear immediate implications, they require intelligent interpretation and understanding, which in turn require intelligent reflection.

We are now in a position to understand why reflective engagement can be seen as an element of moral autonomy. Personal reflective engagement can be carried out only by each individual. This truism nonetheless has an interesting implication. The very activity of moral reflection that an individual engages in necessarily creates a certain moral space between this individual and others. The moral judgment proceeding from his or her reflection and endorsed by him or her may come into conflict with the judgments of other people. The individual may believe that a social convention is morally wrong despite it being generally accepted by society. He or she may adhere to a personal understanding of morality or even challenge the moral understanding of others. From here we may begin to talk about an individual's moral integrity and conscience and move on to stories about how a lone fighter mounts a moral challenge to political authority. Although the reflective engagement of individuals does not function as the justificatory basis of the morality they accept, it nonetheless leaves a mark on the morality lived in their lives. The moral life the agents reflectively endorse and live is properly their own, and has their own stamp on it.

Self-Legislation

Self-legislation requires more than reflective engagement, which is compatible with morality grounded not just in one's own reflection but also in nature, human nature, God, and so on. An individual can still be morally autonomous provided that he or she also reflectively endorses and engages in a morality whose validity is grounded elsewhere.[6] Here the function of reflection is to discover, to know, and to endorse the true morality. The account of morality as self-legislation, however, requires more independence. One well-known example of this account is Kant's conception of moral autonomy. Kant gives a highly special view on what counts as a proper reason for, or grounding of, morality. For Kant, moral law is independent not only of society's conventions or traditions but also of anything external to one's own rationality, including, for instance, nature and human desires—these are sources of heteronomy, not

---

burn, "Evaluations, Projections, and Quasi-Realism," chap. 6 in *Spreading the Word: Groundings in the Philosophy of Language* (Oxford: Oxford University Press, 1984).

6   For some theories, objective morality does not undermine one's autonomy or freedom but serves as the basis of it. Autonomy or freedom *in spite of* morality is license, as Locke famously suggests.

autonomy. It is reason, inherent in one's humanity alone, that gives rise to moral law. Reason does not discover or endorse moral principles derived from elsewhere, it performs the function of legislation—it originates and validates the moral law. Individuals are subject to no authority other than their self-made law based on reason. According to Kant, even obedience to a moral law justified on the basis of human desires and emotions involves the surrender of individual autonomy.

Radical Free Expression of the Individual's Will

If Kant's conception of moral autonomy as self-legislation is rationalist, then this last element conveys an expressivist conception of self-legislation. Truly autonomous agents obey no law other than their own. Although Kant's view of self-legislation apparently adheres to this notion of self-made law, in reality the law is to be made by an abstract self devoid of any particularistic features of a concrete individual. It is not an expression of individuality as such, but of abstract universal reason to which all human beings should submit. In the expressivist view, however, self-legislation is understood as a thoroughly subjective process unconstrained by any factors other than one's own reflection based on one's desires, ambition, and personal circumstances. Morality and moral choices are made by one's self—the existentialist and not the rationalist self, for the latter does not truly represent the individual. Morality and moral choices are therefore necessarily subjective.[7]

Moral Autonomy in Confucian Ethics

Having briefly sketched the elements commonly found in conceptions of moral autonomy, I shall now examine whether any of these elements are present in Confucian ethics. I shall argue that the first two elements, voluntary endorsement and reflective engagement, exist within Confucian ethics, while the last two, self-legislation and radical free expression of the individual's will, are incompatible with it.

Voluntary Endorsement

Voluntary endorsement is a precondition for a moral life. This point is perhaps so obvious that it is often assumed, rather than explicitly argued for, in

---

7   For discussions of the contrast of these two views in moral philosophy, see Raymond Geuss, "Morality and Identity," chap. 6 in Christine M. Korsgaard et al., *The Sources of Normativity*, ed. Onora O'Neill (Cambridge: Cambridge University Press, 1996), 192–93; also especially see Lewis Hinchman, "Autonomy, Individuality, and Self-Determination," in *What Is Enlightenment? Eighteenth-Century Answers and Twentieth-Century Questions*, ed. James Schmidt (Berkeley: University of California Press, 1996), 488–516.

Confucian ethics. Indeed, if this first element of moral autonomy were not deemed to be true, the second element, reflective engagement, would not make any sense. Also, classical Confucians are known to appeal to the idea of voluntary endorsement in other matters of high importance, for example, emphasizing repeatedly that it is desirable for people to voluntarily endorse, and submit themselves to, political authority, and for tribal people to voluntarily submit to the people of higher cultures in the central region of China. Thus, in the absence of an argument that says otherwise, it would be implausible to think that Confucians would not accept the idea of voluntary endorsement of morality.

Nevertheless, there is a more direct way to show that Confucian ethics accepts voluntary endorsement. As I have discussed, for agents to lead moral lives they must be motivated by morality itself rather than coerced. Confucians repeatedly ask us to endorse and embrace morality for its own sake. Throughout *The Analects*, Confucius is reported to be saying that we must desire and be fond of ren, be at peace with ren, and see ren as the most important thing in our lives (*Analects* 4.2, 4.6, 15.9). In addition, Mencius's famous example of the child on the verge of falling into a well (*Mencius* 2A.6) also demonstrates that he understands that acting virtuously is tantamount to acting morally—namely, that preventing a child from suffering constitutes the right reason and proper moral motivation, whereas acting to enhance one's own reputation does not.[8] Xunzi also recognizes that, while the innate nature of human beings does not necessarily motivate them to behave in a morally correct way,[9] there are moral agents such as sages and gentlemen (jun zi) who desire morality and virtues for their own sake and take delight in acting morally (*Xunzi* 2.5, 2.14).

Furthermore, the importance of acting for morality's sake and being properly motivated by morality can be vividly seen in Confucius's negative remark about what he calls "the village worthy" (*xiang yuan*) (*Analects* 17.13). As explained and elaborated by Mencius, the village worthy lack character and real virtues. They follow no moral principle of their own, only the popular trend. They appear to be virtuous but are not really acting for morality's sake. They are just trying "cringingly to please the world" (*Mencius* 7B.37). Confucius says that the village worthy are "the ruin of virtue." Confucius's condemnation of this character type shows that he understands that a moral life has to be led from the inside, by an agent who is voluntarily motivated by morality.[10] As will be seen

8 For an illuminating discussion on this point, see David B. Wong, "Is There a Distinction between Reason and Emotion in *Mencius*?" *Philosophy East and West* 41, no. 1 (1991): 31–44.

9 Xunzi's view on the connection between human nature and moral motivation raises many interpretative and philosophical difficulties. See David B. Wong, "Xunzi on Moral Motivation," chap. 10 in *Chinese Language, Thought, and Culture: Nivison and His Critics*, ed. Philip J. Ivanhoe (Chicago: Open Court, 1996).

10 I thank Lee H. Yearley for drawing my attention to the discussion of the village worthy in *Mencius*. See his illuminating analysis of Mencius's view in "Mencius: Virtues, Their Semblances, and the Role of Intelligent Awareness," in *Mencius and Aquinas: Theories of Virtue and Conceptions*

later, this and other character types mentioned in *Mencius* also have interesting implications with regard to reflective endorsement and civil liberties.

At this point we are in a position to counteract a possible objection to the claim that Confucianism must accept voluntary endorsement of morality. For Confucians, the objection goes, a person can lead a moral life simply by doing the right thing, which does not necessarily require appropriate motivation or correct appreciation of the right reason for action. This is because the moral character of the act is in the nature of the act, not the intentional state of the agent. This objection confuses a moral *act* with a moral *life*. We may grant that an act can be morally right whether it is performed with a proper moral motivation or not. Saving the falling child is the right thing to do, even if an individual does it for the sake of his or her reputation. However, this act does not constitute a moral life or make the individual virtuous. On the contrary, acting without proper motivation shows precisely that an individual lacks virtue. The examples discussed above show that Confucians emphasize the moral motivation of people because for them what is morally significant is the cultivation of moral lives and virtues as a whole, and not merely the performance of right acts. As far as moral lives are concerned, a proper appreciation and endorsement of the demands of morality is absolutely essential. Nevertheless, some might contend that as classical Confucians expect only sages and gentlemen to lead truly moral lives, not the common people, the requirement of voluntary submission is restricted to a small group of people. I shall discuss this objection toward the end of this section.

Reflective Engagement

It is sometimes argued that Confucian thought lacks a distinction between morality and social convention, and that therefore the possibility of individuals being morally autonomous relative to social conventions cannot arise.[11] Since morality is convention, the argument continues, there is little need for moral reflection. Convention is by nature public, and all one needs to do is to follow public norms. This is far from the truth. Although Confucius inherits much of the content of his ethics from the social conventions (rites) of the Zhou dynasty, he does not regard his ethics as being based on convention alone. Confucius does not view rites as external rules that constrain people's behavior and distribute powers and duties, but as a necessary part of the conception of an ideal moral person—the man of ren. Rites are based on a deeper ethical foundation, ren, which is a human quality, an expression of humanity. Ren can be mani-

---

of Courage, SUNY Series: Toward a Comparative Philosophy of Religions (Albany: State University of New York Press, 1990), 67–72.

11   See Chad Hansen, "Punishment and Dignity in China," in *Individualism and Holism: Studies in Confucian and Taoist Values*, ed. Donald J. Munro, vol. 52 of Michigan Monographs in Chinese Studies (Ann Arbor: Center for Chinese Studies, University of Michigan, 1985), 361–63.

fested in different virtues, from personal reflection and examination of one's life to respect, concern, and care for others.

These attitudes and qualities of self-examination, empathetic understanding and caring for others are essential to the spirit and vitality of rites. At the same time, these attitudes and qualities create the possibility of a difference between rites that are lived in the spirit of ren and those that are devoid of it, and conflicts can arise between ren and those rites that fail to express or promote it. Confucius says, "What can a man who is not benevolent do with the rites? What can a man who is not benevolent do with music?" (*Analects* 3.3). Confucius does not dogmatically believe that rites should never change. Although the essence of filial piety or respect for a superior is unchanging, ways of expressing this norm may change. For instance, the essence of filial piety consists in caring for, supporting, and respecting one's parents, but the concrete ways of expressing care and respect may change. Confucius protests, for example, against the extravagant burial practices of his age. Furthermore, he suggests that some rites may seem inappropriate when judged with a deeper ethical perspective or lose their attractiveness in new circumstances.

> The Master said, "A ceremonial cap of linen is what is prescribed by the rites. Today black silk is used instead. This is more frugal and I follow the majority. To prostrate oneself before ascending the steps is what is prescribed by the rites. Today one does so after having ascended them. This is casual and, though going against the majority, I follow the practice of doing so before ascending." (9.3)

> The Master said, "Follow the calendar of the Xia, ride in the carriage of the Yin, and wear the ceremonial cap of the Zhou, but, as for music, adopt the *shao* [music of Emperor Shun] and the *wu* [music of King Wu]." (15.11)

These passages suggest two things about the Confucian attitude toward rites. First, one should not blindly follow rites as endorsed by society or the majority—one should adopt a reflective moral attitude and examine the ethical reason behind a rite to determine whether that rite is appropriate. Second, rites can and should change if the circumstances change. Confucius himself emphasizes that we should learn and select appropriate rites developed in different periods and places. This is, therefore, one reason for the importance of reflective endorsement.

Of course, for classical Confucians some rites are fundamental and should never change. But even these rites should be reflected on rather than followed blindly—and this is the second reason for the importance of reflection. Human life-situations are varied and complex. Rites as norms of conduct are often too general to give precise guidance on how to make concrete moral decisions in particular circumstances. Situations arise that are unique and without precedent, as well as borderline and complex—in which certain rites conflict with others—and these call for reflective judgment and moral discretion. Because of this, Confucians often emphasize moral discretion (*quan*),[12] flexibility (*wu gu*),[13] and timeliness (*shi*),[14] particularly with regard to circumstances in which moral decisions must be made.[15] Moral discretion, flexibility, and timeliness are important qualities that a gentleman ought to develop (*Analects* 9.4, 18.8), and Mencius praises Confucius for being timely in action rather than stubborn and inflexible (*Mencius* 5B.1). Similarly, Xunzi thinks that to strike at the mean in each particular context is not easy, and that individuals must therefore carefully weigh and deliberate the relative merits of different courses of action before making a decision, and try not to be one-sided or prejudiced (*Xunzi* 3.13).

If one has reached the highest point of moral development, one does not need much reflection to know what to do and how to behave correctly. At this point, moral action simply flows naturally from an established virtuous disposition, without difficulty or hesitation. But to reach that stage, one needs a high level of moral training, including learning, reflection, and habituation,[16] and this is the third reason for the importance of reflection. While the three Confucian masters have different views on moral psychology and development, they all emphasize the importance of moral understanding and reflection along with the transforming power of rituals. Confucius and Xunzi hold that an individual develops moral understanding through reflective learning and studying.[17] The conception of moral learning expounded in *The Analects* is one that emphasizes thinking, reflection, imagination, and dynamic deliberation.[18] Xunzi, like Confucius, emphasizes a kind of learning that requires much careful studying, pondering, searching analysis, and understanding.[19] He also clearly thinks that associating with a teacher is more effective than learning from books alone, because the teacher can enhance and illuminate a student's understanding.

---

12   *Analects* 9.30.

13   Ibid., 9.4.

14   *Mencius* 5B.1.

15   For a good discussion on this point, see A. S. Cua, *Moral Vision and Tradition: Essays in Chinese Ethics*, vol. 31 of Studies in Philosophy and the History of Philosophy (Washington, DC: Catholic University of America Press, 1998), 257.

16   The clearest statement on this point is in *The Doctrine of the Mean*, bk. 20.

17   On Confucius's view on this point, see the succinct analysis of William Theodore de Bary, *The Trouble with Confucianism* (Cambridge: Harvard University Press, 1991), 35–37, 83.

18   For example, "If one learns from others but does not think, one will be bewildered. If, on the other hand, one thinks but does not learn from others, one will be imperiled" (*Analects* 2.15); "Learn widely and be steadfast in your purpose, inquire earnestly and reflect on what is at hand, and there is no need for you to look for benevolence elsewhere" (19.6); "When I have pointed out one corner of a square to anyone and he does not come back with the other three, I will not point it out to him a second time" (7.8); "Do I possess knowledge? No, I do not. A rustic put a question to me and my mind was a complete blank. I kept hammering at the two sides of the question until I got everything out of it" (9.8).

19   "The gentleman, knowing well that learning that is incomplete and impure does not deserve to be called fine, recites and enumerates his studies that he will be familiar with them, ponders over them and searches into them that he will fully penetrate their meaning" (*Xunzi* 1.14).

In learning, no method is of more advantage than to be near a man of learning. *The Book of Rites* and *The Classic of Music* present models but do not offer explanation; *The Book of Poetry* and *The Book of History* present matters of antiquity but are not always apposite; *The Spring and Autumn Annals* are laconic, and their import is not quickly grasped. It is just on these occasions that the man of learning repeats the explanations of the gentleman. Thus, he is honored for his comprehensive and catholic acquaintance with the affairs of the world. Therefore it is said: "In learning, no method is of more advantage than to be near a man of learning.[20]

Among the three early Confucian masters, Mencius puts the least emphasis on the role of learning as part of an individual's moral development. This lack of emphasis has to do with his view that people have a basic ethical instinct to act morally, and that moral development is more like the natural growth of a plant than the process of an artifact being crafted. However, even the growth of a natural entity needs nourishing conditions, and Mencius believes that to be able to live a moral life, an individual must exercise certain cognitive abilities, or the abilities of the mind, to develop his or her moral understanding and motivation and make proper judgments.[21] These abilities of the mind include the ability to attend (*si*)[22] to objects and one's feelings toward them, the ability to extend (*tui*)[23] what is attended to other situations, and the ability to weigh circumstances (quan).[24]

The Importance of the Will

Reflective endorsement and engagement create a moral space between the agent who does the reflecting and others. It is possible that others may not share an agent's beliefs about what he or she regards as morally right. It is also possible that the agent may find other people's ways of doing things wrong. In this case, Confucians tell agents to stand firm on the moral position that they reflectively endorse—namely, to act on their independent will. Confucius says, "The three armies may be robbed of their supreme commander, but a common man cannot be robbed of his will [*zhi*]" (*Analects* 9.26).[25] Mencius says

---

20 *Xunzi* 1.10.

21 For discussions on Mencius's views on moral thinking and development, see Philip J. Ivanhoe, "Thinking and Learning in Early Confucianism," *Journal of Chinese Philosophy* 17, no. 4 (1990): 473–93; Kwong-loi Shun, "Self-Reflection and Self-Cultivation," chap. 5, sec. 2, in *Mencius and Early Chinese Thought* (Stanford: Stanford University Press, 1997), 149–53; Wong, "Reason and Emotion in Mencius"; Yearley, "Mencius: True Virtue as a Product of Ethical Reasoning's Use of Extension, Attention, and the Understanding of Resemblances," in *Mencius and Aquinas*, 62–67.

22 *Mencius* 6A.6, 13, 15.

23 Ibid., 1A.7.

24 *Mencius* 1A.7, 4A.17, 7A.26.

25 Huang's translation. D. C. Lau translated *zhi* as "purpose". Stephen Angle is of the view that *zhi* should be translated as "commitment" rather than "will." See his *Sagehood*, 114–15. While the

that the great man remains true to his will and principles even if his cause is not shared by others or if he is in unfavorable circumstances. "He cannot be led into excesses when wealthy and honored or deflected from his will when poor and obscure, nor can he be made to bow before superior force. This is what I would call a great man" (*Mencius* 3B.2). Xunzi, as well, writes, "The exigencies of time and place and considerations of personal profit cannot influence the gentleman, cliques and coteries cannot sway him, and the whole world cannot deter him. . . . Truly this can be called 'being resolute from inner power'" (*Xunzi* 1.14).

The idea of a great man (or woman) having an independent will and remaining true to it against all odds presupposes the belief that one should act on one's own best understanding of morality. A great man is one who forms an independent moral will and takes control of his own moral life. In moral life, he follows nothing but the moral principles that he reflectively endorses and the moral will that he develops. In this sense he is morally autonomous.

The will of a morally autonomous person can be expressed or asserted externally and internally.[26] Externally it creates for individuals a moral space of independence in society—individuals are morally independent of political establishment and social opinions, and their moral will can be asserted antagonistically against them. There is no shortage of remarks and stories in Confucianism about moral heroes who defy what they regard as immoral political authority.[27] Even parental authority, if exercised in an immoral way, should be respectfully disobeyed.[28] Internally the will can be asserted toward oneself positively—in uplifting one's motivation of self-cultivation—or negatively—in bringing forth a sense of shame (*chi*) when failing to live up to one's will. For Confucians, shame is an important moral phenomenon (*Mencius* 7A.6).[29] If individuals feel ashamed of their behavior, this suggests that they at least still have a motivation to live up to what they reflectively endorse, and that the problem is one of weakness of will, which is remediable. Lack of shame, on the other hand, is a sign of complete moral failure. Individuals without a sense of shame have no motivation to act morally. Even if such individuals are made to behave according to moral law, they do not act from a moral standpoint; they do not see the intrinsic importance of leading a moral life.

---

use of "commitment" instead of "will" will not affect much of the substance of my argument here, I think "will" can better help me articulate the points I make below.

26   For an illuminating analysis, see Zhou Jizhi 周繼旨, *Lun Zhongguo gu dai she hui yu chuan tong zhe xue* 論中國古代社會與傳統哲學 [On Traditional Chinese Society and Philosophy] (Beijing: People's Publishing, 1994), 260–79.

27   See de Bary, "Autocracy and the Prophetic Message in Orthodox Neo-Confucianism," chap. 4 in *Trouble with Confucianism*.

28   See *Xunzi* 29, and "Filial Piety in Relation to Reproof and Remonstrance" 諫諍, chap. 15 in *The Book of Filial Piety* 孝經 [*Xiao jing*].

29   For a subtle philosophical analysis of shame in Mencius, see Bryan W. Van Norden, "The Virtue of Righteousness in Mencius," chap. 7 in Shun and Wong, *Confucian Ethics*.

Willing, Not Free Choosing

It is important to note that for Confucians, the moral will is not the free ex-pression of an individual's arbitrary will, but rather the expression of a deter-mination to will what is demanded by the kind of morality the individual re-flectively endorses. Thus Mencius says that the business of a gentleman is to will ren and yi (*Mencius* 7A.33). Individuals do not choose the content of their moral will. It is an independent substance that judges all individuals. Confu-cian ethics cannot accept the third and fourth elements of moral autonomy. It cannot accept the Kantian conception of morality as self-legislation since, in the Confucian view, morality is not legislated by reason but grounded in human nature or Heaven, which are two parts of the same whole. According to some interpretations, Kant's notion of reason as universalizable is a procedur-alist account of moral realism as opposed to various substantive accounts of moral realism, one instance of which, I believe, is the Confucian view of mo-rality.[30] With this distinction we may say that no substantive realist account of morality satisfies the requirement of moral autonomy as understood by the Kantian perspective. (Although some may think that Xunzi gives a rationalist-constructivist account of morality, as opposed to the Mencian naturalistic one, it is still far from the Kantian notion of self-legislation by impartial procedur-alist reason.)

Similarly, Confucian ethics cannot accept the expressivist view that morality is the radical free expression of the individual's will. This view emphasizes free choice and individuality as the true sources of morality, and these are lacking in Confucian ethics. More important, Confucian ethics does not accept that mo-rality is reducible to what individuals would choose given their desires and preferences. Does this imply that the Confucian ethical view of moral life is defective because it does not take free choice as the grounds of morality? This question raises further questions about the role of choice in moral life that go far beyond the scope of this chapter. Nevertheless, I would like to venture a brief, tentative defense of the Confucian view.

We may use our experience of choosing in ordinary life to understand by analogy the phenomenon of fundamental moral choice. When we go into a supermarket, we make many choices. Facing a variety of fruit brands, we rank our options in terms of cost, quality, and other factors. We then select the item that best satisfies our preferences. But very little of this happens in fundamental "moral choices," where we have an experience of willing that involves thinking, understanding, and willfully embracing, rather than picking or selecting. Meir Dan-Cohen puts this point well:

> On [Kant's] view our moral experience does not consist in scanning a more or less arbitrarily delimited range of acceptable moral options and then pick-ing out the most attractive member in the set. When we are in the grip of

---

30 See Korsgaard, *Sources of Normativity*, 36.

moral truth we are moved by its intrinsic value, rather than by its comparative advantage over other acceptable alternatives. Moral choice consists, according to Kant, in my embracing a particular maxim and a course of action
that falls under it. So long as I wilfully embrace the correct maxim I behave
both freely and rationally.[31]

If this account more or less captures our deep moral experience, then what is
essential in making fundamental moral choices is more a matter of "willing"
than "choosing." The Confucian conception of moral autonomy is closer to a
will-conception of autonomy than a *choice*-conception, which also better captures what happens in our fundamental moral choices. Of course, this is not to
suggest that Confucian ethics recognizes no room for moral choice-making.
Confucius himself suggests that in some circumstances it is up to a gentleman
to choose whether to stay in government or to step down when the Way does
not prevail in politics; in either case, the gentleman's choice should be respected
(*Analects* 15.7).[32] In this instance, his choice does play an important role in explaining and justifying his act. Since staying in or leaving politics are both permissible, the fact that the gentleman decides on one way rather than another
has to be explained and justified by his own choice among other things. His
choice is one factor that confers authority on his act. But when we reflect on our
fundamental moral experience—when we ask ourselves whether we should act
in accordance with ren or act as a filial son—it is not that we are to choose between permissible options with different degrees of attractiveness. It is rather
that ren and filial piety both appear to us as necessary, inescapable moral truths
that we ought to grasp and willfully embrace. Some people might insist that this
kind of moral experience can still be described as a matter of "choosing." But
the crucial point is not one of terminology but of moral significance. Unlike the
genuine choice about remaining in politics, this so-called choosing neither
confers moral authority on one's act nor explains one's real motivation. Instead,
from the moral agent's own point of view, it is a matter of moral necessity to act
in accordance with ren.

   Donald Munro has argued that while Confucians have not questioned the
possibility of the individual's independence of will, "*choice-making*, or *willing*,
has not often been at the center of ethical concern. . . . The central problem in
self-cultivation [for Confucians] is not the proper exercise of free choice, as is
hypothesized in so much of Western ethics."[33] Munro does not differentiate between choosing and willing. That choice-making in its popular sense in the West

31   Meir Dan-Cohen, "Conceptions of Choice and Conceptions of Autonomy," *Ethics* 102, no.
2 (1992): 226–27.
32   For a further discussion of the issue of choice in *The Analects*, see Teemu H. Ruskola,
"Moral Choice in the *Analects*: A Way without a Crossroads?" *Journal of Chinese Philosophy* 19, no.
3 (1992): 285–96.
33   See his introduction to *Individualism and Holism*, 12–13. Italics added.

is not central in Confucianism is indeed true.[34] But the same cannot be said for willing. As argued above, Confucianism does put a great deal of emphasis on the importance of willing. The will-conception of moral autonomy seems to capture better the phenomenon of moral choice than the choice-conception.

Before examining the implications of the Confucian conception of moral autonomy, it is necessary to consider one potential challenge to the argument thus far, namely, that although my reconstruction of the Confucian conception may be correct as a description of the moral elite—a minority consisting of gentlemen and sages—the majority of people fall far short of this ideal; and that any implications Confucian moral autonomy has with regard to civil liberties therefore apply only to the moral elite.

This challenge has certain force. Neither Confucius nor Xunzi is optimistic about the ability of the common people to understand the Way and the reasons behind it. However, they do not think the common people need this ability. Society and politics can flourish so long as the moral elite is in power to enforce the Way through rectification of names, education, and legislation (*Xunzi* 22.3e, *Analects* 8.9). Mencius recognizes a greater role of the common people in legitimizing and strengthening political rule than Confucius and Xunzi, and he also seems more optimistic about the people's potential for self-cultivation. But he shares the classical Confucian view that it is sages and gentlemen who can best grasp the Way and who have the capacity, hence responsibility, to put it in practice.

I therefore agree that in classical Confucianism, moral autonomy has significance mainly for moral and political leaders. But my aim is to reconstruct Confucianism for a contemporary purpose, and I think that there are a number of reasons why a contemporary version should at least partially reject the moral elitism of the classical period. For example, the contemporary Confucian perspective retains the classical view that human beings are born equal in their capacity to become moral and that ideally people should receive education that equips them with learning and self-cultivation skills. This egalitarian principle clearly supports equal opportunities of education and office in society. Also, as de Bary observes, classical thinkers link moral education to the task of training political leaders for society, and thus the kind of learning for the gentleman becomes demanding and difficult for ordinary people to attain.[35] De Bary writes, "In [Confucius's] day it is a simple fact that most people do not have the means or the leisure to pursue learning, and especially learning of a kind indispensable to the gentleman as a social and political leader."[36] The learning pre-

---

34 Many scholars have argued this claim. See, for example, Herbert Fingarette, *Confucius: The Secular as Sacred* (New York: Harper and Row, 1972); and Peerenboom, "Confucian Harmony," 245. However, they did not consider the possibility of taking "willing" as an alternative conception of moral choice.

35 de Bary, *Trouble with Confucianism*, 37–39.

36 Ibid., 37–38.

scribed by Confucians for political governance is indeed demanding. It includes detailed and persistent study of the laws, institutions, and rites of the present and the past, and of the writings and deeds of previous Sage Kings and scholars, and in modern terminology it is nothing less than the art and science of government. Today the Confucian conception of moral life, and the reflective abilities required by it, should not be closely linked to this highly specialized, demanding task of political governance attributed to the gentleman. Moral life and moral autonomy should be applicable to everyone and should be lived out in the contexts of the family, workplace, and community. With increased opportunities for education and social mobility, and with the disconnection of moral education and the special task of political governance, the gap between the moral elite and the common people should be considerably narrowed in a modern reconstructed version of Confucian ethics. The discussion in the next section concerning the moral and political implications of Confucian moral autonomy assumes this more egalitarian perspective.

Limited Toleration of Unethical Deeds and Expressions

Does the Confucian conception of moral autonomy have any significant implications regarding issues of civil liberty? I shall argue that although it does provide some good reasons for restraining the use of coercion, and hence for protecting individual freedom in the sense of not interfering in individual lives, the force of these reasons is quite limited. Confucian moral autonomy alone does not provide a secure justification for civil liberties.

There are several features in Confucianism that tend to generate an intolerant attitude toward behavior and expressions regarded as wrong or immoral. First, Confucians put significant emphasis on shared moral vocabularies, beliefs, and principles and regard them as essential to the stability and flourishing of society. Second, they believe that moral agents should take morality as the supreme imperative of their lives—with the other goods (physical, material, or social) giving way to morality in cases where they may conflict. Third, Confucianism is a perfectionist political theory that holds that one of the most important tasks of the state is to promote morality and virtue. These three features combined push Confucianism strongly down the path of intolerance. But, paradoxically, it is also well-known that Confucians do not favor the use of coercive or oppressive measures to foster virtue. I want to suggest that the two elements of moral autonomy that are identified in Confucian ethics, namely, voluntary endorsement and reflective engagement, help prevent Confucianism from sliding easily into oppressive intolerance. Confucius states that legal punishment cannot change an individual's heart or soul; only rites can.

> Guide them by edicts, keep them in line with punishments, and the common people will stay out of trouble but will have no sense of shame. Guide

them by virtue, keep them in line with the rites, and they will, besides having a sense of shame, reform themselves. (*Analects* 2.3)

Why this is so can be seen in light of the voluntary endorsement of morality. One cannot be compelled to become a morally autonomous agent and a virtuous person. To live a virtuous life, agents must see the value of that life. They must willingly endorse virtue, be motivated to live by it—and enjoy that life. "One who is not benevolent cannot remain long in straitened circumstances, nor can he remain long in easy circumstances. '*The benevolent man is attracted to benevolence because he feels at home in it*'" (4.2, italics added). The cultivation of virtue occurs through education and practice in rites—it is rites, not physical force, that make people feel at home with virtue, while the use of force runs the risk of making people lose the sense of shame.

Xunzi, I believe, also understands the limits of coercion in fostering virtues, although he does not explicitly say so. In Xunzi's view, sages and the common people share not only a common human nature but also the same faculties that enable them to grasp and learn the Way and transform their lives through persistent learning and practice. According to him, the reason only a small number of people are sages and gentleman is that the common people are "unwilling" to become sages, and therefore "they cannot be made to do so" (*Xunzi* 23.5b). Xunzi recognizes that there is no direct way to *make* people lead a moral life if they are not willing to do so. The law is not a good instrument of moral edification.

Some other thinkers also take morality to be objective and yet uphold the virtue of tolerance. John Locke's *A Letter Concerning Toleration* is a classic example. Using the idea of voluntary endorsement, Locke argues that while coercion can change a person's outward behavior, it has little ability to correct the individual's inner soul. We should practice toleration because its opposite—persecution or coercion—is ineffective if its goal is to correct people's souls. This argument for toleration, however, is limited in two important ways. First, it may not rule out indirect coercion. Although force might not directly change an individual's heart, it can change the external, social circumstances in which an individual's attitudes and habits are formed and nurtured. If a book, say, Dostoyevsky's *The Brothers Karamazov*, challenges Christianity so powerfully that a Christian reader might suffer a loss of faith,[37] then there is nothing in the idea of voluntary endorsement that can say banning the book is wrong.[38] Although banning a book is not the same as coercing individuals to change their minds, it does prevent people from being exposed to certain influences, and it does not violate the idea of voluntary endorsement. Second, Locke's argument does not rule out direct coercion that is intended to prevent wrong expressions

---

37 To get a sense of the power of the challenge, take a look at the chapter "Rebellion" (bk. 5, chap. 4) in Fyodor Dostoyevsky's *The Brothers Karamazov* (1880).

38 This argument is indebted to Jeremy Waldron, "Locke, Toleration, and the Rationality of Persecution," chap. 4 in *Liberal Rights*.

or acts from having a corrupting influence. If the aim of coercion is to help the coerced to change their lives, then the argument thus far correctly implies that this would be ineffective, for outward force seldom changes the hearts of individuals. However, if the coercion is intended not to help the coerced but rather to prevent them from corrupting other people, then again there is nothing in the idea of voluntary endorsement that can say that such coercion is wrong or ineffective.

Locke's use of voluntary endorsement thus cannot provide a secure basis for toleration. This is as much a problem for Confucians as for Locke. It is hard to deny that there is a strong tendency in Confucianism to adopt an intolerant attitude toward thoughts and expressions it takes to be unethical or wrong. Confucianism tends to treat all ethical perspectives that are at odds with the core substance of the Confucian ideal as "heresies." It also worries about the harmful effects of heresies on social harmony and stability—important values in the Confucian scheme. Furthermore, as a theory of political perfectionism, Confucianism would expect political rulers to help maintain or restore the Way in the face of heretical challenges.[39] One telling example of this tendency is Mencius's attitude toward two schools of thought current in his day.[40] He regards the egocentric philosophy of Yang Zhu as "a denial of one's prince" and the philosophy of Mozi, which preaches universal love, as "a denial of one's father." "If the way of Yang and Mo does not subside and the Way of Confucius does not shine forth, the people will be deceived by heresies and the path of morality will be blocked" (*Mencius* 3B.9). Although Mencius uses very strong words to condemn the Yang and Mo schools of thought, he does not advocate the use of political force to ban them. Instead, he says, whoever can combat them "with words" is a true disciple of the sages.

> I . . . wish to follow in the footsteps of the Three Sages in rectifying the hearts of men, laying heresies to rest, opposing extreme action, and banishing excessive views. I am not fond of disputation. I have no alternative. Whoever can, with words, combat Yang and Mo is a true disciple of the sages. (3B.9)

Mencius does not explain why he asks people to combat heresies with words rather than swords. However, perhaps his attitude is similar to that of Xunzi, who states:

> But now the sages and true kings have passed away and the world is in confusion. Evil doctrines arise, and the gentleman has no power to control the people with and no punishments to prohibit them from evil. Therefore, he must have recourse to persuasive speaking.[41]

---

39 Note that there are different forms of political perfectionism, Confucianism being just one. For a defense of a modern, moderate form, see my "Legitimacy, Unanimity, and Perfectionism."

40 Xunzi is even more hostile to what he regards as heresies. See, for instance, *Xunzi* 4.7, 5.6, 6.9.

41 Watson's translations, *Hsün Tzu* sec. 22, 146 (cf. Knoblock, *Xunzi* 22.3e).

For Xunzi, then, and possibly Mencius as well, the best way to contain and combat heresies is by control and punishment. The use of argument and explanation is merely the second-best solution.

But is there anything in Confucian ethics that can resist such a strong tendency to restrict and punish wrong or unethical expressions? To see where such resistance might come from, consider J. S. Mill's view of the freedom of expression. Mill is concerned with the pursuit of truth. Accepting that there are always falsehoods and half-truths circulating in society, he argues that the best way to combat false doctrines and opinions is through better argument, not suppression. Although Mill gives several reasons for this, we will consider only the one that directly relates to the issue here. An oppressive environment that permits no falsehood or challenges to the truth, Mill argues, is stultifying and not conducive to an enlightened, genuine understanding of the truth itself.

Does the Confucian conception of moral autonomy contain anything that may lead to this Millian position? In my opinion, reflective engagement enables Confucians to walk with Mill for a while, although they eventually part company. In Confucianism, a successful moral life requires the moral agent to be capable of reflective understanding, which in turn requires a kind of moral learning that emphasizes thinking, reflection, extension and imagination, and dynamic deliberation. These qualities of the mind are difficult to develop in an environment where no challenges to received wisdom are allowed, and where no falsity has a chance to be heard and rejected by better arguments. Thinking and reflection prosper in an environment that encourages a certain degree of open-mindedness, rather than blind dogmatism. Banning opposing views or false beliefs does not help people to see the truth more clearly, but merely encourages unreflective acceptance of received views and makes people less capable of reflective understanding. It is only through thorough exposition and criticism of false doctrines that doubts and mistaken thinking can be completely dispelled and people can gain a more genuine and firm understanding of the ethical truth.[42]

It may be instructive to relate this argument to Confucius's remarks on "the village worthy," although Confucius does not make this comparison himself. Confucius clearly despises the village worthy for being disingenuous—appearing to behave uprightly and benevolently but in reality caring only about what people think of them. However, a rigorous and dogmatic moral environment that presses people to conform to an orthodox morality that cannot openly be challenged will tend to develop the village worthy. Although it is possible that Mao's China produced selfless altruistic communists, and that a highly dogmatic, disciplined Christian church produces dedicated Christians, for the

---

42   Just as Mencius's criticism of Gaozi (see *Mencius* 6A) and Xunzi's criticism of Mencius have deepened and enriched later generations' understanding of the issues of human nature and morality.

most part such doctrines produce people who are outwardly good and well behaved but who fall into the same category as the village worthy.

It is even more instructive to relate this argument to the character types that Confucius praises (*Mencius* 7B.37). The ideal character for Confucius is a person who can exercise the best discriminative judgment and follow the Middle Way, or Golden Mean (*zhong yong*). The next most favorable character types are "the wild [*kuang*] and the squeamish [*juan*]," who follow their own moral principles and causes conscientiously, even though their principles and causes do not strike properly at the Golden Mean—going either too far or not far enough. Compared to the village worthy, the wild and the squeamish still have moral characters that are based sincerely on their own moral understanding. They have moral integrity, even if they err. Confucius would recommend these people as friends or associates. The only people whose acquaintance he rejects are the village worthy because of their falseness and lack of real moral character and integrity. A highly oppressive moral environment that permits nothing but orthodoxy and does not allow people to err in their beliefs and ways of life hinders the development of real moral characters like the wild and the squeamish. In such an environment, Confucius would find few to befriend.

Thus far I have tried to bring out the positive implications of Confucian reflective engagement regarding civil liberties. We can see why an oppressive moral community is not desirable even if the sole concern of the community is the promotion of moral life. But the force of this argument of reflective engagement should not be overstated. The argument is much less forceful for rejecting milder forms of suppression, such as mild legal restriction of expression and an ideologically selective schooling system. There are two reasons for this. First, although systematically wiping out heresies and punishing people for having unorthodox views may stultify the minds of individuals, piecemeal banning of extreme and potentially influential views may not. The truth is that both the harmful effects of heresies and people's reflective capacities are a matter of degree. For example, if a powerful heresy is subverting the basic structure of a Confucian society, the legal restriction of this heresy alone need not constitute any serious impediment to the development of people's mental and ethical capacities. In this case the argument of reflective engagement cannot resist legal restriction.[43]

The second reason for the limitation of the reflective engagement argument has to do with the way early Confucians understand the special role and nature of reflective engagement in moral life. Confucius and Xunzi believe that the Way—or basic moral values—was correctly grasped in the past by the sages, and Mencius thinks that it is discernable to everyone through introspection and reflection. The primary task of reflection is not to find the Way by critically assessing all competing thoughts, but rather to help us arrive at a deeper and

43 Note that this is not a utilitarian argument, but merely a consequentialist one that takes the moral environment of a community as an important condition of development of moral life.

more genuine understanding of what is already known. This requires the ability to attend to and reflect on the truth, to understand the canon, and to imaginatively and appropriately extend and apply one's understanding to other life-situations. Although it may not be possible to develop this ability in an oppressive moral environment, its development does not necessarily require the soil of a free, open society in which all ideas can compete on an equal footing. Confucian moral reflection is not identical to free, critical, dialectical thinking.[44] The former, but not the latter, can survive in a circumscribed and ideologically selective school curriculum or moral environment. Perhaps Confucian moral reflection even requires the protection of such an environment. An open society that in principle permits the potential existence of a large number of less desirable ways of life and the circulation of less desirable ideas may not be conducive to Confucian moral reflection.

If the arguments thus far are correct, we have reached the following conclusion: Confucian moral autonomy is not compatible with either an oppressive moral community or a liberal-open society, but is compatible with what may be called a morally conservative environment in which liberties and their restriction are balanced in such a way as to best promote the moral good.

Moral Autonomy versus Personal Autonomy

Up to this point I have tried to give what I think is the strongest case for the importance of the Confucian conception of moral autonomy in matters concerning civil liberties. However, I now want to argue that moral autonomy has nothing more to offer in supporting civil and personal liberties. To see the limitations of moral autonomy, let us first examine what a contemporary liberal in a Western individualistic tradition would say regarding the question of unethical deeds or expressions. A typical liberal position would be that the state has no business interfering with individual freedom unless the expression of this freedom causes harm to others. The justification for this position often draws on some notion of respect for the dignity of individuals, the ideal of individuality, or personal independence. To interfere with an individual's private life and personal activities is to deny respect to that person's dignity or unique individuality. One may argue that dignity and individuality are not genuine values. But if they are, they can offer a more positive and direct, if not conclusive, justification for freedom of action and expression.

Moral autonomy affirms an ideal very different from the liberal notion of autonomy. Moral autonomy emphasizes moral personhood, which is the same for all human beings, rather than individual uniqueness, which differs from individual to individual. Even the Kantian conception of moral autonomy does not take individuality or individual uniqueness as a central idea. For Kant, the

---

44   I owe this point to Chan Sin Yee.

moral autonomy of individuals rests on their rationality, but one individual's rationality is no different from that of any other. It is human rationality that compels each individual to will a moral maxim that all others would also rationally will. As Munro writes, "Kantian autonomy assumes the existence of universal reason, which may imply sameness of moral judgment in all humans. Locked into the *a priori* dictates of such a faculty, the person could be seen as stripped of crucial elements of individuality, thereby losing a portion of his dignity in the process."[45] These two conceptions of dignity are different. The Kantian conception concerns the dignity of moral persons, whereas the liberal conception concerns the dignity of unique individual persons. We should not fault Kantian or Confucian conceptions for not addressing the liberal understanding of dignity or individuality, because their concern is with the moral life of a person. But neither should we think that their conceptions of moral autonomy can give rise to such liberal values as individuality. From the liberal-individualist perspective, what is respected is not merely the common features that define a human being but, more important, the uniqueness of each human individual: a distinct personal identity and path of life history; a unique blend of dispositions, tastes, and talents; a personal ambition in life and perspective on the world. Respect for the dignity of a person includes respect for those features that form the core of individuality.[46]

The idea that lies behind this endorsement of individuality is generally called personal autonomy, as opposed to the Confucian or Kantian notion of moral autonomy. Personal autonomy is the idea that people should be the authors of their own lives. As Steven Wall puts it, personal autonomy "is the ideal of people charting their own course through life, fashioning their character by self-consciously choosing projects and taking up commitments from a wide range of eligible alternatives, and making something out of their lives according to their own understanding of what is valuable and worth doing. . . . In short, autonomous people have a strong sense of their own identity and actively participate in the determination of their own lives."[47]

There are at least two ways to contrast moral and personal autonomy. The first is to see the different ways in which they are valued. In Confucianism the most important aim of a gentleman is to live a moral life of ren and yi. Moral autonomy is valued because it is a *precondition* of living a moral life in a genuine and successful way. One cannot lead a genuine moral life with virtues unless one willingly endorses the moral life. Also, it is difficult to live a moral life successfully if one does not have the reflective capacities necessary to achieve moral autonomy. Therefore the value of moral autonomy is derived from the

45 See Munro's introduction to *Individualism and Holism*, 16.

46 For an interesting comparison of Kantian and expressivist conceptions of respect for persons, see John E. Atwell, "Kant's Notion of Respect for Persons," *Tulane Studies in Philosophy* 31 (1982): 17–30.

47 Steven Wall, *Liberalism, Perfectionism and Restraint* (Cambridge: Cambridge University Press, 1998), 128. See also Raz, "Autonomy and Pluralism," chap. 14 in *Morality of Freedom*.

value of the moral life. Personal autonomy, for many liberals, is an intrinsically valuable ideal on its own, although it can be instrumentally valuable as well. Its value cannot be reduced to the value of the goals that an individual autonomously pursues. Rather, it partially defines a good life and gives value to it. For many liberals, the good life of a person is a life that consists of valuable projects and activities that are autonomously chosen or endorsed by that person.

Second, the conditions of personal autonomy are broader than those of moral autonomy. Personal autonomy requires at least three sets of conditions: (1) an autonomous agent who has the appropriate rational and emotional capacities to make choices; (2) an availability of options that the agent regards as valuable (in the context of modern industrial societies, these normally include the major options of career, marriage, education, association, and religion, which are normally protected in international human rights charters); and (3) an absence of inappropriate interference, such as coercion and manipulation, from others.[48] In contrast, moral autonomy requires only the first and third conditions, not the second one. The ideal of moral autonomy is that moral agents can make moral decisions that they reflectively endorse and act on. Conceptually it is possible to be morally autonomous without having valuable options concerning career, marriage, and so forth.[49] Moral autonomy is also compatible with a narrow range of life choices.

Consider, as an extreme example, the case of moral martyrs in traditional China. Suppose a Confucian gentleman who served in a morally corrupt government faced a dilemma. He must either help perpetuate the immoral practices of a wicked emperor or sacrifice his life in remonstrating and protesting against this emperor (resignation was not an option as the emperor would regard it also as a form of protest). Clearly, although undesirable, the gentleman would regard the second option as the only morally acceptable choice—in choosing to protest and die, the gentleman could preserve his moral autonomy and integrity. Consider the less extreme example of filial children. In traditional China, arranged marriage was the norm, and filial piety required children to accept the choices of their parents. Some may not have liked arranged marriage as such, but they endorsed it as part of a Confucian morality that they regarded as correct. Those filial children who complied with the norm would have their moral autonomy intact, but their personal autonomy would have been restricted by their inability to choose their own marriage partner.

Moral and personal autonomy, therefore, differ in the ways they are valued and in the range of options they require as their conditions. With this in mind,

---

48   Raz, "Autonomy and Pluralism."

49   For a similar understanding of the difference between personal and moral autonomy, see ibid., 370, note 2; and Donald H. Regan, "Authority and Value: Reflections on Raz's *Morality of Freedom,*" *Southern California Law Review* 62 (1989): 1075. Notice that personal and moral autonomy are both what Isaiah Berlin would classify as ideals of positive freedom. The first and second conditions of personal autonomy go beyond the requirement of negative freedom.

we may now proceed to see how the Confucian and liberal perspectives come to justify freedom differently.

Two Theories of Freedom

I would like to propose the following differences between Confucian and liberal theories of individual freedom. In the liberal view, the justification of freedom and toleration of morally dubious behavior come from the same source: personal autonomy.[50] Personal autonomy supports the claim that people should enjoy many civil and personal liberties, for these express and realize personal autonomy. It also rejects all forms of coercive interference, even for the good of the would-be coerced, for coercion infringes on personal autonomy. So the liberal justification of freedom is what I call content-independent—that is, the freedom to do x depends not on the content of x (whether x is good)[51] but on whether x is the autonomous choice of the agent. A Confucian theory, however, gives a content-dependent justification for freedom. Lacking the idea of personal autonomy, Confucians would justify freedom only on the grounds that it allows people to pursue the good. That we should be free to do x is because x is good, not because the freedom to do so expresses or realizes personal autonomy.

The content-independent nature of the liberal justification of freedom explains why its justification for toleration is also content-independent. Since the liberal is not concerned with the content of x (within the limits of not causing harm to others), the fact that x is, from a value standpoint, dubious or worthless does not prevent liberals from endorsing an individual's freedom to do x. The value of x does not affect the value of the freedom to do x, for the latter is secured by personal autonomy. But this strategy is not open to Confucians in their justification for toleration. If x is morally wrong or without value, then this fails to give rise to a content-dependent reason for endorsing the freedom to do x. The freedom to do x when x is *not* good would not have the same kind of value as the freedom to do x when x is good. If we should not interfere with people's freedom to do x, it is mainly because coercion will not help people achieve the good. Coercion frustrates moral autonomy, which is a precondition of the genuine pursuit of the moral good. In this case the freedom to do x is merely tolerated, not positively valued.

---

50 Of course, many liberal justifications of civil liberties also appeal to consequentialist considerations such as the promotion of truth, prevention of corruption, and improvement of public policy. These considerations are no less important than personal autonomy in a full justification, and they could be accepted and employed in a Confucian justification. I emphasize personal autonomy to stress the central difference between liberal and Confucian justifications.

51 I should qualify this, for the content of x is still in one way relevant. If x is an act that would seriously harm others, then liberals might think there should be no freedom to do x. So when I say the liberal justification of the freedom to do x is content-independent, I am assuming that the pursuit of the x in question does not violate the liberal harm principle.

Incorporating Personal Autonomy into
Confucian Ethics and Political Theory

I do not mean to conclude prematurely that the liberal view of personal autonomy and its theory of the value and function of civil liberties is necessarily superior to the Confucian perspective of freedom. Perhaps, as some have argued, an instrumental theory of freedom is all we need to provide the appropriate kind of justification for civil liberties.[52] However, personal autonomy is an important independent value today.[53] I believe a contemporary version of Confucian ethics and political theory should incorporate personal autonomy, as it would make Confucianism more attractive and more adaptable to the conditions of modern society. In this final section I will explain briefly the conception of personal autonomy that a contemporary version of Confucian political theory could adopt, lay out the structure of this reconstructed theory of civil liberties, and tackle one potential obstacle in Confucian ethics for incorporating personal autonomy.

First, I want to specify the kind of personal autonomy that Confucianism could accept. Personal autonomy is a fashionable notion today, with different articulations circulating in both philosophical and popular discourse. There is one particular articulation common in the culture of some Western societies, such as the United States, from which Confucianism should dissociate. This is the notion of personal sovereignty, which finds its best articulation in Joel Feinberg's philosophical writings.[54] The notion of personal sovereignty contains not only the ideal of a person leading an independent life but also a strong moral right to guard against any external action that intrudes on a person's private life. Personal sovereignty is modeled after state sovereignty and is a right so important that it outweighs any form of external interference. Feinberg relies on this notion to reject moralistic or paternalistic interference in a person's life, whether by the state or by other people in society. He places personal sovereignty above all other nonmoral values, such as the well-being of the agent or ethical ideals. In short, personal sovereignty is personal autonomy made nearly absolute. I believe personal sovereignty is a dubious notion, although I will not argue this point here.[55] My present concern is that absorbing this idea into Confucianism would fundamentally change the nature of Confucianism as a political theory. Confucian political theory is perfectionist in the sense that a major aim of the state is to help people pursue a moral life by means of law, education, provision

---

52   See, for example, John H. Garvey, *What Are Freedoms For?* (Cambridge: Harvard University Press, 1996).

53   For a detailed argument for the intrinsic and practical value of personal autonomy, see Wall, "Personal Autonomy and Its Value (I)," chap. 6 in *Liberalism, Perfectionism and Restraint.*

54   Feinberg, *Harm to Self.*

55   For a good critique of Feinberg's notion of personal autonomy as personal sovereignty, see Richard J. Arneson, "Joel Feinberg and the Justification of Hard Paternalism," *Legal Theory* 11, no. 3 (2005): 259–84.

of resources, and the coordination of social groups and their activities. Given its ethical concerns and its conception of the aims of politics, Confucianism would not categorically reject moralistic or paternalistic state interference in people's lives.[56] This major feature of Confucian political theory would have to be abandoned if personal sovereignty were implanted into Confucianism.

The personal autonomy described above is not a moral right but a valuable aspect of a good life. With other propositions it may give rise to certain moral rights, but not in the absolute sense of personal sovereignty. Personal autonomy can exist in degrees—one can be more or less autonomous, and its value need not be absolute. A contemporary version of Confucian political theory could welcome a moderate version of personal autonomy, treating it as one value that competes with, and at times can be outweighed by, such other values as well-being and ethical ideals. This moderate version makes Confucianism sensitive to people's autonomy without categorically placing personal autonomy over and above other values and thus preserves Confucian perfectionism.

The new theory that emerges from this combination gives a strong justification for civil liberties. Liberties are now justified not only by content-dependent considerations—the nature of the particular action in question—but also by a positive respect for the personal autonomy of the agent who chooses to perform that action. This new theory captures the idea that sometimes it is more important for agents to direct their own lives and make their own choices, even if some of those choices may not be wholly desirable. However, it differs from some liberal theories of liberties, in that it in principle allows moralistic and paternalistic considerations in defining the exact scope of liberties. Personal autonomy is a good, but not an absolute good. When an agent's choices are seriously wrong—morally or prudentially—and have dire consequences, this new Confucian perspective would take these considerations into account. It would balance bad outcomes against the good of personal autonomy and the potential drawbacks of coercive interference. This balancing might or might not favor legal intervention, depending on the specific case in question. Xunzi's advice for a gentleman concerning moral reflection and choice may serve as a principle of legislation:

> When a man sees something desirable, he must reflect on the fact that with time it could come to involve what is detestable. When he sees something that is beneficial, he should reflect that sooner or later it, too, could come to involve harm. Only after weighing the total of the one against that of the other and maturely calculating should he determine the relative merits of choosing or refusing his desires and aversions. (*Xunzi* 3.13)

The structure of this new Confucian theory is less tidy than the perspective of classical Confucianism and contemporary mainstream liberalism, but it seems more defensible.

---

56   A contemporary version of Confucianism, however, would favor as much as possible non-coercive public means of promoting the good life (such as subsidizing valuable activities and pursuits and promoting them through school education and mass media).

Suppose we have shown that there is good normative reason for a Confucian theory of civil liberties to incorporate personal autonomy. We now need to consider whether this absorption of a value foreign to Confucian ethics would deeply upset the ethics. Traditional Confucianism endorses a hierarchical system of familial and social relationships, giving a great deal of authority and power to parents, especially the father, in managing the lives of adult children. This system is supported by an elaborate ethics of filial piety. May Fourth thinkers argued that it was this feature of Confucianism that was responsible for the suppression of personal freedom and individuality. Would the inclusion of personal autonomy therefore undermine filial piety and the entire hierarchical system of relationship? I think it would, if filial piety is understood in its traditional form. But I believe there is a strong internal reason to reform and revise the traditional understanding of filial piety, given the conditions of modern society. I will argue that the inclusion of personal autonomy need not be seen as forsaking Confucian ethics, but rather as an internal revision in response to new social circumstances.

From a practical standpoint, personal autonomy is an unavoidable way of life in modern society. One can hardly live a successful life without having the rational and emotional capacities to make choices in many of life's situations. Modern industrial and postindustrial societies are characterized by social and geographic mobility, a multiplicity of occupations, rapid advancement of technology, and effortless communication within and across cultures. Occupations, arts and culture, and ways of life that are attractive and accessible to many individuals now render choice-making a central life activity. Parents may not have a firsthand understanding of the situations their children face. Their experience may no longer be suitable for the task of deliberating about and choosing a child's education, occupation, marriage partner, place of residence, and so forth.

This is a problem that classical Confucianism did not face. Confucianism emerged and developed in a traditional society that changed so slowly that the circumstances for cultivating personal autonomy did not arise. Indeed, personal autonomy would have upset the social and economic system of traditional Chinese clan-based society, in which the authoritative father was essential to the stability of the family—the most important unit of economic production and the basic node in society's network. Granting personal autonomy to adult children would have disrupted this order and threatened the survival of the family. Jeffrey Blustein's description of the difference between premodern and contemporary Europe regarding the issue of parenthood and children also illuminates the case of Confucianism:

> By comparison with the average parent today, parents in pre-industrial Europe did not worry much about the moral values implicit in raising children. There was little mobility out of the family; one's life prospects were largely limited by one's family, and one's station in life was likely to be the same as one's father's. The family was a unit of economic production, and the rights

and responsibilities of parents were defined in terms of whatever was necessary to maintain its productivity. But with the rise of industrialization, the orderly and predictable transmission of occupation and status from parent to child could no longer be assumed, and the education and training appropriate for children had to equip them for success outside the narrow confines of the family. These broad social and economic changes paved the way for some serious rethinking of parenthood.[57]

Unlike parents in premodern societies, the parents of today face tasks that are formidable. The social and economic structure of society makes it impossible for them to dictate their children's choice of career, marriage, education, and so forth. As a result, parents may better help their children by assisting them to make their own choices. Parents hoping to help children live successful lives will need to equip them with the rational and emotional capacities of personal autonomy. Of course, Confucianism wants parents to instill appropriate values and morals in children too, and personal autonomy is just one value among others. Nowadays, however, dictating children's lives, even when they are adult, is not only an unworkable option but also an undesirable one, for it is detrimental to the long-term well-being of the children.[58] Today, therefore, a father with the Confucian virtue of "fatherly love" (ci) should not practice parental authoritarianism, which is incompatible with fatherly love in the context of modern society.

This line of thinking can help explain why the inclusion of personal autonomy is more an internal revision than a total abandonment of Confucian familial ethics. In classical Confucianism filial piety was generally understood to consist of three major moral requirements: respect for one's parents, honoring (or not disgracing) them, and supporting them financially.[59] In traditional China one main expression of respect for parents was to obey parental wishes. This is perhaps the single feature in filial piety that is incompatible with personal autonomy—the other two features are still valuable to many people today and consistent with autonomy. I have suggested that the significance of obedience as an element of respect was based on the social and economic structure of traditional Chinese society, and that once the social conditions changed, this element lost its social importance and attractiveness. Also, practicing this norm of obedience is not conducive to the long-term well-being of children in modern society. Modern Confucians need a new norm to express the more fundamental moral requirement of "respect for one's parents." For example, seeking

57   Jeffrey Blustein, *Parents and Children: The Ethics of the Family* (New York: Oxford University Press, 1982), 3.

58   This is a general statement. Under exceptional circumstances, it may be necessary and appropriate to strongly interfere with adult children's lives if they fail to develop the necessary capacities for autonomy or make autonomous but disastrous decisions.

59   For a detailed analysis of the meaning of filial piety in Confucianism, see Chenyang Li, "Shifting Perspectives: Filial Morality Revisited," *Philosophy East and West* 47, no. 2 (1997): 211–32.

advice from parents when one makes important choices could be seen as respecting one's parents. Moreover, there are other attitudes of respect that can and should remain, such as an attitude of reverence.[60] A contemporary version of filial piety could therefore retain the three traditional requirements: respecting, honoring, and supporting one's parents, although the concrete expression of the first requirement would change.

Another way to argue the case is this: for the sake of his children's well-being, a Confucian father today ought not to wish to practice parental authoritarianism. An interesting implication then follows: if the obedience of adult children is not what Confucian parents themselves wish for, then children cannot be said to not comply with the wishes of their parents. In other words, since the father has no wish to command obedience from his children, the potential conflict between personal autonomy and filial piety dissolves.

Conclusion

It may be helpful to summarize briefly the main claims that I have defended. First, there is a conception of moral autonomy in Confucian ethics that can support a degree of toleration and freedom as the absence of coercion. Second, moral autonomy (Confucian or Kantian) is different from personal autonomy. The two address different concerns, and personal autonomy gives a stronger justification for civil and personal liberties than does moral autonomy. Civil liberties are important because they are instrumentally useful for the promotion of the good, both moral and nonmoral, and are expressive of the ideal of personal autonomy. Third, personal autonomy should be carefully distinguished from the idea of personal sovereignty, and personal autonomy, but not personal sovereignty, should be absorbed into Confucian ethics. Finally, the inclusion of personal autonomy would strengthen the contemporary appeal of Confucianism. It need not be seen as forsaking Confucian ethics, but rather as an internal revision in response to new social circumstances. Emerging from this incorporation is a new perfectionist theory of liberties that recognizes the value of personal autonomy and the importance of the ethical good that liberties instrumentally serve to promote. It is also a theory that attempts to carefully balance the two when they are in conflict.

---

60 The Master says, "Nowadays for a man to be filial means no more than that he is able to provide his parents with food. Even hounds and horses are, in some way, provided with food. If a man shows no reverence, where is the difference?" (*Analects* 2.7). There is still a lot of truth in this famous passage today.

CHAPTER 7

Social Justice as Sufficiency for All

Benevolent Rule: Benevolence or Justice?

In the first part of this book I argued that the Confucian conception of the ideal ruler-ruled relationship is one of mutual commitment—the ruler's commitment to take care of the people and the people's willing submission to or acceptance of the ruler's control. In Confucian political thought, the ruler's commitment to take care of the people is expressed through the image of the benevolent ruler, who protects and promotes the people's good life (especially their material well-being) through a set of social and economic policies that Mencius calls "benevolent rule" (ren zheng). In this chapter and the next, I shall discuss the nature and content of benevolent rule as a set of policies. Specifically, I shall ask whether this set of policies can be called policies of justice. Sometimes when scholars talk about Confucian benevolent rule their focus is on "benevolence" rather than "rule"—the idea seems to be that benevolent rule is motivated by the ruler's benevolence. According to this view, the concept of benevolent rule is simply extended from the concept of benevolence as a virtue and thus lacks an independent status and content. This view seems especially plausible if we accept a traditional interpretation of Confucianism that sees politics as the continuation of personal ethics and the state as the family writ large.[1]

However, this view of benevolent rule, I believe, is one-sided. Although Mencius was the first thinker to coin the term, the main idea and content of "benevolent rule" emerged much earlier, namely, in the Western Zhou dynasty, as recorded in *The Book of History*. As I argue in chapter 1 and appendix 2, Heaven gives a mandate to the ruler who protects and promotes the people's well-being. In this service conception of authority, taking care of the people is not simply a natural expression of the virtuous ruler but an objective requirement for his legitimate authority—a ruler would risk his authority if he failed to take care of the people. *The Book of History* uses the term "protection of the people" (bao min) to characterize the ruler's task or duty. Bao min is the predecessor of ren zheng—Mencius's ideal of benevolent rule and his understanding of Heaven's Mandate, a concept inherited from a long tradition of political thought.

Benevolent rule is thus a prescribed duty of all rulers and a condition for authority. It should not be understood as an open-ended imperfect (Kantian)

1 I challenge this interpretation in "Exploring the Nonfamilial."

duty, much less an optional, supererogatory act of the virtuous ruler. In promoting the idea of benevolent rule to rulers of his times, Mencius sometimes appealed to their benevolent heart, for this seemed to him an effective way to motivate them to accept the concept. But we should not be led to think that benevolent rule is merely a duty of benevolence. Rather, it is first and foremost a *political* duty, an imperative laid down by Heaven, and an objective requirement for legitimate authority.

Mencius understands benevolent rule as a set of social and economic policies that all legitimate rulers must implement. If this set of policies is not simply grounded in the virtue of benevolence, is it also grounded in some consideration of justice? This seems a harder question to answer. As we shall see, one aspect central to the ideal of benevolent rule is the proper distribution of economic resources. The difficulty is to determine whether this proper distribution can be regarded as a just distribution or a requirement of justice. To do this we need to ascertain, first, whether the concept of justice is present in early Confucian thinking, and second, if it is, whether this concept of justice applies to matters of resource distribution.

Most of the limited contemporary writings on Confucian justice argue that Confucianism cannot share the philosophical presuppositions of Western conceptions of justice. A typical strategy that these writings employ is to take John Rawls's theory of justice as a point of reference and argue that his theory presupposes liberal conceptions of persons and communities radically different from those in Confucianism.[2] This kind of discussion, illuminating as it often is, typically concludes without any serious treatment of distributive or social justice. I believe it is not necessary or desirable to reconstruct Confucian views through a comparison with Rawls, for doing so leads us to approach Western and Confucian philosophical visions as diametrically opposed ideal types and distracts us from distributive issues that concern Confucian and Western thinkers alike. Here I hope to explore Confucian justice in a way that assumes the fewest philosophical presuppositions about human nature, personhood, and community.

In the next section I argue that in early Confucian texts the concept of distributive justice, understood as "to each according to his due," is at work in discussions about the distribution of honor, offices, and punishment. In the third section I distinguish between the concepts of distributive and social justice and argue that the historical conditions of pre-Qin China presented distributive issues that naturally fall in the domain of social justice. In addition, Confucian thinkers view society in such a way that matters of economic distribution could be conceived of as issues of social justice. In the fourth and fifth

2   See, for example, Erin M. Cline, "Two Senses of Justice: Confucianism, Rawls, and Comparative Political Philosophy," *Dao* 6, no. 4 (2007): 361–81; Ruiping Fan, "Social Justice: Rawlsian or Confucian?" chap. 7 in *Comparative Approaches to Chinese Philosophy*, ed. Bo Mou, Ashgate World Philosophies Series (Aldershot, UK: Ashgate, 2003).

sections I reconstruct from the main classical texts major principles of distribution and argue that they may form a perfectionist approach to social justice. The key principle of social justice for early Confucians is sufficiency for all, which is neither a libertarian nor an egalitarian conception of justice. The aim of social justice is to enable every member of a community to have sufficient resources to live a good life.

Is There a Concept of Distributive Justice in Confucianism?

Let us start with the classical Greek formula of the idea of justice: "Render to each his due."[3] Although this broad formula leaves what is meant as a person's due open to interpretation, it nevertheless tells us several things. First, it tells us that the concept of justice is *distributive*, namely, that benefits and burdens should be shared among individuals according to certain principles of rightness, rather than according to aggregative ends that make distribution a mere means.[4] Jeremy Waldron has given a nice example to show that the primary concern of justice lies in distribution rather than aggregation. He considers the following news report: "A judge today sentenced five members of an organized crime ring to a total of two hundred years in prison."[5] Waldron says, rightly, that this report is "uninformative" from the angle of justice, for it does not contain information about individual sentences. What justice cares about in this case is not the aggregate outcome of the sentencing but whether each convicted criminal gets the sentence he or she deserves.

The second thing that this classic formula tells us—and this is a corollary of the first—is that the concept of justice is *individual oriented*. "To each his due" expresses a particular way of assessing the rightness of distribution. The distribution of benefit is to be made on the basis of the personal characteristics and circumstances of the individual involved—the person's efforts, contributions, merit, needs, well-being, worth as a person, and so on—and not on the basis of issues that are unrelated to the individual. The same holds for the distribution of burdens. Third and last, the formula tells that the concept of justice is a *moral* one. To give each individual what is due to him or her is a moral requirement, not a matter of personal favor or grace bestowed by the distributor.[6] In sum, the concept of justice embodies a moral concern about how individuals fare—what they ought to receive as their due—in the distribution of benefits and burdens.

Is there such a concept in Confucianism? The answer, I believe, is a clear yes. The most obvious passages in the classical texts that illustrate the concept of justice are those that discuss the justice of punishment and the distribution of

---

3 Beginning here the word "justice" denotes distributive justice unless otherwise stated.
4 See David Miller, *Social Justice* (Oxford: Clarendon Press, 1976), 19–20.
5 Jeremy Waldron, "The Primacy of Justice," *Legal Theory* 9, no. 4 (2003): 275.
6 See Tom D. Campbell, *Justice*, 2nd ed. (London: Macmillan, 2001), 24.

offices. Among pre-Qin masters, Xunzi is the most explicit on the importance of justice or fairness in government affairs. For him the activity of governing has to be "fair" (*ping*) (*Xunzi* 9.19a). "Public-spiritedness and impartiality [*gong ping*] are the balance by which the affairs of government are to be weighed, and the mean of due proportion [*zhong he*] is the marking line by which they are to be measured" (9.2).

Xunzi fleshes out the idea of fairness or impartiality in exactly the same way as the ancient Greek philosophers—namely, by stating that justice or fairness consists in rendering to each person his or her due according to his or her personal characteristics, circumstances, or conduct. "As a general principle, every rank and official responsibility, and each reward or punishment, was given as a recompense that accorded with the nature of the conduct involved" (*Xunzi* 18.3). Therefore "the coming of honor or disgrace must be a reflection of one's inner virtue [de]" (1.5), offices must be matched by appropriate ability, rewards must correspond to achievement, and penalties to offenses (8.3).

It is important to note that for Xunzi, justice involves each person being treated as an independent individual who is separate from other individuals, including family members:

> If rank fits the worth of the individual holding it, there is esteem; where it does not, there is contempt. In antiquity, penal sanctions did not exceed what was fitting to the crime, and rank did not go beyond the moral worth of the person. *Thus, although the father had been executed, his son could be employed in the government; although the elder brother had been killed, the younger could be employed.* . . . *Each was allotted what was his due according in every case to his true circumstances.* (24.3, italics added; see also 24.4)

Nothing could show more clearly that Xunzi understands the individual oriented nature of justice, in the sense that justice concerns the proper treatment of each individual taken separately. Confucius, too, understands this very well. In a story told in *The Annals of Lü Buwei*—a major classical text that incorporated Confucian, Legalistic, Daoist, and Mohist ideas—Confucius is reported to have praised Qi Huangyang's spirit of impartiality (gong), for when Qi recommended people to his duke as candidates for public office, he did so purely on the basis of their merit, and not on the basis of their personal relations with Qi himself. This long passage is worth quoting:

> Duke Ping of Jin questioned Qi Huangyang, saying, "Nanyang is without a commandant. Whom should I appoint?"
> Qi Huangyang replied, "Xie Hu would be suitable."
> Duke Ping said, "Is not Xie Hu an enemy of yours, sir?"
> "Your grace asked who would be appropriate for the office not whether he was the enemy of your servant."
> Duke Ping declared this "Excellent!" and as a result employed Xie Hu. All the people praised the excellence of the decision.

Sometime later Duke Ping again asked Qi Huangyang, "The state lacks a military guardian. Whom should I appoint?"

Qi Huangyang replied, "Wu would be appropriate."

Duke Ping asked, "Is not Wu your own son, sir?"

"Your grace asked who would be appropriate for the office not whether he was my son."

Duke Ping declared this "Excellent!" and as a result employed Wu. All the people praised the excellence of the decision.

When Confucius learned of it, he said, "Excellent indeed were the assessments of Qi Huangyang. When recommending those from without, he did not avoid even personal enemies, and when recommending from within, he did not avoid even his own son."

Qi Huangyang may properly be called *impartial* [gong].[7]

Both Mencius and Xunzi also view justice as a moral imperative that trumps political goals such as the gaining of an empire. Mencius says that it is wrong to "kill one innocent man" or "take what one is not entitled to" in order to gain the empire, for doing so is contrary to rightness (yi) and benevolence (ren) (*Mencius* 2A.2, 7A.33; see also 4B.4). Xunzi is of the same view, namely, that a gentleman (ru) "would not commit a single act contrary to the requirements of justice nor execute a single blameless man, even though he might thereby obtain the empire. Such a lord acts with justice [yi] and faithfulness [xin] toward the people" (*Xunzi* 8.2; see also 11.1a, 4.8). For Mencius and Xunzi, then, justice is a moral constraint on people's pursuit of goals and benefits. Justice is understood as a nonconsequentialist, nonutilitarian idea.

If my analysis is correct, Confucianism does contain a concept of (distributive) justice, and this concept is the same as the Greek one: namely, to render to each person his due. Like the Greek concept, Confucian justice is distributive, individual oriented, and moral.

Is There Room for a Concept of Social Justice in Confucianism?

From Distributive to Social Justice

We have seen that in the Confucian texts the concept of distributive justice exists in discussions about the distribution of honor, offices, and punishment. But what about economic matters like the distribution of land or other forms of material goods such as grains? Do Confucian thinkers also approach economic matters from the perspective of justice? In particular, is there a concept of eco-

---

7 John Knoblock and Jeffrey Riegel, trans., *The Annals of Lü Buwei* (Stanford: Stanford University Press, 2000), bk. 1, chap. 5, sec. 4 (hereafter 1.5.4). Italics added. Unless otherwise stated, all translations and notation of *The Annals of Lü Buwei* 呂氏春秋 [*Lüshi chun qiu*] are Knoblock and Riegel's.

nomic justice or social justice in Confucianism? Is the distribution of material resources a matter of justice for Confucians?

The Confucian concept of justice reconstructed so far is close to the traditional Western concept of justice in that it links justice with a person's merit or desert. Some theorists argue that this traditional Western concept—sometimes called a *meritorian* perspective of justice[8]—is very different from the modern concept of economic or social justice. The former confines the scope of the concerns of justice to the civil sphere (offices, honor, and punishment), while the latter extends it to the economic sphere (material goods).[9] Samuel Fleischacker argues that major thinkers in the Western tradition from Aristotle to Adam Smith held the traditional, meritorian concept of justice, and that they would reject the concept of social justice, for they did not believe that it was the poor's due, merit, or desert to receive allocation of material goods from society or the state.[10] Modern theorists of social justice (of the egalitarian kind), however, take the opposite view. They believe that justice morally entitles each member of a society to a certain level of material goods, and that it is the responsibility of society—of which the government is the agent—to provide all members of society with these material goods.

The Centrality of Material Goods to People's Lives

According to Fleischacker, premodern Western thinkers tend to hold some of the following views about the nature or origin of poverty, any one of which can block a transition from the traditional concept of distributive justice to the modern concept of social justice:

- Poverty is a punishment for sin.
- Poverty is a natural evil which cannot be overcome by human efforts.
- Material things are of no consequence, hence the poor and the rich can live equally good lives without any change in their material condition.
- Poverty is a blessing, enabling one to learn humility or to turn away from material obsessions.[11]

If a society does not believe that poverty is bad for an individual or that anything can or should be done to alleviate it, then poverty (or the distribution of

8   See Campbell, "What Is Justice?" chap. 1 in *Justice*.

9   For a contrast of civil justice and social justice, see J. A. Passmore, "Civil Justice and Its Rivals," chap. 2 in *Justice*, ed. Eugene Kamenka and Alice Erh-Soon Tay (London: Edward Arnold, 1979).

10   Samuel Fleischacker, introduction to *A Short History of Distributive Justice* (Cambridge: Harvard University Press, 2004). For criticisms of Fleischacker's account of premodern Western views of justice, see, for example, Siegfried Van Duffel and Dennis Yap, "Distributive Justice before the Eighteenth Century: The Right of Necessity," *History of Political Thought* 32, no. 3 (2011): 449–64.

11   Fleischacker, *Distributive Justice*, 9. Fleischacker mentions other views on poverty as well, but they are less relevant for my purposes here and so are not included.

material goods) will not be considered a subject of concern for justice. Confucianism holds none of the four views above. No doubt Confucian thinkers expect people of high virtue to live nobly, whether in poverty or riches, and to take pride and delight in virtue rather than in material possessions (*Analects* 1.15, *Mencius* 7A.21, *Xunzi* 2.5, 12.3). Yet none of them states that material goods are of no consequence to people's lives. Quite the contrary, the people's desire for material goods and wealth is viewed as natural and, if pursued within moral boundaries, is also seen to be legitimate. Confucius says,

> Wealth and rank are what every man desires . . . poverty and low station are what every man dislikes. (*Analects* 4.5)

> If wealth were a permissible pursuit, I would be willing even to act as a guard holding a whip outside the market place. If it is not, I shall follow my own inclinations. (7.12)

Mencius affirms even more explicitly the centrality of material goods to the lives of ordinary people. In a well-known passage he says that people who lack stable, sufficient material possessions will go astray, and that it is the responsibility of the ruler to prevent them from falling into the trap of poverty and illegal acts:

> Only a gentleman can have a constant heart in spite of a lack of constant means of support. The people, on the other hand, will not have constant hearts if they are without constant means. Lacking constant hearts, they will go astray and fall into excesses, stopping at nothing. To punish them after they have fallen foul of the law is to set a trap for the people. How can a benevolent man in authority allow himself to set a trap for the people? (*Mencius* 1A.7)

Material goods, in Mencius's view, not only are important to keep people from going astray; they are necessary conditions for them to live a good life. Immediately following the passage above he says:

> Hence when determining what means of support the people should have, a clear-sighted ruler ensures that these are sufficient, on the one hand, for the care of parents, and, on the other, for the support of wife and children, so that the people always have sufficient food in good years and escape starvation in bad; *only then does he drive them toward goodness*. (1A.7, italics added)

For Mencius, material goods enable individuals to support both their own physical existence and that of their family, and thus fulfill important ethical duties. Moreover, having sufficient material means to support their families, people "learn, in their spare time, to be good sons and good younger brothers, loyal to their prince and true to their word, so that they will, in the family, serve their fathers and elder brothers, and outside the family, serve their elders and superiors" (1A.5). This is what constitutes Mencius's conception of the good life, for which material goods are an important, necessary condition.

The Circumstances of Social Justice

I have shown that in the view of Confucian thinkers, material goods are important to the good life, and people's desire for them is natural and legitimate. But this is not sufficient to establish that such a concern for material goods is, or can be, part of a concern of social justice. As David Miller has argued, we need some premises about the kind of society that can give rise to the circumstances of social justice. "If we do not inhabit bounded societies, or if people's shares of goods and bads do not depend in ways we can understand on a determinate set of social institutions, or if there is no agency capable of regulating that basic structure, then we no longer live in a world in which the idea of social justice has any purchase."[12] If we follow Miller's understanding of the circumstances of social justice here, then we need to show that Confucian thinkers understand society as territorially bounded, structured by institutions, and regulated by human agency.

In a moment I shall show that Mencius and Xunzi do see society as a scheme for the division of labor in the production and distribution of goods that are necessary for the well-being of each and every member. This scheme is regulated by rules enforced by a ruler and his government, and fairness and entitlements concerning resource distribution are questions of importance within such a scheme. But first it is important to look at the historical conditions in which the two thinkers developed their conceptions of society.[13] While their prescriptions for society contain a good ideal of idealism, they corresponded to, and were made possible by, the historical conditions of their times. Drawing on Cho-yun Hsu's *Ancient China in Transition*,[14] I shall briefly sketch the changing nature of society in the pre-Qin period and highlight the characteristics relevant to concerns of social justice.

Ancient China in the early Spring and Autumn (Chunqiu) period (772–475 BCE) was marked by clear and deep social stratification based primarily on political rank. At the top were the rulers of states. Immediately below were the nobles or aristocrats. These were relatives of the rulers or hereditary heads of prestigious clans that had kin relations with the rulers' families and were also landlords who occupied high positions in government. In the lowest level of the ruling group were the literati (*shi*), who were retainers to their lords and did not

12 David Miller, *Principles of Social Justice* (Cambridge: Harvard University Press, 1999), 6.

13 Confucius's conception of society is much less developed than that of the other two, so he is not included in the discussion.

14 Cho-yun Hsu 許倬雲 [Xu Zhuoyun], *Ancient China in Transition: An Analysis of Social Mobility, 722–222 B.C.* (Stanford: Stanford University Press, 1965). See also Yuri Pines, "The Literati," chap. 3 in *The Everlasting Empire: The Political Culture of Ancient China and Its Imperial Legacy* (Princeton: Princeton University Press, 2012).

see themselves as constituting an independent social group. Below the ruling group were the commoners. This level mostly consisted of peasants but also included merchants and artisans, who were expected to follow the lead of the political elite in social and political affairs.

From the late Spring and Autumn period to the Warring States period, interstate wars and interfamilial struggles within states brought rapid and significant social changes throughout China. Several aspects of social mobility in that period are especially relevant to our purposes:

1. The appearance of a new type of state and the rise of the intelligentsia. The downfall of noble ministerial houses created a vacuum for political talent. This meant, on the one hand, that rulers were able to wield power directly but, on the other, that they had to recruit commoners to serve as ministers and advisers to help them win or consolidate power in interstate wars. As Hsu describes, "At the start of the [Warring States] period a new type of state appeared—a state in which the ruler wielded despotic power and ministers could be brought into and discharged from a bureaucratic system that selected and promoted competent men and rejected the unqualified."[15] This was the social background for the prominence of the principle of personal merit and desert (in terms of moral and intellectual caliber) with regard to the distribution of offices in early Confucianism, especially in Xunzi's thought.

2. The emergence of urban cities and commercialization. The political unification of large areas of territory and the relative security of travel led to "the change in the function of cities from that of mere fortified strongholds to that of industrial-commercial centers."[16] In the cities the use of metallic money for exchange was common; occupational specialization and differentiation proliferated; a new social stratum of wealthy and sometimes politically influential merchants emerged along with prospering trades and commercial activities.

3. The widening of economic inequality. The expansion of state territories and changes in the land policies and tax system facilitated the private possession of land. "Land became concentrated in the hands of fewer people because of heavy taxation, high rent, and usury, which caused farmers in desperate financial straits to sell their land to whoever could buy it."[17] Those who lost their land usually became hired field laborers with low wages. Some became tenants of the new landlords and were charged up to 50 percent of their crop yield for rent.[18]

It was against this historical background that Mencius and Xunzi developed their understanding and vision of political society. Responding to the major

15   Hsu, *Ancient China in Transition*, 105–6.
16   Ibid., 137.
17   Ibid., 138–39.
18   Ibid., 113.

social issues of their day, they went to great lengths to discuss issues such as poverty, differentiation of social roles and functions, inequality of income and status, and the distributive role of government. Both thinkers view society as an interdependent complex that requires specialization and differentiation of occupation in the political and economic spheres. Both think that trade between "the hundred crafts" is necessary to satisfy everyone's needs (*Mencius* 3A.4, 3B.4; *Xunzi* 4.12, 11.5b). But, realizing that unregulated free trade can result in monopoly, excessive profits, and what contemporary theorists today have called "the tragedy of the commons" in forestry and fishing,[19] they also believe that government interference in economic activity is necessary (*Mencius* 1A.3, 2B.10; *Xunzi* 9.16b). More important, as will be shown, Mencius and Xunzi both believe that rulers and their governments have the capacity and the obligation to ensure fairness or equity in the management of government and economic affairs by enforcing the right kinds of laws and policies in taxation, distribution of land, and social welfare.

To sum up, the historical conditions of pre-Qin China presented distributive issues that naturally fall within the domain of social justice, and Confucian thinkers did look at society in such a way that it is *possible to conceive* that they viewed society's distributive impact on people's well-being as a concern of social justice. However, whether these thinkers framed this concern as one of justice is a further question that requires a detailed analysis of the texts.

Distributive Principles

In this section I argue that the principle subscribed to by Mencius and Xunzi is one that is today sometimes called the principle of sufficiency with regard to the government's responsibility for the material well-being of the people—namely, that people who are badly off have first priority for care; inequality of wealth and income beyond the threshold of sufficiency does not matter; the proper principle for the distribution of offices, occupational positions, and emolument is one of merit and contribution; and natural inequality in talents does not give rise to moral concerns.

Sufficiency for All

Mencius is keenly aware of the seriousness of poverty and wealth inequality in his times. He refers to the situation where some people have food "so plentiful as to be thrown to dogs and pigs," while "men drop dead from starvation by the

19   "If it is the season when the grasses and trees are in the splendor of their flowering and sprouting new leaves, axes and halberds are not permitted in the mountain forest so as not to end their lives prematurely or to interrupt their maturation. If it is the season when the giant sea turtles, water lizards, fish, freshwater turtles, loach, and eels are depositing their eggs, nets and poisons are not permitted in the marshes so as not to prematurely end their lives or to interrupt their maturation" (*Xunzi* 9.16b).

wayside" (*Mencius* 1A.3). He also says, "Nowadays, the means laid down for the people are sufficient neither for the care of parents nor for the support of wife and children. In good years life is always hard, while in bad years there is no way of escaping death" (1A.7). Part of the cause is the unequal distribution of land and the inability of the government to take proper measure to redistribute land or provide the poor with material subsistence. Mencius therefore takes the equity of land distribution to be the first task of a benevolent government:

> *Benevolent government must begin with land demarcation.* When boundaries are not properly drawn [*zheng*], the division of land according to the well-field system[20] and the yield of grain used for paying officials cannot be equitable [*jun, ping*]. For this reason, despotic rulers and corrupt officials always neglect the boundaries. Once the boundaries are correctly fixed, there will be no difficulty in settling the distribution of land and the determination of emolument. (*Mencius* 3A.3, italics added)

In modern terms, Mencius's point is that economic justice is the backbone of good governance. But what counts as an equitable distribution of land?

The following two passages would appear to indicate that an equitable distribution of land is regarded as being an equal distribution of land *sufficient* for each person to live a good life.

> Hence, when determining what means of support the people should have, a clear-sighted ruler ensures that these are *sufficient*, on the one hand, for the care of parents, and, on the other, for the support of wife and children, so that the people always have sufficient food in good years and escape starvation in bad; only then does he drive them toward goodness. (*Mencius* 1A.7, italics added)

Mencius goes on to explain the amount of land needed for ensuring material sufficiency to King Xuan of Qi:

> If you wish to put this into practice, why not go back to fundamentals? If the mulberry is planted in every homestead of five *mu*[21] of land, then those who are fifty can wear silk; if chickens, pigs and dogs do not miss their breeding season, then those who are seventy can eat meat; if each lot of a hundred *mu* is not deprived of labor during the busy season, then families with several mouths to feed will not go hungry. (*Mencius* 1A.7; see also 1A.3)

Mencius further elaborates on the "well-field (*jing*) system,"[22] which he regards as the first task of benevolent government:

---

20 The notion of the "well-field system" will be explained below.

21 D. C. Lau notes in his translation: "As a *mu* is one nine-hundredth part of a square *li*, it works out to be somewhat less than 200 square meters." See his *Mencius*, 9.

22 D. C. Lau has the following note to explain the notion of *jing*: "As can be seen from the sequel, when a piece of land is divided into nine parts, it looks like the Chinese graph [jing] 井. Hence the system is known as [*jing*]-fields. The common translation of the term as 'well-fields,'

A *jing* is a piece of land measuring one *li* square, and each *jing* consists of 900 *mu*. Of these, the central plot of 100 *mu* belongs to the state, while the other eight plots of 100 *mu* each are held by eight families who share the duty of caring for the plot owned by the state. Only when they have done this duty do they dare turn to their own affairs. (*Mencius* 3A.3)[23]

Although Mencius states that this is a rough outline only, and that it is up to the ruler to make adjustments, it seems clear that the well-field system contains three related principles:

1. Sufficiency: Each household should have an amount of land that is sufficient for the material well-being and ethical life of its members.
2. Equality (as a corollary of the first principle): The amount of land to be allocated should be more or less the same for every household of commoners (officials receive more land because they make a greater contribution to society).
3. Government obligation: It is the duty of the government to ensure that the land demarcation is "properly drawn" (zheng) and the division of land according to the well-field system is "equitable" (jun).

Like Mencius, Xunzi subscribes to the principle of sufficiency and regards it as central to benevolent government (*Xunzi* 9.5, 10.2, 12.6). He makes reference to something like Mencius's well-field system as a basis for sufficiency:

A people that are not made prosperous will have no means of caring for the needs of their essential natures. . . . Hence, the way to make families prosperous is to allot five *mu* "lots" for the abode and one hundred *mu* for the fields, to devote one's attention to their concerns, and not to rob them of the time required for their fields. (*Xunzi* 27.52)

However, apart from land distribution, Xunzi also talks about income from jobs and assignments as another basis for sufficiency. He advises a ruler thus:

Employ the people so that they are certain to succeed in their assigned tasks; make certain that *the profits from their assigned tasks are sufficient to provide a means of living for them*. In all these to cause income to match outgo in regard to clothing, food, and the hundred other necessities of life so that with certainty the harvest surplus will be stored up at the proper season is called the "art of calculating what fits each respective station." (*Xunzi* 10.3a, italics added)

There is an important point to note about Mencius's understanding of government obligation, namely, his belief that if people die of starvation under a

---

being based on the accident that the word [*jing*] means 'a well,' is somewhat misleading, but I have kept it as it has become the standard translation." See ibid., 111.

23 It seems that the one-ninth to the state or the public is not very different from the classic Western tithe, or one-tenth.

ruler, then that ruler not only has failed in his obligation to care for them but also has behaved no differently from if he had killed them:

> Now when food meant for human beings is so plentiful as to be thrown to dogs and pigs, you fail to realize that it is time for collection, and when men drop dead from starvation by the wayside, you fail to realize that it is time for distribution. When people die, you simply say, "It is none of my doing. It is the fault of the harvest." *In what way is that different from killing a man by running him through*, while saying all the time, "It is none of my doing. It is the fault of the weapon." Stop putting the blame on the harvest and the people of the whole Empire will come to you. (*Mencius* 1A.3; see also 1A.4; italics added)

How to make sense of this strong condemnation of a ruler's failure to help the needy? One possible answer is that Mencius believes it is the people's due to have sufficient means to live a good life, and that the government should supply this through prudent management and proper policies. The failure of the ruler to help the needy, therefore, is a serious failure of justice, namely, having no regard for the people's due in economic distribution. This issue, however, raises some important questions: What does Mencius believe is the moral foundation of the distribution of resources? Is the foundation one of justice? Unfortunately Mencius does not provide a direct answer. But I believe that from the ideas of Mencius discussed above, we can construct a perfectionist theory of justice that justifies the distributive role of government as a duty of justice. This is a perfectionist theory because its ultimate basis is a certain conception of the good life. This theory tries to link up Mencius's conception of the good life and the distributive role of government and social justice. It runs like this:

1. It is morally important that every human person can live a good life.
2. Living a good life requires sufficient material resources.
3. The natural world provides human beings with enough material resources to meet the material needs of everyone.
4. The availability of and access to the resources of the natural world depend on a well-ordered structure in which the ruler (or government) plays a critical role. A well-ordered structure requires a proper set of laws and policies in land distribution, taxation, and the management of common-pool resources such as forests and fish.
5. The fact that people's access to material resources is affected by how the ruler sets up and manages social and legal rules gives rise to the ruler's duty of justice.
6. In setting up distributive rules and institutions, the ruler has a duty of justice to provide everyone with a fair share of material resources (according to the sufficiency principle) because everyone has the capacity to lead a good life (and therefore has worth and need). In a well-ordered

society, any person can claim it is his or her due to have sufficient material resources. If the ruler fails to maintain a well-ordered structure even though natural resources are sufficient, and if as a result some people die of starvation while others have excessive wealth, then the ruler has actively committed a serious injustice (on a par with killing the starved) rather than merely a wrong in failing to help them.

7. The duty of justice is not just the responsibility of the ruler alone. Everyone has a part in contributing to government revenue through the working of public land in the well-field system or paying other forms of tax. In other words, everyone has some responsibility in providing for everyone's due. In modern language we can say that everyone has both a claim to the justice of material sufficiency and an obligation to work to provide that sufficiency for all.

As many of the statements above are drawn from Mencius, or are at least consistent with his ideas, this perfectionist theory of justice can properly be called Mencian. This theory helps us see why the sufficiency principle can be a principle of social justice.

Priority for the Badly Off

If sufficiency for all is the proper distributive goal for society and government, then it seems to follow that those who are farther below the threshold of sufficiency than others should have priority in receiving proper treatment from the government. This is exactly the position Mencius and Xunzi take. Both thinkers say that there are disadvantaged groups of people who cannot normally help themselves:

Old men without wives, old women without husbands, old people without children, young children without fathers—these four types of people are the most destitute and have no one to turn to for help. Whenever King Wen put benevolent measures into effect, he always gave them first consideration. (*Mencius* 1B.5)

Those who have one of the Five Defects [i.e., those who are deaf, dumb, physically disabled, armless, suffering from dwarfism] should be raised up and gathered in so that they can be cared for. They should be given official duties commensurate with their abilities and employment adequate to feed and clothe themselves so that all are included and not even one of them is overlooked. (*Xunzi* 9.1)

Select good and worthy men for office, promote those who are honest and reverent, reward filial piety and brotherly affection, gather under your protection orphans and widows, and offer assistance to those in poverty and need. (*Xunzi* 9.4)

Notice that they do not prescribe helping those who are badly off only through handouts. Assistance can also take the form of jobs protected by a level of wage sufficient for subsistence. As Xunzi notes, people with disabilities "should be given official duties commensurate with their abilities and employment adequate to feed and clothe themselves." The next chapter will give a more detailed analysis of how the government and other actors should help the needy.

Merit and Contribution

As seen in the second section, for Mencius and Xunzi the salary or income from one's productive activity should be based on one's merit or contribution. They do not believe in equality of outcome. Some people may legitimately get a greater reward or possess more wealth than others because of their merit or contribution. Xunzi writes that the amount and substance of one's emolument should fit one's "station":

> The ancient kings acted to control men with regulations, ritual, and moral principles, in order thereby to divide society into classes, creating therewith differences in status between the noble and base, disparities between the privileges of age and youth, and the division of the wise from the stupid, the able from the incapable. *All of this caused men to perform the duties of their station in life and each to receive his due; only after this had been done was the amount and substance of the emolument paid by grain made to fit their respective stations.* (*Xunzi* 4.12, italics added)

> When a man of ren occupies the highest position, farmers labor with all their energy to exhaust the potential of their fields, merchants scrutinize with keen eyes to get the utmost from their goods, the various artisans use their skills to the fullest in making utensils and wares, and the officials, from the knights and grand officers up to the feudal lords, all execute fully the functions of their offices with ren, generosity, wisdom, and ability. This may be called "perfect peace." *So though one may have as his emolument the whole world, he need not consider it excessive, and though one be only a gatekeeper, receptionist, guard, or nightwatchman, he need never think his salary too meager. Anciently it was said: Unequal yet equivalent, bent yet obedient, not the same yet uniform. This refers to the constant relationships of mankind.* (4.12, italics added)

Note that Xunzi is not advocating a discriminatory, class-based hierarchy of society. Rather, he presents a hierarchy of status and emolument that is defined with reference to people's ability, not their family background. In fact, Xunzi is an advocate of class mobility based on merit. He writes:

> Although they be the descendants of kings and dukes or knights and grand officers, if they are incapable of devotedly observing the requirements of ritual and moral principles, *they should be relegated to the position of com-*

moners. Although they be the descendants of commoners, if they accumulate culture and study, rectify their character and conduct, and are capable of devotedly observing the requirements of ritual principles and justice, *they should be brought to the ranks of a prime minister, knight, or grand officer.* (9.1, italics added)

Mencius also endorses contribution or merit as the basis of emolument. He says one should be paid in accordance with one's work or contribution (*gong*), not one's intention (*Mencius* 3B.4). He stresses in particular that a gentleman who gives advice to the ruler deserves emolument, even though he does not engage in a productive activity like that of farmers and carpenters. This is because helping to make the prince secure and honored and to educate people to be dutiful is also a form of contribution (7B.32).

We have seen that once the level of material sufficiency has been attained, Mencius and Xunzi do not object to economic inequalities that arise from personal factors such as merit and contribution, which are largely based on the possession of abilities (moral character and intelligence). Neither thinker is a "luck egalitarian," one who believes that those who become worse off than others through no fault of their own should be compensated. Instead, both believe that desert should be based on a person's achievement and contribution.

Interestingly (and controversially), both men believe that human beings are born with the same nature and natural talents. "In natural talent, inborn nature, awareness, and capability, the gentleman and the petty man are one" (*Xunzi* 4.8). What accounts for the eventual differences in ability and moral development are two factors, one personal and the other social. The personal factor is the extent to which a person is willing to think, learn, and cultivate himself (*Mencius* 6A.17, *Xunzi* 4.8, 4.10, 23.5b). The social factor is a person's environment and the customs of his community. "The habituation of custom modifies the direction of will and, if continued for a long time, will alter a person's substance" (*Xunzi* 8.11; see also 4.8). Mencius also says that a person's surroundings can transform his temperament (*qi*) (*Mencius* 7A.36). Although people's achievements depend in part on the environment and customs they grow up in, neither thinker asserts that those made worse off by such uncontrollable factors should be compensated. I suspect that even if they were shown that people are born with different levels of talent, they would still not choose to endorse luck egalitarianism.

Toward a Confucian Perfectionist Perspective on Social Justice

The main principles of a rudimentary Confucian perspective on social justice can be summarized as follows:

1. Sufficency for all: Each household should have an amount of resources sufficient to live a materially secured and ethical life.

2. Priority to the badly off: People who fall below the threshold of sufficiency—those who have special needs and are badly off—should have priority in being taken care of.
3. Merit and contribution: Offices and emolument should be distributed according to an individual's merits and contributions; any subsequent inequality of income is not illegitimate.

This perspective on social justice is perfectionist, for the (early) Confucian conception of the good life is at work in several stages of the above reconstruction. First, according to a perfectionist view, the aim of social justice is to enable every member of a community to live a good life. As the Confucian conception of the good life requires material resources, these are an important issue for distributive justice. Second, the perfectionist view also explains in part why the distributive principle is one of sufficiency rather than equality (as an intrinsic value). Because social justice aims to enable everyone to live a good life, what is morally important is whether each person has enough resources to lead a good life, not whether each has the same amount.

Third, being a perfectionist view, the Confucian conception of the good life sets a rough but objective standard for sufficiency—it is defined not by the amount of resources one needs to pursue one's subjective conception of the good life (for example, to be a billionaire), but by how much people generally need to feel materially secure enough to pursue the higher, ethical life. It is difficult to be precise on the exact amount of resources needed for this purpose. But I think a Confucian perspective would take a clear stance on the following. On the one hand, the standard of sufficiency would not be "material abundance" or "affluence," for one does not need riches to cultivate virtues and practice social relationships, and it may be argued that the pursuit of affluence distracts people from the ethical good. On the other hand, the standard of sufficiency would also not be a "bare minimum," for people having only a bare minimum to sustain their lives exist at the precarious edge of poverty and starvation and as a result do not have a sufficient sense of security to be able to engage in moral learning. In Mencius's view, an appropriate level of sufficiency would be equivalent to what we may call a "decent material life"—namely, that those who are fifty can wear silk and those who are seventy can eat meat. Abstract application of this standard to a modern society is clearly not feasible, as the standard may vary from society to society and can only be determined by considering the specifics of the society in question.

Fourth, from a perfectionist perspective, it is worth examining Mencius's choice of land as the main resource for distribution and his idea of the well-field system. Land is not only a place for shelter but also an important "means of production." However, being a means of production, it cannot be compared with a cash or welfare handout that the recipient can immediately use. The recipient must labor to reap its value. To use modern terminology, justice cannot be achieved through direct welfare handouts (with the exception of welfare handouts to those who are badly off). If we put this in the larger picture of Mencius's social ideal represented by the well-field system, we can begin to understand the kind of regime of justice that Mencius envisages. As we shall see in the next chapter, what Mencius envisages is not just a regime of justice but also a regime of care. Social justice provides an equitable economic foundation for the pursuit of the good life; in caring for others, whether the others are from one's own family or other families/social networks, benevolence is expressed and virtuous relationships developed and sustained. According to this perfectionist view, justice and care are not opposing demands but are nicely integrated by a conception of the good life. More will be said about this in the next chapter.

In sum, the Confucian perfectionist perspective gives social justice an *aim* (the promotion of the good life), a *standard* (sufficiency for all), and a *proper place* in the larger ideal social system (the integration of justice and care, with input from the family, social networks, and government). Needless to say, much more work needs to be done to develop this perspective into a full-fledged theory for modern times and to provide a philosophical defense of this perspective against competing theories of justice. For now I will simply point out that the Confucian perspective I have outlined bears striking resemblance to the position of a recent group of theorists who challenge the egalitarian theory of justice and have developed an alternative perspective that is sometimes called the "doctrine of sufficiency."[24] Like the doctrine of sufficiency, a Confucian perspective will need to defend itself against opponents from either end of the spectrum of social justice theories. At one end is the libertarian, who argues that it is not a matter of justice or moral right for society to provide any level of material assistance whatsoever to those who are economically badly off. At the other end is the egalitarian, who argues that economic inequality above the level of sufficiency still needs to be corrected as far as justice is concerned. No verdict can be made on the reasonableness of the Confucian perspective until these challenges have been examined.

---

24 The most influential defense of this alternative perspective is Harry Frankfurt, "Equality as a Moral Ideal," *Ethics* 98, no. 1 (1987): 21–43. Other important discussions include Elizabeth S. Anderson, "What Is the Point of Equality?" *Ethics* 109, no. 2 (1999): 287–337; and Roger Crisp, "Equality, Priority, and Compassion," *Ethics* 113, no. 4 (2003): 745–63. For a critical discussion of the doctrine of sufficiency, see Paula Casal, "Why Sufficiency Is Not Enough," *Ethics* 117, no. 2 (2007): 296–326; for a defense, see Yitzhak Benbaji, "The Doctrine of Sufficiency: A Defence," *Utilitas* 17, no. 3 (2005): 310–32.

CHAPTER 8

Social Welfare and Care

In chapter 7 we saw that Mencius's well-field system is first and foremost about fair distribution of land—namely, that the government has a duty of justice to distribute to every household sufficient land to provide a decent standard of living. In this sense it is appropriate to say that social justice is the foundation of the well-field system. The well-field system, however, is a multilayered system of provision, in which the family and the village or commune also have specific roles to play. Mencius's vision is not of a nanny state that takes care of every aspect of people's lives from the cradle to the grave but of a social system regulated by several principles, such as justice as sufficiency, personal responsibility, care and voluntary help, and merit and contribution. Although many of the details are today no longer relevant, I believe that the basic principles are still plausible and appealing to modern societies. In the following I shall reconstruct the different layers of Mencius's thought and discuss the appeal and limitations of each in turn. Whenever possible, I shall also try to briefly highlight the policy implications of these principles for contemporary societies.

The Multilayer System

First Tier of Care: The Family

If the foundation tier of the well-field system is social justice, the tier above that, the first tier, is the tier of care and help from the family or household, the most important basic social unit in the well-field system. Mencius says that when people in the well-field system have enough land to plow and enough harvest to feed and clothe themselves, they will "learn, in their spare time, to be good sons and good younger brothers . . . they will, in their family, serve their fathers and elder brothers, and outside the family, serve their elders and superiors" (*Mencius* 1A.5).

The family is also the most important social unit in Confucian ethics. It is where people develop and exhibit their most natural and immediate affection and love. Mencius says that young children naturally know love for their parents, and when they grow they will naturally respect their elder brothers (*Mencius* 7A.15). If an individual is in need of help, the most natural and appropriate source of help would be the individual's own family, the prime site of care and love. Moreover, for Confucians it is the ethical responsibility of each individual to take care of his or her family members. Filial piety (*xiao*), the most important Confucian virtue, consists of the duty to financially support and care for one's parents (*Mencius* 4B.30, *Analects* 2.7). Similarly, parental love (ci) requires parents to be kind to their young children and take good care of them (*Mencius* 6B.7). If a son is able to provide care and help to his parents, it would be a serious wrong to pass this responsibility to other people or to the government.

I believe Confucians would support the idea that, when basic justice is secured, the responsibility for social welfare resides first and foremost with the family. Only when this first tier of help fails to deliver should other tiers be considered. This idea would seem to help explain two phenomena apparent in some East Asian societies: the first is that, traditionally, Chinese people typically prefer to seek help from their family rather than from the government;[1] and the second is that China, Taiwan, and Singapore currently have legislation to the effect that parents who are unable to support themselves have the right to demand support from their children if they have come of age and are financially able to provide it. The idea behind the legislation is not that the government has no responsibility to help older people but that, from a Confucian point of view, it is the duty of adult children to care for their elderly parents.[2]

Second Tier: Communities and Social Networks

To serve as the second tier of help, Mencius envisages a network of *communal* relationships. In his proposal of a method of land distribution for the well-field system, Mencius expects the eight households that form the system's basic unit to provide each other with mutual aid:

> Neither in burying the dead, nor in changing his abode, does a man go beyond the confines of his village. If those who own land within each *jing* befriend one another both at home and abroad, help each other to keep watch, and succor each other in illness, they will live in love and harmony. (*Mencius* 3A.3)

The idea of mutual aid among fellow villagers coheres well with another famous saying of Mencius's: "Treat the aged of your own family in a manner befitting their venerable age and extend this treatment to the aged of other families; treat your own young in a manner befitting their tender age and extend this to the young of other families" (*Mencius* 1A.7). If family members constitute first-tier caregivers, then neighbors constitute the second tier.

---

1   See Lau Siu-kai, *Society and Politics in Hong Kong*, Hong Kong Series (Hong Kong: Chinese University Press, 1982), esp. chaps. 3 and 4.

2   For a more detailed discussion on the rights of older people from a Confucian perspective, see my "Confucian Perspective on Human Rights," 235–36.

The implications of this proposal for modern urban societies may be somewhat unclear.[3] But the basic notion holds true. The concept of mutual aid need not presuppose a well-field system but any small community or group in which people interact with each other on a regular basis. The fellow villagers of Mencius's time could be modern relatives, neighbors, friends, or even colleagues. In principle, such communities can "befriend one another both at home and abroad, help each other to keep watch, and succor each other in illness." From the perspective of Confucian benevolence, assistance given by those with whom we have social ties is preferable to governmental help. This form of assistance comes with care and concern and may also be more effective because the caregiver understands the needs and problems of the one who seeks assistance. Also, giving assistance provides an important opportunity for the caregiver to act virtuously and for both parties to develop a valuable relationship. Confucian benevolence and virtuous relationships are expressed, developed, and sustained through caring and concern.

However, even when judged in Confucian ethical terms, this seems somewhat idealistic. The problem is that, as an ethical theory, Confucianism is uncertain and vague on what one may reasonably expect from one's neighbors and friends. It is true that for Confucians, an individual's care and concern for others should reach beyond the gateway of his or her home. Mencius even explicitly asks us to extend the care that we give to members of our own family to the members of other families. Yet Mencius is equally explicit in warning us not to confuse benevolence with the Mohist doctrine of equal concern for all, which he heavily criticizes. For Mencius it is natural and legitimate for a man to love his brother's son more than his neighbor's newborn baby (*Mencius* 3A.5); he also believes that if an individual treats his neighbor's father in exactly the same way that he treats his own father, as Mozi asks, he is, in effect, denying his own father (3B.9). Confucians believe in a graded form of love for others, not impartial concern for all.

The difference between Confucian and Mohist thinking on this issue can also be characterized in another way. Mohist thinking seems close to the utilitarian notion of the ideal impartial observer, who attempts to see things from an impersonal point of view and to treat people impartially. Confucian ethical thinking, however, starts from a personal point of view, namely, imagining and inferring the needs of others from one's own. Confucius says that a benevolent person is one who "helps others to establish themselves insofar as he himself wishes to establish himself, and gets others there insofar as he himself wishes to get there. The ability to take as analogy what is near at hand can be called the method of benevolence" (*Analects* 6.30). Benevolence is thus motivated, but also limited, by one's natural desires, concerns, and imagination. The analogical method takes the personal point of view as the natural and trustworthy starting

---

3   For implications in rural areas, see Daniel A. Bell, "Confucian Constraints on Property Rights," chap. 9 in *Confucianism for the Modern World*.

place for ethical reflection and therefore has to allow much room for individual variation. As people's desires to receive help and their willingness to give vary greatly from individual to individual, it follows that there would be a great deal of indeterminacy as to how much one might legitimately be expected to help others and how much assistance one might expect from others. Confucius says that if there were a man who gave extensively to others and brought help to the multitude, this would no longer be a matter of benevolence. He would be a *sage* (*sheng*) (6.30). Thus what we are certain of is only that benevolence requires more than familial love but much less than the ideal of a sage. Confucianism says little about exactly where the requirement of benevolence should lie between these two poles, and perhaps, given the "method of benevolence," it is impossible to specify the different degrees of concern for people outside of one's family.

The moral indeterminacy of benevolence is carried into Mencius's multitier system of assistance. Ideally, social networks and ties in the second tier would play a vital role in the provision of welfare assistance, but Confucians cannot confidently say exactly how much mutual aid may be reasonably expected from this source.[4] This second tier is therefore not as reliable as the familial and governmental tiers, which Mencius envisages as carrying definite responsibilities.[5] This perhaps explains why there was never any law in traditional China that compelled people to help their neighbors, whereas there were, and still are, laws enforcing filial piety in societies with a Confucian heritage. Confucian moral psychology may be less idealistic than Mohist moral psychology. Yet the indeterminacy that follows from this moral psychology prevents Confucians from giving a persuasive account of the ethical and institutional guidelines for mutual aid based on social networks and communities.

Third Tier: The Government

The third tier in the multilayer system of welfare assistance is the government, which serves as a kind of a last resort. There are two main sets of people for whom assistance from the government is necessary. The first are those who are unable to help themselves and have no family to turn to. The following conversation between Mencius and King Xuan of Qi is revealing. The king asked, "May I hear about Kingly government?" and Mencius replied:

> Formerly, when King Wen ruled over Qi, tillers of land were taxed one part in nine; descendants of officials received hereditary emoluments; there was

---

4   For a related but somewhat different discussion of this issue, see David B. Wong, "Universalism versus Love with Distinctions: An Ancient Debate Revived," *Journal of Chinese Philosophy* 16, no. 3–4 (1989): 251–72.

5   Unlike in the second tier, the responsibilities of family and government are not vague. Adult children are expected to give all they can to help maintain their parents. The government is also expected to step in to provide for basic subsistence when the alternatives fail.

inspection but no levy at border stations and market places; fish-traps were open for all to use; punishment did not extend to the wife and children of an offender. *Old men without wives, old women without husbands, old people without children, young children without fathers—these four types of people are the most destitute and have no one to turn to for help. Whenever King Wen put benevolent measures into effect, he always gave them first consideration.* (*Mencius* 1B.5, italics added)

This passage illustrates that even when a government does its best to provide the basic conditions for people to be prosperous, there will always be some who are unable to make a living and have no family to fall back on—these people are, in Mencius's words, old men without wives, old women without husbands, old people without children, and young children without fathers. Mencius says that these are the most destitute and have no one to turn to for help and thus should be given first consideration from the government. To use modern terminology, these are "the worst off" to whom the government should give first priority.[6]

The question of whether it is better for those in need to turn to their fellow villagers for assistance in the absence of a suitable adult family member, rather than to the government, is not addressed by Mencius, and to answer it requires elaboration and extension of what is said in the text. One possible answer is that if a person—old or young—is unable to support himself or herself and has no adult family members to turn to for support, the burden of assistance that would be placed on the person's neighbors, if they were to support him or her for life, would be too great to bear—especially in situations where the neighbors are not well-off themselves. In agricultural economies, for instance, production is heavily affected by contingent natural factors such as weather and land fertility. There are times when peasants do not reap sufficient harvests to maintain a good life for themselves. This second tier, therefore, may not always be able to provide adequate long-term, stable assistance to the old and young who have no direct family support.

The second set of people in need of governmental assistance are those who are too poor to even plow their land or those living in hunger because of poor harvests due to natural causes. If there are large numbers of these people, perhaps only a government can provide sufficient aid to them.[7] Mencius suggests

6 Which does not necessarily mean "absolute" priority as understood in Rawls, *A Theory of Justice.*

7 In principle, members of a community could establish a granary to support each other. But even this is not a safe guarantee, for sometimes an entire community, or all the communities in a region, suffer for long periods of time from bad harvests and natural disasters. The idea of voluntary community granaries is explored in William Theodore de Bary, "The Community Compact," chap. 5 in *Asian Values and Human Rights: A Confucian Communitarian Perspective* (Cambridge: Harvard University Press, 1998). Their history, however, was not well documented. From a historical point of view, government-funded and -managed community granaries were more prevalent than voluntary ones. See the discussion below.

to King Xuan of Qi that on a tour of inspection in spring, he should "inspect plowing so that those who have not enough for sowing may be given help"; and on a tour of inspection in autumn he should "inspect the progress of harvesting so that those who are in need may be given aid" (*Mencius* 1B.4). On another occasion, Mencius explicitly says that in good times a government should prudently collect resources through taxation (in terms of money or goods such as grains) so that it has sufficient resources to help the most needy when times are bad (1A.3). As seen in the previous chapter, Mencius thinks a government that fails to assist those dying of starvation is morally responsible for their death, and that a responsible government is always prepared for bad harvests and natural disasters.

Confucian thinkers never question that the government, or the ruler, should take up this role of last resort. Early Confucian masters hold that the foremost duty of government is to provide welfare assistance to its subjects and improve their material well-being. This duty is implied by both the Confucian service conception of authority and the ideal ruler-ruled relationship as reconstructed in chapter 1—namely, that a ruler has legitimate authority only if he protects and promotes the well-being of the people, and a harmonious relationship with the people can be sustained only if the ruler identifies with the people and shares their happiness and suffering (*Mencius* 1A.2, 1B.4). To ignore the suffering of the people is to alienate oneself as a ruler from the people.

Of course, in the final analysis, the duty to help the needy does not fall solely on the ruler but also on the people. The ruler or the government is not an independent actor with its own resources to perform all welfare tasks. The burden of public welfare provision must also be borne by the people. The Mencian perspective of social justice reconstructed in chapter 7 provides a justification for the people's duty. The ruler has a duty of justice to provide everyone with a fair share of material resources, and he does so through maintaining a well-ordered social structure supported by a proper set of laws and policies in land distribution, taxation, and the management of common-pool resources such as forest and fish. This well-ordered structure, however, is possible only if the people who receive their fair share of resources also contribute to government revenue by working the public land in the well-field system or through some form of tax. In other words, the people's claim to justice in terms of material sufficiency is inseparable from their obligation to work to provide that sufficiency for all. The idea that people have an obligation to work to provide sufficiency for all is recognized by the well-field system, as every household must plow the public or communal land before they work on their own.

According to Chen Huan-Chang, the author of the important but neglected book *The Economic Principles of Confucius and His School*, Mencius's principle of giving special favor to the four classes of the needy (as mentioned in *Mencius* 1B.5), and the poor in general, was indeed put into practice in China. Chen notes that in the Song dynasty the central government established a granary in each district to store rice that came from the public land as rent. Each of the four classes of needy people were given rice and sometimes clothes and other food. In the Ming dynasty (1368–1644) there were decrees to support the destitute. For example, in 1386 a decree was made to the effect that

> Among poor people, if the age was above eighty, five pecks of rice, three pecks of wine, and five catties of meat were given to each of them monthly. If the age was above ninety, one roll of silk and one catty of cotton were added to this amount annually. Those who owned some farm land were not given rice. To all the Four Classes—widower, widow, orphan, the solitary— six bushels of rice were given annually.

Similarly, in the Qing dynasty every district had an almshouse maintained by the government, and officials who failed to fulfill their welfare responsibilities were punished. "According to the *Law Code of the Tsing [Qing] Dynasty*, if the officials do not support the Four Classes, the very sick person and the infirm and superannuated who need public support, they shall be punished with sixty blows of the long stick." This demonstrates, Chen claims, that the Confucian idea that government has a responsibility to help the needy and poor "has been put into actual law, and its effects differs only because of the efficiency of administration."[8]

From Principles to Institutions

Let us take stock. If our previous discussion is not far off the mark, Confucian ethics would endorse the following principles:

1. Welfare assistance should first be provided on the basis of family and social network ties. We can give several points to support this principle.[9] First, family members have the primary responsibility to take care of each other. Second, family and social networks are often built on affection and care. Third, affection and care are genuine only if they are voluntary. A welfare assistance system has a better chance of manifesting the value of care if it is based on the voluntary commitment of the caregiver. Fourth, a family-based or community-based system can respond more effectively to the various needs of individuals than a system based on bureaucratic regulations. Finally, this system may have the desirable consequence of strengthening family and community ties.
2. Welfare entitlements sanctioned by government should be seen as a fallback support. Governmental assistance is first and foremost necessary when the familial and communal tiers break down. There are unfilial

---

8   Chen Huan-Chang 陳煥章 [Chen Huanzhang], *The Economic Principles of Confucius and His School*, 2 vols. (New York: Columbia University, 1911), 2:599.

9   Some of these points can be supported by Confucian ethics. Some, like the final two, are based only on judgments about the probable effects of welfare systems.

children and uncaring parents. There are communities that lack strong ties and mutual concern. An ethics of benevolence would not want the weak and vulnerable to be left behind. As Confucian benevolence demands that we help these people, one way to do so is by supporting the government that acts as our agent. Governmental assistance is also necessary when the first two tiers cannot provide sufficient assistance. Consider the example of care for older people. There are many older people whose quality of life depends on long-term care. However, adult children today find it a heavy burden to take care of their aging parents as their jobs demand a great deal of time and energy, and men and women alike need to work in order to cover family expenses. In such situations, even filial children may not be able to help their parents as much as they want to, in which case government-based social services would be welcome and even necessary (especially if social networks are also unable to offer sufficient help).

3. Welfare entitlements systems should avoid encouraging people to shirk their personal responsibility of caring for family members. While accepting a welfare safety net sanctioned by the government, Confucians would be worried by the growing trend of people becoming reliant on the government. It has been noted that in Western welfare states, "too many people have come to think of their welfare, and their neighbors' welfare, as the government's problem."[10] Active governmental involvement runs the risk of encouraging people to shirk their personal and communal responsibilities. It may also render superfluous valuable voluntary charity groups and mutual aid associations in modern industrial societies. In my opinion, while the government should provide the minimal safety net, it is also highly desirable, from a Confucian point of view, to have a safety net package that induces people to contribute voluntarily and to do so in the spirit of care. (This preference can further be linked to the general tendency in Confucianism to rely more on people's voluntary actions than on government sanctions and legal coercion.) People too often assume that the end of personal responsibility means the beginning of governmental responsibility. But this is not true. We should, and can, tap the resources of the family, charity groups, voluntary associations, mutual aid societies, and the general public.

A Proposal

I argued earlier that Confucian ethics suffers from considerable indeterminacy regarding the extent of moral responsibility we have toward our neighbors and

10   See David Schmidtz, "Mutual Aid," chap. 4 of pt. 1 in David Schmidtz and Robert E. Goodin, *Social Welfare and Individual Responsibility*, ed. R. G. Frey (Cambridge: Cambridge University Press, 1998), 64.

strangers. Although the lack of a clear moral guideline makes it impossible for us to know exactly what is expected of us and what we can expect of others, I believe we must live with this theoretical uncertainty; nevertheless, good institutions may reduce the uncertainty in practice. The best way to deal with this uncertainty is to create welfare institutions that can induce maximal personal contributions from people and yet give them a choice to decide whether to participate. A primarily voluntary scheme would reduce the need to rely on extensive welfare taxation, which, from a Confucian viewpoint, has an unclear moral basis. In this section, I shall consider how we could improve modern welfare mechanisms in light of the Confucian principles reconstructed above.

The standard method of financing governmental social services in modern welfare states is through involuntary taxation. This is done either through compulsory deductions from monthly paychecks (as in many Western countries) or through a one-off compulsory tax payment (as in Hong Kong). When paying taxes, most people do not appear to think they are doing good for others. Instead, most seem only to experience pain in seeing their money forcibly taken away. In addition, the entire process is not only involuntary but also impersonal. Taxpayers do not know where their tax money is spent, and welfare recipients do not know from whom they are receiving help. The two groups of people seldom consider the existence of each other, and the existing welfare mechanisms deliberately prevent them from having any contact. The only agent that either side is in touch with is the government authority. In Hong Kong, for example, older people receive their pensions through impersonal processes like bank transfers. They experience nothing remotely close to care and concern. Rightly or wrongly, then, many taxpayers and welfare recipients feel victimized or humiliated by the welfare state.

I will now propose a tentative way of improving this situation.[11] The core of my proposal is a new mechanism that encourages people's voluntary participation and the active involvement of charity and social welfare groups. Instead of compulsory taxation, voluntary donation would be the major source of revenue. Instead of bureaucratic agencies, voluntary groups would be encouraged to assume the responsibility of delivering as many welfare services as possible. The central aspect of the mechanism would be that each year, when taxpayers receive their tax forms, they would also receive a booklet containing an outline of all qualified (or certified) voluntary social services groups (with details of whom they help, the programs and activities they organize, a breakdown of what they spent in the previous year, and their projected costs for the coming year), along with an assessment of the efficiency of each groups. This booklet would be prepared by a government authority or independent agency. Taxpay-

---

11   Another way, more suitable to the countryside than the urban city, is to try to provide an environment in which communal mutual aid societies can survive and flourish. For stimulating discussions of mutual aid societies in traditional China and Korea, see de Bary, "The Community Compact"; and Chang Yun-Shik, "Mutual Help and Democracy in Korea," chap. 4 in *Confucianism for the Modern World*.

ers would then be asked for voluntary donations to one or more of these groups according to their own choice and would receive tax breaks for the donations made. In the entire process, the government would mainly play the role of a middle agent, providing trustworthy information and effective coordination. The social services groups receiving revenue from this process would be required to provide opportunities for taxpayers to visit their offices and ask questions about their work. It would be in the interest of these groups to make these opportunities attractive to taxpayers.

Would this proposal work? The proposal is based on two key empirical assumptions, which, if true, would suggest that the proposal is feasible. First, it assumes that people are to some degree altruistic. As Mencius says, people have a compassionate heart. Many of us experience something close to Mencius's falling child example: watching TV news about people in situations of need or natural disaster, we are often moved and feel the urge to help by making donations. However, this urge rarely results in action. The main reason—other than weakness of will—is lack of trust, and this is the second assumption. Since we often do not have trustworthy, detailed information about the groups that claim to help people and that request public donations, there is a risk that our money may not go safely into the hands of the needy. Note that this problem of trust is reducible to a problem of information—if an individual knew for certain that a group was doing well, that individual might be less hesitant to donate. There is no free-riding problem in voluntary donation since, given the first assumption, people want to help whether others are helping or not. If the sacrifice requested is not substantial, most people would want to contribute because they feel that they are doing the right thing and feel good doing so. (I assume, of course, that the amount each person is motivated to donate is what he or she feels comfortable with.)

The government's main role, therefore, would be to solve the problem of information. The government would collect information about each of the groups to assess and grade their performance, just as a government inspects and assesses the hygiene of restaurants, or a government's own auditing department assesses the performance of other departments. Performance would be assessed in terms of the percentage of donations received going to administrative costs in relation to the percentage going to beneficiaries, and the cost-effectiveness of the group's programs and activities. (If the assessment is performed by a public agency rather than a governmental department, then part of the donation the government receives would go to financing it.) Taxpayers would thus receive not only useful information that would motivate them to donate but also reliable information about the performance of the groups.

However, the government would also need to ensure fair distribution of donations. Since this mechanism relies on individual choice, it is likely that the distribution of donations would be uneven across groups, and that some needy people would receive little support. To address this problem, the government could take a percentage of total donations. In addition, when choosing where their money should go, people could be asked to choose not individual groups as such but different aid packages that combine a whole range of groups.

This model of voluntary donation is quite similar to that of United Way.[12] Created in 1887 in Denver, the movement has spread to forty-one countries and territories and is now one of the world's largest privately supported nonprofits. Its mission is "to improve lives by mobilizing the caring power of communities around the world to advance the common good." United Way helps people by funding a vast network of some 1,800 community-based organizations called local United Ways. Each organization is independent, separately incorporated, and run by local volunteers. United Way raises funds to support local partner agency service providers. In total, voluntary contributions to United Ways support approximately 45,000 agencies and chapters in the United States. For example, the organization generated an estimated US$5.14 billion in 2011, which was used for human services ranging from disaster relief, emergency food and shelter, and crisis intervention to day care, physical rehabilitation, and youth development. Each group receiving funds is a nonprofit, tax-exempt charity run by volunteers, and each submits to an annual, independent financial audit. Because of the wide network of volunteers and the simplicity of corporate payroll deduction, general and administrative costs took up only 8 percent of United Way's expenses in 2011.[13]

The apparent success of United Way provides an empirical basis for the viability of the model I propose here. Both models work with similar aims and methods, except that the central agency in my model is the government or a publicly authorized independent agency. The advantage of the latter over a private institution is that the public agency, precisely because of its source of authority, is able to express, in a symbolic way, public support for the importance of voluntary help and mutual caring.

However, the example of United Way also shows that this kind of voluntary welfare scheme is not sufficient to meet the welfare needs of people. Realistically it is likely that the model proposed here might not generate enough revenue to support a welfare safety net for all, and thus the traditional method of governmental taxation would still be necessary. This proposed mechanism is not meant to replace taxation for welfare purposes. It only aims to diminish our need for it. Nevertheless, even within a compulsory taxation scheme, we could

---

12   I first heard of this organization from a passenger sitting next to me when I was flying from Boston to Seoul to attend a conference. In a casual but intellectually charged chat, I was explaining to this passenger the main ideas of my paper and in particular this model of voluntary welfare. To my delight and distress, the passenger then immediately told me that the United States United Way was very close to my proposal. The passenger was an American information technology businessman who happened to be interested in social sciences and, surprisingly, Confucianism.

13   United Way, http://www.liveunited.org; 2011 Annual Report, United Way Worldwide, http://unway.3cdn.net/f58b3b8a9b4f33a573_tvm62lh6v.pdf; and "Basic Facts about United Way," a fact sheet provided by the organization as reported on CNSNews.com, July 7, 2008, http://cnsnews.com/node/5459.

still create room for choice—for example, one could have the choice of giving 10 percent of one's tax contribution to a charity group (or area) or an aid package.[14] This method, though compulsory in nature, does to some degree encourage taxpayers to reflect and deliberate on the needs of the needy.

To conclude, this model has a number of virtues. It is not unrealistically ambitious; it encourages people to share the plight of the unfortunate; it allows people to choose to help those they most care about; it promotes the development of voluntary social service groups;[15] and it increases the opportunity for interaction between the benefactor and the beneficiary, thereby fostering a culture of care and benevolence.

Conclusion

Having completed my reconstruction of the Confucian perspective on social justice and welfare in this and the previous chapter, the main principles of this rudimentary Confucian perspective can be summarized as follows:

1. Justice as sufficiency for all: Each household should have a sufficient amount of resources (or land, according to Mencius) to live a materially secure and ethical life.
2. Mutual aid: Beyond the foundation of social justice, families and social networks are the first and second tier of care and help for people in need.
3. Government's welfare assistance: When the needs of the badly off cannot be met by the first two tiers, the government should provide direct welfare assistance.
4. Merit and contribution: Offices and emolument should be distributed according to people's merits and contributions. Inequality of income that arises from this source is not illegitimate.

If we put all these principles together, we see a social ideal that nicely integrates justice, care, personal responsibility, and individual merit into a coherent system. The first principle combines justice with personal responsibility—justice requires equitable land distribution by the government, but members of a household must work together and labor hard to be able to harvest well. The second principle shows that caring is an important part of the social ideal. For the Confucian conception of the good life, assistance coming from family and social ties is preferable to governmental help, for it stems from caring and concern, and may be more effective because the caregiver better understands the needs and problems of those who seek assistance. More important, mutual aid

14   I thank Daniel A. Bell for this suggestion.
15   Today's charity groups, especially smaller ones, often find it difficult to survive precisely because of the information problem and the fact that they need human resources and revenue for fund raising and public relations. This proposed mechanism would help reduce this need.

is an important opportunity for the caregiver to engage in virtuous activity and for both parties to develop a valuable relationship. When mutual aid fails, or is not sufficient to help the needy, the ideal of care requires the government to step in and provide direct welfare assistance, so the third principle comes into action. Finally, the fourth principle makes room for economic inequality arising from differential efforts and merit of individuals. The Confucian social ideal is a regime of justice and care—one that does not eliminate personal responsibility or individual merit.

Confucian Political Perfectionism

The Project

Throughout this book I have attempted to develop a viable alternative for governance that can simultaneously retain the spirit of the Confucian ideal of society and politics and effectively deal with problems arising from nonideal situations. In the Confucian ideal society, the virtuous and competent are chosen to work for the common good; people conduct affairs in sincerity and faithfulness with the aim of cultivating harmony; rulers care for the people, and the people trust them and willingly submit to their rule; rulers ensure that there are sufficient resources for the people to lead a materially secure and ethical life; people look after not only their own family members but also others outside their family; and society gives special care and support to the unfortunate. Running through this ideal society is an ethic of public-spiritedness and mutual care, understood as an ethic of benevolence and righteousness, from which virtuous relationships spring and flourish.

Confucians are acutely aware that reality often falls far short of this lofty ideal—righteousness can give way to selfishness and moral impropriety, and leaders can succumb to the temptations of power and fame. Yet they refuse to abandon this ideal, for it expresses what is right and noble in humanity. To give up the ideal is to give up faith in humanity. For Confucians, governance must be based on benevolence and a kind of moral cultivation promoted through rites and education. They reject the Legalist strategy because it places little faith in humanity and relies solely on punishment and reward to regulate behavior. This is not to say that Confucians would never use force for social regulation, only that the use of force is always secondary to ethical means that are more in keeping with the Confucian ideal. Confucians thus face a difficult situation: on the one hand they cannot agree with the Legalist strategy; on the other, they acknowledge that their preferred means of benevolence, rites, and moral cultivation sometimes fail to regulate the misbehavior of the people and political elites.

This book has examined modern Western institutions of liberal democracy as alternative methods of structuring politics and society. Under appropriate social and economic conditions, the institutions of liberal democracy—limited government, democratic elections, human rights, and civil liberties—seem to be more effective than other political systems in restraining political power, preventing blatant corruption, and compelling elected officials to work for the well-being of the people and heed their opinions.[1] In adopting liberal democratic institutions for Confucian purposes, the central issue is whether these institutions can express the aspirations of the Confucian political ideal and what role they can play in bridging the gap between the Confucian ideal and reality. Several of the previous chapters have dealt with this issue. My main philosophical strategy has been to adopt a political perfectionist approach to tackle the interplay between Confucian ideals and liberal democratic institutions. A political perfectionist approach takes the human good, or so-called conception of the good life, as the basis for evaluating a social and political order. It justifies "the right" by reference to "the good," to use contemporary philosophical terminology. This approach decouples liberal democratic institutions from those popular liberal philosophical packages that place the right prior to the good and base liberal democratic institutions on fundamental moral rights or principles, such as popular sovereignty, political equality, human rights, and individual sovereignty.

In adopting liberal democratic institutions to tackle the problems of nonideal situations, I have reconstructed a normative approach that I call "Confucian political perfectionism." This approach looks at a series of fundamental political issues, such as political authority, democracy, human rights, civil liberties, social justice, and social welfare, in a way that differs from that of mainstream liberal democratic philosophies. Confucian political perfectionism not only provides a different philosophical justification for liberal democratic institutions, it also assigns them different roles and combines them with Confucian values wherever appropriate. However, I have not treated Confucian political values and principles as fixed points of reference that cannot be revised or rejected. Some changes have to be made to make the Confucian political vision more appealing to and appropriate for the context of modern society. For example, I have dropped the Confucian monistic conception of political authority to give room to the idea of limited government with checks and balances, and I have added a moderate notion of personal autonomy as a new basis for civil liberties. The end result of my reconstruction is, I hope, an outline—and no more than an outline—of a nuanced yet coherent new Confucian political philosophy. In the following section I restate this outline by drawing from the analyses and conclusions of the previous chapters and explain how perfectionism runs through the reconstruction. In the final section I discuss and evaluate different ways to promote Confucian political perfectionism in a modern pluralistic society.

---

1 Democracy seems to work well only in relatively advanced social and economic conditions and may not work well in developing countries. See Randall P. Peerenboom, *China Modernizes: Threat to the West or Model for the Rest?* (New York: Oxford University Press, 2007).

The Philosophy of Confucian Political Perfectionism

Political Authority

Political authority is a foundational issue in politics. The way in which political authority is conceived and justified has important bearings on how we understand the purposes of politics, the relations between the state and the people, and the design of political institutions. According to the Confucian perfectionist approach I outline here, political authority and the political rights of individuals are not a matter of moral entitlement. The foundation of political morality is the good life, and the virtues and ethical relationships that constitute the good life, rather than political rights. No individual or group possesses any natural right to rule—whether it be a particular ruler or the people as a whole. For Confucianism, political authority is not something that can be owned by a ruler, or something that grants him the right to treat his people and territory as belonging to him. Political authority refers instead to a legitimate right to govern within a jurisdiction. That right is always conditional on the ruler's (or the political system's) ability to protect and promote the well-being of the people. Political authority exists only for this purpose. Its justification therefore depends on its ability to serve this purpose well. Borrowing a term from Joseph Raz, I have called this the service conception of authority.

Although the people collectively possess no more natural political right to rule than any individual, they are not passive subjects with no role in legitimizing authority. Another important basis of authority, other than the service conception, is the ideal relational approach. According to this approach, an authoritative political relation is marked by a mutual commitment on both sides—the rulers are committed to serve the people and the ruled willingly submit to the rulers. The trust and voluntary submission of the people thus play an important part in constituting authority. For this reason the Confucian perfectionist approach makes two important connections between authority and the good life. First, authority instrumentally promotes the well-being of the people. Second, the authoritative relationship itself contributes to the good life, for its constitutive mutual commitment of care and support make the relationship ethically valuable and satisfying.

The authority of political leaders thus ultimately resides in the "hearts of the people"—that is, true authority can only be accepted, recognized, and willingly complied with by the people. External forces such as sheer might will not give a ruler true authority. Even an institutional office of authority cannot guarantee the officeholder true authority. Precisely because authority is constituted by the attitudes and commitment of both the ruler and the ruled, political authority is a precarious and fragile relationship that can be easily undermined if either side withdraws its constitutive attitudes and commitments. In the Confucian view, political leaders have to strive hard to forge and maintain this relationship—

they should care for the people, gain their trust, and win their hearts. This holds true for political systems of all types. The key message Confucianism sends to existing rulers—elected or otherwise—is that they should continually remind themselves of the fragility of their authority and devote themselves wholeheartedly to serving the people.

Limited Government and Separation of Powers

Although the Confucian service conception of authority and its ideal relational approach have a natural affinity with the idea of limited government, the former does not necessarily imply the latter. In fact, early Confucian thinkers embraced a conception of monistic and supreme authority, believing that the power of a Sage King with perfect moral virtue and perfect capacity of judgment needs no limitations: such a Sage King will always care for the people and make the best political judgments to promote their well-being, and any limitations imposed on his power would be a disabling constraint of his creativity. In reality, however, as such Sage Kings rarely exist, authority can be misused or exercised arbitrarily by rulers who are not so virtuous or competent. To prevent this from happening, authority should be limited or restrained in ways that protect the people. For this reason, any view that endorses the service conception of authority would be also inclined to defend limited government of some kind in nonideal situations, whether the government takes the form of a monarchy or a democracy.

The Confucian perfectionist view of politics and the good life also lends support to limited government. The aim of Confucian politics is to encourage and enable all individuals to live the good life, which is understood not as life lived according to the subjective preferences of individuals, but as life lived as an expression of humanity, or Dao, embodied in virtues and social relationships. The Confucian perfectionist conception of the good life can thus serve as a higher principle to evaluate politics. Dao-based perfectionist politics shares the spirit of the idea of limited government, in that both presuppose fundamental principles of morals and politics that (1) are not subject to the mere likes and dislikes of people and should not be changed by the politics of the day, and (2) should be put into effect to enable a government to pursue its proper tasks and to prevent abuse of power.

The Confucian political perfectionism that I advance here endorses not only limited government but also the separation of powers. The separation of powers is desirable on both epistemic and practical grounds. In nonideal situations, as no single virtuous person possesses a full understanding of the Way, we need a political system that allows individuals with different virtues to compete together and complement each other's strengths in order to achieve a balanced view of the Way and to put this into practice. The separation of powers is an institutional method that allows and promotes complementarity and competition between different visions of the Way. In addition, the separation of powers curbs power corruption. Confucians have long understood that virtue is in fact a form of power—a virtuous leader can persuade, inspire, and transform others. In nonideal situations, Confucians should agree with Montesquieu and Arendt that "even virtue stands in need of limitation,"[2] for it is a form of power too. Virtue must be opposed to virtue, just as power must be opposed to power.

Democracy

Confucian political perfectionism understands the value of democracy in a unique way. It rejects a rights-based approach that values democracy for its ability to realize popular sovereignty or the moral principle of political equality. It also rejects the ownership conception of political authority, whether ownership resides with the Sage King, the monarch, or the people. Instead, it justifies any authority by its service to the people. Accordingly, no individual has a fundamental moral right to a share in political authority. Any institutional arrangement of political authority is to be assessed in part by its contribution to the well-being of the people. The right to vote grants citizens a share in political authority. Their rights therefore need to be justified by reference to the good of the people (including voters and nonvoters in a community). In this sense there is no natural citizenship, just as there is no natural rulership.

Confucian perfectionism does not, however, adopt a purely instrumental view of democracy. In this theory democracy's value lies in its expression of another political ideal that Confucianism endorses, namely, the ideal political relationship marked by mutual commitment and trust, in which whoever exercises political power is committed to governing the people in a trustworthy and caring manner, and those whose exercise of political power is limited to the vote and other less extensive means express their willing endorsement and support for those who have the responsibility to govern. Democracy can be understood as a political system that best expresses such an ideal political relationship. The point of democratic elections is to select those who are public-spirited and trustworthy and to make explicit the public's endorsement and support of those who are elected. While other kinds of political systems can also express this ethically attractive political relationship, democracy provides the most direct and explicit form of institutional expression.

Democratic elections can perform both expressive and instrumental functions. In ideal situations, they express the ideal political relationship. In nonideal situations where politicians are motivated by self-interest as well as public interest, democratic elections can reward with reelection those who serve the people and remove those who fail to do so. The relative importance of the ex-

---

2 Arendt, *On Revolution*, 143.

pressive and instrumental functions of democratic elections depends on the relative dominance of public-interested vis-à-vis self-interested motivations. If the nonideal situation is within tolerable bounds, the expressive (selection) function should be primary and the protective (sanction) function secondary. Elections can thus address problems of reality and at the same time tally with the aspirations of the Confucian perfectionist ideal.

While democracy can help express and promote Confucian values, Confucian perfectionism can also work to the advantage of democracy. A well-functioning democracy needs a virtuous citizenry to ensure that it does not degenerate into a form of highly antagonistic politics based on narrow self-interests. I have argued that the cultivation of Confucian morals, as a form of humanity-based moral education, may well be more effective than liberal civic education in instilling the virtues that promote the health of democratic institutions and processes. According to the Confucian conception of moral education, people should cultivate certain virtues whether or not they choose to participate in public affairs. These virtues—respect, reverence, sincerity, lenience, truthfulness, industry, and beneficence—make individuals better people and offer them guidance in their interactions with family members, friends, colleagues, or fellow citizens. As such, Confucian moral education provides a stronger incentive for citizens to cultivate civility and a more comprehensive foundation of virtues than liberal civic education, which focuses primarily on developing critical thinking and the knowledge of public affairs, and citizens' rights and duties.

Confucian political perfectionism can also provide some reflection on how to select virtuous and competent people to serve in politics. The Confucian conception of authority does not entail any particular design of political institutions and insists only that they be designed to attract virtue and talent to work for the good of the people. If democratic elections do not furnish an adequate number of high-caliber politicians, or if they discourage politicians from making policies that are conducive to the long-term interests of the people, Confucian perfectionism would encourage people to consider alternative institutions to supplement democracy. I have suggested, by way of example, a second chamber of legislature whose members are selected by colleagues. Such a second chamber could contribute to governance through discussing and passing bills, discussing government budgets and spending, balancing the views of the democratically elected chamber, and monitoring the government. Its more important function, however, would be educational. If the second chamber were filled with politicians thought to be of high quality (i.e., virtuous and competent), they could serve as role models for other politicians and the entire citizenry. The manner with which they debated on public affairs, the viewpoints they brought into public discussion, and the judgments and decisions they made could have an educational effect on others. The second chamber would not only be a governing institution in its own right but also play an important part in the moral education of the society at large.

Human Rights and Civil Liberties

Confucian perfectionism adopts a similar two-track approach to human rights. As Confucians believe that human dignity or human worth consists in human beings' capacity for benevolence and righteousness, not in their possession of rights, human rights do not play an important role in the ideal society. Such rights are also not constitutive of human virtues. In an ideal situation, people are more or less virtuous and act in the spirit of benevolence. People in virtuous relationships do not think of themselves as subjects possessing rights upon which they make claims against their partners. Rather they think of themselves as participating in a relationship of reciprocal commitment or of mutual caring. To introduce the considerations of rights is inappropriate to such a relationship, as it would motivate individuals to see the interests of other members more as limitations on their personal rights than as interests that should be promoted for the common good.

In nonideal situations, however, human rights are an important fallback apparatus to protect fundamental human interests. According to the Confucian perfectionist view, we should strive to resolve conflicts first by means of education, mediation, and compromise in order to preserve the spirit of mutual caring and trust. But when virtuous relationships break down and mediation fails to reconcile conflicts, human rights are important instruments for the vulnerable to protect themselves against exploitation and harm from powerful actors, particularly the state. In nonideal situations human rights and virtues are important and mutually dependent. Despite the fact that virtues may occasionally slip or fail, and their use is thus somewhat precarious in protecting human interests, they are prerequisite for guiding the conduct of right-holders in the exercise of their rights. Virtues help prevent people from misusing their rights.

In contemporary Western societies there is a tendency in public and academic discourse to stress the language of rights sometimes to the near exclusion of concern for relationships. Contemporary rights talk often eclipses the traditional moral vocabularies of the common good, virtues, and duties and has become the main moral currency for tackling social problems. In the Confucian perfectionist perspective, human rights function as both normative principles and legal instruments, but their legal function is more significant. To avoid the pitfalls of a discourse focused largely on rights, the Confucian perfectionist perspective prefers to keep the list of human rights as legal instruments short, restricting it to civil and political rights such as the right to freedom from torture and arbitrary detention and arrest; equality before the law; the right to a fair trial; and the right to freedom of peaceful assembly and association. A short list containing civil and political rights is preferable not because social and economic needs are less important, but because these rights are more suitable for legal implementation, while the promotion of economic rights requires sound economic institutions and policies that cannot be easily captured by legal human rights language. Confucian perfectionism also makes the provision of basic needs central to the legitimacy of any political authority. More important, the adoption of civil and political rights redresses an otherwise strong tendency within traditional Confucianism to overempower political leaders. It thus reduces the chance of political corruption and despotism, which, according to Mencius, is the chief cause of severe poverty and famine. In short, a robust set of civil and political rights and the legal apparatus necessary to enforce those rights protects not only the physical security and freedom of the people but also their fundamental material needs and interests.

While Confucian political perfectionism embraces civil and political liberties, its stance toward liberties in cultural and moral matters—or autonomy in the personal sphere—is less straightforward. One of the most forceful modern challenges to Confucian ethics is that it does not recognize the value of individual personal autonomy. Confucian ethics does have the value of individual moral autonomy, in the sense that the moral agent must voluntarily accept the demands of morality and reflectively engage in the moral life. Traditional Confucian moral autonomy, however, was compatible with only a narrow range of life choices in study, career, marriage, and other areas of personal life. To cope with the demands of a fast-changing, pluralistic society, Confucian ethics should incorporate a moderate notion of personal autonomy, defined as enabling an individual to develop a personal identity, fashion his or her character, and chart a unique path in life. Such a concept of personal autonomy functions not as a moral right but as a valuable aspect of a good life. It is a matter of degree—one can be more or less autonomous, and this value need not be absolute. Personal autonomy competes with, and at times can be outweighed by, other values such as well-being and other ethical ideals. Personal autonomy differs from the strong liberal right of personal sovereignty, which forbids any restriction of this right regardless of other values. A Confucian perfectionist ethics that incorporates moderate personal autonomy is sensitive to the pluralism of values and ways of life in modern society. A Confucian perfectionist theory of liberties recognizes the value of personal autonomy as well as the importance of the ethical good that liberties instrumentally serve to promote. It attempts carefully to balance the two when they conflict.

Social Justice and Welfare

Central to Confucian political thought is the ruler's commitment to care for the people and to practice benevolent rule. This commitment does not arise simply from the benevolent character of the ruler. Rather, it is the ruler's political obligation, a condition for authority. I have argued that the policies of benevolent rule, in particular distributive policies regarding land and other material resources, can be conceived as policies of social justice. Confucian thinkers believe that the natural world provides human beings with adequate material resources to meet the material needs of everyone. Rulers have a duty of justice to maintain a well-ordered social and economic structure that provides everyone with sufficient resources to live a materially secured life. If the ruler fails to maintain the well-ordered structure even though natural resources are sufficient, and if, as a result, some people die of starvation while others have excessive wealth, then the ruler has actively committed a serious injustice (on a par with killing the starved, as Mencius puts it) rather than merely failed to help them.

Unlike contemporary liberal theories that ground justice on equality or individual rights, a Confucian perfectionist perspective on social justice views the aim of social justice as enabling every member of a community to live a good life. What is morally important is whether each person has sufficient resources to lead a good life, not whether each has the same amount. The Confucian perfectionist conception of the good life also sets a rough but objective standard for sufficiency that is not defined by the amount of resources one needs to pursue one's subjective conception of good life, but by how much people generally need to feel materially secure enough to pursue the higher, ethical life.

Justice as sufficiency for all is only part of the larger Confucian perfectionist social ideal. Mencius's well-field system, for example, is a multilayered system of provision in which the family, the village or commune, as well as the government all have specific roles to play. Mencius does not envisage a nanny state that takes care of every aspect of people's lives from the cradle to the grave, but a social system regulated by several principles such as justice, sufficiency, mutual aid, personal responsibility, care and voluntary help, and merit and contribution, all of which are still plausible and appealing to modern people. The sufficiency principle combines justice with personal responsibility: although justice requires equitable land distribution by government, members of a household must work together and labor hard in order to be able to reap a good harvest. For the Confucian conception of the good life, assistance that stems from mutual aid, through the family and social ties, is preferable to assistance from the government, for it stems from caring and concern. It may ultimately also be more effective because a caregiver connected by relatively close ties better understands the needs and problems of the one seeking assistance. More significant, mutual aid is an important opportunity for the caregiver to engage in virtuous activity and for both parties to develop a valuable relationship. However, if mutual aid fails or is not sufficient to help the needy, the ideal of care requires the government to step in to provide direct welfare assistance. Finally, the principle of merit and contribution allows for economic inequality arising from differential efforts and merit of individuals. Thus the Confucian social ideal integrates justice and care, recognizing both individual merit and personal responsibility.

The Politics of Confucian Political Perfectionism

Confucian perfectionism is designed as a political philosophy for modern times. It incorporates a number of basic institutions of liberal democracy but grounds them on Confucian perfectionism and shapes them by redefining their roles and functions. Where possible and necessary, it alters those institutions in light of Confucian values. Yet Confucianism has never been a pure philosophy; it is a praxis that aims to translate thought into action, transforming people's moral lives and building a good social and political order. Some practical questions are worth asking: In what ways can this new Confucian political philosophy be translated into action in modern times? Given that the traditional institutions that made Confucianism a state orthodoxy disintegrated in the twentieth century, what kinds of agents and institutions can be employed today to turn a philosophy into a praxis that has a meaningful impact on society? Should people make use of whatever political resources and power available (through political parties in power or enlightened benevolent autocrats) to promote Confucian philosophy and implement its vision in society? Today those East Asian societies that have been influenced by Confucian culture have undergone modernization and become pluralistic societies marked by a diversity of religions, philosophies, and ideologies. Should Confucianism, which is only one of the many competing forms of ideological discourse in these societies, be actively and publicly promoted to become a powerful agent of change? And what relevance does Confucianism have for non-Asian societies, including Western liberal democratic ones?

I think that Confucianism can be actively and publicly promoted in society. It can be promoted by citizens in civil society, businesspeople in commerce, and even politicians and state officials in the political arena. Some liberals have argued that the state and its officials should take a neutral stance toward competing conceptions of the good life, whether Confucian, Christian, Buddhist, Marxist, or Liberal. I believe, though I have no space to argue here, that state neutrality is a mistaken doctrine, and that the state can promote conceptions of the good life in a suitable way, as I shall explain below.[3] Nevertheless, the return of Confucianism as a state orthodoxy is not a desirable or feasible goal in a pluralistic society. We should distinguish between two kinds of political perfectionism, and hence two ways of promoting Confucianism. In extreme perfectionism the state adopts a comprehensive doctrine of the good life as the basis of state policy. Following John Rawls,[4] by "comprehensive doctrine" I mean a conception of the good life that involves a systematic theorization about human life, which explains why certain things are good for human life, ranks these good things according to a certain hierarchy, specifies concrete ways to realize them, and ties them to a tradition of thought distinct from other traditions. Traditional Confucianism does contain a comprehensive conception of the good life in this sense. In the moderate perfectionism that I espouse here, however, the state may appeal only to specific judgments about the good life, not comprehensive doctrines.[5] The state should promote specific valuable good

---

3 See Chan, "Legitimacy, Unanimity, and Perfectionism."
4 See John Rawls, *Political Liberalism* (New York: Columbia University Press, 1993), 59.
5 I have defined "moderate perfectionism" in "Legitimacy, Unanimity, and Perfectionism," 10–20.

things, such as the arts, family life, and basic human virtues, and discourage people from ways of life that are highly deficient in these things. Moderate perfectionism does not seek to make fine-grained comparative judgments on many different ways of life. It looks at the broad social trends and environments that undermine or promote the good life and considers if any state action is necessary to create conditions conducive to its pursuit. Thus, we may distinguish two ways of promoting Confucianism: one is to promote Confucianism as a comprehensive doctrine and try to implement it as a comprehensive package; the other is to promote Confucianism in a piecemeal way as suggested by moderate perfectionism.[6]

Promoting Confucianism as a comprehensive doctrine is, I believe, undesirable because it damages civility. In modern pluralistic societies, citizens live according to various ways of life and beliefs, including different religions. Civility is of crucial importance for this kind of society. Civility is the attitude of fellow citizens toward each other that shows a concern for the *common bond* despite differing opinions or conflicts of interest. Civility tries to diminish conflict by seeking *common ground* underlying opposing opinions and a *common good* transcending partisan interests. To seek a common ground and a common good, civility requires citizens to be open-minded, to justify opinions with reasons that others can share, to attempt to limit the extent and depth of moral disagreement, and to be willing to make compromises if full agreement cannot be achieved. Civility is at odds with "ideological politics" based on comprehensive doctrines. As Edward Shils observes, ideological politics are "obsessed with totality." Those who practice it believe that "they alone have the truth about the right ordering of life—of life as a whole, and not just of political life," and that "sound politics require a doctrine which comprehends every event in the universe, not only in space but in time. . . . Ideological politics are the politics of 'friend-foe,' 'we-they,' 'who-whom.' Those who are not on the side of the ideological politician are, according to the ideologist, against him."[7] Ideological politics destroy the common bond of citizens and deny the value of civility.

Confucianism as a comprehensive doctrine constitutes a form of ideological politics that must be rejected if we regard civility as an important virtue. In an open society, the promulgation of comprehensive doctrines is not only allowed by law but also actively supported by civil society, resulting in a vibrant but at times volatile marketplace of ideas. Inevitably conflict and struggle will arise from the free exchange of views and free pursuit of interests. To maintain civic concord, citizens must exercise self-constraint, and no group should attempt to

6 For an interesting use of the idea of moderate perfectionism in contemporary Confucian political philosophy, see Stephen C. Angle, "Sages and Politics: A Way Forward," chap. 11 in *Sagehood*, and "Conclusion: The Shape of Confucian Virtue-Ritual-Politics," chap. 8 in *Contemporary Confucian Political Philosophy*.

7 Edward Shils, *The Virtue of Civility: Selected Essays on Liberalism, Tradition, and Civil Society*, ed. Steven Grosby (Indianapolis: Liberty Fund, 1997), 26–28.

impose its own worldview and system of values on others in a winner-take-all fashion.[8]

Civility is also an important virtue in Confucianism, although the Confucian definition of civility is not identical to the modern ideal of an open society. As we have seen in chapter 4, the Confucian gentleman or exemplary person is not imposing or competitive but maintains harmony with others without compromising his principles. The exemplary person practices civility by deferring and yielding to others. The Master said, "If rulers are able to effect order in the state through the combination of observing ritual propriety [li] and deferring to others [rang], what more is needed? But if they are unable to accomplish this, what have they to do with observing ritual propriety?" (*Analects* 4.13).[9] Confucian gentlemen want to effect order in society through ritual propriety, but they do so with a readiness to defer and yield to others in order to preserve social harmony. "The gentleman seeks harmony not sameness" (13.23).[10] This is the Confucian spirit of civility. In a society without this spirit, people will press their claims or demands to the fullest, competing positions will harden, and conflicts and hostility will escalate. In political competition, if people practice rang, the winner will not take all, in either gesture or substance, and the loser will thus not be devastated and find opportunities for revenge.

In short, neither the modern nor the Confucian understanding of civility lends support to the promotion of comprehensive perfectionism through political means in a modern pluralistic society. However, both understandings of the virtue of civility are compatible with moderate perfectionism because civility does not require citizens to abandon their values or attachments or refrain from appealing to them in politics. In Shils's view, "civility is compatible with other attachments to class, to religion, to profession, but it regulates them out of respect for the common good."[11] Similarly, we can say that civility is compatible with our attachments to values and moral principles, and that it asks us only to judge these things on their own merits, to regulate disagreements with mutual respect and a readiness to find common ground, and to limit disagreements by making specific rather than comprehensive judgments. Moderate perfectionism exhibits and promotes this approach to political life. It appeals to specific values and virtues that are generally regarded as desirable for their own sake, and that can be found in many forms of the good life. Moreover, moderate perfectionism does not seek to give a consistent ranking of values and virtues

---

8   I have discussed the importance of civility in greater detail in the unpublished paper "In Defense of Moderate Perfectionism" (2009). It has been published in Chinese as "Wei wen he yuan shan zhu yi bian hu" 為溫和圓善主義辯護, in *Pu bian yu te shu de bian zheng: zheng zhi si xiang de tan jue* 普遍與特殊的辯證：政治思想的探掘 [Between the Universal and the Particular: Explorations in Political Philosophy], ed. Sechin Yeong-Shyang Chien 錢永祥 (Taipei: Research Center for Humanities and Social Sciences, Academia Sinica, 2012), 1–24.

9   Translation from Ames and Rosemont.

10   Translation adapted from Ames and Rosemont.

11   Shils, *Virtue of Civility*, 49.

or to assign them relative weight: none is regarded as primary or ultimate. More important, *the acceptance of these values and virtues need not presuppose any particular comprehensive doctrine* as they are compatible with a great many such doctrines and are widely accepted by many people in modern society. Because moderate perfectionism is specific and piecemeal, the contest between citizens over individual legislation or public policy will also be specific and piecemeal. Unlike ideological politics, which are obsessed with the totality of truth, moderate perfectionism does not fashion a winner-take-all politics based on clashes of comprehensive doctrines—the gains of the winners and the losses of the losers are limited, and their positions can reverse in different policy domains.

The Confucian perfectionism in political philosophy and politics that I espouse thus takes the form of moderate perfectionism. As a moral philosophy Confucianism may develop its conception of the good life comprehensively and rigorously. However, as a political or public philosophy for modern times, this conception should not be derived from a comprehensive doctrine of the good. It should offer a list of items that constitute the good life and good social order—such as valuable social relationships, practical wisdom and learning, sincerity, harmony, social and political trust and care, moral and personal autonomy, and economic sufficiency and self-responsibility—and explore the implications of these items for social and political arrangements. This is what I have attempted to do in this book through a process of theorizing that is bottom-up rather than top-down. Rather than starting with a comprehensive doctrine and applying it to politics in the modern context, I have examined the specific Confucian values and principles relevant to each political issue under discussion, assessed the attractiveness and implications of these values and principles for modern times, revised or rejected them where necessary, and further developed or integrated them with other values and principles as appropriate. The outcome of these discrete analyses and reconstructions is, I hope, an outline of a coherent and systematic political philosophy that is recognizably Confucian, but one that has not been reached by applying a comprehensive doctrine.[12]

In accordance with this stance, the promotion of Confucian political perfectionism should be done in a piecemeal and moderate way. In public political discourse, one should not present Confucianism as a complete and packaged conception and ask people to accept policy proposals as implications of that package. One should not, for example, argue that filial piety should be pro-

---

12   For an example of a top-down application of a comprehensive doctrine in contemporary Confucian political philosophy, see Jiang Qing 蔣慶, "A Confucian Constitutional Order," pt. 1 in *A Confucian Constitutional Order: How China's Ancient Past Can Shape Its Political Future*, trans. Edmund Ryden, ed. Daniel A. Bell and Ruiping Fan (Princeton: Princeton University Press, 2013). For my critique of Jiang's comprehensive Confucianism and his reply, see chap. 4, "On the Legitimacy of Confucian Constitutionalism," and chap. 8, "Debating with My Critics," of the book, respectively. Part of the third section of the present chapter is drawn from this critique of Jiang.

moted *because* it is a central element in Confucianism. To argue this way is to ask others to accept the authority of Confucianism as a philosophy. Moderate perfectionism requires us to justify Confucian values in terms that do not require prior acceptance of Confucianism, and that can be shared by others who do not necessarily accept other elements within Confucianism. The core values of Confucianism such as virtues, human ethical relations, the mutual commitment of the ruler and the ruled, the principle of benevolent politics, and fair rewards and punishments in the political system can be accepted or understood by many people without their adopting Confucianism as a comprehensive doctrine.

In discussing concrete legislative or policy issues, one may analyze step-by-step the insights of relevant Confucian values so as to compare and incorporate them with other values outside Confucianism. In the process of promoting Confucian values, we must engage in discussion in a language and manner that citizens of the modern world can understand and accept. Moderate perfectionism does not require ideological control by the state; instead it demands a high level of freedom of speech so that citizens can freely assess Confucianism and discuss policy in a rational manner. This free and democratic process will decide which Confucian values, if any, should be promoted or adopted as the grounds for legislation. If Confucian values are adopted in such a manner, Confucianism will win only in regard to specific policies, and its advocates will not use political power to impose a winner-take-all comprehensive package over other schools of thought. If social discussion and political procedure are conducted fairly, then those who lose out in democratic competition this time will still have the chance to regain political victory in the future. In this light, the moderate promotion of Confucian values preserves civility among citizens in a pluralistic society.

One may wonder to what extent a society can be called "Confucian" if the legislative and policy-making process is guided by moderate perfectionism. The answer is that the actual extent of Confucian influence in a society will and always should be determined by the continuous process of democratic discussion and policy making over time. Just as human society is always changing, so should Confucianism. As it changes and adapts to the needs of today's societies, it can provide a guide not only to those Asian societies whose cultures have been steeped in Confucian practice and thought, but also to other societies whose cultures may benefit from contemplating, and perhaps applying in practice, the deepest principles of Confucian thought.

APPENDIX 1:
Notes on Scope and Methods

I shall explain the scope and methods of my critical reconstruction of Confucian political thought, starting with a brief note on the Confucian tradition. Confucianism as a tradition of thought began life in China more than 2,500 years ago. Although its core ideas can be traced back to the teachings of Confucius, the tradition is not thought to have wholly originated with Confucius himself. In fact, the original Chinese term for Confucianism, *ru jia*, does not refer to Confucius (Kongzi or Master Kong) but to a school of *ru*. In the times before Confucius, ru referred to professional experts in religious rituals and ceremonies. In the Spring and Autumn period, ru became associated with men of learning and education who taught rituals, history, poetry, music, mathematics, and archery in official and private education.[1] Confucius was regarded as an outstanding ru of his time. Confucius himself stressed that he was not an inventor of any radically new vision of ethics or ideal society, but only a transmitter of the old tradition—the rites, social and political values, and metaphysical and religious orientations developed in the early Zhou dynasty—as expounded in the Five Classics (*The Book of Poetry, The Book of History, The Book of Rites, The Book of Changes*, and *The Spring and Autumn Annals*).[2]

The Five Classics were the primary source of Confucian learning as well as the primary source of official education from the Han dynasty to Tang dynasty. It was not until the Song dynasty that *The Analects* came to be used alongside the Five Classics. And it was the influence of neo-Confucian philosopher Zhu Xi (1130–1200 CE) that led to *The Analects, Mencius,* and two chapters from *The Book of Rites* (*The Great Learning* and *The Doctrine of the Mean*)—together known as the Four Books—becoming the basic textbooks for Confucian learning and the subject of scholarly studies of Confucian thought throughout the world up to now.[3]

---

1   For a balanced overall account of different scholarly views of the meanings and origins of ru and a hypothesis synthesizing these various views, see Yao, *Introduction to Confucianism*, 16–21. See also Nylan, *Five "Confucian" Classics*, 364–65.

2   Early traditions of commentary believe that Confucius compiled and edited the Five Classics, but this view has been disputed in modern scholarship. For discussions of the Five Classics' relation to Confucius, see Nylan, *Five "Confucian" Classics*, 8–10, and Yao, *Introduction to Confucianism*, 52–54.

3   For the evolution of the Five Classics and the Four Books, see Yao, *Introduction to Confucianism*, 57–67, and Nylan, "Introduction to the Five Classics," chap. 1 in *Five "Confucian" Classics*.

Confucius handed down no systematic philosophy. Nor is *The Analects*, a record of Confucius's ideas and teaching compiled primarily by his disciples and later scholars, a treatise of ethics. Nevertheless it was Confucius who most creatively interpreted the tradition that he inherited, gave it new meaning at a time when it had become rigid, and expounded it so effectively that his views influenced a great number of generations of ru. *The Analects* left a number of basic questions undeveloped, such as those about human nature, the metaphysical grounds of ethics, and the proper organization of the state. It was Mencius and Xunzi who filled in the details more systematically and developed the old tradition with further new interpretations, and it is the thoughts of these three thinkers together that constitute the classical tradition of Confucian thought. Confucianism has continued to evolve over time, in part as a response to the political needs of the time (as in Han Confucianism), and in part as a response to the challenges of other schools of thought (as in Song-Ming Confucianism). Han Confucianism developed Confucian ethics and politics into a comprehensive worldview and a practical philosophy for statecraft, drawing heavily on the early classics and, to a lesser extent, on Daoist and Legalist schools of thought. Song-Ming Confucianism turned its inquiry inward to the human mind to meet the challenges of Buddhism and constructed robust theories of the inner life of individuals.[4] No matter what innovations were made in these later developments, however, classical Confucianism, especially the Mencius strand, has been recognized as the canon of the tradition—a canon that later thinkers claimed only to have appreciated, vindicated, and enriched in the same way Confucius claimed only to have enriched the tradition that existed before him. In this sense a deep respect for tradition—a fundamental belief that the sages in the past had already pinpointed the right direction—has always been a salient mark of Confucianism.

The tenets of Confucianism that I examine for their contributions in terms of a modern Confucian political philosophy are limited to those from the pre-Qin period, in particular, *The Analects*, *Mencius*, and *Xunzi*, which contain many social and political ideas relevant to the purposes of this book. Obviously a single study cannot cover the 2,500-year-long tradition of Confucianism without doing injustice to its breadth and complexity. Nevertheless these works, the first two especially, have constituted the paradigm and basis for critical reflection in the Song-Ming period and after. In addition to these three primary texts, I also refer to other texts, especially certain chapters in *The Book of History*. *The Book of History* is arguably the most important source for understanding ancient Chinese political ideas. Many early Confucian political ideas—such as virtuous rule, care for the people, and Heaven's Mandate—can be traced back to *The Book of History*. The work was compiled in different ways at different

---

4 For an accessible account of the historical development of Confucianism, see "Evolution and Transformation—A Historical Perspective," chap. 2 in Yao, *Introduction to Confucianism*. For a more philosophical introduction, see Shu-Hsien Liu 劉述先 [Liu Shuxian], *Understanding Confucian Philosophy: Classical and Sung-Ming* (Westport, CT: Praeger, 1998).

times, and its authenticity has been under persistent dispute throughout the centuries. I am inclined to a contemporary view that in the so-called Modern Script version of *The Book of History*, a majority of the Zhou chapters could be dated back to early to late Zhou period, while a majority of the Yao and Shang chapters possibly date back to the Qin unification and after.[5] When I discuss the concept of Heaven's Mandate in appendix 2, I mostly draw on the more "authentic" Zhou chapters. Occasionally I also refer to *The Book of Rites* (most likely compiled and edited in early Western Han dynasty [206 BCE–9 CE]),[6] *The Annals of Lü Buwei* (Qin dynasty), and *Chun qiu fan lu* (Western Han), texts that contain ideas from Confucian and other schools of thought. My justification for using certain passages in these texts is that these passages are either often cited by later Confucians or contain ideas that fit with, or can reinforce, the Confucian ideas that I discuss.

What hermeneutical method would be most appropriate to the critical reconstruction of a traditional philosophy? There are at least three methods commonly used to study ancient thinkers, whether Eastern or Western.[7] These methods differ in how closely they follow the thinker's own aims, concepts, and techniques in interpreting and evaluating the thinker's thought.

The first, and strictest, method, which may be called "classical scholarship," tries to understand an ancient thinker "in his own terms and within his own context."[8] It starts with the problem as the thinker sees it and evaluates his solutions not by any external perspective but by assessing the internal consistence of the arguments and the reasons given to support the conclusions. When modern readers find it difficult to understand a concept or an argument presented by the thinker, help should be sought from the contexts within which the thought was developed, including the thinker's life experience and the intellectual, social, and cultural contexts of the thinker's times. The primary techniques of this method are literal exegesis and intellectual history.[9]

The second method may be called "philosophical reconstruction." It tries to "understand the text not only on its own terms but also by applying external concepts, theories, and techniques."[10] This method aims to bring an ancient thinker's views to bear on questions that he himself may not have asked but that are of interest to contemporary theorists. For this method the primary interest

5   For this view, see Nylan, *Five "Confucian" Classics*, 127–36. For a similar view, see also *Shang shu yi zhu* 尚書譯注 [Modern Chinese Translation and Commentary of *The Book of History*], comp. Li Min 李民 and Wang Jian 王健 (Shanghai: Shanghai gu ji chu ban she 上海古籍出版社, 2004), preface, 29–33.

6   See Nylan, *Five "Confucian" Classics*, 174–75.

7   The following threefold distinction is indebted to David Charles, *Aristotle's Philosophy of Action* (London: Duckworth, 1984), ix–x; and Fred D. Miller, Jr., *Nature, Justice, and Rights in Aristotle's Politics* (Oxford: Clarendon Press, 1995), 21–22.

8   Miller, *Nature, Justice, and Rights*, 21.

9   Recent examples of classical scholarship are, in the field of Chinese philosophy, Shun's *Mencius and Early Chinese Thought*, and in Chinese political thought, Pines's *Envisioning Eternal Empire*. Pines describes his historical method in pages 6–9.

10   Miller, *Nature, Justice, and Rights*, 21.

in an ancient thinker is contemporary rather than historical, and comparative rather than exegetical. It does not simply interpret what is said in a text but extends and develops it to a point where comparison with contemporary perspectives is possible. The ultimate interest is to critically assess the contemporary philosophical significance of a certain ancient view. The primary techniques of this method are conceptual analysis and comparative methodology.[11]

The third method may be called "philosophizing within a tradition."[12] Adopting this method involves original philosophizing within the broad framework of a philosophical tradition. Certain basic tenets of a tradition of thought are taken as the points of departure and developed into a new perspective previously not explored by thinkers in that tradition. The primary interest of this method is not accurate exegesis of an ancient thought or critical assessment of its contemporary philosophical significance but active contribution to the contemporary development of a tradition of thought. The theories resulting from such philosophizing are often denoted by the prefix "neo" (e.g., neo-Confucianism) to emphasize the fact that they are new developments within a broad tradition.

Many students of ancient Chinese or Western philosophy employ more than one of these methods and techniques in their study. This book assesses the contemporary relevance of early Confucian political thought and attempts to bridge the gap between the Confucian ideal and the reality of modern circumstances. For these purposes I adopt philosophical reconstruction as the main method and make use of the other two methods where appropriate. Employing philosophical reconstruction helps to ascertain the contemporary significance of Confucianism by placing it in the context of modern philosophy and politics and assessing it in comparison with modern viewpoints. In advancing an understanding of Confucian ideas, I draw on works in classical scholarship. And in further developing Confucian political thought, I make use of the method of philosophizing within a tradition. I will now elaborate on this method by discussing first the particular understanding of the nature of Confucianism that this method presupposes and second the stages that this method consists of.

It is important to note that a central presupposition behind this method of philosophical reconstruction is a certain understanding of the nature of Confucianism. This understanding treats Confucianism not as an organic unity but as a complex tradition that can be somewhat deconstructed into different elements and perhaps different levels. It also rejects the antitraditionalist view—argued by those such as Chen Duxiu—that Confucianism is a thoroughly outdated philosophy that should be replaced by Western ethics.

According to the antitraditionalists, any attempt to revise and modernize Confucianism for modern purposes is bound to fail as, in their view, Confu-

---

11 I would put the following recent works in the category of philosophical reconstruction, although they employ other methods as well: Angle's *Sagehood* and Fan's *Reconstructionist Confucianism*.

12 Miller, *Nature, Justice, and Rights*, 21.

cianism is an organic whole that cannot be deconstructed or reconstructed. This stance is supported by what might be called an "ideal-type strategy" to understand the nature of Confucianism as an ethical system. The construction of an ideal type, to make use of a phrase coined by Max Weber, is a strategy that enables people to better understand and compare social realities that are often complex, fuzzy, vague, and difficult to theorize about. An ideal-type strategy first captures certain features of a complex reality from a particular point of view (to facilitate theoretical understanding and comparison) and then constructs an idealized description of that reality by artificially drawing precise and clear conceptual boundaries around these features and ignoring those that do not fit the construct. Chen Duxiu, for example, constructed the following ideal types for the Western and Chinese ethical systems: the Western system upholds individual freedom, human rights, and equality—all of which are elements of what Chen calls the "grand spirit of individualism"; while the Chinese system is the mirror image of the Western one, namely, a rigid, hierarchical social and political order structured along the lines of a feudalistic family and clan, one that rejects individual independence and equality before the law and preaches authoritarianism.[13]

The advantage of the ideal-type strategy is that it helps to define more readily the distinctive features of the two systems under comparison. With an ideal-type understanding of Western and Confucian ethical systems as holistic entities, it is easy to conclude that they are mutually incompatible. However, the strategy also runs the risk of "essentializing" traditions of thought, turning them into rigid schemes of ideas that are tightly interlocked, whereas in reality variations of themes and emphases generally coexist, with the exact meanings of the distinctive features of a tradition of thought constantly reinterpreted and debated by friends and critics of that tradition. More significantly, most traditions of thought have multiple levels that may not always fit well together, thus creating room for internal adjustment, revision, and innovation. For this reason I am convinced that a better strategy is one that is presupposed by the method of philosophical reconstruction, namely, one that holds that a complex tradition of thought such as Confucianism is multilevel and multifaceted and has evolved dynamically over time.

In the literature on Confucian thought, there are different ways of understanding Confucianism as a multilevel tradition, especially with regard to its ethics. Some regard the notion of ren as the most fundamental level, virtues as the second or intermediate level, and rites as the third or surface level.[14] Others take both ren and li (rites) as fundamental and mutually defining, claiming that

13 Chen, *De sai er xian sheng*, see esp. "Dong xi min zu," 25–29, and "Kongzi zhi dao," 56–62.

14 Examples of a multilevel approach to Confucian ethics are Lau Kwok-keung, "An Interpretation of Confucian Virtues and Their Relevance to China's Modernization," in *Confucianism and the Modernization of China*, ed. Silke Krieger and Rolf Trauzettel (Mainz: v. Hase & Koehler Verlag, 1991), 210–28; and Wong Wai-ying 黃慧英 [Huang Huiying], "Ru jia lun li ge ceng mian de shi jian" 儒家倫理各層面的實踐 [The Practice of Confucian Ethics at Different Levels], chap. 12 in

both give content to and shape virtue.[15] Still others take the notion of li itself as multilevel, encompassing cosmic principles, virtues, and behavioral rituals.[16] There is no need for this book to adopt any particular interpretation. Suffice it to mention that the book does not to give an ideal-type construction of Confucian ethics and politics and but adopts a piecemeal approach that is sensitive to the fact that there are different elements at different levels of the tradition. This piecemeal approach raises a series of questions: Can a particular element at a particular level be revised to accommodate modern insights? Is that element worth keeping? Can it be combined with new ideas to form a new synthesis? Note that two holistic ideal types cannot be combined or mixed without losing their internal coherence or purity, but the concrete elements of two complex, dynamic, evolving traditions can be. The piecemeal approach, I believe, is more conducive to creative thinking and reconstruction than the ideal-type one. It is also more helpful in addressing practical and normative issues in modern times.

The piecemeal method of philosophical reconstruction can be deconstructed into the following stages.

Stage 1: Question Setting

How would Confucianism consider an issue, philosophical or practical? Some of the issues examined in this book—such as political authority and social welfare—are discussed in traditional Confucianism. Others—such as human rights and democracy—are issues that have only arisen in contemporary times. For contemporary issues, the following types of questions will be asked: Would Confucianism accept the ideas and types of human rights as commonly understood today? Would Confucianism accept democracy as an intrinsic value and a political institution?

Stage 2: A Conceptual Analysis of the Key Terms Involved in the Question

Concepts such as "human rights," "democracy," and "justice" are analyzed and defined. Defining a concept is often a theoretically controversial matter. One needs to be sensitive to the possibility of different interpretations of such concepts and try to choose a definition that does not prejudicially favor Confucianism or its competing modern viewpoints.

Ru jia lun li: ti yu yong 儒家倫理: 體與用 [Confucian Ethics: Ti and Yong] (Shanghai: Joint Publishing, 2005).

15 See Kuang, *Kongzi ping zhuan*, 193–98.

16 Yeung, "Shi fei qu zhi," chap. 7 in *Xian mei yu he le*.

Stage 3: Interpretation and Extrapolation

The major texts in Confucianism are analyzed to see if they contain the concepts or direct answers to the questions under consideration. If the texts contain no direct views on the questions, other views from the texts are extended and their implications brought to bear on the questions. To avoid selective interpretation, the texts must be comprehensively surveyed. For example, in analyzing whether the idea of human rights is compatible with Confucianism, the analysis should consider not only those passages that favor the compatibility view but also passages that may point to difficulties in making the two compatible. In addition, the views extracted from the texts should be presented coherently, unless different parts of the text themselves imply contradictory views on a particular issue.

Stage 4: Comparison

The reconstructed view of Confucianism is compared with the views of contemporary schools of thought (e.g., liberalism). However, as each school of thought may comprise different strands that hold different views on the issues concerned, it is imperative not to oversimplify the complexity of either of the two traditions being compared. Similarities should be considered as well as differences, points of agreement as well as points of divergence.

Stage 5: Evaluation, Revision, and Development

The validity, truth, or attractiveness of the reconstructed Confucian view is examined in comparison with other views. Here there is no neutral or unquestionable criterion to judge the acceptability of any views. Just as for any original philosophizing, independent philosophical argumentation must be employed to support all judgments. Such a process of evaluation helps determine which elements in the Confucian views are still valid and which are no longer relevant; which should be dropped, revised, kept, or further developed; and how. There will be considerable original philosophizing at this stage, but throughout the process there is a self-awareness of how the revision comes about, how much is changed, and how much is kept. At the end of the reconstruction, the extent to which the overall outlook of the reconstructed philosophy is "Confucian" depends on its details, namely, which core elements are kept or developed and which are dropped. The continuation with its traditional past is a matter of degree and open to interpretation.

APPENDIX 2:

Against the Ownership Conception of Authority

This appendix develops the ideas presented in the first section of chapter 1. In the history of political ideas, Eastern or Western, political authority, defined as a legitimate right to rule at the highest level within a jurisdiction, has been given different names: rulership, lordship, kingship, emperorship, imperium, dominium, tianming, tian zi, sovereignty, people's sovereignty, presidency, and so forth. However, the different names also suggest that the nature of political authority can be viewed from different perspectives. In this appendix I shall look at one of these perspectives in detail—the ownership perspective or dominium. From this perspective, political authority is viewed as something that a ruler can personally own and pass on at his own will, and as the right that enables him to claim entitlement to the resources and people within his jurisdiction. In traditional China many critics as well as defenders of the imperial system viewed the power of an emperor (*huang quan*) as his private property (*si chan*): the people living under the rule of an emperor were said to be the emperor's subjects (*wang min*), the land was seen as the emperor's land (*wang tu*), and both people and land existed to serve the emperor. The throne was also regarded as private property that could be inherited by the emperor's son (*jia tian xia*).[1] This ownership perspective of political authority was also prominent in Europe in the sixteenth century and after. The Roman private law concept of dominium (ownership) was frequently invoked in the sixteenth century to define the nature of political authority, that is, the royal rights and powers attached to the crown were thought to be the king's own property and as such could be passed on to his heirs by the ordinary rules of succession. The king was a dominus, who held not only the final right to rule (i.e., to make and execute

---

1 For detailed analyses of this view of political authority in traditional China, see Liu Zehua 劉澤華, *Wang quan zhu yi yu si xiang he she hui* 王權主義與思想和社會 [Royalism, Thought, and Society], vol. 3 of *Zhongguo zheng zhi si xiang shi ji* 中國政治思想史集 [Collection of the History of Chinese Political Thought], 3 vols. (Beijing: People's Publishing, 2008); and Wang Yi 王毅, "Zhongguo huang quan tong zhi 'zi min' ren shen he cai chan de fa quan zhi du ji qi yu xian zheng fa li de bei ni" 中國皇權統治"子民"人身和財產的法權制度及其與憲政法理的悖逆 [The Personal and Property Rights of "Subjects" under Chinese Imperial Rule and the Paradox of the Constitutional Principles Concerning These Rights], chap. 12 in vol. 2 of *Zhongguo huang quan zhi du yan jiu* 中國皇權制度研究 [The Study of the Institution of Royalism in China], 2 vols. (Beijing: Peking University Press, 2007).

laws) within his jurisdiction, as defined by the Roman public law notion of imperium, but also dominium, or ownership, of the land within the king's territorial jurisdiction, and in extreme cases dominium over the people as well.[2]

Although the notion of the king as a dominus has long been rejected in the West, the conception of dominium has remained a dominant perspective for understanding political authority or sovereignty. It has been argued that "critics of royal absolutism simultaneously wanted to deny dominium to the crown, while still clinging to the concept of dominium in their vision of the constitution."[3] The absolute royal rights and powers that once belonged to the king are now understood as belonging to the people or the state, and hence we have the idea of popular sovereignty or state sovereignty. The people are now the sovereign—the dominus—whose will or consent is the final basis of the state's authority, and the state, being the agent of the people, wields the same rights and entitlements as those once attached to the royal domain.

How did early Confucianism understand the nature of political authority? Interestingly, there seems to be textual support within Confucianism to see political authority either as the personal property of the ruler or as something that belongs to the people (an embryonic version of popular sovereignty), and there are scholars who have argued for one or the other of these interpretations. I shall argue that there is no good basis to ascribe either to early Confucianism, and that Confucianism rejects a dominium conception of political authority, whether the dominium is vested in a person or a people. Similar to the Roman concept of imperium, Confucian political thought discusses political authority in reference to the final legitimate right to rule under Heaven (or within a jurisdiction), with no implication that there is any form of ownership claim attached to the rulership. The purposes of this appendix, however, are not purely negative. The criticism of the ownership interpretations of political authority paves the way for developing a Confucian conception of political authority that is, hopefully, philosophically interesting and plausible for modern times. Such a conception can further serve as a critical basis for evaluating political institutions and processes in modern society. These two tasks are pursued in chapters 1–3.

2   For an excellent discussion of the dominium conception of authority and sovereignty, see Daniel Lee, "Private Law Models for Public Law Concepts: The Roman Law Theory of Dominium in the Monarchomach Doctrine of Popular Sovereignty," *The Review of Politics* 70, no. 3 (2008): 370–99. In his discussion of the legal foundations of the British empire from 1576–1640, Ken MacMillan defines imperium as "independent and absolute sovereignty" and dominium as the "right to possess and rule territory under its jurisdiction"; see his *Sovereignty and Possession in the English New World: The Legal Foundations of Empire, 1576–1640* (Cambridge: Cambridge University Press, 2006), 6.

3   Lee, "Private Law Models," 383. For a contemporary statement of the conception of dominium in the context of international relations, see Friedrich Kratochwil, "Sovereignty as *Dominium*: Is There a Right of Humanitarian Intervention?" chap. 2 in *Beyond Westphalia? State Sovereignty and International Intervention*, ed. Gene M. Lyons and Michael Mastanduno (Baltimore: Johns Hopkins University Press, 1995).

Land and People

As I said in chapter 1, the best starting point to look at the early Confucian perspective of political authority is the idea of tianming, which expresses the notion that the right to rule is based on Heaven's Mandate. The concept of tianming raises more questions than answers, however:

1. Content. What does tianming consist of? What exactly does tianming amount to in terms of political rule—what rights or entitlements does a ruler blessed with tianming possess?
2. Purpose. What is the purpose of investing a person with tianming?
3. Basis. On what basis, if any, does Heaven choose a person or a group of persons to receive tianming?
4. Process. Through what process does Heaven choose or make known its choice of the person or group of persons to receive tianming?
5. Condition. Can a mandate be taken back once it is given? Under what conditions, if any, would a legitimate ruler lose his tianming?
6. Succession. Does the idea of tianming have anything to say about succession? Can a legitimate ruler pass his tianming on to another person of his own choice?

The questions concern the different facets of political authority: its meaning, source, condition, purpose, and succession. I shall start with the questions related to content: What exactly does tianming amount to in terms of political rule? What rights or entitlements does a ruler have by possessing it? By examining these questions, we should be able to answer the others as well. One strand of interpretation says tianming is something that can be personally owned by a ruler, like a piece of property that can be owned by a property owner. Let us call this the ownership interpretation. According to this view, tianming is private property in two separate senses. First, it can be owned and transferred. The ruler who possesses tianming has the right to pass it on to anyone he chooses to succeed his rule: the owner of the throne decides who inherits it. Second, tianming gives the ruler an ownership right to the territory and the people who are under his jurisdiction. The land and the people belong to the ruler, in the same sense as private property belongs to its owner.[4]

As evidence to support the ownership interpretation, we can refer to *The Book of History*, which talks about tianming in a manner that suggests that it does give a ruler ownership of territory and people. The Duke of Zhou said that Heaven had given his ancestors "the Middle Kingdom [China] with its people and territories."[5] There is also a common saying that first originated from *The Book of Poetry*: "Under the wide Heaven, all is the king's land; within

---

4 Conceptually the two senses are distant and not logically connected, but they came together in a dominium conception of authority in China and Europe in premodern times.

5 "Zi cai" 梓材 (Catalpa Timbers) chapter.

the sea-boundaries of the land, all are the king's servants."[6] The saying is generally taken to mean precisely what the ownership interpretation affirms: that the land and people under a ruler's jurisdiction belong to the ruler. Furthermore, it seems that the general acceptance of hereditary succession in the classical texts can best be explained by the idea that rulership is something that can be owned and hence transferred at the owner's choice—if a ruler did not own his Heaven-mandated right to rule, he could not legitimately pass it on to his heir. Contemporary neo-Confucian philosopher Mou Zongsan (1909–95), for example, takes hereditary succession as an act of privatizing *tian xia* (the world ruled by a ruler).[7] He argues that the early Confucian conception of tianming slides into an endorsement of hereditary succession in the hands of Mencius, thereby turning political authority into a form of private property, and this is not the direction of development that best realizes Confucianism's goals.[8] Similarly, Mencius and Xunzi's endorsement of revolt or revolution, in Mou's understanding, also implies that individuals can possess political authority.[9] Contemporary Chinese political theorist Shih Yuan-Kang echoes Mou in saying that traditional Chinese thought treats "political authority or the state as property that can be transferred." He further argues that even the principle of giving away the throne to a virtuous and competent person who is not a member of the ruler's family for the benefit of the people (i.e., the principle of abdication) presupposes that *tian xia* is a *thing* that can be taken or given away.[10]

I shall criticize this interpretation and argue for an alternative one. In the full sense of the term, an ownership right to a thing comprises a bundle of rights, including the right to keep it from others' interference, the right to use it (or leave it unused), the right to benefit out of its use, the right to transfer it to someone else (by selling or giving it freely), and the right to destroy it. Not every ownership right in reality contains this full set of rights, but the fewer rights it contains, the less it resembles an ownership right, and the more reason we have to use another concept to characterize it. The alternative interpretation

---

6   "Bei shan" 北山 (Northern Hill) chapter. Translations adapted from James Legge, *The Chinese Classics*, vol. 4 (London: Trübner, 1871; repr., Hong Kong: Hong Kong University Press, 1960); 1871 edition available at http://books.google.com/books?id=TsKwKUq95LYC (first half of vol. 4), http://books.google.com/books?id=L8ZRsTC1miAC (second half of vol. 4). All translations of *The Book of Poetry* 詩經 [*Shi jing*] are adapted from Legge's.

7   Mou Zongsan 牟宗三 [Mou Tsung-san], *Zheng dao yu zhi dao* 政道與治道 [The Principles of Politics and Governance], rev. ed. (Taipei: Student Book 台灣學生書局, 1987), 12.

8   Ibid., 132–34.

9   Ibid., 17, 133.

10   Shih Yuan-Kang 石元康, "Tian ming yu zheng dang xing—cong Weibo de fen lei kan ru jia de zheng dao" 天命與正當性—從韋伯的分類看儒家的政道 [Heaven's Mandate and Political Legitimacy—An Examination of Confucian Theory of Legitimacy from Weber's Typology], in *Zheng zhi li lun zai Zhongguo* 政治理論在中國 [Political Theory in China], ed. Joseph Chan 陳祖為 and Leung Man-to 梁文韜 (Hong Kong: Oxford University Press, 2001), 55. My own translation.

that I shall argue for states that tianming is not an ownership right as defined above, but *a legitimate right to govern* within a jurisdiction. It rejects the two aspects of the ownership interpretation: that the right to govern can be owned and hence transferred, and that it gives rise to a set of ownership rights with regard to the territory and people living under the jurisdiction.

Let me start with the second aspect. In *The Book of History*, the Duke of Zhou says at least twice that Heaven had given his ancestors "the Middle Kingdom with its people and territories."[11] However, this phrase itself is ambiguous and open to two interpretations: (1) that the ruler is given the right to govern the people and make use of the resources within the jurisdiction of the Middle Kingdom; or (2) that the land and people within that jurisdiction belong to the ruler. The latter interpretation implies the former, but not the other way round. To determine the precise meaning, we must examine what purposes, privileges, responsibilities, and conditions go with Heaven's Mandate when it is given to a ruler. For example, if one of the conditions for a ruler to receive and maintain tianming is the ability and willingness to protect and serve the people over whom he rules, then this clearly conflicts with the ownership interpretation that maintains that the people are there to serve the ruler, just as property is to be used for the benefit of its owner. Many passages in *The Book of History* suggest that the way to ensure continuity of Heaven's Mandate is for the ruler to "practice virtue" and "protect the people" (bao min).[12] Further, if a ruler failed to protect his people, or harmed them, the mandate would be lost.

> The wise, through not thinking, become foolish, and the foolish, by thinking, become wise. Heaven for five years waited kindly, and forbore with the descendant (of Tang), to see if he would indeed prove himself the ruler of the people; but there was nothing in him deserving to be regarded. Heaven then sought among your numerous regions, making a great impression by its terrors to stir up someone who would look (reverently) to it, but in all your regions there was not one deserving of its favoring regard. But there were the kings of our Zhou, *who treated well the multitudes of the people, and were able to sustain the burden of virtuous (government).* They could preside over (all services to) spirits and to Heaven. Heaven thereupon instructed us [the kings of Zhou], and increased our excellence, made choice of us, and gave us the decree of Yin, to rule over your numerous regions.[13]

The passage above shows that the possession of tianming is not permanent but conditional on the ruler's virtues and virtuous rule (*de zhi*)—namely, his disposition and willingness to care for the people and protect them. The Duke of Zhou warns further that tianming is unpredictable because good governance is

---

11 "Zi cai" 梓材 (Catalpa Timbers) chapter. See also "Kang gao" 康誥 (Announcement to the Prince of Kang) chapter.

12 "Zi cai" 梓材 (Catalpa Timbers) chapter.

13 "Duo fang" 多方 (Numerous Regions) chapter; italics added, brackets in the original.

hard to achieve. A ruler should not assume that once the mandate is given to him, he will be able to keep it indefinitely. He has to have utmost seriousness and an utmost sense of responsibility in discharging his job, which is to bring order, peace, and well-being to his people. He underscores his point by repeating his key words a second time.

> We should by all means survey the dynasties of Xia and Yin. I do not presume to know and say, "The dynasty of Xia was to enjoy the favoring decree of Heaven just for (so many) years," nor do I presume to know and say, "It could not continue longer." The fact simply was that for want of the virtue of reverence, the decree in its favor prematurely fell to the ground. (Similarly), I do not presume to know and say, "The dynasty of Yin was to enjoy the favoring decree of Heaven just for (so many) years," nor do I presume to know and say, "It could not continue longer." The fact simply was that for want of the virtue of reverence, the decree in its favor fell prematurely to the ground. The king has now inherited the decree—the same decree, I consider, which belonged to those two dynasties. Let him seek to inherit (the virtues of) their meritorious (sovereigns).[14]

> The king says, "O Feng, I make you this long announcement, not (for the pleasure of doing so); but the ancients have said, 'Let not men look into water; let them look into the glass of other people.'[15] Now that Yin has lost its appointment, ought we not to look much to it as our glass, (and learn) how to secure the repose of our time?"[16]

The protection and promotion of the people's well-being is such an important condition that the best explanation for its centrality is that it is the very purpose of the decree itself. This reading might be challenged by arguing that, in the eyes of the ruler, the protection of the people may be regarded as merely a means to sustaining his throne, a necessary condition rather than the purpose of his rule. But this reading is incompatible with many passages, in which rulers are asked or expected to respect virtues (*jing de*) and practice virtuous rule (*de zheng*), thus showing genuine concern and love for the people in the same way a father shows love for his son.

One might still argue for the ownership interpretation by qualifying the ownership right with all the uncertainty, condition, and purpose that we have discussed regarding the nature of Heaven's Mandate. It might be said that even a highly qualified and restricted ownership is still a form of ownership. But this seems to stretch the term to an extent that it can barely be recognized as ownership—after all, is it an ownership right in any real sense of the word when it is

---

14   "Shao gao" 召誥 (Announcement of the Duke of Shao) chapter; brackets in the original.

15   As suggested by the anonymous referee, this sentence might be better translated as "Men should not mirror themselves in water but in other people."

16   "Jiu gao" 酒誥 (Announcement about Drunkenness) chapter.

so conditional, fragile, and unstable, and when its purpose benefits not the owner (ruler) but the owned (the ruled)?[17]

But if we look again at the saying "Under the wide Heaven, all is the king's land; within the sea-boundaries of the land, all are the king's servants," does it actually mean, as the ownership interpretation affirms, that the land and people under a ruler's jurisdiction are the property of the ruler? A closer examination of the context in which the saying appears tells us that it does not. This saying originated from the poem chapter "Bei shan" in *The Book of Poetry*, in which the author, an officer working for the king, complains that the duties ascribed to him are much heavier than those given to other officers. What this poem says is that since the king has universal jurisdiction and no shortage of officers to serve him, why must the author alone bear so heavy a responsibility that he no longer has time to serve his parents, while others are delegated easy tasks and live restful lives? It is, more than anything else, a complaint about unfair distribution of work.

> I ascend that northern hill,
> And gather the medlars.
> An officer, strong and vigorous,
> Morning and evening I am engaged in service.
> The king's business is not to be slackly performed;
> And my parents are left in sorrow.

> Under the wide Heaven,
> All is the king's land.
> Within the sea-boundaries of the land,
> All are the king's servants.
> His great officers are unfair,
> Making me serve thus as if I alone were worthy.

> My four horses never halt;
> The king's business allows no rest.
> They praise me as not yet old;
> They think few like me in vigour.
> While the backbone retains its strength,
> I must plan and labour in all parts of the kingdom.

> Some enjoy their ease and rest,
> And some are worn out in the service of the State;
> Some rest and loll upon their couches,
> And some never cease marching about.

---

17 If we are to use private law language, the people's sovereignty should be understood as a *usufructuary* right, which is not a right of ownership or possession but only a right to use and enjoy within constraints, including, in this case, the constraints of the principle of the common good and justice for all. I thank Lusina Ho for suggesting this concept.

The "unfairness" interpretation above is confirmed by a passage in *Mencius* in which the saying is quoted. In this passage Xian Qiumeng asks Mencius whether Shun should appoint Yao—who was supposed to pass his rulership to Shun before his death—as a minister once Shun became the ruler. Xian claims, citing *The Book of Poetry*, that "Under the wide Heaven, all is the king's land; within the sea-boundaries of the land, all are the king's servants"; therefore Yao, after stepping down as ruler, should be appointed as minister to Shun, since everyone is a minister to Shun the sovereign king. Mencius replies by saying that the quoted passage should not be taken out of context and gives the same "unfairness" interpretation. He says:

> This is not the meaning of the ode, which is about those who were unable to minister to the needs of their parents as a result of having to attend to the king's business. They were saying, "None of this is not the king's business. Why are we alone overburdened?" Hence in explaining an ode, one should not allow the words to get in the way of the sentence, nor the sentence to get in the way of the sense. (*Mencius* 5A.4)

The saying is also quoted in *Xunzi*, where it is taken to support only the notion that the Son of Heaven enjoys the highest authority in the world.

> That the Son of Heaven has no mate informs men that he is without peer. That within the Four Seas there are no ceremonies which treat him as a guest informs men that there is no one to match him. . . . An Ode says: Under the vastness of Heaven, there is no land that is not the king's land. To the far shores of the earth, none are not royal servants. (*Xunzi* 24.1)

The saying conveys the notion of the universal jurisdiction of the Son of Heaven and the supreme authority he enjoys, not the ruler's universal ownership of the land (or the people). As seen in chapter 7, not only does Mencius not think that the land belongs to the ruler, he views the equity of land distribution as the first task of a benevolent government, holding that each household should be entitled to an amount of land sufficient for living a decent material life (*Mencius* 3A.3, 1A.3). Xunzi also follows Mencius in this regard (*Xunzi* 27.52).

The Throne

I hope I have provided enough textual evidence and analysis to reject the second aspect of the ownership interpretation concerning the ownership of land and people. But what about the first aspect, which says that a legitimate claim to govern is "owned" by a ruler and hence can be freely transferred to others? As I argued above, abdication to the virtuous (*shan rang*) and hereditary succession seem to be two instances that support the ownership conception of tianming rather than the service conception. I shall examine each of these in turn.

According to the ownership interpretation, when the ruler abdicates his throne and gives it to a virtuous and wise successor, this act itself suggests that tianming, the right to rule, is something that the ruler owns and may freely transfer.[18] After all, the ruler must first have the right to give before he can legitimately give and the successor legitimately receive. But this is a misunderstanding of the nature of shan rang, a misunderstanding that arises from an incorrect description of the process and justification of the legitimacy of the successor as envisaged by Mencius. The following passage from *Mencius* about the process of shan rang clearly asserts that "the emperor cannot give the empire to another."

Wan Chang said, "Is it true that Yao gave the empire to Shun?"

"No," said Mencius. "The emperor cannot give the empire to another."

"In that case who gave the empire to Shun?"

"Heaven gave it him."

"You say Heaven gave it him. Does this mean that Heaven gave him detailed and minute instructions?"

"No. Heaven does not speak but reveals itself through its acts and deeds."

"How does Heaven do this?" . . .

"In antiquity, Yao recommended Shun to Heaven and Heaven accepted him; he presented him to the people and the people accepted him. . . ."

"May I ask how he was accepted by Heaven when recommended to it and how he was accepted by the people when presented to them?'

"When he was put in charge of sacrifices, the hundred gods enjoyed them. This showed that Heaven accepted him. When he was put in charge of affairs, they were kept in order and the people were content. This showed that the people accepted him. Heaven gave it to him, and the people gave it to him. Hence I said, 'The emperor cannot give the empire to another.'" (*Mencius* 5A.5)

In the process of abdication, the sole role of the ruler is to recommend a successor to Heaven; it is Heaven who gives the right to rule to the successor, and it does so according to the criterion discussed above—namely, that what justifies the successor's political legitimacy is his possession of qualities and experience necessary for taking up the important and onerous task of governing for the sake of the people. Mencius takes the acceptance shown by Heaven and the people as evidence of fulfillment of such a criterion. This is why Yao took great care to test Shun, and Shun took great care to test Yu, before they abdicated their right to rule. Although the act of passing on the right to rule is necessary, this does not make it akin to a transfer of property.

How shall we interpret monarchical heredity in this light? If a monarch can pass his throne to his first son (or occasionally a younger brother) on the basis of blood relation rather than personal merit, this seems to suggest that tian-

---

18   Shih, "Tian ming yu zheng dang xing," 55.

ming can be owned and transferred according to one's own wishes. Mencius and later Confucians tried to reconcile this by saying that it is Heaven's choice whether to adopt shan rang or heredity as the method of succession, and that Heaven has an independent and ultimate will on this. Mencius says, "If Heaven wished to give the empire to a good and wise man, then it should be given to a good and wise man. But if Heaven wished to give it to the son, then it should be given to the son" (*Mencius* 5A.6). Here Mencius is saying that it is up to Heaven to decide whether governance should be passed to the son of a ruler or a good and wise man. This seems to suggest that Heaven may decide this matter using a case-by-case approach rather than according to a general rule that favors one over the other. However, Mencius later shifts to a general endorsement of heredity as the principle of succession favored by Heaven.[19] He says,

> A common man who comes to possess the empire must not only have the virtue of a Shun or a Yu but also the recommendation of an emperor. That is why Confucius never possessed the empire. On the other hand, he who inherits the empire is only put aside by Heaven if he is like Jie or Zhou. That is why Yi, Yi Yin, and the Duke of Zhou never came to possess the empire. (5A.6)

Without further explanation as to why Heaven favors the heredity principle, the appeal to the will of Heaven could easily be viewed as an intellectually empty device for justifying the status quo. What is called for is a justification of hereditary succession that (1) does not presuppose the ruler's ownership of the throne and (2) is consistent with the requirement that authority must serve the people. Later Confucians have tried to make such a justification by pointing to the stability and effectiveness of political rule under a hereditary monarchical regime, given the conditions in premodern China. At this time, basically three modes of succession existed: abdication, heredity, and coup or revolution (democracy by universal suffrage not being considered an option in premodern China). Of the three options, heredity was regarded as the most reliable method for ensuring stability and effectiveness.

Abdication to the good and wise impels a search for the suitable person—a process that could easily create contention, competition, and instability. In fact, abdication has often been invoked in traditional China as an excuse to topple rulers and seize power.[20] Confucians were also well aware that few sages existed. Revolution or coup is by nature too unpredictable, disruptive, and costly to be regarded as a viable standard method of succession. Heredity, therefore, promises the most stability, for its norm of succession allows little room for differing interpretations. Establishing a norm in which the first son of an emperor auto-

---

19   Mou Zongsan noted this shift in his *Zheng dao yu zhi dao*, 132–33.

20   For a discussion of the problems of abdication in theory and practice, see Sun Kuang-te 孫廣德 [Sun Guangde], *Zhongguo zheng zhi si xiang zhuan ti yan jiu ji* 中國政治思想專題研究集 [Collection of Study of Chinese Political Thought] (Taipei: Laureate Book, 1999), 3–10; and Yang Yongjun 楊永俊, *Shan rang zheng zhi yan jiu* 禪讓政治研究 (Beijing: Academy Press 學苑出版社, 2005).

matically succeeds his throne ensures that no other members of the royal family, or self-proclaimed sages and their followers, can viably challenge the legitimacy of the new ruler. Nevertheless, how can hereditary succession ensure effective governance? To illustrate that heredity is not necessarily an ineffective way of ensuring that those who inherit the throne have the ability to govern, late Confucians argue that there are, in effect, few very evil people just as there are few great sages.[21] As most people are average in their virtues or abilities, differing only in degree, there is, therefore, a high chance that the son of the emperor will be of average virtue; and Confucians believe that even a person of average virtue could become an effective ruler, given the right conditions.

One such condition is tradition.[22] Confucians believe that a new ruler inherits not just the throne but also the success of previous rulers, the implication being that the new ruler should emulate the conduct of the early emperors of a dynasty and learn from their experiences, laws, policies, and institutions, as it was these things that enabled the dynasty to receive and keep the mandate to rule.[23] In addition, according to the Confucian conception, virtues and wisdom could be taught and acquired through habituation and practice. Princes were groomed from early childhood to learn the responsibilities of a ruler and underwent rigorous education and training to learn the art and science of governance.[24] Once enthroned, they were also assisted by a team of experienced and competent ministers that was led by the prime minister and chosen on the basis of merit. To be sure, the relationship between monarchy and meritocratic bureaucracy fluctuated in the long imperial history of China. In good times the two sides worked in good partnership; in bad times one side dominated the other or the two sides vied bitterly for power.[25] Nevertheless, it seems right to think that, on the whole, meritocratic ministers and officials have helped maintain the stability of the hereditary monarchy, contributed to meritorious governance, and served as "checks and balances" against emperors.[26]

At the institutional level, hereditary succession appears to imply sufficient condition for conferring legitimacy and to confirm the view that heredity is an

---

21 Sun, *Zhongguo zheng zhi si xiang*, 14.

22 See Wang Fuzhi 王夫之 [Chuanshan Xiansheng 船山先生], *Si shu xun yi xia* 四書訓義下 [Interpreting the *Four Books* vol. 2], vol. 8 of *Chuanshan quan shu* 船山全書 [Complete Works of Chuanshan], ed. Chuanshan quan shu bian ji wei yuan hui 船山全書編輯委員會 [Editorial board of the *Chuanshan quan shu*] (Changsha: Yuelu 嶽麓書社, 1996), 593–600.

23 Some scholars have argued that the rites of the ancestors served the function of what we today call the constitutional conventions that rulers are generally expected to follow. See Hahm Chaihark, "Constitutionalism, Confucian Civic Virtue, and Ritual Propriety," chap. 1 in Bell and Chaibong, *Confucianism for the Modern World*.

24 For a discussion of a case of the early education of an emperor, Ming dynasty's Wan-Li (1563–1620), see "The Wan-Li Emperor," chap. 1 in Ray Huang, *1587, A Year of No Significance: The Ming Dynasty in Decline* (New Haven: Yale University Press, 1981), 9–12.

25 See Huang, "A World without Chang Chü-cheng," chap. 3 in ibid.

26 For an account of this position, see Yuri Pines, "The Literati," chap. 3 in *The Everlasting Empire*.

expression of the privatization of the throne and the world under Heaven (*jia tian xia*). But if the account above is plausible, we see that Confucians justify hereditary succession not as confirmation of the ownership interpretation of authority but as a better alternative to abdication and revolution, namely, a better way to maintain effective rule and service for the people. In addition, Confucians believe that at the institutional level, the heredity mechanism alone is not sufficient but must be embedded within a larger institutional setup that includes a strong respect for tradition and rituals as constitutional conventions, a sound political education for the monarch's family, and a meritocratic system for the employment of officials (ministers and magistrates). Furthermore, all the usual conditions associated with tianming, such as virtuous practices and promotion of the people's well-being, also apply to the heirs of throne, who are deemed illegitimate if they perform their duties poorly. According to the Confucian view, hereditary monarchy is not so much about passing on the glory and privileges of the ruler as about passing on the heavy responsibility of governance. The prince has no choice but to assume the duties of a ruler, and it is expected that he will behave in a way that fits the role and manner of a responsible ruler. Authority is first and foremost a matter of responsibility.

To summarize, I have argued against the ownership interpretation of tianming. Tianming is a justified right to govern rather than an ownership right: the right to govern is not owned by the claim-holder, nor can it be freely transferred to others; the right does not give the claim-holder the ownership right to a territory or people. The justified right to govern is no more than the power to make and implement laws and policies within a certain territorial jurisdiction. To use the jargon of Roman law, Confucianism understands political authority as imperium, not dominium.

The People as the Dominus?

If Confucianism rejects the notion that political authority is something that can be owned by a single person or family, does it accept that "the people" can own it? If political authority at the highest level—referred to by some Western scholars as dominium or sovereignty—does not reside with the ruler or the royal family, does it reside with the people? After all, a dominium requires a dominus to preside over it. Some interpretive arguments maintain that Confucianism tends to see the people as the dominus, in that it views embryonic democratic ideas such as "people's sovereignty" or "people's consent" as a necessary condition of political legitimacy. Perhaps the most famous statement of this position can be found in *Manifesto to the World's People on Behalf of Chinese Culture*, coauthored by four leading Chinese Confucian scholars in the 1950s: Carsun Chang (Zhang Junmai), Tang Junyi, Xu Fuguan, and Mou Zongsan.[27] These

---

27 An abbreviated English version of the manifesto has been published under the title "A Manifesto for a Re-appraisal of Sinology and Reconstruction of Chinese Culture," in Carsun Chang

scholars argue that traditional Chinese systems of thought, especially Confucianism, contain "democratic seeds" that can develop into a clear, unmistakable demand for democracy as a set of political institutions. These four highly regarded thinkers have influenced several generations of scholars in Taiwan and Hong Kong, and the following analysis is based on a selection of their main arguments, as well as those of later scholars who share this line of thought. I shall argue against this interpretation.

In arguing that Confucianism contains ideas that could be regarded as relating to fundamental democratic rights, many scholars, including the four above, appeal to two popular ideas in traditional Chinese political discourse: *tian xia wei gong* (a public and common spirit ruled all under the sky) and *tian xia fei yi ren zhi tian xia ye, tian xia zhi tian xia ye* (the world does not belong to one person but the whole world). But in what sense are these ideas democratic? Some argue that they express the democratic idea of popular sovereignty. To examine the legitimacy of this assertion, let us look in turn at these two ideas and the contexts in which they appear.

Tian Xia Wei Gong

The notion of *tian xia wei gong* appears in the famous passage about the Confucian ideal social order—the Grand Union—in *The Book of Rites*. Confucius says:

> When the Grand Dao was pursued, *a public and common spirit ruled all under the sky* [*tian xia wei gong*]; they chose men of talent, virtue, and ability for public service. . . . They did not treat only their own parents as parents, nor treat only their own sons as sons. Provision was secured for the aged till their death. . . . People showed kindness and compassion to widows, orphans, childless men, and those who were disabled by disease, so that they were all sufficiently provided for. . . . Possessions were not wastefully discarded, nor were they greedily hoarded. . . . In this way selfish schemings were discouraged and did not arise. Robbers, thieves, and rebellious traitors were unknown, and doors remained open and unlocked. Such was the Grand Union." ("Li yun," *Book of Rites*, italics added) [28]

In this passage I believe that James Legge, the translator of *The Book of Rites*, has captured the meaning of *tian xia wei gong* well by translating it as "a public and common spirit ruled all under the sky." The passage makes no mention of where political authority or sovereignty lies, or who possesses it, but instead describes the ideal world as a place in which people act in a "public and common spirit"

張君勱 [Zhang Junmai], *The Development of Neo-Confucian Thought*, vol. 2 (New York: Bookman Associates, 1962). For further bibliographical details of the manifesto and a detailed analysis of its views, see Albert H. Y. Chen, "Is Confucianism Compatible with Liberal Constitutional Democracy?" *Journal of Chinese Philosophy* 34, no. 2 (2007): 195–216.

28 Author's translation after consulting translations by Legge as well as Chai and Chai.

to promote the common good. In the ideal world people care not only for their own family members but for others as well; they do not pursue power and opportunity to satisfy selfish interests but impartially select talented and virtuous individuals to run the community's affairs for the benefit of everyone. This interpretation of *gong* (i.e., "for the benefit of the public") does not refer to the "ownership" of sovereign power in the ideal world but suggests instead an ideal of the common good and impartiality.

Some scholars, however, have argued that *tian xia wei gong* should be understood in contradistinction with *tian xia wei jia*, a notion that appears in the subsequent paragraph of the chapter cited above in *The Book of Rites* and refers, among other things, to the situation in which political authority is inherited along the family line (i.e., that political authority belongs to the emperor and his family). When contrasted with *tian xia wei jia*, the meaning of *tian xia wei gong* implies that political authority, or the world, belongs to everyone in the world or the people, that is, it is publicly owned—hence the idea of popular sovereignty.[29]

The paragraph is as follows:

> Now that the Grand Dao has fallen into disuse and obscurity, *hereditary families rule over the whole land* [*tian xia wei jia*]. People love only their own parents as parents, and cherish only their own sons as sons. Goods and labor serve self-interests. Noblemen believe in their right to hereditary power. ("Li yun," *Book of Rites*, italics added)[30]

There are several points in reply to this interpretation. First, the passage does not denounce *tian xia wei jia* as illegitimate—to do so would run contrary to the strong Confucian endorsement of hereditary monarchy during the Three Dynasties (Xia, Shang, Zhou) when it was praised as a model of political rule, with Zhu Xi even calling it "the model of the Sage King, the law of '*gong tian xia*.'"[31] What later Confucians denounced was the abuse of political authority that began in the Qin dynasty, when emperors began to exercise their power to benefit themselves and their families rather than the people. It was in this sense that a real opposition was drawn between *gong tian xia* and *si tian xia* (i.e., whether the ruler acts impartially for the people or acts selfishly for himself and his family). So, while in the passages above, *tian xia wei gong* and *tian xia wei jia* represent two different ways of transferring political authority, and while the former is doubtless portrayed as more ideal than the latter, they were never understood as being in opposition. Here *tian xia wei gong* does not imply that political authority belongs to the people, but that the social and political order, including the selection of the ruler, should work for the benefit of everyone. Based on this principle, the selection of the truly virtuous and competent was

29   See Deng Xiaojun 鄧小軍, *Ru jia si xiang yu min zhu si xiang de luo ji jie he* 儒家思想與民主思想的邏輯結合 [The Logical Integration of Confucian and Democratic Thought] (Chengdu: Sichuan People's Publishing, 1995), 260–64.

30   Author's translation after consulting translations by Legge as well as Chai and Chai.

31   *Zhuzi yu lei* 朱子語類, cited in Zhang, *Min ben si xiang*, 2:525. My own translation.

therefore preferable to hereditary succession. The passage above about the Grand Union does not, however, suggest that this selection should be made by the people. In fact, *The Book of History* describes the selection as being made by the outgoing ruler and his ministers. In the same way, *tian xia wei jia* implies that the social and political order was primarily based on the principle of partiality, including the transfer of political authority according to the rule of heredity. But it is important to note that in this lesser ideal, people still follow rites, and the social relationships were governed by li such that harmony was still possible between people. In particular, rulers were said to be "very attentive to the rules of propriety, thus to secure the display of righteousness, the realization of sincerity, the exhibition of errors, the exemplification of benevolence, and the discussion of courtesy, showing the people all the normal virtues" ("Li yun," *Book of Rites*).The implication was that only if the practice of partiality was done without regard to rites, and only if the ruler put his interests above those of the ruled and thus failed to show benevolence to the people, would this fallen situation be unacceptable.

The account above is further confirmed by Mencius's endorsement of both heredity and abdication. He quoted Confucius's point that both methods of succession reflected the same meaning or were based on the same principle: "Confucius said, 'In Tang and Yu succession was through abdication, while in Xia, Yin and Zhou it was hereditary. The basic principle was the same'" (*Mencius* 5A.6). The principle underlying both methods of selection is Heaven's Mandate, which, according to the interpretation in the first section above implies that both methods are justifiable if they contribute to effective political rule for the betterment of the people.

In my belief, *tian xia wei gong* and *tian xia wei jia*, and the two methods of political succession, do not represent two ways of locating ultimate political authority or sovereignty: one with the people and the other with the ruler and his family. Rather, they represent two ways of governance: the most ideal being one in which absolute impartiality is practiced, and the other, the lesser ideal, in which a lesser degree of impartiality is practiced (i.e., partiality constrained by fundamental principles of rituals and benevolence).

Tian Xia Fei Yi Ren Zhi Tian Xia Ye, Tian Xia Zhi Tian Xia Ye

Let us look now at the second saying, *tian xia fei yi ren zhi tian xia ye, tian xia zhi tian xia ye* (the world does not belong to one person but the whole world), which some argue suggests a notion of common ownership or popular sovereignty. The phrase appears in *The Annals of Lü Buwei*, in the "Honoring Impartiality" (Gui gong) chapter that is often cited by later Chinese scholars. It says in part:

> *The world does not belong to one person; it belongs to the whole world* [*tian xia fei yi ren zhi tian xia ye, tian xia zhi tian xia ye*]. The harmony of the Yin and Yang forces does not favor growth in only one species of thing, the sweet

dews and seasonable rains are not partial to one thing, and so the ruler of the myriad people does not show favoritism toward a single individual. (*Annals of Lü Buwei* 1.4.2, italics added)

When Duke Huan acted with impartiality [gong], set aside selfish interests and private aversions, and used Master Guan, he became the most important of the Five Lords-Protector. When he acted in pursuit of selfish interests, showed favoritism to those he loved, and used Shudao, maggots crawled out from under his door. (1.4.3)

What this passage clearly suggests is that the forces of the world (yin and yang) do not favor particular individuals or groups but give blessings to every living thing on earth. Similarly, political rule should practice impartiality and public-spiritedness by promoting the good of everyone without prejudice or discrimination. The contrast to this ideal is political favoritism and partiality, which is the subject of the next chapter, "Dispensing with Selfish Partiality" (Qu si). Similar to the passage in *The Book of Rites*, this passage also suggests nothing about popular sovereignty, mentioning only the importance of impartiality (gong) in political rule. The beginning paragraph of the "Honoring Impartiality" chapter lays out quite clearly this conception of impartiality as a fair way to govern the world:

In the past, when the ancient Sage Kings governed the world, they invariably made impartiality their first priority, because if they acted impartially, the world would be at peace. . . . As a general principle, the establishment of a ruler develops out of his impartiality. Thus the *Hong fan* says:

Be neither partial nor partisan;
The way of the king is all encompassing.
Be neither partial nor biased;
Adhere to the king's rules.
Be not on good terms just with some;
Cleave to the king's way.
Be not on bad terms just with some;
Keep to the king's road. (1.4.1)

Like *The Book of Rites*, the "Dispensing with Selfish Partiality" chapter commends abdication as an expression of "perfect impartiality."

Heaven covers all without partiality; Earth bears all up without partiality; the sun and moon shine on all without partiality; the four seasons alternate without partiality. Each bestows its Power, and the myriad things attain thereby mature form. (1.5.1)

When Yao, who had ten sons, did not share the empire with them but passed it to Shun and when Shun, who had nine sons, did not share the empire with them but passed it to Yu, both acted with perfect impartiality. (1.5.3)

However, the principle of abdication is not equivalent to the principle of popular sovereignty. The former is an ideal not because it is an expression of the people's ownership of the world or of sovereignty but because political authority is given to the one who is most suited to use it for the benefit of everyone in the world. I would go further and argue that *The Annals of Lü Buwei* takes a much more radical stance on the question of possession or ownership; that it rejects the very idea of possession at a fundamental level, maintaining that the ruler does not possess the world or his throne, human beings cannot claim to possess it, and even Heaven and Earth, the creators of myriad things, cannot claim to possess it. The notion that human beings do not enjoy a privileged place in the scheme of things in the world can be seen in this paragraph:

> A man of Chu who had lost his bow and was unwilling to search for it, said: "A man of Chu lost it and a man of Chu will find it, so why should I search for it?" When Confucius learned of this, he said, "Omit 'Chu' and the comment will be proper." When Lao Dan learned of this, he said, "Omit 'a man' and it will be proper." Thus, it was Lao Dan who attained perfect impartiality. (1.4.2)

The idea that even Heaven and Earth, the creators of life, do not claim possession is suggested in the subsequent paragraph:

> Heaven and Earth are so great that while they give life they do not raise anything as their own, and while they bring things to completion they do not possess them. The myriad things all receive their blessings and obtain their benefits, but no one knows whence they first arose. So it is with the Power of the Three August Ones and the Five Sovereigns. (1.4.2)

It seems quite clear that *The Annals of Lü Buwei* adopts what I have called a nondominium conception of the world—that the world and its myriad things are not the possession or property of anyone, be it a ruler, a people (like the people of Chu), the human species (ren), or even Heaven and Earth. Rather, the world exists to benefit everyone and everything so that the "myriad things attain thereby mature form" (1.5.1). The sentence "The world does not belong to one person; it belongs to the whole world" (*tian xia fei yi ren zhi tian xia ye, tian xia zhi tian xia ye*) is not a statement about dominium or ownership; it is about impartiality. The meaning of the second part of the sentence (*tian xia zhi tian xia ye*) is something like this: "The world exists for the myriad things on earth." Applying this understanding to the issue of political authority, one can argue that political authority is not a form of property to be possessed by anyone (a person or a people), to be used to benefit a possessor, or to be used at the will of the possessor. It should not be conceived as dominium but simply as imperium—the right to governance—with the purpose of governance being to benefit the myriad things through impartiality. The conception of popular sovereignty as dominium is not found in *The Annals of Lü Buwei*, nor can it be derived from the idea of gong as developed in *The Book of Rites* or *The Annals*.

Heaven's Mandate Expressed through the Acceptance or Consent of the People

Confucianism views the ultimate source of political authority as residing with Heaven. A legitimate political ruler is one who receives a mandate to rule from Heaven. However, Mencius, who most explicitly endorses the Heaven's Mandate theory, also holds that this mandate is revealed through *the people's acceptance*. For some scholars, this emphasis on the people's acceptance or consent represents a democratic value or principle. As we have seen above, the most explicit statement of this theory is *Mencius* 5A.5:

> "In antiquity, Yao recommended Shun to Heaven and Heaven accepted him; he presented him to the people and the people accepted him. . . ."
>
> "May I ask how he was accepted by Heaven when recommended to it and how he was accepted by the people when presented to them?"
>
> "When he was put in charge of sacrifices, the hundred gods enjoyed them. This showed that Heaven accepted him. When he was put in charge of affairs, they were kept in order and the people were content. This showed that the people accepted him."

In this passage, Mencius says that Heaven speaks through the gods (through the acceptance of religious sacrifices) and through the people. Heaven's acceptance of a ruler can be seen in the acceptance of the people and the gods (as demonstrated by the acceptance of sacrifices without event). Later Mencius goes further and says, "Heaven sees with the eyes of its people; Heaven hears with the ears of its people" (5A.5). Some scholars argue that this strong emphasis on the people's acceptance and opinions as the basis of the Heaven's Mandate, and hence rightful rule, reflects a democratic value or principle. In another passage Mencius also says that the people's acceptance is the basis of successful political rule:

> Mencius said, "It was through losing the people that Jie and Zhou lost the empire, and through losing the people's hearts that they lost the people. There is a way to win the empire; win the people and you will win the empire. There is a way to win the people; win their hearts and you will win the people. There is a way to win their hearts; amass what they want for them; do not impose what they dislike on them. That is all. The people turn to the benevolent as water flows downwards or as animals head for the wilds." (4A.9)

For Mencius, Heaven reveals its choice through the people. Any ruler who hopes to attain stable rule must win the people's hearts. Acceptance from the people is necessary for the ruler's political legitimacy. Among all the ideas in Confucianism examined so far, this one comes closest to the idea of democracy. But "the people's acceptance" does not imply democracy as an institution or a fundamental principle. The fact that a political system has the acceptance of the people does not make the system democratic. For example, it is possible that the people may accept a system of monarchy so long as the monarch's performance is satisfactory to them. Neither does acceptance imply popular sovereignty. Popular sovereignty, at least the modern version that is part of democratic theory, must be expressed through certain *institutions* or *procedures*, such as the legal right to amend a constitution and the right to vote. The people's acceptance of political authority, as such, is not an institutional expression of popular sovereignty.[32] To illustrate the distance between Confucian consent and democracy, let us look again at Mencius. In Mencius's view, if the ruler is benevolent, morally upright, and able to deliver basic services to the people, the people will accept him as the legitimate ruler (*Mencius* 4A.9, 5A.5). Mencius sees a unity of the Way and the will (or heart) of the people (4A.9). If a ruler practices the Way in his governance, he will gain the hearts of the people and their voluntary submission. For Mencius and other classical Confucian masters, the people's wishes and wants, to which any benevolent ruler must give first priority, are as clear and stable as objective human needs. The people desire sufficient material subsistence, protection of private land and property, low taxation, leisure time to enjoy basic human relationships, and a virtuous leader who can serve as an exemplary model for their moral lives. The problem for Confucians is not that it is difficult to ascertain the wants and needs of the people, but that in reality rulers do not often put the people's needs as their first priority. However, Confucians believe that if a ruler can deliver the goods and satisfy the people's wants, the people's approval is almost automatic: "The people turn to the benevolent as water flows downwards or as animals head for the wilds" (4A.9). A benevolent, virtuous monarch will automatically obtain the people's approval, and hence approval is consistent with a monarchy where the subjects have no rights whatsoever to participate in politics. In fact, as some scholars have similarly argued, the people may just function as "indicators of Heaven's approval," like a "barometer of the ruler's competence"[33] or "thermometers, measuring the quality of rule and thereby indicating the presence or absence of legitimate authority."[34]

We may thus conclude that the Confucian ideas above do not necessarily express fundamental democratic ideas or imply such principles as popular sovereignty.

Conclusion

In sum, I have argued that for early Confucianism, political authority is not a form of property to be owned by a ruler, nor does it grant a ruler any right to

---

32 Similarly, the fact that the people are regularly consulted by their government does not imply that they have the institutional right to participate in decision making on public affairs.

33 Tiwald, "A Right of Rebellion," 278, 272. Tiwald also gives an argument, convincing in my view, against a modern view that Mencius thinks people have a right to revolt.

34 Angle, *Contemporary Confucian Political Philosophy*, 40.

treat his people and territory as his ownership. Authority is also not something that can be owned by the ruled. According to the Confucian view, the ultimate source of political authority lies with Heaven, as Heaven's will and choice is the basis of legitimate authority—Heaven selects the ruler, grants him the mandate to rule, and removes him if he fails to serve the people and promote their well-being (hence the Heaven's Mandate view). However, as many commentators have noted, the early Confucian conception of Heaven gradually evolved from being a deistic notion before the Zhou period to a more or less moral-transcendental one in the Spring and Autumn and Warring States periods and thereafter.[35] Thus the will of Heaven became over time less analogous with the wishes and deeds of a personal deity and more a set of objective cosmological principles and ethical values that regulate the order of the universe and guide human action. If Heaven is objectified and its will stripped of intentionality, the conception of Heaven as the supreme sovereign loses practical significance. Heaven becomes a higher law that rulers and the common people should follow, rather than an absolute sovereign whose will is hard to predict. Such a conception of Heaven, when applied to politics, lends support to the idea of limited government rather than absolute divine right. This is discussed further in chapter 2.

I conclude that Confucianism rejects the dominium or ownership conception of authority. Political authority in Confucian terms means imperium, namely, a legitimate right to govern within a jurisdiction that is conditional on its ability to protect and promote the people's well-being. Political authority exists for this purpose, and its justification depends on its ability to serve this purpose.

35   See Chen Lai 陳來, "Tianming" 天命 [Heaven's Mandate], chap. 5 in *Gu dai zong jiao yu lun li—ru jia si xiang de gen yuan* 古代宗教與倫理—儒家思想的根源 [Ancient Religion and Ethics—The Origin of Confucian Thought], SDX & Harvard-Yenching Academic Library (Beijing: SDX Joint Publishing, 1996); Yuri Pines, "Heaven and Man Part Ways: Changing Attitudes toward Divine Authority," chap. 2 in *Foundations of Confucian Thought: Intellectual Life in the Chunqiu Period, 722–453 B.C.E* (Honolulu: University of Hawaii Press, 2002).

BIBLIOGRAPHY

Ames, Roger T. *Confucian Role Ethics: A Vocabulary.* Hong Kong: Chinese University Press, 2011.

———. "Rites as Rights: The Confucian Alternative." In *Human Rights and the World's Religions,* edited by Leroy S. Rouner, 199–216. Notre Dame: University of Notre Dame Press, 1988.

Anderson, Elizabeth S. "What Is the Point of Equality?" *Ethics* 109, no. 2 (1999): 287–337.

Angle, Stephen C. *Contemporary Confucian Political Philosophy.* Cambridge: Polity Press, 2012.

———. *Sagehood: The Contemporary Significance of Neo-Confucian Philosophy.* New York: Oxford University Press, 2009.

Arendt, Hannah. *On Revolution.* London: Penguin, 2006.

Aristotle. *Nicomachean Ethics.*

Arneson, Richard J. "Joel Feinberg and the Justification of Hard Paternalism." *Legal Theory* 11, no. 3 (2005): 259–84.

———. "The Supposed Right to a Democracy Say." Chap. 11 in *Contemporary Debates in Political Philosophy,* edited by Thomas Christiano and John Christman. Oxford: Wiley-Blackwell, 2009.

Atwell, John E. "Kant's Notion of Respect for Persons." *Tulane Studies in Philosophy* 31 (1982): 17–30.

Barber, Benjamin R. "The Real Present: Institutionalizing Strong Democracy in the Modern World." Chap. 10 in *Strong Democracy: Participatory Politics for a New Age.* Berkeley: University of California Press, 1984.

Barry, Brian. *Democracy, Power and Justice: Essays in Political Theory.* Oxford: Clarendon Press, 1989.

Beetham, David. "Liberal Democracy and the Limits of Democratization." In *Prospects for Democracy: North, South, East, West,* edited by David Held, 55–73. Stanford: Stanford University Press, 1993.

Bell, Daniel. "The Old War: After Ideology, Corruption." *New Republic.* August 23 and 30, 1993, 20–21.

Bell, Daniel A. *Beyond Liberal Democracy: Political Thinking for an East Asian Context.* Princeton: Princeton University Press, 2006.

———. *China's New Confucianism: Politics and Everyday Life in a Changing Society.* Princeton: Princeton University Press, 2008.

———. "Confucian Constraints on Property Rights." Chap. 9 in *Confucianism for the*

Modern World, edited by Daniel A. Bell and Hahm Chaibong. Cambridge: Cambridge University Press, 2003.

———. "Just War and Confucianism: Implications for the Contemporary World." In *Confucian Political Ethics*, edited by Daniel A. Bell, 226–56. Princeton: Princeton University Press, 2008.

———. "Toward Meritocratic Rule in China? A Response to Professors Dallmayr, Li, and Tan." *Philosophy East and West* 59, no. 4 (2009): 554–60.

Benbaji, Yitzhak. "The Doctrine of Sufficiency: A Defence." *Utilitas* 17, no. 3 (2005): 310–32.

Besley, Timothy. "Political Selection." *Journal of Economic Perspectives* 19, no. 3 (2005): 43–60.

Billante, Nicole, and Peter Saunders. "Six Questions about Civility." Occasional Paper 82 (July 2002). Centre for Independent Studies.

Blackburn, Simon. *Spreading the Word: Groundings in the Philosophy of Language.* Oxford: Oxford University Press, 1984.

Blustein, Jeffrey. *Parents and Children: The Ethics of the Family.* New York: Oxford University Press, 1982.

Brennan, Geoffrey, and James Buchanan. "Predictive Power and the Choice among Regimes." *Economic Journal* 93, no. 369 (March 1983): 89–105.

Brennan, Geoffrey, and Alan Hamlin. *Democratic Devices and Desires.* Cambridge: Cambridge University Press, 2000.

Brennan, Jason. *The Ethics of Voting.* Princeton: Princeton University Press, 2011.

Burnheim, John. *Is Democracy Possible? The Alternative to Electoral Politics.* Berkeley: University of California Press, 1985.

Callan, Eamonn. *Creating Citizens: Political Education and Liberal Democracy.* Oxford: Clarendon Press, 1997.

Campbell, Tom D. *Justice.* 2nd edition. London: Macmillan, 2001.

Caney, Simon. "Sandel's Critique of the Primacy of Justice: A Liberal Rejoinder." *British Journal of Political Science* 21, no. 4 (1991): 511–21.

Caplan, Bryan. *The Myth of the Rational Voter: Why Democracies Choose Bad Policies.* Princeton: Princeton University Press, 2007.

Carter, Robert E. *Dimensions of Moral Education.* Toronto: University of Toronto Press, 1984.

Casal, Paula. "Why Sufficiency Is Not Enough." *Ethics* 117, no. 2 (2007): 296–326.

Chai, Ch'u, and Winberg Chai, eds. and trans. *The Sacred Books of Confucius and Other Confucian Classics.* New Hyde Park, NY: University Books, 1965.

Chan, Joseph 陳祖為. "A Confucian Perspective on Human Rights for Contemporary China." Chap. 9 in *The East Asian Challenge for Human Rights*, edited by Joanne R. Bauer and Daniel A. Bell. Cambridge: Cambridge University Press, 1999.

———. "Democracy and Meritocracy: Toward a Confucian Perspective." *Journal of Chinese Philosophy* 34, no. 2 (2007): 179–93.

———. "Exploring the Nonfamilial in Confucian Political Philosophy." Chap. 3 in *The Politics of Affective Relations: East Asia and Beyond*, edited by Hahm Chaihark and Daniel A. Bell. Lanham, MD: Lexington, 2004.

———. "Hong Kong, Singapore, and 'Asian Values': An Alternative View." *Journal of Democracy* 8, no. 2 (1997): 35–48.

———. "In Defense of Moderate Perfectionism." Unpublished manuscript. 2009.

———. "Legitimacy, Unanimity, and Perfectionism." *Philosophy and Public Affairs* 29, no. 1 (2000): 5–42.

———. "On the Legitimacy of Confucian Constitutionalism." Chap. 4 in Jiang Qing 蔣慶, *A Confucian Constitutional Order: How China's Ancient Past Can Shape Its Political Future*, translated by Edmund Ryden, edited by Daniel A. Bell and Ruiping Fan. Princeton: Princeton University Press, 2013.

———. "Notes on the Methods of Philosophical Reconstruction." Unpublished notes. 2012.

———. "Political Authority and Perfectionism: A Response to Quong." *Philosophy and Public Issues* 2, no. 1 (2012): 31–41.

———. "Raz on Liberal Rights and Common Goods," *Oxford Journal of Legal Studies* 15, no. 1 (1995): 15–31.

———. "Thick and Thin Accounts of Human Rights: Lessons from the Asian Values Debate." Chap. 3 in *Human Rights and Asian Values: Contesting National Identities and Cultural Representations in Asia*, edited by Michael Jacobsen and Ole Bruun. Vol. 6 in Democracy in Asia series. Surrey, UK: Curzon, 2000.

———. "Wei wen he yuan shan zhu yi bian hu" 為溫和圓善主義辯護 [In Defense of Moderate Perfectionism]. In *Pu bian yu te shu de bian zheng: zheng zhi si xiang de tan jue* 普遍與特殊的辯證：政治思想的探掘 [Between the Universal and the Particular: Explorations in Political Philosophy], edited by Sechin Yeong-Shyang Chien 錢永祥, 1–24. Taipei: Research Center for Humanities and Social Sciences, Academia Sinica, 2012.

Chan, Joseph, and Elton Chan. "Confucianism and Political Leadership." In *The Oxford Handbook of Political Leadership*, edited by Paul 't Hart and R.A.W. Rhodes. Oxford: Oxford University Press, forthcoming.

Chan, Wing-tsit, comp. and trans. "Legalism." Chap. 12 in *A Source Book in Chinese Philosophy*. Princeton: Princeton University Press, 1969.

Chang, Carsun 張君勱 [Zhang, Junmai]. *The Development of Neo-Confucian Thought*. Vol. 2. New York: Bookman Associates, 1962.

Chang, Yun-Shik. "Mutual Help and Democracy in Korea." Chap. 4 in *Confucianism for the Modern World*, edited by Daniel A. Bell and Hahm Chaibong. Cambridge: Cambridge University Press, 2003.

Charles, David. *Aristotle's Philosophy of Action*. London: Duckworth, 1984.

Chen, Albert H. Y. "Is Confucianism Compatible with Liberal Constitutional Democracy?" *Journal of Chinese Philosophy* 34, no. 2 (2007): 195–216.

———. "Mediation, Litigation, and Justice: Confucian Reflections in a Modern Liberal Society." Chap. 11 in *Confucianism for the Modern World*, edited by Daniel A. Bell and Hahm Chaibong. Cambridge: Cambridge University Press, 2003.

Chen, Duxiu 陳獨秀. *De sai er xian sheng yu she hui zhu yi: Chen Duxiu wen xuan* 德賽二先生與社會主義：陳獨秀文選 [*Mr Democracy and Mr Science and Socialism:*

Selected Writings of Chen Duxiu], edited by Wu Xiaoming 吳曉明. Shanghai: Shanghai Yuan Dong 上海遠東, 1994.

Chen, Huan-Chang 陳煥章 [Chen Huanzhang]. *The Economic Principles of Confucius and His School.* 2 vols. New York: Columbia University Press, 1911.

Chen, Lai 陳來. "Tianming" 天命 [Heaven's Mandate]. Chap. 5 in *Gu dai zong jiao yu lun li—ru jia si xiang de gen yuan* 古代宗教與倫理—儒家思想的根源 [Ancient Religion and Ethics—The Origin of Confucian Thought]. SDX and Harvard-Yenching Academic Library. Beijing: SDX Joint Publishing, 1996.

Ci Jiwei 慈繼偉. "Cong zheng dang yu shan de qu fen kan quan li zai xian dai xi fang he ru jia si xiang zhong de cha yi" 從正當與善的區分看權利在現代西方和儒家思想中的差異 [The Right, the Good, and the Place of Rights in Confucianism]. In *Guo ji ru xue yan jiu* 國際儒學研究 [International Confucian Studies], vol. 6. Beijing: China Social Sciences Press, 1999.

Cline, Erin M. "Two Senses of Justice: Confucianism, Rawls, and Comparative Political Philosophy." *Dao* 6, no. 4 (2007): 361–81.

CNSNews.com. "Basic Facts about United Way." July 7, 2008. http://cnsnews.com/node/5459.

Confucius. *The Analects of Confucius*, translated by Simon Leys. New York: Norton, 1997.

———. *The Analects of Confucius: A Philosophical Translation*, translated by Roger T. Ames and Henry Rosemont, Jr. New York: Ballantine, 1998.

———. *Confucius: The Analects*, translated by D. C. Lau. Revised bilingual edition, Hong Kong: Chinese University Press, 1992.

———. *The Analects of Confucius*, translated by Chichung Huang. New York: Oxford University Press, 1997.

Constitution of India. Article 60, "Oath or Affirmation by the President." http://lawmin.nic.in/olwing/coi/coi-English/coi-indexEnglish.htm.

Creel, Herrlee Glessner. *The Western Chou Empire.* Vol. 1 of *The Origins of Statecraft in China.* Chicago: University of Chicago Press, 1970.

Crisp, Roger. "Equality, Priority, and Compassion." *Ethics* 113, no. 4 (2003): 745–63.

Cua, A. S. *Moral Vision and Tradition: Essays in Chinese Ethics.* Vol. 31 of Studies in Philosophy and the History of Philosophy. Washington, DC: Catholic University of America Press, 1998.

———. "The Status of Principles in Confucian Ethics." *Journal of Chinese Philosophy* 16, no. 3–4 (1989): 273–96.

Dan-Cohen, Meir. "Conceptions of Choice and Conceptions of Autonomy." *Ethics* 102, no. 2 (1992): 221–43.

de Bary, William Theodore. *Asian Values and Human Rights: A Confucian Communitarian Perspective.* Cambridge: Harvard University Press, 1998.

———. *The Trouble with Confucianism.* Cambridge: Harvard University Press, 1991.

Deng, Xiaojun 鄧小軍. *Ru jia si xiang yu min zhu si xiang de luo ji jie he* 儒家思想與民主思想的邏輯結合 [The Logical Integration of Confucian and Democratic Thought]. Chengdu: Sichuan People's Publishing, 1995.

DeVitis, Joseph L., and Tianlong Yu, eds. *Character and Moral Education: A Reader.* New York: Peter Lang, 2011.

Diamond, Larry. *Developing Democracy: Toward Consolidation.* Baltimore: Johns Hopkins University Press, 1999.

Dostoyevsky, Fyodor. *The Brothers Karamazov.* 1880.

Dworkin, Ronald. *Is Democracy Possible Here? Principles for a New Political Debate.* Princeton: Princeton University Press, 2006.

Eliasoph, Nina. "Civil Society and Civility." Chap. 18 in *The Oxford Handbook of Civil Society*, edited by Michael Edwards. New York: Oxford University Press, 2011.

Estlund, David M. *Democratic Authority: A Philosophical Framework.* Princeton: Princeton University Press, 2008.

Fan, Ruiping. *Reconstructionist Confucianism: Rethinking Morality after the West.* Dordrecht: Springer, 2010.

———. "Social Justice: Rawlsian or Confucian?" Chap. 7 in *Comparative Approaches to Chinese Philosophy*, edited by Bo Mou. Ashgate World Philosophies Series. Aldershot, UK: Ashgate, 2003.

Fearon, James D. "Electoral Accountability and the Control of Politicians: Selecting Good Types versus Sanctioning Poor Performance." Chap. 2 in *Democracy, Accountability, and Representation*, edited by Adam Przeworski, Susan C. Stokes and Bernard Manin. Cambridge: Cambridge University Press, 1999.

Feinberg, Joel. *Harm to Self.* Vol. 3 of *The Moral Limits of the Criminal Laws.* New York: Oxford University Press, 1986.

———. "The Nature and Value of Rights." *Journal of Value Inquiry* 4, no. 4 (1970): 243–60.

Fingarette, Herbert. *Confucius: The Secular as Sacred.* New York: Harper and Row, 1972.

Fleischacker, Samuel. Introduction to *A Short History of Distributive Justice.* Cambridge: Harvard University Press, 2004.

Frankfurt, Harry. "Equality as a Moral Ideal." *Ethics* 98, no. 1 (1987): 21–43.

Frey, Bruno S. "A Constitution for Knaves Crowds Out Civic Virtues." *Economic Journal* 107, no. 443 (July 1997): 1043–53.

Galston, William A. "Realism in Political Theory." *European Journal of Political Theory* 9, no. 4 (2010): 385–411.

Garvey, John H. *What Are Freedoms For?* Cambridge: Harvard University Press, 1996.

Geuss, Raymond. "Morality and Identity." Chap. 6 in *The Sources of Normativity*, by Christine M. Korsgaard et al. edited by Onora O'Neill. Cambridge: Cambridge University Press, 1996.

Gongyang Commentary on The Annals of Spring and Autumn 公羊傳 [Gongyang zhuan].

Griffin, James. *On Human Rights.* New York: Oxford University Press, 2008.

Gutmann, Amy, and Dennis Thompson. *Democracy and Disagreement.* Cambridge: Harvard University Press, 1996.

Hahm, Chaihark. "Constitutionalism, Confucian Civic Virtue, and Ritual Propriety."

Chap. 1 in *Confucianism for the Modern World*, edited by Daniel A. Bell and Hahm Chaibong. Cambridge: Cambridge University Press, 2003.

Hampton, Jean. *Political Philosophy*. Boulder: Westview Press, 1997.

Hansen, Chad. "Punishment and Dignity in China." In *Individualism and Holism: Studies in Confucian and Taoist Values*, edited by Donald J. Munro, 359–83. Ann Arbor: Center for Chinese Studies, University of Michigan, 1985.

He, Baogang. "Knavery and Virtue in Humean Institutional Design." *Journal of Value Inquiry* 37, no. 4 (2003): 543–53.

Hinchman, Lewis. "Autonomy, Individuality, and Self Determination." In *What Is Enlightenment? Eighteenth-Century Answers and Twentieth-Century Questions*, edited by James Schmidt, 488–516. Berkeley: University of California Press, 1996.

Howard, Rhoda E. "Dignity, Community, and Human Rights." Chap. 4 in *Human Rights in Cross-Cultural Perspectives: A Quest for Consensus*, edited by Abdullahi Ahmed An-Na'im. Philadelphia: University of Pennsylvania Press, 1992.

Hsiao, Kung-chuan 蕭公權 [Xiao Gongquan]. *Zhongguo zheng zhi si xiang shi* 中國政治思想史 [The History of Chinese Political Thought]. Taipei: Chinese Culture University, 1980.

Hsu, Cho-yun 許倬雲 [Xu Zhuoyun]. *Ancient China in Transition: An Analysis of Social Mobility, 722–222 B.C.* Stanford: Stanford University Press, 1965.

Huang, Ray. *1587, A Year of No Significance: The Ming Dynasty in Decline*. New Haven: Yale University Press, 1981.

Hume, David. "Of the Independency of Parliament." Essay 6 in pt. 1 of *Essays: Moral, Political and Literary*, edited by Eugene F. Miller. Revised edition. Indianapolis: Liberty Fund, 1987. http://files.libertyfund.org/files/704/0059_Bk.pdf.

Ihara, Craig K. "Are Individual Rights Necessary? A Confucian Perspective." Chap. 1 in *Confucian Ethics: A Comparative Study of Self, Autonomy, and Community*, edited by Kwong-loi Shun and David B. Wong. Cambridge: Cambridge University Press, 2004.

Ivanhoe, Philip J. *Confucian Moral Cultivation*. 2nd edition. Indianapolis: Hackett, 2000.

———. "Thinking and Learning in Early Confucianism." *Journal of Chinese Philosophy* 17, no. 4 (1990): 473–93.

Jackson, Robert. *Sovereignty: The Evolution of an Idea*. Cambridge: Polity Press, 2007.

Jiang, Qing 蔣慶. *A Confucian Constitutional Order: How China's Ancient Past Can Shape Its Political Future*, translated by Edmund Ryden, edited by Daniel A. Bell and Ruiping Fan. Princeton: Princeton University Press, 2013.

Kant, Immanuel. *Critique of Pure Reason*. Translated and edited by Paul Guyer and Allen Wood. Cambridge: Cambridge University Press, 1998.

Kline, T. C., III, and Philip J. Ivanhoe, eds. *Virtue, Nature, and Moral Agency in the Xunzi*. Indianapolis: Hackett, 2000.

Kratochwil, Friedrich. "Sovereignty as *Dominium*: Is There a Right of Humanitarian Intervention?" Chap. 2 in *Beyond Westphalia? State Sovereignty and International Intervention*, edited by Gene M. Lyons and Michael Mastanduno. Baltimore: Johns Hopkins University Press, 1995.

Kuang, Yaming 匡亞明. *Kongzi ping zhuan* 孔子評傳 [A Critical Biography of Confucius]. Nanjing: Nanjing University Press, 1990.

LaFollette, Hugh. *Personal Relationships: Love, Identity, and Morality*. Oxford: Blackwell, 1996.

Lai, Karyn L. *An Introduction to Chinese Philosophy*. Cambridge: Cambridge University Press, 2008.

Lau, Kwok-keung. "An Interpretation of Confucian Virtues and Their Relevance to China's Modernization." In *Confucianism and the Modernization of China*, edited by Silke Krieger and Rolf Trauzettel, 210–28. Mainz: v. Hase & Koehler Verlag, 1991.

Lau, Siu-kai. *Society and Politics in Hong Kong*. Hong Kong Series. Hong Kong: Chinese University Press, 1982.

Lee, Daniel. "Private Law Models for Public Law Concepts: The Roman Law Theory of Dominium in the Monarchomach Doctrine of Popular Sovereignty." *Review of Politics* 70, no. 3 (2008): 370–99.

Lee, Seung-hwan. "Liberal Rights or/and Confucian Virtues?" *Philosophy East and West* 46, no. 3 (1996): 367–79.

Legge, James. *The Chinese Classics: With a Translation, Critical and Exegetical Notes, Prolegomena and Copious Indexes*. 5 vols. London: Trübner, 1861–1872.

———. *The Lî Kî. Part 3–4 of The Texts of Confucianism*. Vols. 3–4 of *The Sacred Books of China*. Vols. 27–28 of *The Sacred Books of the East*, edited by Max Müller. Oxford: Clarendon Press, 1885. http://oll.libertyfund.org/index.php?option=com_staticxt&staticfile=show.php%3Ftitle=2014&Itemid=27.

———. *The Shû King, The Religious Portions of the Shih King, The Hsiâo King*. Part 1 of *The Texts of Confucianism*. Vol. 1 of *The Sacred Books of China*. Vol. 3 of *The Sacred Books of the East*, edited by Max Müller. Oxford: Clarendon Press, 1879. http://oll.libertyfund.org/index.php?option=com_staticxt&staticfile=show.php%3Ftitle=2162&Itemid=27.

Li, Chenyang 李晨陽. "Confucian Value and Democratic Value." *Journal of Value Inquiry* 31, no. 2 (1997): 183–93.

———. "Min zhu de xing shi he ru jia de nei rong—zai lun ru jia yu min zhu de guan xi" 民主的形式和儒家的內容—再論儒家與民主的關係 [Democracy as Form and Confucianism as Content—Revisiting the Relationship between Confucianism and Democracy]. In *Ru xue: xue shu, xin yang he xiu yang* 儒家：學術、信仰和修養 [Confucianism: Scholarship, Faith, and Self-Cultivation], edited by Liu Xiaogan 劉笑敢, 131–46. Vol. 10 of *Zhongguo zhe xue yu wen hua* 中國哲學與文化 [Journal of Chinese Philosophy and Culture]. Shanghai: Lijiang chu ban she 漓江出版社, 2012.

———. "Shifting Perspectives: Filial Morality Revisited." *Philosophy East and West* 47, no. 2 (1997): 211–32.

———. "Where Does Confucian Virtuous Leadership Stand?" *Philosophy East and West* 59, no. 4 (2009): 531–36.

Li, Min 李民, and Wang Jian 王健, trans. and comp. *Shang shu yi zhu* 尚書譯注 [Modern Chinese Translation and Commentary of The Book of History]. Shanghai: Shanghai gu ji chu ban she 上海古籍出版社, 2004.

Lin, Yü-sheng. *The Crisis of Chinese Consciousness: Radical Antitraditionalism in the May Fourth Era*. Madison: University of Wisconsin Press, 1979.

———. "The Evolution of the Pre-Confucian Meaning of *Jen* 仁 and the Confucian Concept of Moral Autonomy." *Monumenta Serica: Journal of Oriental Studies* 31 (1974–75): 172–204.

———. "Reflections on the 'Creative Transformation of Chinese Tradition.'" In *Chinese Thought in a Global Context: A Dialogue between Chinese and Western Philosophical Approaches*, edited by Karl-Heinz Pohl, 73–114. Leiden: Brill, 1999.

Liu, Shu-Hsien 劉述先 [Liu Shuxian]. *Understanding Confucian Philosophy: Classical and Sung-Ming*. Westport, CT: Praeger, 1998.

Liu, Shujun 劉樹軍. "Chuan tong wu de si xiang de ji ben nei rong" 傳統武德思想的基本內容 [The Basic Content of Traditional Wu De Thought]. In *Chuan tong wu de ji qi jia zhi chong jian* 傳統武德及其價值重建 [The Reconstruction of Traditional Wu De and Its Values], 87–96. Changsha: Central South University Press, 2007.

Liu, Zehua 劉澤華. *Wang quan zhu yi yu si xiang he she hui* 王權主義與思想和社會 [Royalism, Thought, and Society]. Vol. 3 of *Zhongguo zheng zhi si xiang shi ji* 中國政治思想史集 [Collection of the History of Chinese Political Thought]. 3 vols. Beijing: People's Publishing, 2008.

Locke, John. "Second Treatise of Government." In *Two Treatises of Government*, edited by Peter Laslett. 3rd edition. Cambridge: Cambridge University Press, 1988.

Lü Buwei. *The Annals of Lü Buwei*, translated by John Knoblock and Jeffrey Riegel. Stanford: Stanford University Press, 2000.

Lu, Zhaolu. "Fiduciary Society and Confucian Theory of *Xin*—On Tu Wei-ming's Fiduciary Proposal." *Asian Philosophy* 11, no. 2 (2001): 85–101.

Lu Zhi 陸贄. "Qing xutaisheng zhang guan gu jian shu li zhuang" 請許台省長官舉薦屬吏狀 [A proposal to allow ministers to select their own staff]. *Wikisource*. http://zh.wikisource.org/zh-hant/%E8%AB%8B%E8%A8%B1%E5%8F%B0%E7%9C%81%E9%95%B7%E5%AE%98%E8%88%89%E8%96%A6%E5%B1%AC%E5%90%8F%E7%8B%80.

Lucas, John R. *Democracy and Participation*. Harmondsworth, UK: Penguin, 1976.

MacIntyre, Alasdair. *After Virtue: A Study in Moral Theory*. London: Duckworth, 1981.

MacMillan, Ken. *Sovereignty and Possession in the English New World: The Legal Foundations of Empire, 1576–1640*. Cambridge: Cambridge University Press, 2006.

Madison, James. "The Alleged Tendency of the New Plan to Elevate the Few at the Expense of the Many Considered in Connection with Representation." No. 57 in Alexander Hamilton, James Madison, and John Jay, *The Federalist Papers*, edited by Clinton Rossiter. With introduction and notes by Charles R. Kesler. New York: Signet Classic, 2003.

———. "Virginia Ratifying Convention." Vol. 1, chap. 13, document 36, of *The Founders' Constitution*, edited by Philip B. Kurland and Ralph Lerner. Chicago: University of Chicago Press, 2000. http://press-pubs.uchicago.edu/founders/documents/v1ch13s36.html/.

Mansbridge, Jane. *Beyond Adversary Democracy*. Chicago: The University of Chicago Press, 1983.

———. "Clarifying the Concepts of Representation." *American Political Science Review* 105, no. 3 (August 2011): 621–30.

———. "A 'Selection Model' of Political Representation." *Journal of Political Philosophy* 17, no. 4 (2009): 369–98.

Mansbridge, Jane, James Bohman, Simone Chambers, David Estlund, Andreas Føllesdal, Archon Fung, Cristina Lafont, Bernard Manin, and José Luis Martí. "The Place of Self-Interest and the Role of Power in Deliberative Democracy." *Journal of Political Philosophy* 18, no. 1 (2010): 64–100.

March, James G., and Johan P. Olsen. *Rediscovering Institutions: The Organizational Basis of Politics*. New York: Free Press, 1989.

McCubbins, Mathew D., and Thomas Schwartz. "Congressional Oversight Overlooked: Police Patrols versus Fire Alarms." *American Journal of Political Science* 28, no. 1 (1984): 165–79.

Mencius. Translated by D. C. Lau. Revised bilingual edition, Hong Kong: Chinese University Press, 2003.

Meyer, Michael J. "When Not to Claim Your Rights: The Abuse and the Virtuous Use of Rights." *Journal of Political Philosophy* 5, no. 2 (1997): 149–62.

Mill, John Stuart. *Considerations on Representative Government*. In *Utilitarianism, On Liberty, Considerations on Representative Government*, edited by H. B. Acton. London: J. M. Dent & Sons, 1972.

Miller, David. *Principles of Social Justice*. Cambridge: Harvard University Press, 1999.

———. *Social Justice*. Oxford: Clarendon Press, 1976.

Miller, Fred D., Jr. *Nature, Justice, and Rights in Aristotle's Politics*. Oxford: Clarendon Press, 1995.

Montesquieu, Baron de. *The Spirit of the Laws*. New York: Hafner, 1949.

Mou, Zongsan 牟宗三 [Mou Tsung-san]. *Zheng dao yu zhi dao* 政道與治道 [The Principles of Politics and Governance]. Revised edition. Taipei: Student Book 台灣學生書局, 1987.

Munro, Donald J. "Introduction." *Individualism and Holism: Studies in Confucian and Taoist Values*, edited by Donald J. Munro. Ann Arbor, MI: Center for Chinese Studies, University of Michigan, 1985.

Mutz, Diana C. *Hearing the Other Side: Deliberative versus Participatory Democracy*. New York: Cambridge University Press, 2006.

Nylan, Michael. *The Five "Confucian" Classics*. New Haven: Yale University Press, 2001.

Obama, Barack. *The Audacity of Hope: Thoughts on Reclaiming the American Dream*. New York: Three Rivers Press, 2006.

Offe, Claus. "Designing Institutions in East European Transitions." In *The Theory of Institutional Design*, edited by Robert E. Goodin, 199–226. Cambridge: Cambridge University Press, 1996.

———. "How Can We Trust Our Fellow Citizens?" In *Democracy and Trust*, edited by Mark E. Warren, 42–87. Cambridge: Cambridge University Press, 1999.

———. "Institutional Design." In *Encyclopedia of Democratic Thought*, edited by Paul Barry Clarke and Joe Foweraker, 363–69. London: Routledge, 2001.

Office of the President of the Republic of China (Taiwan): Inaugural Ceremony of the

Thirteenth-Term (May 2012). "Swearing-in Ceremony." http://www.president.gov .tw/Portals/0/president520/English/oath.html.

Passmore, J. A. "Civil Justice and Its Rivals." Chap. 2 in *Justice*, edited by Eugene Kamenka and Alice Erh-Soon Tay. London: Edward Arnold, 1979.

Peerenboom, Randall P. *China Modernizes: Threat to the West or Model for the Rest?* New York: Oxford University Press, 2007.

———. "Confucian Harmony and Freedom of Thought: The Right to Think versus Right Thinking." Chap. 13 in *Confucianism and Human Rights*, edited by William Theodore de Bary and Tu Weiming. New York: Columbia University Press, 1998.

———. "What's Wrong with Chinese Rights? Toward a Theory of Rights with Chinese Characteristics." *Harvard Human Rights Journal* 6 (1993): 29–57.

Pharr, Susan J. and Robert D. Putnam, eds. *Disaffected Democracies: What's Troubling the Trilateral Countries?* Princeton: Princeton University Press, 2000.

Philp, Mark. *Political Conduct.* Cambridge: Harvard University Press, 2007.

Pines, Yuri. *Envisioning Eternal Empire: Chinese Political Thought of the Warring States Era.* Honolulu: University of Hawaii Press, 2009.

———. *The Everlasting Empire: The Political Culture of Ancient China and Its Imperial Legacy.* Princeton: Princeton University Press, 2012.

———. *Foundations of Confucian Thought: Intellectual Life in the Chunqiu Period, 722–453 B.C.E.* Honolulu: University of Hawaii Press, 2002.

Pye, Lucian 白魯恂. "Ru xue yu min zhu" 儒家與民主 [Confucianism and Democracy], trans. Chen Yinchi 陳引馳. Chap. 3 in *Ru jia yu zi you zhu yi* 儒家與自由主義 [Confucianism and Liberalism], edited by Harvard-Yenching Institute and SDX Joint Publishing, 172–83. SDX and Harvard-Yenching Academic Series. Beijing: SDX Joint Publishing, 2001.

Quinn, Frederick, ed. *The Federalist Papers Reader and Historical Documents of Our American Heritage.* Santa Ana, CA: Seven Locks, 1997.

Rawls, John. *Political Liberalism.* New York: Columbia University Press, 1993.

———. *A Theory of Justice.* Cambridge: Harvard University Press, 1971.

Raz, Joseph. *The Morality of Freedom.* Oxford: Clarendon Press, 1986.

Regan, Donald H. "Authority and Value: Reflections on Raz's *Morality of Freedom.*" *Southern California Law Review* 62 (1989): 995–1095.

Rescher, Nicholas. *Ethical Idealism: An Inquiry into the Nature and Function of Ideals.* Berkeley: University of California Press, 1992.

Robeyns, Ingrid. "Ideal Theory in Theory and Practice." *Social Theory and Practice* 34, no. 3 (2008): 341–62.

Rosemont, Henry, Jr. "State and Society in the *Xunzi*: A Philosophical Commentary." Chap. 1 in *Virtue, Nature, and Moral Agency in the Xunzi*, edited by T. C. Kline III and Philip J. Ivanhoe. Indianapolis: Hackett, 2000.

———"Why Take Rights Seriously? A Confucian Critique." Chap. 10 in *Human Rights and the World's Religions*, edited by Leroy S. Rouner. Notre Dame: University of Notre Dame Press, 1988.

Ruskola, Teemu H. "Moral Choice in the *Analects*: A Way without a Crossroads?" *Journal of Chinese Philosophy* 19, no. 3 (1992): 285–96.

Sachsenmaier, Dominic, and Jens Riedel, with Shmuel N. Eisenstadt, eds. *Reflections on Multiple Modernities: European, Chinese and Other Interpretations*. Leiden: Brill, 2002.

Salls, Holly Shepard. *Character Education: Transforming Values into Virtues*. Lanham, MD: University Press of America, 2006.

Sandel, Michael J. *Democracy's Discontent: America in Search of a Public Philosophy*. Cambridge: Harvard University Press, 1996.

Schmidtz, David. "Mutual Aid." Chap. 4 of pt. 1 in David Schmidtz and Robert E. Goodin, *Social Welfare and Individual Responsibility*, edited by R. G. Frey. Cambridge: Cambridge University Press, 1998.

Sen, Amartya K. "Democracy as a Universal Value." *Journal of Democracy* 10, no. 3 (1999): 3–17.

Shih, Yuan-kang 石元康. "Tian ming yu zheng dang xing—cong Weibo de fen lei kan ru jia de zheng dao" 天命與正當性—從韋伯的分類看儒家的政道 [Heaven's Mandate and Political Legitimacy—An Examination of Confucian Theory of Legitimacy from Weber's Typology]. In *Zheng zhi li lun zai Zhongguo* 政治理論在中國 [Political Theory in China], edited by Joseph Chan 陳祖為 and Leung Man-to 梁文韜. Hong Kong: Oxford University Press, 2001.

Shils, Edward. *The Virtue of Civility: Selected Essays on Liberalism, Tradition, and Civil Society*, edited by Steven Grosby. Indianapolis: Liberty Fund, 1997.

Shultziner, Doron. "Human Dignity: Functons and Meanings." Chap. 7 in *Perspectives on Human Dignity: A Conversation*, edited by Jeff Malpas and Norelle Lickiss. Dordrecht: Springer, 2007.

Shun, Kwong-loi. "Conception of the Person in Early Confucian Thought." Chap. 8 in *Confucian Ethics: A Comparative Study of Self, Autonomy, and Community*, edited by Kwong-loi Shun and David B. Wong. Cambridge: Cambridge University Press, 2004.

———. "*Jen* and *Li* in the *Analects*." *Philosophy East and West* 43, no. 3 (1993): 457–79.

———. *Mencius and Early Chinese Thought*. Stanford: Stanford University Press, 1997.

Simmons, A. John. "Ideal and Nonideal Theory." *Philosophy and Public Affairs* 38, no. 1 (2010): 5–36.

———. *On the Edge of Anarchy: Locke, Consent, and the Limits of Society*. Princeton: Princeton University Press, 1993.

Skinner, Quentin. "The Rediscovery of Republican Values." Chap. 2 in *Renaissance Virtues*. Vol. 2 of *Visions of Politics*. Cambridge: Cambridge University Press, 2002.

Stemplowska, Zofia. "What's Ideal about Ideal Theory?" *Social Theory and Practice* 34, no. 3 (2008): 319–40.

Su, Dongpo 蘇東坡. "Memorial to His Majesty Emperor Shengtsung" 上神宗皇帝萬言書. In *Lin Yutang Chinese-English Bilingual Edition: Selected Poems and Prose of Su Tungpo*, translated by Lin Yutang. Taipei: Cheng Chung Book, 2008.

Sun, Kuang-te 孫廣德 [Sun Guangde]. *Zhongguo zheng zhi si xiang zhuan ti yan jiu ji* 中國政治思想專題研究集 [Collection of Study of Chinese Political Thought]. Taipei: Laureate Book, 1999.

Sun, Xidan 孫希旦. *Liji ji jie* 禮記集解 [Collected Commentaries on the *Book of Rites*]. Beijing: Zhonghua, 1989.

Sunstein, Cass R. "Beyond the Republican Revival." *Yale Law Journal* 97, no. 8 (1988): 1539–90.

Swift, Adam. "The Value of Philosophy in Nonideal Circumstances." *Social Theory and Practice* 34, no. 3 (2008): 363–87.

Tan, Sor-hoon. "Authoritative Master Kong (Confucius) in an Authoritarian Age." *Dao* 9, no. 2 (2010): 137–49.

———. "Beyond Elitism: A Community Ideal for a Modern East Asia." *Philosophy East and West* 59, no. 4 (2009): 537–53.

———. "The *Dao* of Politics: *Li* (Rituals/Rites) and Laws as Pragmatic Tools of Government." *Philosophy East and West* 61, no. 3 (2011): 468–91.

Tang, Junyi 唐君毅 [Tang, Chun-i]. "Min zhu li xiang zhi shi jian yu ke guan jia zhi yi shi" 民主理想之實踐與客觀價值意識. Chap. 20 in *Zhong hua ren wen yu dang jin shi jie* 中華人文與當今世界. Taipei: Dongfang ren wen xue hui 東方人文學會, 1975.

Teng, Ssu-yü, and John K. Fairbank. *China's Response to the West: A Documentary Survey, 1839–1923*. Cambridge: Harvard University Press, 1954.

Tiwald, Justin. "Confucianism and Human Rights." Chap. 22 in *Handbook of Human Rights*, edited by Thomas Cushman. Abingdon, UK: Routledge, 2011.

———. "A Right of Rebellion in the *Mengzi*?" *Dao* 7, no. 3 (2008): 269–82.

Tomasi, John. "Individual Rights and Community Virtues." *Ethics* 101, no. 3 (1991): 521–36.

Tu, Wei-ming. "The Fiduciary Community." Chap. 3 in *Centrality and Commonality: An Essay on Confucian Religiousness*. Albany: State University of New York Press, 1989. Revised edition of *Centrality and Commonality: An Essay on Chung-yung*. Honolulu: University of Hawaii, 1976.

United Nations. "The Universal Declaration of Human Rights." http://www.un.org/en/documents/udhr/.

United Way. http://www.liveunited.org.

United Way Worldwide. Annual Report 2011. http://unway.3cdn.net/f58b3b8a9b4f33a 573_tvm62lh6v.pdf

Van Duffel, Siegfried, and Dennis Yap. "Distributive Justice before the Eighteenth Century: The Right of Necessity." *History of Political Thought* 32, no. 3 (2011): 449–64.

Van Norden, Bryan W. "The Virtue of Righteousness in Mencius." Chap. 7 in *Confucian Ethics: A Comparative Study of Self, Autonomy, and Community*, edited by Kwong-loi Shun and David B. Wong. Cambridge: Cambridge University Press, 2004.

Vermeule, Adrian. "Hume's Second-Best Constitutionalism." *University of Chicago Law Review* 70, no. 1 (2003): 421–37.

Waldron, Jeremy. *Liberal Rights: Collected Papers 1981–1991*. Cambridge: Cambridge University Press, 1993.

———. ed. *Nonsense upon Stilts: Bentham, Burke and Marx on the Rights of Man*. London: Methuen, 1987.

———. "The Primacy of Justice." *Legal Theory* 9, no. 4 (2003): 269–94.

Wall, Steven. *Liberalism, Perfectionism and Restraint*. Cambridge: Cambridge University Press, 1998.

———. "Perfectionism in Moral and Political Philosophy." *Stanford Encyclopedia of Philosophy*. Edited by Edward N. Zalta. Winter 2012 edition. http://plato.stanford.edu/archives/fall2008/entries/perfectionism-moral/.

Wang, E 王鍔. *Liji cheng shu kao* 《禮記》成書考 [An Investigation on the Creation of *The Book of Rites*]. Beijing: Zhonghua, 2007.

Wang, Fuzhi 王夫之 [Chuanshan Xiansheng 船山先生]. *Si shu xun yi xia* 四書訓義下 [Interpreting the *Four Books* vol. 2]. Vol. 8 of *Chuanshan quan shu* 船山全書 [Complete Works of Chuanshan], edited by Chuanshan quan shu bian ji wei yuan hui 船山全書編輯委員會 [Editorial board of the Chuanshan Quan shu]. Changsha, China: Yuelu Publishing 嶽麓書社, 1996.

Wang, Yi 王毅. "Zhongguo huang quan tong zhi "zi min" ren shen he cai chan de fa quan zhi du ji qi yu xian zheng fa li de bei ni" 中國皇權統治"子民"人身和財產的法權制度及其與憲政法理的悖逆 [The Personal and Property Rights of "Subjects" under Chinese Imperial Rule and the Paradox of the Constitutional Principles Concerning These Rights]. Chap. 12 in vol. 2 of *Zhongguo huang quan zhi du yan jiu* 中國皇權制度研究 [The Study of the Institution of Royalism in China]. 2 vols. Beijing: Peking University Press, 2007.

Weithman, Paul. "Political Republicanism and Perfectionist Republicanism." *Review of Politics* 66, no. 2 (2004): 285–312.

Wong, David B. "Is There a Distinction between Reason and Emotion in *Mencius*?" *Philosophy East and West* 41, no. 1 (1991): 31–44.

———. "Universalism versus Love with Distinctions: An Ancient Debate Revived." *Journal of Chinese Philosophy* 16, no. 3–4 (1989): 251–72.

———. "Xunzi on Moral Motivation." Chap. 10 in *Chinese Language, Thought, and Culture: Nivison and His Critics*, edited by Philip J. Ivanhoe. Chicago: Open Court, 1996.

Wong, Wai-ying 黃慧英 [Huang Huiying]. "Ru jia lun li ge ceng mian de shi jian" 儒家倫理各層面的實踐 [The Practice of Confucian Ethics at Different Levels]. Chap. 12 in *Ru jia lun li: ti yu yong* 儒家倫理: 體與用 [Confucian Ethics: Ti and Yong]. Shanghai: Joint Publishing, 2005.

Woodruff, Paul. *Reverence: Renewing a Forgotten Virtue*. New York: Oxford University Press, 2001.

Xu, Fuguan 徐復觀. "Ru jia zheng zhi si xiang de gou zao ji qi zhuan jin" 儒家政治思想的構造及其轉進 [The Structure and Transformation of Confucian Political Thought]." In *Xue shu yu zheng zhi zhi jian* 學術與政治之間 [Between Academics and Politics], 47–60. Revised edition. Taipei: Taiwan Student Book, 1985.

Xunzi. *Basic Writings of Hsün Tzu*, translated by Burton Watson. New York: Columbia University Press, 1963.

———. *Xunzi: A Translation and Study of the Complete Works*, translated by John Knoblock. 3 vols. Stanford: Stanford University Press, 1988–94.

Yao, Xinzhong 姚新中. *An Introduction to Confucianism*. Cambridge: Cambridge University Press, 2000.

Yang, Yongjun 楊永俊. *Shan rang zheng zhi yan jiu* 禪讓政治研究. Beijing: Academy Press, 2005.

Yearley, Lee H. *Mencius and Aquinas: Theories of Virtue and Conceptions of Courage*. Albany: State University of New York Press, 1990.

Yeung, Anthony Kwok-wing 楊國榮. "Shi fei qu zhi: ren li gong cheng de jia zhi guan" 是非曲直：仁禮共成的價值觀 [Right and Wrong, Straight and Crooked: Co-Realization of *Ren* and *Li* and Its Value System]. Chap. 7 in *Xian mei yu he le—Dui sheng ming yi yi de ni liu tan suo* 顯魅與和樂—對生命意義的逆流探索 [Revealing the Sacred Dimension of Life and Enjoying Harmony: A Search for the Meaning of Life]. Hong Kong: Joint Publishing HK, 2010.

Yu, Tianlong. *In the Name of Morality: Character Education and Political Control*. Vol. 26 of *Adolescent Cultures, School, and Society*. New York: Peter Lang, 2004.

Yu, Ying-shih. "The Idea of Democracy and the Twilight of the Elite Culture in Modern China." In *Justice and Democracy: Cross-cultural Perspectives*, edited by Ron Bontekoe and Marietta Stepaniants, 199–215. Honolulu: University of Hawaii Press, 1997.

Zakaria, Fareed. "The Debt Deal's Failure." *Time Magazine*. August 15, 2011, 22.

Zhang, Dainian 張岱年. *Key Concepts in Chinese Philosophy*, translated and edited by Edmund Ryden. New Haven: Yale University; Beijing: Foreign Languages Press, 2002. Originally published in Chinese as *Zhongguo gu dian zhe xue gai nian fan chou yao lun* 中國古典哲學概念範疇要論 [A Handbook of Categories and Concepts in Classical Chinese Philosophy]. Beijing: Academy of Social Sciences, 1989.

Zhang, Fentian 張分田. *Min ben si xiang yu Zhongguo gu dai tong zhi si xiang* 民本思想與中國古代統治思想 [People-Based Thought and Ancient Chinese Thought on Governance]. 2 vols. Tianjin: Nankai University Press, 2009.

Zhou, Jizhi 周繼旨. *Lun Zhongguo gu dai she hui yu chuan tong zhe xue* 論中國古代社會與傳統哲學 [On Traditional Chinese Society and Philosophy]. Beijing: People's Publishing, 1994.

INDEX

abdication. *See* political authority: abdication

Adams, John, 63

Ai, Duke of Lu (魯哀公), 3

Ames, Roger T., 48n4, 115–116n 7, 119n10

The Analects (論語), 205–6; and autonomy, 13, 137, 141, 144; on the common people, 11; on filial piety, 159n60, 179; on gentleman, 15, 91, 98, 140; on golden rule, 118; on governance, 38, 40–41, 45, 53, 62; and Grand Union, 7, 9; on harmony, 91–93; and ideal and nonideal means, 13, 124–25, 145–46; on litigation, 124; on material sufficiency, 166, 179; on moral cultivation, 11, 100, 140; on mutual care, 7; on punishment, 17, 147–48; on *ren*, 15, 94, 97–98, 118, 137, 139, 180; on rites, 9, 13, 17, 139, 202; and selection for public office, 105; on straightness, 125; on trust and trustworthiness, 41; on the village worthy, 13, 137; on the Way, 3, 14; on wealth, 166; on willing submission, 38. *See also* Confucius

Anderson, Elizabeth S., 177n24

Angle, Stephen C., xi n2, 2n3, 44n32, 63n33, 72n18, 93n31, 141n25, 201n6, 208n11, 231n34

Arendt, Hannah, 34, 34n12, 63, 63n34, 63n36, 195, 195n2

Aristotle, 134, 165, 207n7

Arneson, Richard J., 32n9, 155n55

Atwell, John E., 152n46

authority. *See* political authority

autonomy. *See* personal autonomy

Barber, Benjamin R., 95–96n39

Barry, Brian, 84, 84n5

Beetham, David, 83, 83n3

Bell, Daniel, 107n67

Bell, Daniel A., xi n1, 17n25, 103, 103n53, 104, 104n56, 104n58, 104n59, 105n60, 108n68, 125n25, 128n32, 180n3, 189n14

Benbaji, Yitzhak, 177n24

benevolence (*ren* 仁), 9, 10–13, 15–16, 20, 38–39, 45, 102, 114, 118, 120–24, 137, 140n18, 143–44, 147, 152, 164, 177, 180, 185, 189, 191, 197; cannot be brought about by punishment, 66; explained, 4, 138–39, 180–81; in Grand Union and Small Tranquility, 8–9, 227; relationship with rites (*li*), 49, 49n6, 139, 209. *See also The Analects*: on *ren*; benevolent rule

benevolent rule (*ren zheng* 仁政), 2, 39, 45, 49, 198; and economic distribution, 161; as an objective political duty, 160–61; and the well-field system, 129

Besley, Timothy, 75n26, 75n29

Billante, Nicole (and Peter Saunders), 91n22

Blackburn, Simon, 134n5

Blustein, Jeffrey, 157, 158n57

The Book of History (尚書), 28, 29, 31n7, 37, 50n12, 52, 73, 93, 141, 160, 205–7, 215, 217, 227

The Book of Poetry (詩經), 50n12, 141, 205, 215–16, 219–20

The Book of Rites (禮記), 5, 17, 48, 50n12, 60, 141, 205, 207; "Li yun" (禮運) chapter, 5, 8–10, 73, 93, 225–29

Brandeis, Louis, 32, 89

Brennan, Geoffrey (and Alan Hamlin), 79, 79n42; (and James Buchanan), 72n19

Brennan, Jason, 79n44, 89, 89n15, 89n16

Buchanan, James, 72n19, 75n26

Burke, Edmund, 77–78

Burnheim, John, 87–88

247